BY THE EDITORS OF
CONSUMERGUIDE

W9-CCE-814

CURES
FROM THE
KITCHEN

JJ DeSpain
Linnea Lundgren
Michele Price Mann

pil

Publications
International, Ltd.

JJ DeSpain writes about health, consumerism, and senior issues for national magazines in the United States and Canada. A former critical-care nurse, she is a college instructor, coauthor of *Government Secrets,* and author of *Life-Saving Health Secrets, Inside Info,* and *Money Secrets.*

Linnea Lundgren has more than ten years of experience researching, writing, and editing for newspapers and magazines. She is the author of four books, including *Living Well with Allergies.*

Michele Price Mann is a freelance writer who has written for such publications as *Weight Watchers* magazine and *Southern Living* magazine. Formerly assistant health and fitness editor at *Cooking Light* magazine, her professional passion is learning and writing about health issues.

Consultant: **Ara Der Marderosian, Ph.D.**

Illustrator: **Jeff Moores**

ACKNOWLEDGMENTS:
Pages 12, 88, 90, 117, 126, 140, 164, 224, 244, 277: Excerpts from *The Complete Book of Ayurvedic Home Remedies,* by Vasant Lad. Copyright © 1998 by Vasant Lad. Reprinted with permission of Harmony Books, a division of Random House. For more information on Ayurveda visit www.ayurveda.com.

Page 38: Excerpt from *The People's Pharmacy Guide to Home & Herbal Remedies,* by Joe and Teresa Graedon. Reprinted with permission.

Page 48: Excerpt from *Mayo Clinic Guide to Self-Care,* by Philip T. Hagen. Reprinted with permission.

Pages 51, 152: Excerpts from *Folk Remedies from Around the World,* by John Heinerman. Reprinted with permission.

Pages 51, 53, 63, 64: Excerpts from *Healing Power of Food,* by Amanda Ursell. Reprinted with permission.

Pages 52, 118, 221: Excerpts from *Heinerman's Encyclopedia of Healing Herbs and Spices,* by John Heinerman. Copyright © 1996. Reprinted with permission of Prentice Hall Direct.

Page 62: Excerpt from The American Dental Association Web site, www.ada.org. Reprinted with permission.

Pages 67, 108: Excerpts from *The Complete Home Wellness Handbook,* by John Edward Swartzberg. Reprinted with permission.

Page 75: Excerpt from *Natural Folk Remedies,* by Lelord Kordel. Reprinted with permission.

Pages 101, 102, 118, 152: Excerpts from *Miracle Food Cures from the Bible,* by Reese Dubin. Copyright © 1999. Reprinted with permission from Elsevier Science.

Page 139: Excerpt from *Cider Vinegar: The Natural Remedy,* by Margaret Hills. Reprinted with permission.

Pages 177, 183, 184: Excerpts from the American Heart Association Web site, www.americanheart.org. Reprinted with permission.

Page 178: Excerpt from *The Thrifty Living Newsletter,* www.urbanext.uiuc.edu/thriftyliving, by Drusilla Banks, nutrition & wellness educator, University of Illinois Extension. Reprinted with permission.

Page 243: Excerpt from *Hoosier Home Remedies,* by Varro E. Tyler. Reprinted with permission.

Page 264: Excerpt from *The Doctors Book of Home Remedies for Preventing Disease.* Reprinted with permission.

Page 278: Excerpt from *The Complete Home Healer* by Angela Smyth. Copyright © Angela Smyth 1991. Reprinted with permission of The Lisa Eveleigh Literary Agency.

Louis Weber, CEO
Publications International, Ltd.
7373 North Cicero Avenue
Lincolnwood, Illinois 60712

Manufactured in U.S.A.

8 7 6 5 4 3 2 1

ISBN: 1-4127-1114-2

Contents

Contents *continued*

Introduction

What's cookin' in the kitchen? A lot
more than you might expect. But
we're not talking about meals here.
What we've cooked up
are hundreds of
cures, treatments,
and preventatives
for both everyday
and serious health problems—
all using ingredients you can find
in your own kitchen.

Think of the kitchen as a personal
pharmacy that you can visit in your bathrobe and slippers, 24 hours
a day, 7 days a week. Open up the cupboards, peek into the refrigerator, and scan the pantry. Got baking soda? Vinegar? Tea? Milk?
Honey? These are just some of the simple items that are the basis
for scores of problem-solving remedies you'll find in this book—
remedies that have stood the test of time as well as contemporary
ones based on the latest scientific information.

Cures from the Kitchen covers 80 health problems, from allergies
to yeast infection. Each profile includes a short explanation of the
causes and symptoms of the condition, followed by a host of remedies for it based on ingredients from your kitchen. The remedies are
listed according to where they are typically found: the cupboard,
the spice rack, the refrigerator, the sink... even the junk drawer.

So next time you or a loved one suffers from a health problem,
check out the kitchen first. With *Cures from the Kitchen*, you'll find a
whole pharmacy at your feet... er, slippers.

Allergies
BREATHING EASIER

Allergies can be called a haywire response of the immune system. Normally, the immune system guards against intruders it considers harmful to the body, such as certain viruses and bacteria. That's its job. However, in allergic people, the immune system goes a bit bonkers. It overreacts when you breathe, ingest, or touch an otherwise harmless substance. The benign culprits triggering the overreaction, such as dust, pet dander, and pollen, are called allergens.

The body's first line of defense against invaders includes the nose, mouth, eyes, lungs, and stomach. When the immune system reacts to an allergen, these body parts become great battlegrounds. Symptoms include runny nose; sneezing; watery, swollen, or red eyes; nasal congestion; wheezing; shortness of breath; a tight feeling in the chest; difficulty breathing; coughing; diarrhea; nausea; headache; fatigue; and a general feeling of misery. Symptoms can occur alone or in combination.

What Causes Allergies?

Blame your genes. The tendency to become allergic is inherited, and allergies typically develop before age 30. What you become allergic to is based on what substances you are exposed to and how often you are exposed to them. Generally, the more you are exposed to an allergen, the more likely it is to trigger a reaction.

Unfortunately, there is no cure for allergies. But there are ways to ease your long-suffering sinuses and skin.

FROM THE CUPBOARD

BAKING SODA. One-half cup baking soda poured into a warm bath is an old New England folk remedy for soothing hives. Soak for 20 to 30 minutes.

TEA. Allergy sufferers throughout the centuries have turned to hot tea to provide relief for clogged-up noses and irritated mucous membranes. One of the best for symptom relief is mint tea, which has been used by the Chinese to treat allergies since the seventh century. Mint's benefits extend well beyond its delicious smell. Mint's essential oils act as a decongestant, and substances within the mint contain anti-inflammatory and mild antibacterial constituents. To make mint tea: Place ½ ounce dried mint leaves in a 1-quart jar. Fill two-thirds of the jar with boiling water and steep for five minutes (inhale the steam). Let cool, strain, sweeten if desired, and drink.

FROM THE FREEZER

ICE. Wrap a washcloth around some ice cubes and apply them to your sinuses for instant relief and refreshment.

FROM THE REFRIGERATOR

MILK. Milk does the body good, especially when it comes to hives. Wet a cloth with cold milk and lay it on the affected area for 10 to 15 minutes.

WASABI. If you're a hay fever sufferer and sushi lover combined, this remedy will please. Wasabi, that pale-green, fiery condiment served alongside California rolls, is a member of the horseradish family. Anyone who has taken too big a dollop of wasabi or plain old horseradish knows how it makes sinuses and tear ducts spring into action. That's because allyl isothiocyanate, a constituent in wasabi, promotes phlegm flow and has antiasthmatic properties. The tastiest way to get in those allyl isothiocyanates is by slathering horseradish on your sandwich or plopping wasabi onto your favorite sushi. The last, harder-to-swallow option is to purchase grated horseradish and take ¼ teaspoon during an allergy attack.

FROM THE SPICE RACK

BASIL. To help ease an allergic reaction or hives, try dousing the skin with basil tea, a traditional Chinese folk remedy. Basil contains high amounts of an antiallergic compound called caffeic acid. Place 1 ounce dried basil leaves into 1 quart boiling water. Cover and let cool to room temperature. Use the tea as a rinse as often as needed.

WHEN TO CALL THE DOCTOR

You can't always tell whether what's bothering you is an allergy or an infection, intolerance, or a specific disease. So check with your doctor if you experience any of the following:

- Nasal problems that cause secondary symptoms, such as chronic sinus infections, nasal congestion, or difficulty breathing
- Symptoms that last for several months
- Inability to get relief from over-the-counter medications or unacceptable side effects from them, such as drowsiness
- Symptoms that interfere with your daily activities or decrease your quality of life
- Any of these symptoms, which can be warning signs of asthma: struggling to catch your breath; wheezing and coughing, especially at night or after exercise; shortness of breath; chest tightness

SNEEZE AND THE WORLD SNEEZES WITH YOU

When it comes to seasonal allergic rhinitis (hay fever), take comfort in the fact that you aren't alone in your misery. At least 35.9 million people in the United States suffer from hay fever symptoms.

SPEEDY SNEEZES

Blink and you just might miss that sneeze. Sneezing, a reflex beyond your control, is caused by the irritation of nerve endings in the nose and mucous membranes. A sneeze can whip out at 100 miles per hour—quicker than you can grab a tissue to catch it. Also, your eyes will naturally close when one approaches, so yes, you will blink and miss it.

SALT. Nasal irrigation is a very effective allergy-management tool that's done right at the sink every morning. It uses a mixture of salt water to rid the nasal passages of mucus, bacteria, dust, and other gunk, as well as to soothe irritated passageways. All you need is 1 to 1½ cups lukewarm water (do not use softened water), a bulb (ear) syringe, ¼ to ½ teaspoon salt, and ¼ to ½ teaspoon baking soda. Mix the salt and baking soda into the water, and test the temperature. To administer, suck the water into the bulb and squirt the saline solution into one nostril while holding the other closed. Lower your head over the sink and gently blow out the water. Repeat this, alternating nostrils, until the water is gone.

Nasal irrigation isn't a pretty sight, yet it works wonders on sore noses and rids the passages of unwanted stuff.

FROM THE STOVE

STEAM. Breathing steam refreshes and soothes sore sinuses, and it helps rid the nasal passages of mucus. While it takes some time, it will make you feel wonderful! Boil several cups of water and pour into a big bowl (or a plugged sink). Place your head carefully over the bowl and drape a towel over yourself. Breathe gently for 5 to 10 minutes.

When you're finished breathing steam, use the hot water for a second purpose. Let the water cool until warm, saturate a washcloth, and hold it on the sinuses.

MORE DO'S AND DON'TS

- Pass up the milk. When allergies act up, skip that extra-large, whole-milk latte, since dairy products thicken mucus. Try herbal tea instead.
- Shampoo before bedtime. During pollen prime time, the hair acts as one gigantic magnet, attracting flying pollen and stray mold spores. When you lie down, these hair hitchhikers drop onto the pillow and are quickly inhaled, causing allergy symptoms that night or the next morning. To avoid sleeping in pollen, wash your hair before bedtime.

Alzheimer's Disease
ALLEVIATING SYMPTOMS

Alzheimer's disease (AD) is everyone's worst nightmare. Most diseases destroy either a physical or a mental function. Alzheimer's seizes both, slowly and steadily destroying memory, logical thought, and language. Simple tasks— how to eat or comb hair—are forgotten, and once AD sets in there's no turning back the clock.

The disease is named for Dr. Alois Alzheimer, a German doctor who, during an autopsy in 1906, discovered physical changes in the brain of a woman who had died of a strange mental illness. He found plaques and tangles in her brain, signs that are now considered hallmarks of AD.

A Progressive Disease

AD is one of a group of brain disorders called dementia, which are progressive degenerative brain syndromes that affect memory, thinking, behavior, and emotion. Alzheimer's is the most common cause of dementia: Between 50 and 60 percent of all cases of dementia can be attributed to Alzheimer's.

Early symptoms include difficulty remembering names, places, or faces and trouble recalling things that just happened. Personality changes and confusion when driving a car or handling money are also early symptoms. Eventually mild forgetfulness progresses to problems in comprehension, speaking, reading, and writing. And physical breakdown occurs, too, partly because tasks such as eating and drinking are simply forgotten or too difficult to accomplish.

While we don't know the cause of AD yet, we do know that there are dietary and environmental factors. And a stealth virus that lies dormant for years is being studied as a possible cause. So is heredity. Aluminum has been suspected as a possible cause, but the jury is still out. Most researchers believe that if aluminum plays a role in the development of AD, it is a minor one.

Since we don't know what causes AD, we also do not yet have a cure for it. However, the picture is not as bleak as it was a decade ago.

WHEN TO CALL THE DOCTOR

- When memory becomes a problem
- When normal reasoning and decision-making turns difficult
- When the ability to recall simple, everyday tasks is a struggle
- When friends or family mention that there's a noticeable change in personality or memory
- When there is disorientation about time and place

EXERCISE EATING RESTRAINT

Recent studies indicate that the less you eat, the slower you age. "Old-age genes" may actually stop functioning when daily calories are cut back by as little as 25 percent. Some of these genes that switch off may be linked to AD.

Research is turning up some remedies that can help alleviate symptoms as well as slow the advancement of the disease. And the good news is that many of these can be found right in your kitchen.

FROM THE CUPBOARD

There are lots of good cures in here, not only for appetite and health, but for hygiene, which can become a problem as AD progresses and personal care becomes difficult.

BAKING SODA. Since many brands of toothpaste on the market contain aluminum, perhaps try a mixture of powdered salt and baking soda. This combination makes an excellent toothpaste that can help whiten teeth and remove plaque, which contributes to cavities and gum disease. To make the mixture, pulverize salt in an electric coffee mill, or spread some on a cutting board and roll it with a pastry rolling pin, crushing it into a fine, sandlike texture. Mix 1 part crushed salt with 2 parts baking soda, then dip a dampened toothbrush into the mixture and brush teeth. Keep the powder in an airtight container in your bathroom.

MEAL SUPPLEMENTS. These meal-in-a-can beverages are easy to drink, and they're fortified with vitamins and minerals.

SEEDS. Pumpkin, sesame, and sunflower seeds are packed with essential fatty acids necessary for brain function.

SESAME OIL. Depression associated with AD may be relieved with nose drops of warmed sesame oil. Use about 3 drops per nostril, twice a day. Some say you can also help relieve depression by rubbing a little of that warmed sesame oil on the top of the head and bottoms of the feet.

VINEGAR. For incontinence, clean the genital area thoroughly with equal parts vinegar and water. For a homemade deodorant, since many store-bought brands contain aluminum, combine equal amounts of water and vinegar. Dab lightly under the arms. This will not stop perspiration, but it will control odor. Cider vinegar can help relieve itchy skin. Add

8 ounces apple cider vinegar to a bathtub of warm water. Soak for at least 15 minutes.

WHEAT GERM OR POWDERED MILK. Add to foods for extra protein.

FROM THE REFRIGERATOR

BLUEBERRIES. New evidence suggests they contain an antioxidant that may slow down age-related motor changes, such as those seen in Alzheimer's.

BOTTLED WATER. Because tap water may contain aluminum, pure bottled well or spring water may be a more brain-safe beverage. A water filter works, too. Call your water company to ask about an analysis of your water.

CARROTS. These are loaded with beta-carotene, which is a memory booster. Carrot and beet juice are good for the memory, too. So are okra and spinach.

CITRUS FRUITS. These fruits are loaded with vitamin C, which is believed to help protect brain nerves. Berries and some vegetables, including peppers, sweet potatoes, and green leafy vegetables, are also rich sources of vitamin C.

STATISTICS ON ALZHEIMER'S

According to statistics from the Alzheimer's Disease Education & Referral Center:

• Up to 4 million Americans have Alzheimer's.

• AD usually begins after age 60.

• AD increases with age; 3 percent of the population ages 65 to 75 have AD, and up to 50 percent of those age 85 are afflicted.

• The number of people with AD doubles every 5 years after age 65.

• Those with a sibling who has AD have a 50 percent chance of developing it.

• People who smoke more than 1 pack of cigarettes a day are 4 times more likely to develop AD as those who don't smoke.

EGGS. It doesn't matter how you eat them. Eggs are loaded with vitamin A, which may protect brain cells and enhance brain function. Other vitamin A-rich foods include liver, spinach, milk, squash, and peaches.

FISH. Fatty acids, which AD sufferers often lack, are important in keeping those brain nerves healthy. Fish are high in fatty acids (that's why they're often called "brain food"), so it's a good idea to eat fish several times a week. Good choices include salmon, mackerel, sardines, and anchovies.

GREEN LEAFY VEGETABLES. These are high in folic acid, which may stimulate cognitive function. Other good sources of folic acid include beets, black-eyed peas and other legumes, brussels sprouts, and whole-grain foods.

ORANGE JUICE. This is another way to up your vitamin C intake, but don't combine it with buffered aspirin. The two, taken together, form aluminum citrate, which is absorbed into the body five times faster than normal aluminum.

ACCIDENT REMEDIES FROM THE PANTRY

People with Alzheimer's will eventually begin to have embarrassing bathroom accidents. Here are some simple, straight-from-the-pantry cleaners that will take care of those situations.

- For cleaning urine accidents, rinse the carpet, bedding, or upholstery immediately with warm water. Then mix 3 tablespoons white vinegar and 1 teaspoon liquid soap. Apply solution to stained area and leave on 15 minutes. Rinse and rub dry.

- For carpet and upholstery shampoo, use an eggbeater to combine 1 quart water, ¼ cup mild powdered detergent, and 1 tablespoon white vinegar. Whip until a stiff foam forms. Gently rub solution into fabric or carpeting, then remove soiled foam with a dull knife. Follow with a rinse of clean water.

RED VEGETABLES. Research from the Netherlands suggests that people who eat large amounts of dark red, yellow, and green vegetables may reduce their risk of dementia by 25 percent.

SOY PRODUCTS. Studies suggest that isoflavones found in soy protein may protect postmenopausal women from AD. Try these: soy milk over cereal, soy meat substitutes, tofu frozen treats. And substitute tofu for ricotta or cream cheese in recipes. Dietary guidelines suggest 20 to 25 grams soy protein a day.

FROM THE SPICE RACK

Many people with AD experience a decrease in taste, so spice up that food to tempt the taste buds and appetite. Chili powder, pepper, sage, oregano—anything that tastes good and makes food interesting will work. Don't overload on salt, though.

ALMOND EXTRACT. This contains vitamin E. Try baking some almond cookies.

CURRY. New research suggests that curcumin, an antioxidant and anti-inflammatory compound in turmeric, a spice used in yellow curry, might prevent AD. This could explain why India has one of the lowest rates of AD in the world.

GINGER. This spice can stimulate a poor appetite. Try some ginger tea or gingersnaps, or chop up some fresh ginger and mix it with a little lime juice and a pinch of rock salt, then chew. It will not only increase appetite but thirst, too.

LEMON OIL. Steep a few drops of lemon or peppermint oil in hot water, then inhale. These are aromatherapy stimulants; they can perk up those suffering typical AD symptoms such as lethargy or depression.

SAGE. For depression associated with AD, drink a tea made with ½ teaspoon sage and ¼ teaspoon basil steeped in 1 cup hot water twice a day.

SALT. For dry skin that occurs with age: After a shower or bath, and while the skin is still wet, sprinkle salt onto your hands and rub it all over the skin. Then rinse. This salt massage will remove dry skin and make skin more smooth to the touch. It will also invigorate the skin and get circulation moving. Try this first thing in the morning to help you wake up. If the skin is itchy, soak in a tub of salt water. Just add 1 cup table salt or sea salt to bathwater. This solution will also soften skin and encourage relaxation.

TURMERIC. Curcumin, an antioxidant and anti-inflammatory compound in this spice, has been found to reduce the number of plaques in the brain of mice and thus may slow the progression of Alzheimer's.

MORE DO'S & DON'TS

- Don't serve foods with pits or bones.

- Always check the temperature of food before you serve it. Hot and cold sensations can be numbed in people with AD, but they can still get burned.

- Don't serve foods with a mixture of textures. They may be hard to swallow.

- Serve foods that require little chewing, such as soups, ground meat, and applesauce.

- Serve several smaller meals instead of three main meals.

- Select favorite foods, especially if the appetite is poor. And keep in mind that as the disease progresses, food preferences may change.

- Play music at meals. Mealtimes can be stressful and music is relaxing. Choose songs from the patient's youth or that hold a special memory.

BANANA BASICS

For those with Alzheimer's, the banana is a nutritional miracle. One of the most common problems plaguing people with AD is low fluid intake. Those with the disease simply forget to drink, or they choose not to in order to avoid bathroom emergencies and accidents. The result is dehydration, which can cause a loss of potassium, which in turn contributes to confusion. The simple solution for restoring essential potassium is to force fluids—water or sports drinks with potassium—but that's often easier said than done. So the next best solution grows in bunches, is easy to eat, and tastes great.

Here are the banana facts you need to know:

- One ripe, medium-size banana supplies about 13 percent of the body's daily need for potassium.

- Bananas are a great source of fast energy. Very ripe bananas are loaded with sugar, about 23 grams, which is digested quickly and converted into energy. Ripe bananas are not recommended for people with diabetes.

- Bananas are easy to chew and swallow, which can be very important in AD since these functions may become impaired.

Anemia
BUILDING YOUR BLOOD

Anemia is a condition in which your red blood cell count is so low that it can't carry enough oxygen to all parts of your body. Not having enough oxygen in the blood is like trying to drive a car with no oil. Your car may run for a while, but you'll soon end up with a burned-out engine. In the same way that oil nourishes your car's engine, oxygen provides needed nourishment for your body's tissues (organs, muscles, etc.), and if they aren't getting enough of that vital sustenance, you'll start feeling weak and tired. A short climb up the stairs will leave you breathless, and even a couple days of rest won't perk you up. If that describes how you feel, check with your doctor. If you do have anemia, you should take action as soon as possible. And you need to be sure you don't have a more serious condition.

Anatomy of Anemia

Your red blood cells are the delivery trucks of the body. They carry oxygen throughout your blood vessels and capillaries to feed tissues. Hemoglobin, the primary component of red blood cells, is a complex molecule and is the oxygen carrier of the red blood cell.

The body works very hard to ensure that it produces enough red blood cells to successfully carry oxygen but not too many, which can cause the blood to get too thick. Red blood cells live only 90 to 120 days. The liver and spleen get rid of the old cells, though the iron in the cells is recycled and sent back to the marrow to produce new cells.

When you're diagnosed with anemia it usually means your red blood cell count is abnormally low, so it can't carry enough oxygen to all parts of your body, or that there is a reduction in the hemoglobin content of your red blood cells. Anemia's not a disease in itself but instead is considered a condition. However, this condition

WHEN TO CALL THE DOCTOR

• At the first sign of any of the following symptoms: weakness, unexplained fatigue, shortness of breath. That's because anemia can mask a more serious disease.

can be a symptom of a more serious illness. That's why it's always important to check with your doctor if you think you may be anemic.

The Most Common Causes of Anemia

There are many types of anemia. Some rare types are the result of a malfunction in the body, such as early destruction of red blood cells (hemolytic anemia), a hereditary structural defect of red blood cells (sickle-cell anemia), or an inability to make or use hemoglobin (sideroblastic anemia). The most common forms of anemia are the result of some type of nutritional deficiency and can often be treated easily with some help from the kitchen. These common types of anemia are:

- Iron deficiency anemia. Iron deficiency anemia happens when the body doesn't have enough iron to produce hemoglobin, causing the red blood cells to shrink. And if there's not enough hemoglobin produced, the body's tissues don't get the nourishing oxygen they need. Children younger than three years of age and pre-menopausal women are at highest risk for developing iron deficiency anemia. Most young children simply don't get enough iron in their diet, while heavy menstrual periods are the most common cause of iron deficiency anemia in women who are premenopausal. In addition, during pregnancy a woman's blood volume increases three times, boosting iron needs. Contrary to popular belief, men and older women aren't at greater risk for iron deficiency anemia. If they do end up developing the condition, it's most often the result of an ulcer.

- Vitamin B12 deficiency anemia. While iron deficiency anemia produces smaller than usual red blood cells, a vitamin B12 deficiency anemia

FASCINATING FACT
Women have fewer red blood cells per cubic centimeter than men.

ANEMIA: FOR WOMEN ONLY?

Is anemia a gender-biased condition? The answer is yes. While men are not immune from the condition, premenopausal women and adolescent girls are at highest risk for nutritional deficiency anemias. Why?

Menstruation Magic. Blood loss is a major cause of iron deficiency anemia, and because women lose blood through their menstrual cycle every month, they are more at risk for becoming anemic.

Pregnancy Power. Women's blood volume increases so much during pregnancy, they literally carry around almost three pints of extra blood. The body needs more iron to adequately supply red blood cells.

Dieting Downside. Most women end up sacrificing iron-rich foods, such as meats, to make the scale go down.

DAILY IRON, VITAMIN B$_{12}$, AND FOLIC ACID REQUIREMENTS			
	IRON	VITAMIN B$_{12}$	FOLIC ACID
Men (age 14–51+)	15 mg	2.4 mcg	400 mcg
Women (age 14–51+)	12 mg	2.4 mcg	400 mcg
Pregnant women	30 mg	2.6 mcg	600 mcg

produces oversized red blood cells. This makes it harder for the body to squeeze the red blood cells through vessels and veins. It's like trying to squeeze a marble through a straw. Vitamin B$_{12}$-deficient red blood cells also tend to die off more quickly than normal cells. Most people get at least the minimum amount of B$_{12}$ that they need by eating a varied diet. If you are a vegetarian or have greatly limited your intake of meat, milk, and eggs for other health reasons, you may not get enough of the vitamin in your diet. Many older people are more at risk for vitamin B$_{12}$ deficiency; in fact, 1 out of 100 people older than 60 years of age are diagnosed with pernicious anemia (a vitamin B$_{12}$ deficiency that is caused by a lack of intrinsic factor). This age-group is at increased risk because they are more likely to have conditions that affect the body's ability to absorb vitamin B$_{12}$. Surgical removal of portions of the stomach or small intestine; atrophic gastritis, a condition that causes the stomach lining to thin; and diseases such as Crohn's can all interfere with the body's ability to absorb vitamin B$_{12}$. But the most common cause of vitamin B$_{12}$ deficiency anemia is a lack of a protein called intrinsic factor. Intrinsic factor is normally secreted by the stomach; its job is to help vitamin B$_{12}$. Without intrinsic factor, the vitamin B$_{12}$ that you consume in your diet just floats out as waste. In some people, a genetic defect causes the body to stop producing intrinsic factor. In other people, an autoimmune reaction, in which the body mistakenly attacks stomach cells that produce the protein, results in a lack of intrinsic factor. Pernicious anemia can be particularly dangerous because it causes neurological problems, such as difficulty walking, poor concentration, depression, memory loss, and irritability. These can usually be reversed if the condition is treated in time. Unfortunately, in the case of pernicious anemia, the stomach cannot absorb the vitamin no matter how much B$_{12}$-rich food you eat. Treatment requires B$_{12}$ injections, usually once a month, that bypass the stomach and shoot the vitamin directly into the bloodstream.

• Folic acid deficiency anemia. A deficiency of folic acid produces the same oversized red blood cells as a vitamin B$_{12}$ deficiency. One of the most common causes of folic acid deficiency anemia is simply not getting enough in the diet. The body doesn't store up folic acid for long periods like it does many other nutrients, so if you aren't getting enough in your diet, you will quickly become deficient. Pregnant women are most at risk for folic acid anemia because the need for folic acid increases by two-thirds during pregnancy. Adequate folic acid intake is essential from the start of pregnancy because it protects against spinal defects in the fetus.

Symptoms of Anemia

Symptoms of more severe anemia include rapid heartbeat, dizziness, headache, ringing in the ears, irritability, pale skin, restless legs syndrome, and confusion. A vitamin B_{12} or folic acid deficiency may even cause your mouth and tongue to swell. These symptoms may sound scary, but the most common forms of anemia are easily treated, especially if caught early.

SUPER SUPPLEMENTS

Though most people can get adequate amounts of iron, vitamin B_{12}, and folic acid through their diet, experts believe that people who are at highest risk for nutrient deficiency anemias can benefit from taking supplements. If you are at higher-than-usual risk for a deficiency of iron, vitamin B_{12}, or folic acid, discuss it with your doctor, take a good look at your diet, and follow these recommendations.

- Take it on empty. The iron you absorb from supplements can be decreased by as much as 50 percent if you eat food with your supplement. Absorption is best when iron is taken on an empty stomach and washed down with juice or water.

- Don't overload. The government has done extensive testing on how much of a nutrient is adequate for a healthy diet. Overdoing the amounts can be harmful instead of beneficial. For example, taking too much folic acid may mask symptoms of pernicious anemia. Follow the Recommended Dietary Allowances (RDAs) guideline and you can't go wrong.

- Be a label reader. Be cautious when choosing a supplement, and be sure that it meets your unique needs. Some vitamin supplements don't contain any folic acid at all. And some may contain large amounts of nutrients that you don't need, which can not only be a waste of money but, depending on the nutrients, also harmful to your health. In addition, be sure to check the expiration date on the bottle; you don't want to buy a 500-count bottle of a once-a-day supplement that expires in six months!

IRON'S ABSORPTION EQUATION

How much iron you absorb depends on the kind of iron in the food and what other nutrients the food contains. There are two types of iron, heme and non-heme. Heme, found primarily in foods of animal origin, is much more easily absorbed than non-heme iron, found primarily in plant products. But if you eat a vitamin C-rich food or a food rich in heme iron with your non-heme iron food, your body will absorb more iron.

- Sources of mostly heme iron: beef liver, lean sirloin, lean ground beef, skinless chicken, pork
- Sources of non-heme iron: fortified breakfast cereal, pumpkin seeds, bran, spinach
- Sources of vitamin B_{12}: salmon (3 ounces) 2.6 mcg, beef tenderloin (3 ounces) 2.5 mcg, yogurt (1 cup) 1.4 mcg, shrimp (3 ounces) 1.3 mcg
- Sources of folic acid: spinach (½ cup) 130 mcg, navy beans (½ cup) 125 mcg, wheat germ (¼ cup) 80 mcg, avocado (½ cup) 55 mcg, orange 45 mcg

Symptoms of mild to moderate anemia:
- weakness
- fatigue
- shortness of breath

Symptoms of moderate to severe anemia:
- rapid heartbeat
- dizziness
- headache
- ringing in the ears
- pale skin (especially the palms of your hands), pale or bluish fingernails
- hair loss
- restless legs syndrome
- confusion

Symptom specific to severe vitamin B_{12} or folic acid deficiency anemia:
- swelling of the mouth or tongue

Symptoms specific to pernicious anemia:
- numbness, tingling
- depression and/or irritability
- memory loss

Because all but pernicious anemia are the result of a nutritional deficiency, the best ways to treat them can be found in the kitchen.

FROM THE CUPBOARD

BLACKSTRAP MOLASSES. Consider covering waffles or pancakes in a little molasses. Blackstrap molasses has long been known to be a nutritional powerhouse. Containing 3.5 mg of iron per tablespoon, blackstrap molasses has been used in folk medicine as a "blood builder" for centuries.

DRY CEREAL. Fix yourself a bowl of your favorite cereal (go for one without the sugar and the cartoon characters on the box), and you'll be waging a battle against anemia. These days many cereals are fortified with a nutrient punch of iron, vitamin B12, and folic acid. Check the label for amounts per serving, pour some milk over your flakes, and dig right in.

FROM THE REFRIGERATOR

BEEF LIVER. Beef liver is rich in iron and all the B vitamins (including B12 and folic acid). In fact, beef liver contains more iron per serving—5.8 mg per 3 ounces—than any other food. Other animal sources of iron include eggs, cheese, fish, lean sirloin, lean ground beef, and chicken.

BEETS. Beets are rich in folic acid, as well as many other nutrients, such as fiber and potassium. The best way to prepare beets is to nuke 'em in the microwave. Keep the skin on when cooking, but peel before eating. The most nutrient-dense part of the beet is right under the skin.

SPINACH. Dark green leafy vegetables contain loads of iron and folic acid, so choose your leaves carefully. Iceberg lettuce is mostly water and is of little nutritive value. Spinach, on the other hand, has 3.2 mg of iron and 130 mcg of folic acid per ½ cup.

MORE DO'S AND DON'TS

- If you're a vegetarian or have cut way down on your intake of meats, milk, and eggs, be sure that you're getting adequate amounts of iron and vitamin B12 in your diet. With such a diet, you are at greater risk for nutritional deficiency anemias because iron from plant sources isn't absorbed as well as iron from animal sources and because vitamin B12 is found almost exclusively in animal foods.

- Eat foods rich in vitamin C at the same time that you eat whole grains, spinach, and legumes to increase absorption of the iron they contain.

- Drink coffee or tea between meals rather than with meals, because the caffeine in these beverages reduces iron absorption.

BAD BLOOD

For centuries before bad blood took on quite a different meaning, folk medicine experts used it in a more literal sense. Even current folk medicine wisdom believes that if you're feeling run-down, you might be suffering from "bad blood." Folk healers use "blood builders" to help restore needed nutrients to the body and the blood to good standing. Two of the most common "blood builders": beets and molasses.

Anxiety

QUASHING THE QUIVERS

Anxiety is a feeling everyone experiences sooner or later. Perhaps you're sitting in the waiting room, anticipating the horse-size needle your doctor has waiting for you on the other side of the door. Or you've spent all day cooking but the look on your mother-in-law's face says your best efforts were wasted. Or you really hate your job.

These very different experiences can bring on anxiety and its typical symptoms:

- heart palpitations
- sense of impending doom
- inability to concentrate
- muscle tension
- dry mouth
- sweating
- queasy, jittery feeling in the pit of the stomach
- hyperventilation

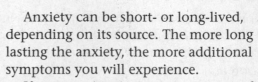

WHEN TO CALL THE DOCTOR

- If you're chronically experiencing severe symptoms: chest pain, shortness of breath or hyperventilation, dizziness, headache
- If your anxiety has progressed to panic attacks
- If you begin to alter your life in order to avoid situations that make you feel anxious

Anxiety can be short- or long-lived, depending on its source. The more long lasting the anxiety, the more additional symptoms you will experience.

If your anxiety is a reaction to a single, isolated event—the shot the doctor is about to give you—your anxiety level will decrease and your symptoms will disappear after the event. If your anxiety is from friction between you and your mother-in-law, you're likely to experience anxiety for a period of time before and after you see her. In this case, the symptom list probably has grown to include diarrhea or constipation and irritability.

Then there's that job, a source of anxiety that never leaves you. You dread getting up in the morning because you have to go to work, dread going to bed at night because when you wake up you have to go to work, dread the weekend because when it's over you'll have to go to work. When the source of your anxiety is ever-present, you can probably add the following to the list of symptoms: chest pain, over- or under-eating, insomnia, loss of sex drive.

All three situations described above are types of everyday anxiety, or as some would put it, the cost of living. But the cost can be huge, taking its toll on you physically, mentally, and emotionally.

What Causes Anxiety?

Essentially, anxiety is part of the "fight or flight" mechanism, a carryover from our ancient ancestors. They were hunters as well as the hunted; ready to attack or run from an attack. Their anxiety kept them alive, kicking in when adrenaline was released into the bloodstream. That big ol' bear was breathing down our ancestor's neck, and his adrenaline surged as a warning, causing his liver to release energy-stimulating sugars into his system to ready him for the fight. That was definitely an anxiety-filled situation, but that warning system was, and still is, necessary for today's emergencies.

Trouble is, we experience the manifestations of the "fight or flight" mechanism even when it's not really necessary. Certainly, your mother-in-law's visit isn't pleasant, but it's not life threatening, either. You feel your muscles knot up at the very mention of her name. That, in itself, isn't a problem. But when anxiety is severe or prolonged, the powerful "fight or flight" chemicals can damage your body's organs. Eventually, anxiety can cause chronic illnesses, such as headaches and high blood pressure.

While emotion is most often at the root of anxiety symptoms, they can be caused by physical problems as well. Rule out the following before assuming your symptoms are stress-related:

• Hyperthyroidism, which may produce symptoms that resemble those of anxiety

TIPS ON CUTTING THE CAFFEINE

Because caffeine can cause anxiety, and caffeine addiction symptoms mimic anxiety, this good-morning pick-me-up is at the head of the no-no list. But cutting it out all at once can cause withdrawal symptoms, including anxiety, irritability, headache, and fatigue.

To stop, cut back gradually until you are caffeine free and have no withdrawal symptoms. If you do experience withdrawal symptoms, especially as you near the end of all caffeine consumption, continue drinking 1 cup of a caffeinated beverage daily, then gradually cut back on that.

DON'T IGNORE CHEST PAINS!

Symptoms of hyperventilation may actually be the signs of other more serious health problems such as diabetes, heart disease, or thyroid disease. If you experience chest pains, numbness, shortness of breath, or dizziness, call your doctor or 9-1-1 immediately. Remember; a heart attack is a life-threatening medical emergency!

• Heart disorders, which can cause rapid heartbeat, often associated with anxiety

• Caffeine, which can produce nervous symptoms even in moderate amounts

• Premenstrual syndrome (PMS)

• Diet pills

• Anemia

• Diabetes

• Hypoglycemia

So now that you know what anxiety can do, it's time to learn what you can do to control it. Mild anxiety can be treated successfully at home with some soothing remedies from the kitchen.

FROM THE CUPBOARD

ALMONDS. Soak 10 raw almonds overnight in water to soften, then peel off the skins. Put almonds in blender with 1 cup warm milk, a pinch of ginger, and a pinch of nutmeg. Drink at night to relax before bedtime.

BAKING SODA. Add ⅓ cup baking soda and ⅓ cup ginger to a nice warm bath. Soak in the tub for 15 minutes to relieve tension and anxiety.

OIL. Sesame oil is great, but sunflower, coconut, or corn oil will work, too. For a wonderful, anxiety-busting massage, heat 6 ounces oil until warm, not hot. Rub over entire body, including your scalp and the bottoms of your feet. Use the oil as a massage before the morning bath to calm you down for the day's activities. If anxiety is keeping you awake, try using it before you go to bed, too.

FROM THE FREEZER

ICE. This is for muscle tension associated with anxiety. Wrap ice or a bag of frozen vegetables in a kitchen towel and apply it to tight muscles.

FROM THE REFRIGERATOR

CELERY AND ONIONS. This Hoosier remedy may calm your nerves. Eat 2 cups celery, onions, or a mixture of the two, raw or cooked, with your meals for a week or two. Both vegetables contain large amounts of potassium and folic acid, deficiencies of which can cause nervousness.

ORANGE. The aroma of an orange can reduce anxiety. All you have to do to get the benefits is peel an orange and inhale. You can also drop the peel into a small pan or potpourri burner. Cover with water and simmer. When heated, the orange peel will release its fragrant and calming oil.

ORANGE JUICE. For a racing heart rate associated with anxiety, stir 1 teaspoon honey and a pinch of nutmeg into 1 cup orange juice and drink.

FROM THE SPICE RACK

ROSEMARY. Once used by early Californians to rid themselves of "evil spirits," rosemary has a calming effect on the nerves. Make a tea by adding 1 to 2 teaspoons of the dried herb to 1 cup boiling water; steep for 10 minutes, then drink. Inhaling rosemary can be relaxing, too. Burn a sprig, or use rosemary incense to ease anxiety.

MORE DO'S & DON'TS

- Keep a diary to track and eliminate events that might trigger anxiety. Also make note of foods, since some of the things you eat may be responsible for the symptoms.

- Indulge in noncompetitive exercising, such as walking, bicycling, or swimming. It's good for you both physically and emotionally.

- Meditate, pray, indulge in a mental flight of fantasy. Do whatever it takes to give your mind a break.

- Breathe in, breathe out. Slowly, deeply. This is relaxing.

- Chat it away. With a friend, a psychotherapist, a clergyman. Talking about your anxiety can help relieve it.

- Make a mental list and check it twice. This is simply an exercise in repetitive thinking that can distract you from what's causing the anxiety.

FOLK REMEDY HERBAL CURES

These may not be found in your kitchen supplies, but if you experience frequent anxiety, it might be wise to give them an honored place of their own in the cupboard or drawer.

Warning! If you are taking any medication, whether it's over-the-counter or prescription, do not use any herbal remedy without first consulting your doctor. These cures can have bad side effects when mixed with other drugs!

Catnip. You may keep this one around for Fluffy, but it can help alleviate human anxiety. Make a tea by steeping 3 teaspoons catnip in 1 cup boiling water for 10 minutes. Sweeten to taste and drink three times a day.

Chamomile. This calms the nerves and aids in getting to sleep. When you feel anxious, simply steep 1 tablespoon chamomile flowers in 1 cup water for 15 minutes, then strain and drink as needed. Breathe in its aroma, too, for a soothing effect. Use chamomile in an aroma lamp, sachet, or potpourri. However, since chamomile contains pollen, be careful if you have allergies.

Ginseng. Simmer the root on low heat in enough water to cover the root twice. When half the water is evaporated, remove from heat to cool. Strain and drink twice a day. You can also buy ginseng extracts that readily dissolve in hot water.

Arthritis
PROTECTING YOUR JOINTS

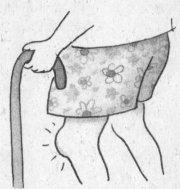

Arthritis means inflammation of the joints. To the millions of Americans afflicted by one of the 100 varieties of arthritis, every day can be painful. The two most prevalent forms of arthritis are osteoarthritis and rheumatoid arthritis.

Osteoarthritis (OA), the most common form, is the result of joint cartilage wearing down over time. When the durable, elastic tissue is gone, bones rub directly against one another. This causes stiffness and dull pain in the weight-bearing joints (hips, knees, and spine) and in the hands. The elderly are most susceptible to OA, but athletes and those in jobs requiring repetitive movements are also very vulnerable.

Rheumatoid arthritis (RA) is the inflammation of the joint lining. The cause is unknown, but it is thought that the symptoms are the result of the body turning against itself. Symptoms of RA vary from individual to individual. In its mildest form, it causes minor joint discomfort. More often, however, the inflammation causes painful, stiff, swollen joints, and in prolonged cases, severe joint damage. Unlike OA, whose symptoms are joint-specific, RA tends to cause body-wide symptoms such as fatigue, fever, and weight loss.

While it's typically thought that old age puts one at risk for arthritis, this isn't the case with RA. RA usually develops between the ages of 20 and 50 and is more common in women than in men.

Waking up with a stiff back or swollen finger joint doesn't necessarily indicate arthritis; however, should pain, stiffness, or swelling last more than two weeks, you may have arthritis. Other symptoms include:

• Swelling in one or more joints

• Early morning stiffness

• Recurring pain or tenderness in a joint

• Inability to move a joint normally

WHEN TO CALL THE DOCTOR

• When stiffness and pain last more than a few weeks

• If joint pain is accompanied by unexplained weight loss, fever, or weakness

• If the pain is severe enough to disrupt your daily routines and well-being

DUCKS AREN'T THE ONLY ONES WHO QUACK

Millions of people suffer from arthritic pain, and many arthritis sufferers will do just about anything to stop the suffering. Such desperation brings out the quacks who equate vulnerability with profit and promote miracle arthritic cures for a high price. Tread carefully when it comes to seeking arthritis treatment outside the established medical realm or you may suffer both physically and financially.

- Remember, there is no cure for arthritis. Beware any person, food, drug, liquid, therapy, or vacation retreat that promises a cure.
- Watch for words such as "Secret Formula," "Special Product," or "Quick, Simple Cures." All are sure signs of quackery.
- Look closely at products displayed in magazines. Is the article you're reading an "advertorial," written and paid for by the product's manufacturer, or was it written by an objective source?
- Beware testimonials, especially when the person "testifying" only uses a first name and last initial.

- Redness or warmth in a joint
- Unexplained weight loss, fever, or weakness accompanied by joint pain

There is no cure for arthritis, but many kitchen-crafted remedies can help ease the pain.

FROM THE CUPBOARD

ASPARTAME. Drink to pain relief with a sugar-free soda pop. A research experiment published in the scientific journal *Clinical Pharmacology and Therapeutics* noted that aspartame—an artificial sweetener found in brands Equal and NutraSweet—provides relief that's comparable to anti-inflammatory agents. Ask your doctor about the study and exactly how much you should drink.

EPSOM SALTS. Magnesium sulfate, otherwise known as Epsom salts, is commonly used to relieve aching joints and reduce swelling. Mix a few heaping tablespoons into the bathwater and soak. More localized soaks are sometimes necessary, especially for the feet. Rest painful feet in a tub of warm water combined with 2 tablespoons Epsom salts. Relax for 15 minutes, pat your tootsies dry, and massage them with your favorite lotion.

FROM THE REFRIGERATOR

DAIRY PRODUCTS. Some medicines used to treat arthritis can lead to a loss of calcium from the bones, resulting in osteoporosis. To counteract this

A PERSEVERANT PAINTER

"For me a picture has to be something pleasant, delightful, and pretty, yes, pretty. There are enough unpleasant things in the world without us producing even more."—
PIERRE-AUGUSTE RENOIR

How true his words were. Renoir, the famous 19th-century French artist, painted nearly 6,000 works of art while at the same time battling severe rheumatoid arthritis, truly one of the "unpleasant things in the world." Later in life, when the disease seriously took hold, he still painted daily, despite being unable to pick up a paintbrush without assistance. (Brushes had to be placed between his fingers.) Even after he was bedridden and paralyzed, Renoir persevered, using his mind in place of his fingers. Many of his sculptures never touched the master's hands. Instead he verbally guided his assistants on what to create until he was satisfied with the outcome.

effect (and to keep healthy in general) make sure you get enough calcium in your diet. A cup of low-fat yogurt, for instance, supplies 300 to 400 mg calcium—about one-third of your daily requirement. Calcium-fortified orange juice will also help you meet your daily calcium needs.

FOOD. Decreasing arthritis pain and stiffness may be as easy as eliminating certain foods from your refrigerator and, thus, from your diet. However, the deduction process is a bit difficult, requiring time and observation. There are no set guidelines for this remedy. Rather, it is intuitive. Do you ache more after eating a certain food? Keep a food diary, record what you've eliminated from your diet that week, and rate your discomfort level. There are no guarantees, but you may discover that certain foods contribute to stiffness.

GAMMA LINOLENIC ACID. Recent research suggests that high doses of an omega-6 essential fatty acid, known as gamma linolenic acid (GLA), can help reduce joint inflammation. You'll find GLA in some plant seed oils, such as evening primrose and borage, and in black currants. Research also indicates that the benefits of GLA may be enhanced by supplementation with omega-3 fatty acids, which are plentiful in cold-water fish. You can also take GLA supplements; 1,800 mg a day is recommended for rheumatoid arthritis.

FROM THE SINK

HOT AND COLD COMPRESSES. Hot and cold compresses are the simplest remedies for relieving stiff and painful joints. Which to choose depends on what feels good to you...and may depend on the temperature outside.

Heat—in the form of a hot, moist towel—combats pain by relaxing muscles and joints and decreasing stiffness. A heating pad or a warm bath or shower will also do the trick. Cold compresses put the chill on joints "hot" from inflammation, common with rheumatoid arthritis. Cold helps, too, when you need to pinpoint a specific joint for pain relief.

Constructing a cold compress is as easy as running cold water in the sink and soaking a washcloth in it. You can also fill up a plastic bag with crushed ice or use a frozen package of vegetables (peas are perfect). If you use ice, wrap the cold pack in a towel to prevent developing a "freezer burn" on your skin. Apply to sore spots.

FROM THE SUPPLEMENT SHELF

CALCIUM. The Recommended Dietary Allowance is 1,000 mg calcium per day for women prior to menopause and 1,200 to 1,500 mg after menopause. Men require 800 mg per day. If you don't get enough calcium in your diet, be sure to supplement to protect your bones.

GLUCOSAMINE. Glucosamine supplements, often found in products that contain a combination with chondroitin, help relieve the pain and may slow the joint degeneration associated with osteoarthritis. The recommended dosage is 500 mg of glucosamine three times a day. It usually takes two to three months of supplementation to achieve optimal results. Ongoing supplementation is required to maintain this benefit.

MORE DO'S AND DON'TS

Kitchen cures don't only come from the spice rack or stove. Little adjustments in the kitchen itself may make a big difference in protecting arthritic joints from injury or excessive strain.

- Buy kitchen drawer knobs with long, thin handles. These require a looser, less stressful grip.

- More padding means less pain. On tools that require a grip, such as brooms and mops, add a layer of thin foam rubber around the handles and fasten with tape.

- Use lightweight pots and pans with comfortable handles.

- Utilize a pair of long-handled pinchers (or a gripper) to pick up objects on the floor.

- Transport groceries or heavy items from car to kitchen using a wagon or cart.

- Use loops made of soft but strong fabric or rope to pull the refrigerator and oven doors open without strain.

Asthma

WEATHERING THE WHEEZE

Recent statistics about asthma don't paint a pretty picture. The disease now affects 17 million people in the United States—that's an increase of 2.5 million people in five years. Asthma is the number one cause of chronic illness in kids, affecting more than 5.5 million children. Despite this discouraging news, there is reason to be hopeful if you are one of the millions of asthmatics across the country. As the numbers of asthma cases continue to climb, researchers are even more determined to find asthma's causes and develop more effective treatments.

Breathing Basics

When you take a breath, the air goes from your mouth or nose to the windpipe (or trachea). It then travels to the lungs. It first enters the lungs through the bronchi, a group of tubes that branch off from the windpipe. The bronchi then branch off into bronchioles. Imagine a car driving from the interstate to a state highway to a country road and you get the picture.

Asthma happens when the bronchi and bronchioles come in contact with a foreign invader, or asthma "trigger." There are many different triggers, and each person has his own set. Once a foreign material enters the body, the airways quickly become inflamed, causing the muscles that rest on the outside of the airways to tighten and narrow. This allows a thick mucus to enter the airways. The mucus causes swelling and makes it very difficult to breathe. The classic symptoms of an asthma attack include wheezing, tightening in the chest, dry coughing, and increased heart rate—symptoms that are frightening to experience and to observe.

THE COST OF ASTHMA

In 1998, asthma's estimated cost in the United States was a whopping $11.3 billion. This includes direct costs, such as hospitalization and medical bills, and indirect costs such as lost workdays and school days. (Asthma is responsible for 9 million lost workdays every year.)

Asthma's Instigators

About half of all asthma attacks are caused by allergies. The most common allergens are dust mites, cockroaches, chemicals, pollen, mold, and animal dander.

In addition to allergens, asthma triggers include:

- Tobacco smoke. There is a direct relationship between secondhand smoke and asthma. It's especially bad for children and teenagers to be around tobacco smoke.

- Exercise. Working out, especially outside in the cold, can cause exercise-induced asthma. This is not an excuse for people with asthma to shy away from exercise; they just need to consult the doctor about how to control the attacks.

- Weather. Cold air can act as an asthma trigger. But other weather conditions such as rain, wind, or a sudden change in the weather can cause an attack.

- Chemicals. This includes chemical fumes, such as from paint or perfume, and chemical additives, such as the sulfites that are used as preservatives in food. Any of these can trigger an asthma attack in susceptible people.

- Respiratory infections. Colds, sinus infections, even the flu can predispose one for or aggravate asthma. It's a good idea for asthmatics to get a flu shot each year.

- Stomach acid. Excess stomach acid can irritate the esophagus lining and create a reaction in the lungs that may cause an attack.

- Pregnancy. One-third of pregnant women with asthma get worse, but one-third of pregnant women with asthma get better, too. And one-third remain the same.

- Emotional stress. Though a stressful day at work won't cause an asthma attack, it can aggravate the condition.

- Drugs. Some people with asthma are sensitive to certain drugs. The most common culprits are aspirin and nonsteroidal anti-inflammatory drugs (NSAIDs).

WHEN TO CALL THE DOCTOR

Asthma attacks can be deadly. Each year there are more than 5,300 deaths from asthma. Those deaths are preventable, but you need to know when to take quick action. Get to an emergency room fast if you have any of these symptoms:

- If breathing gets difficult, especially if your neck, chest, or ribs pull in every time you take a breath, or if you have a feeling of suffocation

- If nostrils begin to flare

- If walking or talking is a chore

- If fingernails or lips turn blue

- If you are dizzy

- If ears, palms, genitals, or soles of feet begin itching

- If you have hives

- If you have a feeling of imminent doom

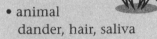
Though there are many natural ways to help asthma sufferers breathe easier, experts say that your best bet to attack your asthma is combining certain natural remedies with prescription anti-inflammatories and bronchodilators. Here are some helpful remedies right from the kitchen.

FROM THE CUPBOARD

COFFEE. The caffeine in regular coffee can help prevent and treat asthma attacks. Researchers have found that regular coffee drinkers have one-third fewer asthma symptoms than those who don't drink the hot stuff. And caffeine has bronchodilating effects. In fact, caffeine was one of the main anti-asthmatic drugs during the 19th century. Don't load up on java, though. Three cups a day provides the maximum benefit.

ONIONS. Onions are loaded with anti-inflammatory properties. Studies have shown that these properties can reduce the constriction of the airways in an asthma attack. Use cooked onions, as raw onions are generally too irritating.

FROM THE DRAWER

CHEESECLOTH. Put a fine cheesecloth over each room's heat outlet. This homemade dust filter can help freshen the air in your home. Commercial stick-on fine filters are also available.

FROM THE REFRIGERATOR

CHILI PEPPERS. Hot foods such as chili peppers open up airways. Experts believe this is because peppers stimulate fluids in the mouth, throat, and lungs. The increase in fluids thins out the mucus formed during an asthma attack so it can be coughed up, making breathing easier. Capsaicin, the stuff that makes hot peppers hot, acts as an anti-inflammatory when eaten and a bronchodilator when inhaled in small doses.

ORANGE JUICE. Vitamin C is the main antioxidant in the lining of the bronchi and bronchioles. Research discovered that people with asthma had low levels of vitamin C and that eating foods that had at least 300 mg of vitamin C a day—equivalent to about 3 glasses of orange juice—cut wheezing by 30 percent.

SALMON. Fatty fish such as sardines, salmon, mackerel, and tuna contain omega-3 fatty acids. These fatty acids seem to help the lungs react better to irritants in people who have asthma and may even help prevent asthma in people who have never had an attack. Studies have found that kids who eat fish more than once a week have one-third the chance of getting asthma as children who don't eat fish. And researchers found that people who took fish oil supplements, equivalent to eating 8 ounces of mackerel a day, increased their ability to avoid a severe asthma attack by 50 percent.

YOGURT. Vitamin B_{12} can improve the symptoms of asthma and seems to be even more effective in asthma sufferers who are sensitive to sulfite. Studies have found that taking 1 to 4 micrograms (mcg) works best as protection against asthma attacks. The current RDA for vitamin B_{12} is 2.4 mcg for adults. One cup of yogurt has 1.4 mcg of the lung-loving vitamin.

FROM THE SPICE RACK

PEPPERMINT EXTRACT. Here's a folk remedy for a homemade vaporizer. Put 1 quart nonchlorinated water in a stainless steel, glass, or enamel pan, and put it on the stove. Add 10 drops peppermint extract or peppermint oil and bring to a boil. Simmer for about 1 hour, until all the water is gone. The volatile oil will saturate the room air.

MORE DO'S AND DON'TS

- Take it easy on the salt. Salt tends to make the airways more sensitive to triggers.

- Consider a vegan diet. Getting rid of animal products in the diet helps asthma by eliminating many food allergens (cow's milk, for example) and, if you add asthma-aiding nutrients such as vitamin C to your diet, you can greatly improve asthma symptoms.

- Watch out for other foods, such as eggs, some types of fish, nuts, chocolate, and sodas, all of which can cause allergy attacks, especially in children. An attack precipitated by something you ate will most likely occur within an hour of eating the suspect food.

Athlete's Foot

FIGHTING THE FUNGUS

Athlete's foot itches, burns, and is downright ugly to look at. But it's not a condition unique to athletes. Blame the misnomer on the ad man who gave it its name in the 1930s. In fact, athlete's foot, or *tinea pedis*, is the most common fungal infection of the skin. This fungus loves moist places, especially the soft, warm, damp skin between the toes. Certainly the athlete's locker room environment, with its steamy showers, is a good place for the fungus to thrive. But tinea pedis is actually present on most people's skin all the time, just waiting for the right opportunity to develop into an infection.

Who Gets It?

So what causes athlete's foot to rear its ugly little fungal head? Skin that's irritated, weakened, or continuously moist is primed for an athlete's foot infection. And certain medications, including antibiotics, corticosteroids, birth control pills, and drugs that suppress immune function, can make you more susceptible. People who are obese and those who have diabetes mellitus or a weakened immune system, such as those with AIDS, also are at increased risk. And some people may be genetically predisposed to developing athlete's foot.

Anyone can get athlete's foot—and most people will at some time in their lives. Teenage and adult males, though, are the most susceptible. They're at the top of the fungus-footed list. Who's at the bottom? The following are those who are least likely to succumb:

WHEN TO CALL THE DOCTOR

- If the infection gets worse no matter what you do
- If one or both feet swell
- If you see pus in the cracks
- If the fungus spreads to your hands or elsewhere
- If you see an obvious change in color in your toenails, especially the nail of your big toe
- If you develop pain in the feet along with angry-looking inflammation, general malaise, fever, or chills. Your athlete's foot could be turning into a much more serious condition called cellulitis, which MUST be treated by a physician immediately.

- People who spend a lot of time barefoot
- Women
- Children under the age of 12

Signs and Symptoms

Just because you're not in the high risk category doesn't mean you're safe. Here's how you can tell whether you have an athlete's foot infection:

- Itching, scaling, red skin
- Red, cracking, peeling skin between the toes
- Dry, flaking skin
- Blisters
- Unpleasant and unusual foot odor

Keep It From Spreading

In extreme cases, the fungus that causes athlete's foot can spread to other moist areas of the body, such as the groin and even the armpits. So take precautions when coming into contact with that athlete's foot. Be sure to wash your hands with soap and water after contact. Keep your linens and towels clean, and never wear the same pair of socks twice without first washing them. You can also spread athlete's foot with contaminated sheets, towels, and clothing.

There are any number of antifungal creams on the market that can rid you of your foot fungus. They're costly, and you may have to buy several tubes or cans before the problem is cleared. So before you trudge off to the pharmacy on those poor, itchy feet, try some of the following kitchen concoctions.

FUNGUS TOENAIL

Yep, the creeping athlete's foot fungus can creep right on up to your toenail if your infection goes untreated long enough. Called tinea unguium, toenail fungus turns the nail yellowish or brown and makes it thicken and crack. As the fungus grows, the nail will give off a foul odor. Eventually the toe under and around the nail can start to throb as the infection takes a firm hold and pus builds up in the irritated areas.

Athlete's foot is easily treated but not so fungus toe. It may respond to any of the kitchen remedies in this profile or to an over-the-counter or prescription antifungal treatment. But occasionally the nail must be surgically removed. The simplest solution is to treat the initial athlete's foot infection as soon as it appears to keep it from spreading.

FROM THE CUPBOARD

BAKING SODA. Sprinkle baking soda directly into your shoes to absorb moisture.

CORNSTARCH. Rub cornstarch, which absorbs moisture, on your feet. Very lightly browned cornstarch is even better because any moisture content already contained in the cornstarch is removed, allowing for better absorption. To brown, sprinkle cornstarch on a pie plate and bake at

FASCINATING FACT
Feet have more sweat glands than any other area of the body. On a good day, they can sweat up to ½ cup each.

325°F for a few minutes, until it looks brownish. Cool, then dab some on your feet and toes.

GARLIC. Eat some garlic, as it has antifungal properties. You can also swab the affected area with garlic juice or oregano oil twice a day.

If your toenail appears to have the fungus, use this recipe, which is usually effective:

Crush 1 clove garlic and mix with a few drops of olive oil to make a paste. Apply to the nail and leave on for 15 to 30 minutes, then clean it off in warm, soapy water. Dry feet thoroughly. Repeat daily. Because the fungus can return, you may wish to continue with this treatment for several weeks after it has disappeared to ward off another fungal visit.

IMMUNE-BOOSTING FOODS. Because low immunity can make you more susceptible to a fungal infection, diets rich in immune-boosting foods might make it possible for you to tiptoe through the shower without getting infected. These foods might help: garlic, sweet potatoes, whole-grain breads, sunflower seeds, onions, and rice. (See also "From the Refrigerator" below for more immune-boosting foods.)

SALT. Soak your infected foot in warm salt water, using 1 teaspoon salt for each cup of water, for ten minutes. Dry your foot thoroughly, then dab some baking soda between your toes.

TEA. The tannic acid in tea is soothing and helps dry the foot and kill the fungus. Make a foot soak by putting 6 black tea bags in 1 quart warm water.

VINEGAR. Soak your feet in 1 cup vinegar to 2 quarts water for 15 to 30 minutes every night. Or make a solution of 1 cup vinegar to 1 cup water, and apply it directly to the affected areas with a cotton ball. If the infection is severe and the skin is raw, the solution will sting. Make sure your feet are completely dry before putting on your socks or slippers.

Cider vinegar can also be used as a remedy. Mix equal parts apple cider (or regular) vinegar and ethyl alcohol. Dab on the affected areas.

FROM THE REFRIGERATOR

IMMUNE-BOOSTING FOODS. Low immunity can make you more susceptible to a fungal infection, so include some of these immune-boosting foods in your diet: broccoli, red meats, and scallions. (See also "From the Cupboard" above for more immune-boosting foods.)

LEMON. Squeeze the juice from a lemon and mix it with 2 ounces water. Rinse your feet with the lemon water to help prevent sweaty foot odor.

YOGURT. One of the greatest of all fungus-fighting foods in your fridge is yogurt that contains acidophilus. It doesn't matter what the flavor is as long as the yogurt contains the active bacteria (check the label; it will tell you). Acidophilus helps control vaginal and oral yeast, but it may give other fungi a pretty good fight. And if nothing else, it tastes good and is good for you, too!

FROM THE SPICE RACK

CINNAMON. A good soak in a cinnamon tea foot bath will help slow down the fungus. Boil 8 to 10 broken cinnamon sticks in 4 cups water, then simmer for five minutes. Let steep for another 45 minutes. Soak your feet for 15 to 30 minutes. Repeat daily as needed.

MORE DO'S AND DON'TS

- Don't wear tight-fitting or watertight shoes. Skip shoes made of plastic and rubber, too. The best shoe choices are those made of natural materials that "breathe," such as leather.

- Don't share or swap shoes with anybody. If you find yourself with a pair of someone else's vintage shoes, treat them with antifungal powder before you put them on.

- Wear sandals or thongs on your feet in fungus-harboring public places such as beach showers and locker rooms; don't go barefoot.

- Set your shoes outside to air on a warm, sunny day. This will help dry them out and kill the fungus. Alternate shoes every day.

- When selecting socks, try both natural and synthetic fabrics to see which keep your sweaty feet the driest. You may wish to try synthetic sock liners to absorb the moisture and keep it away from your skin.

- Give your socks a double washing in extra hot water to kill the fungal spores.

- Make sure to dry thoroughly between your toes after bathing. That's where athlete's foot usually starts.

- Go barefoot as often as you can. This will get your foot outside the moist shoe environment, where fungus loves to lurk. It's best to go barefoot indoors, though, as you are less likely to cut, scrape, or otherwise injure your feet.

AVOID THIS HOUSEHOLD REMEDY

One of the oldest folk remedies for athlete's foot is to soak your tootsies in diluted bleach water. The remedy called for using ¼ cup bleach for each quart of water. You were supposed to make enough to cover your feet and soak them for 20 minutes.

The theory was that the bleach solution would dry out the skin and kill the infection. And it will do that. But the chlorine in the bleach is a harsh chemical, and it can cause skin damage while not necessarily killing the fungus. Be cautious about using chemicals and solvents such as bleach and alcohol. They may do more harm than good, despite the fact that many natural remedy practitioners still swear by the bleach treatment.

Back Pain
ANSWERING THE ACHE

People are bad to their backs, crouch-
ing over keyboards for eight hours,
struggling to lift heavy objects, or
quickly transforming themselves from
sedentary office workers to weekend
warriors. Whatever the action, the
back often can't handle such stress,
and it reacts with pain.

Almost everyone will experience
back pain once in their life. Lower
back pain has many causes, including
common muscle strain and more
serious problems with the bones in the spine (vertebrae) and the disks of
shock-absorbing material that separate them. Why is the lower back such
a glutton for punishment? Unlike the upper back, it isn't supported by
the rib cage, and many people don't exercise the back and the supporting abdominal muscles as they should.

Back pain remedies rely primarily on rest, strengthening and stretching exercises, and modification of daily routine. However, the kitchen
shelves do hold a few ingredients that can help get that back back into
shape.

FROM THE CUPBOARD

CHAMOMILE TEA. Daily stress can turn back muscles into a knot. Luckily,
chamomile tea offers some calming relief to soothe tense muscle tissue.
During a break or after work, treat yourself to a steaming mug. Steep
1 tablespoon chamomile flowers in 1 cup boiling water for 15 minutes.
Or, you can use a prepackaged chamomile tea. Drink 1 to 3 cups a day.

Warning! Chamomile contains allergy-inducing proteins related to
ragweed pollen. Ask your doctor about drinking chamomile if you are
allergic to ragweed. Packaged tea may be safer to drink than tea made
from the flowers. Your doctor can advise you.

EPSOM SALTS. Epsom salts ease back pain by reducing swelling. Fill your
bathtub as usual and add 2 cups salts. Soak for 30 minutes.

RICE. Fill a clean, thick sock with 1 cup uncooked rice and place in the
microwave for 30 to 60 seconds on medium-low. Check the temperature
and apply to the back.

From the Freezer

Cold compresses. Cold compresses or ice packs should be applied immediately after back strain or injury. When the back suffers injury, blood rushes to the damaged area. Even though the resulting swelling is normal, too much inflammation can increase pain and lengthen your recovery period. An icy application reduces inflammation and helps numb pain. To make a cold compress, pack a few crushed cubes of ice into a plastic, reclosable bag, cover with a washcloth or towel, and apply to the back for 15 minutes. Take it off for 30 minutes, and then replace it for 15 more minutes. (A bag of frozen vegetables also works well. Wrap them in a towel, too.)

(Hot compresses can be used 48 hours after the injury. See "From the Stove," page 38, and the "Rice" section, page 36.)

From the Refrigerator

Ginger root. Fragrant ginger root has long been known to cure nausea, but can it cure back pain, too? Ginger does contain anti-inflammatory compounds, including some with mild aspirinlike effects. When your back aches, cut a 1- to 2-inch fresh ginger root into slices and place in 1 quart boiling water. Simmer, covered, for 30 minutes on low heat. Cool for 30 minutes. Strain, sweeten with honey (to taste), and drink.

Milk. Bone up on milk. Women especially should take care to include plenty of calcium in their diets. (Older women are at greater risk for developing osteoporosis, the disease of eroding bones.) Calcium helps build strong bones and protect the spine from osteoporosis.

From the Spice Rack

Cayenne pepper. How 'bout some hot stuff for your back? Cayenne pepper pulls no punches in delivering a hot and healing back pain remedy. Cayenne pepper (and all peppers for that matter) contains capsaicin, the fiery source of its heat. Capsaicin causes nerve endings to release substance P, a chemical that transmits pain signals from the body to the brain. When the nerve endings have lost all of their substance P, no pain signals can be transmitted back to the brain. Voilà! You feel no pain.

When to Call the Doctor

- When the pain radiates from your lower back to the buttocks or down your legs
- If you experience numbness in the leg, foot, groin, or rectal area
- If the back pain is accompanied by fever, nausea, vomiting, stomachache, weakness, or excessive sweating
- If you lose control of your bowel and/or bladder functions
- When the pain is intense
- When a back injury is cramping your lifestyle

To make a cayenne back rub, place 1 ounce cayenne pepper into 1 pint boiling water. Simmer for 30 minutes, remove from heat, and add a pint of rubbing alcohol. Cool and use when needed.

You can also make a pepper poultice by mixing cayenne pepper with flour and water to form a paste. Spread onto muslin, wrap up, and apply to the back.

Warning! Never apply cayenne pepper directly to the skin or you may suffer a burn or blisters. Do not touch your eyes while handling cayenne pepper, and always wash your hands well after handling peppers of any sort. Better yet, wear disposable rubber gloves.

Capsaicin ointment, 0.025 percent, is also available over the counter.

ROSEMARY. Rosemary's leaves are packed with these anti-inflammatory substances: carnosol, oleanolic acid, rosmarinic acid, and ursolic acid, all of which work to ease swollen tissues. To make a tea that relieves pain: Place ½ ounce dried rosemary leaves into 1 quart boiling water. Cover and steep for 30 minutes. Drink 1 cup tea at bedtime and another cup before eating breakfast.

FROM THE STOVE

HOT COMPRESSES. You can begin to apply heat to your back 48 hours after an injury. Warmth relaxes tight muscles, increases blood flow, and feels terrific. Soak a washcloth in water that you've heated on the stove, use a heating pad, or take a hot shower or bath.

LEARN TO LIFT

Working in the kitchen requires more lifting, bending, and standing than you may think. You lug in the groceries, reach to put them away, lift a heavy saucepan from the cabinet, stand over the stove for an hour. Here are some back-saving tips to use when in the kitchen.

- Always stand with your feet shoulder-width apart. This gives you a solid base of support. If you'll be peeling potatoes for hours, place one leg on a stool or a heavy book to relieve back strain.
- Keep knees slightly bent. Never lock your knees.
- Suck that stomach in! Abdominal muscles help support your back.
- When lifting, position the person or object close to your body, and lift using your leg muscles. Squat; don't bend at the waist.
- Try not to twist and turn when lifting. To move, point your toes in the direction you want to move and pivot in that direction.
- Push, don't pull, grocery carts, baby buggies, or anything with wheels.
- Wear flat shoes or heels no higher than one inch.
- Don't think you're Hercules. Ask for assistance if an item is too heavy or too awkward to lift alone.

MORE DOS AND DON'TS

- Get some ZZZs. If you're not in the kitchen working on back pain cures, head to bed! Bed rest can help relieve muscle strain. Back muscles work all day to hold you erect; lying down takes the stress off. Be sure to lie flat on your back with two pillows underneath your knees. But don't overdo it. Doctors rarely recommend extended bed rest for sore backs anymore. More than a day or two of rest may actually prolong your recovery. If you are still in too much pain to walk after two days, call your doctor.

> ### FASCINATING FACT
> Back pain affects 31 million Americans and is spread evenly between men and women. No age is immune, but it is most common in middle age.

- Relax! When you're tense, so are those back muscles. Try some relaxation exercises, such as closing your eyes, breathing deeply, and counting backward from 100.

- Sit in comfort. Are your kitchen chairs padded? Does your car seat support the small of your back? Comfort should always come first wherever you park yourself. Buy inexpensive cushions for wooden or metal chairs and a small cushion for the car seat. Watch how you sit, too. It is better to lean back at an angle of 110 degrees than to sit straighter than an arrow.

- Less is more: Maintaining your ideal weight helps take pressure off back muscles. The less you have to carry, the less burden to the supporting muscles and bones. Additionally, beer bellies and pendulous abdomens can cause you to become sway-backed, which only serves to accentuate back pain.

Bad Breath

HALTING HALITOSIS

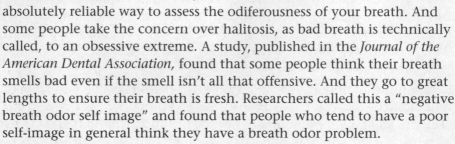

Most people are worried about having bad breath—they don't want their breath to walk into a room before they do. That's why Americans spend a billion dollars a year on mints, mouthwash, and minty-fresh toothpastes. They hope that these will prevent others from recoiling every time they speak.

Concern and awareness about the possibility of bad breath is certainly normal, and even desirable. But the truth is, there is no absolutely reliable way to assess the odiferousness of your breath. And some people take the concern over halitosis, as bad breath is technically called, to an obsessive extreme. A study, published in the *Journal of the American Dental Association,* found that some people think their breath smells bad even if the smell isn't all that offensive. And they go to great lengths to ensure their breath is fresh. Researchers called this a "negative breath odor self image" and found that people who tend to have a poor self-image in general think they have a breath odor problem.

WHEN TO CALL THE DOCTOR

If you have chronic bad breath and your dentist gives your mouth a clean bill of health. Make an appointment with your doctor to rule out any other conditions that might be causing your bout with foul breath. Some specialists now treat chronic halitosis.

Harboring Halitosis?

Only about 25 percent of the population deal with chronically bad breath. Are you one of them? You can try breathing into a handkerchief, running floss through your mouth, or licking the back of your hand, waiting a few minutes, and then sniffing. The Japanese have even tried to develop an electronic breath-sniffing device. But the truth is, people are immune to their own odors, offensive or not. So have a spouse or a (really) close, honest friend sniff your breath (use the same friend who always tells you when you have green stuff in your teeth) and give you the verdict.

More than likely, your fears of halitosis are all in your head. But if you discover your breath does have an unpleasant odor, there is usually a very treatable reason. Ninety percent of bad breath is a result of bacteria from something you ate setting up house in your mouth. Even when you brush and floss regularly, you can still miss some food particles. This can cause smelly breath. Other reasons for bad breath include

- Potent foods. Garlic and onions, among other foods, contain sulfur compounds that move on to the lungs after they're absorbed in the bloodstream. Unfortunately, during the move the chemicals that make these foods so tasty and pungent stick around. And they don't smell so great as you whisper sweet nothings into your sweetheart's ear. In some cultures, however, garlic and onion are so common in the food that they're considered desirable aromas even on the breath.

- Periodontal (gum) disease. Caused by a buildup of plaque on the teeth, periodontal disease can result in chronically bad breath.

- Dry mouth. Saliva is the mop of the mouth. It cleanses and removes potentially smelly particles. When you don't produce enough saliva, you end up with bad breath. That's why when you wake up in the morning, you go running for the nearest toothbrush. You produce less saliva while you sleep, and that causes you to wake up with icky breath.

- Hunger. If you haven't eaten in a while, you develop a very distinctive breath smell. Some scientists believe this happens because pancreatic juices pass into the stomach when a person doesn't eat for some time. This is another factor in morning breath.

- Smoking. Tobacco is a major factor in bad breath. Ever heard the saying, "Kissing a smoker is like licking an ashtray"? There's a reason for that. Tobacco causes bad breath, stains the teeth, and interferes with your ability to taste food. Tobacco also irritates gum tissue, making smokers more likely to suffer periodontal disease.

FIVE STEPS TO FRESH BREATH

- Brush teeth twice a day and floss regularly.
- Use your toothbrush to brush your tongue after you've brushed your teeth.
- Chew sugarless gum or candy to keep your mouth moist.
- Rinse your mouth with water after you eat.
- Chew on parsley after eating.

FASCINATING FACT

Believe it or not, most people can tell, within 95 percent accuracy, if a person is a man or woman by the way their breath smells.

IS MOUTHWASH WORTH IT?

 As much as most people would like to think mouthwash gets rid of offending odors, it only covers odors temporarily (from 20 minutes to 2 hours). Look for mouthwashes that contain cetylpyridinium chloride (CPC); essential oils of lime, cinnamon, or cloves; zinc chloride; or chlorhexidine. These compounds neutralize odors and/or inhibit bacterial growth.

ANCIENT REMEDIES FOR BAD BREATH

Yes, bad breath has been a bane of existence for centuries. According to the Academy of General Dentistry, ancient Greeks rinsed with white wine, aniseed, and myrrh. Italians created a mouthwash of sage, cinnamon, juniper seeds, root of cypress, and rosemary leaves.

• Sinus infections and stuffy noses can cause smelly breath.

• Other, more serious illnesses can cause distinctive breath odors. People with kidney failure may have breath that smells like urine. Liver failure can cause a "fishy" breath smell. And fruity breath can signal diabetes.

• Some prescription drugs can cause bad breath.

• Certain fish, such as anchovies, and seaweed are high in "fishy" amine odors.

FROM THE CUPBOARD

BAKING SODA. Baking soda is a great way to clean your teeth and get fresh breath. For fresher breath, sprinkle some baking soda into your palm, dip a damp toothbrush into the baking soda, and brush.

If brushing with plain baking soda sounds icky, try adding a little artificial sugar, such as saccharine or aspartame. Or you can make your own toothpaste: Mix 3 parts baking soda with 1 part salt; add 3 teaspoons glycerin and 10 to 20 drops of your favorite flavoring (peppermint, wintergreen, anise, cinnamon); add enough water to make a paste.

To create a tooth powder, mix 3 parts baking soda with 1 part salt. Add a few drops of peppermint or wintergreen oil.

SUGARLESS GUM OR CANDY. To keep your mouth moist and increase saliva flow, the American Dental Association suggests chewing sugarless gum or sucking on sugarless candy. These are made with sorbitol, mannitol, or xylitol (sugar alcohols), which do not support oral bacterial growth.

FROM THE FAUCET

WATER. Water is essential for fresher breath. Swish water around your mouth for at least 20 seconds to loosen food particles and clean your mouth. Water may even work as well as mouthwash in removing trapped food particles and keeping your breath fresh.

FROM THE REFRIGERATOR

FRESH VEGETABLES. Fresh vegetables, such as carrots and celery, fight plaque and keep your breath smelling nice.

PARSLEY. Parsley is not just for decoration. It's long been used as a breath neutralizer. Parsley won't get rid of bad breath, but it may help mask the garlic shrimp you had for dinner.

FROM THE SPICE RACK

AROMATIC SPICES. Chewing on the seeds of aromatic spices such as clove, cardamom, or fennel after meals is a common practice in South Asia and the Middle East. The seeds of these spices contain antimicrobial properties that can help halt bad breath.

MORE DO'S AND DON'TS

- Reduce stress. Stress can dry out your mouth, causing bad breath.

- If you wear dentures, don't sleep with them. Give them a through cleaning, and leave them out until morning.

- Practice good oral hygiene. Brush your teeth twice a day to remove plaque and food particles that can cause bad breath (and tooth decay!). Be sure to brush your tongue or use a tongue scraper. And floss once a day to clean trapped particles from between your teeth.

TOP TEN BREATH OFFENDERS FROM THE KITCHEN

Garlic
Raw onions
Cabbage
Horseradish
Eggs
Broccoli
Brussels sprouts
Fish
Red meat
Coffee

FASCINATING FACT

The average person produces more than two quarts of saliva a day.

Bites and Stings
REDUCING THE REACTION

With billions of bugs out there, you're bound to get bit or stung sometime in your life. Typically, the worst reactions are to bees, yellow jackets, hornets, wasps, and fire ants. Other nasty creatures, such as blackflies, horseflies, black or red (not fire) ants, and mosquitoes, also bite and sting, but their venom usually does not cause as intense a reaction. No matter who attacks, once you're zapped the body reacts with redness, itching, pain, and swelling at the bite site. These symptoms may last for a few minutes or a few hours. Thankfully, relief is as close as the kitchen.

Warning! The remedies apply to bites and stings from the insects listed above. A health provider should treat those from snakes, spiders, scorpions, ticks, centipedes, and animals.

FROM THE CUPBOARD

ACTIVATED CHARCOAL. This can help draw out toxins that cause inflammation, swelling, and itching. To make a paste, open up 2 to 3 capsules of charcoal, mix with enough water to make a paste, and apply to the affected area. After 30 minutes, wipe the paste off with a wet cloth.

BAKING SODA. Itching can be tamed by applying a paste of 3 teaspoons baking soda to 1 teaspoon water directly to the site. This remedy is especially good for ant bites and bee stings, both of which are acidic in nature.

VINEGAR: 10,000 YEARS OLD AND GOING STRONG

The virtues of vinegar have long been played out in history. Hippocrates extolled its medicinal qualities, the Babylonians used it as a preservative, and the Roman legionnaires swilled it down before doing battle.

MEAT TENDERIZER. Meat tenderizers contain the enzyme papain that, when applied immediately, degrades the venom and reduces swelling. Use an unseasoned brand, mix a few teaspoons with a few drops of water, and apply the paste to the sting. Time is of the essence with this technique. Once the venom proteins penetrate deep into the skin, it's too late for the tenderizer to reach and degrade them.

TEA BAGS. Soak a tea bag in water to use as a poultice. Or when you make hot or iced tea, save the used tea bag in the refrigerator for a few days to use as a poultice. The tannic acid in tea helps decrease the swelling from a sting.

Black tea is the most effective. Apply cooled tea bags to bites and stings as needed.

FROM THE FREEZER

ICE. Ice or any cold compress does triple first-aid duty by diminishing the itch, reducing inflammation, and easing the pain of bites and stings. Put crushed ice into a plastic bag (or use a bag of frozen vegetables), wrap it in a towel, and apply to the site for 20 minutes.

FROM THE PANTRY

VINEGAR. No matter whether it's the white or the apple cider variety, vinegar turns insect sting pain into a thing of the past. Pour it on the affected site or mix it with baking soda to make a paste that you can apply to the bitten area. Out of vinegar? Try applying straight lemon juice instead.

FROM THE REFRIGERATOR

GARLIC. You might not get kissed, but you might not get bitten either if you eat your onions and garlic regularly. Just like humans, stinging insects are attracted to or repulsed by odors in their environment. Perhaps it is to your advantage not to smell so sweet. Some people believe that by eating pungent foods such as onions and garlic, the smell of your sweat changes, sending out a signal to insects that you stink. While this theory hasn't been tested, it can't hurt to add an extra onion to your burger or an extra garlic clove to spaghetti sauce. Just remember to have mouthwash or gum on hand if you plan to talk to others!

ONION. Get a tissue, a knife, and an onion for this sting remedy. An onion (or a garlic clove) contains antibiotic and anti-inflammatory substances that minimize infections and swelling from bites and stings. Slice the onion in half, dab your crying eyes with the tissue, and hold the onion on the bite site for five to ten minutes. Resist the urge to recycle the onion in your sandwich.

FROM THE SILVERWARE DRAWER

KNIFE. Bees and yellow jackets leave evidence behind when they strike: their barbed stinger. It's not a pleasant sight to see this pulsating barb

WHEN TO CALL THE DOCTOR

Most victims just yell, "Ouch!" once they've been stung or bitten. However, for the five percent of the population allergic to insect bites and stings, such an incident is more than an "ouch." It is life threatening. Seek medical attention immediately should any of these allergic reaction symptoms occur:

- Hives
- Severe itching
- Swelling throughout the body
- Tightness and swelling of the throat
- Breathing difficulty
- A sudden drop in blood pressure
- Dizziness
- Unconsciousness
- Cardiac arrest

THE WHO AND WHY BEHIND THE STING

Stinging insects belong to the order hymenoptera, which includes wasps, bees, and ants. The stinger is a modified egg-laying apparatus, so only females do the dirty deed. Most hymenopterans would rather flee than fight, but when it comes to social hymenopterans, such as yellow jackets, fire ants, and honeybees, they'll fight to the end to defend the nest or hive.

puncturing the skin and releasing venom. Carefully and gently remove the stinger by scraping it off with a knife blade. Don't reach for the tweezers or tongs. Squeezing and grabbing the stinger causes more venom to be pumped into the victim. After removing the stinger, apply a topical antiseptic such as alcohol or Betadine.

FROM THE SINK

SOAP. Some kitchen cures are right under your nose. Take plain old bar soap for instance. Besides keeping you squeaky clean, soap helps relieve the bite of the ubiquitous mosquito. Wet the skin and gently rub on soap. Rinse well. Be sure to use only nondeodorized, nonperfumed soap. Fancy, smelly soaps may irritate the bite area.

MORE DO'S AND DON'TS

• Don't forgo those flip-flops! Walking barefoot in the grass—a favorite nesting, resting, and grazing ground for stinging insects—invites a bite.

• Wear long-sleeved shirts and pants outside to reduce skin exposure.

• Don't dry clothing outside. Flying, stinging insects might get caught in the laundry and be brought inside.

• Don't look like a flower. That bright, floral shirt may be attractive to a bee. And, since we're on the floral theme, avoid smelling like a rose, too. Perfumes, lotions, and hair sprays smell sweet to stinging insects.

Boils

SIMMERING THEM DOWN

Boils have been a problem since the beginning of time. These painful bumps even got a mention in the Bible as one of the ten plagues used to convince the Egyptians to let the Israelites go. Even today, boils make people cringe. They are painful and unattractive. The good news is, though they look and feel awful, most boils are harmless. And, ironically enough, most of the treatments for boils have been around since the Egyptian doctors found themselves dealing with a boil epidemic.

Debunking the Furuncles

Boils start out harmless enough, but they become monsters overnight. Typically, a red spot or pimplelike knot you notice on your underarm one day turns into a swollen, painful lump the next. Boils, or furuncles as they're known in medical circles, are a result of a bacterial infection, usually staphylococcus, setting up house in a hair follicle. The bacteria gets an open-door invitation when the hair follicle is traumatized. This can happen from a blockage, such as might occur from an oily ointment or lotion, or from irritation, as can happen when clothing rubs against the follicles. People who tend to get boils frequently are staph carriers and therefore physiologically more prone to get boils. Other problems such as acne, dermatitis, diabetes, and anemia can increase your risk of contracting the staphylococcus bacterial overgrowth. Men are more likely than women to get boils.

Boils can appear on any part of the body that has hair follicles, but they usually occur on the face, scalp, underarm, thigh, groin, and buttocks. Boils vary from small, pimple-size sores to large, painful lumps, but they are typically larger than one-half inch in diameter.

The lifetime of a boil is about two weeks. During that time the boil will grow quickly, fill with pus, and burst. After it drains, the boil needs a little tender loving care as it begins to heal.

A cluster of boils is called a carbuncle. These are most frequently found at the back of the neck or the thigh. Carbuncles are more serious than boils and are frequently accompanied by fever and fatigue. There may be whitish, bloody discharge from the carbuncle. Carbuncles require medical attention.

WHEN TO CALL THE DOCTOR

The bacterial infection that causes boils can spread to your lymphatic system and to your bloodstream. If this happens you will need to take antibiotics or to have the boil drained. You should seek medical attention if

- Redness is beginning to expand around the boil
- A red streak is radiating from the boil
- There is pain in the lymph glands near the boil
- You have more than one boil
- You have a boil on your face, especially on or near your nose, cheek, eye, or lip
- Your boil is larger than a quarter

FROM THE CUPBOARD

CORNMEAL. Cornmeal doesn't have medicinal properties per se, but it is absorptive, making it an effective treatment for boils. Bring ½ cup water to a boil in a pot, and add cornmeal to make a thick paste. Apply the cornmeal mush as a poultice to the boil, and cover with a cloth. Repeat every one to two hours until the boil comes to a head and drains.

JELLY JAR. "Cupping" a boil, or applying suction to a boil by placing a cup or jar over the infected area, is an age-old treatment for boils. Boil a cup in a pot of water for a few minutes. Using tongs, take the cup out of the pot and let it cool down a bit before putting it over the boil (if the cup is too cool, there won't be any suction). As the cup cools over the boil, the suction brings blood and circulation to the area. Blot and wash pus away.

SALT. A saltwater compress can do wonders for soothing a boil. Salt is antimicrobial, and it osmotically dries the area to promote healing. Add 1 teaspoon salt to 1 quart boiling water and let cool to a warm temperature. Apply the compress for 30 minutes every few hours to speed up the demise of the boil.

FROM THE REFRIGERATOR

BACON. The fat and salt content of salt pork are believed to help bring boils to a head. Roll some salt pork or bacon in salt and place the meat between two pieces of cloth. Apply the cloth to the boil. Repeat throughout the day until the boil comes to a head and drains. This can be messy.

EGGS. The whites of hard-boiled eggs were used for treating boils in the 19th century. After boiling and peeling an egg, wet the white and apply it directly to the boil. Cover with a cloth.

MILK. Heat 1 cup milk and slowly add 3 teaspoons salt (adding the salt too quickly can curdle the milk). Simmer the milk for ten minutes. Then add flour or crumbled bread pieces to thicken the mixture. Divide the mixture into 4 poultices and apply 1 poultice to the boil every half-hour.

ONION. The pungent onion has antiseptic chemicals and acts as an antimicrobial and irritant to draw blood and "heat" to the boil. Cut a thick slice of onion and place it over the boil. Wrap the area with a cloth.

Change the poultice every three to four hours until the boil comes to a head and drains.

FROM THE SPICE RACK

NUTMEG. Nutmeg stimulates circulation in the body, which can help your body fight the bacterial infection in your boil. Stir ½ teaspoon ground nutmeg into 1 cup hot water and drink.

MORE DO'S AND DON'TS

- Don't squeeze or break the boil open, no matter how tempting that may be. Give the boil time to come to a head and rupture on its own. If you take matters into your own hands, you risk spreading the infection and creating more painful problems.

- Be sure to wash any towels, compresses, or clothes that have touched the boil. Otherwise, these items can spread the infection.

- Don't buy over-the-counter products that say they can draw out the fluid in boils. These just irritate the boil and cause it to burst prematurely. This can cause the bacteria-infested pus to spread in the body and possibly get into the bloodstream.

BANISHING THE BOIL

Since boils have been around for centuries, there are plenty of ancient herbal remedies for getting rid of your boil.

- **Burdock.** Burdock, which helps bring circulation to the surface of the skin, is used around the world for treating boils. Put 1 ounce dried ground burdock in 1 quart water. Bring the water to a boil and let simmer on low for 30 minutes. Drink 4 cups hot burdock tea each day until the boil comes to a head and drains. You can also apply a poultice of fresh boiled burdock leaves directly to the boil.

- **Chamomile.** Chamomile contains antiseptic, antibacterial, and anti-inflammatory properties. To make a poultice, place ½ ounce chamomile flowers in a 1-pint canning jar and cover with boiling water. Cover the jar and let sit for 15 minutes. Strain and apply the hot leaves directly to the boil. Cover the mash with a cloth, keeping it moist with the strained liquid. Keep the leaves on for 20 minutes; repeat every 2 to 3 hours.

- **Chrysanthemums.** Japanese researchers have discovered that chrysanthemum flowers contain properties that inhibit staphylococcus bacteria. Try drinking chrysanthemum tea to prevent boils or use as a poultice.

- **Tea tree oil.** Tea tree leaves contain a potent oil that has considerable antiseptic properties and is a very effective skin disinfectant. Research has proved that tea tree oil speeds the healing of boils because it inhibits staphylococcus. Tea tree oil is especially useful because it doesn't irritate the skin as it cleanses. Apply tea tree oil directly to the boil two or three times a day.

Bronchitis
CONTROLLING THE COUGH

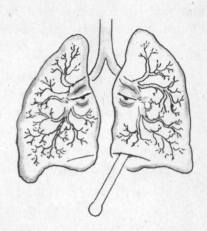

That nasty cold has been hanging on much longer than it should, and day by day it seems to be getting worse. Your chest hurts, you gurgle when you breathe, and you're coughing so much yellow, green, or gray mucus that your throat is raw. These symptoms are letting you know that your cold has probably turned into a respiratory infection called bronchitis, an inflammation of the little branches and tubes of your windpipe that also makes them swell. No wonder breathing has become such a chore. Your air passages are too puffy to carry air very easily.

Acute bronchitis can include these other symptoms, too:

• Wheezing

• Shortness of breath

• Fever or chills

• General aches and pains

• Upper chest pain

Bronchitis is not contagious since it's a secondary infection that develops when your immune system is weakened by a cold or the flu. Some people are prone to developing it, some are not. Those at the top of the risk list have respiratory problems already, such as asthma, allergies, and emphysema. People who have a weakened immune system also are more prone to bronchitis. But anyone can develop it, and most people do at one time or another.

Under most circumstances, bronchitis will go away on its own once the primary infection is cured. But in those few days when you have it, it can sure be miserable. Here are a few tips from the kitchen that can relieve some of the symptoms.

FROM THE CUPBOARD
ALMONDS. These little cure-all nuts have loads of vitamins and nutrients, and they are known to help everything from mental acuity to sexual vitality. Rich in potassium, calcium, and magnesium, almonds are espe-

cially known for their healing powers in respiratory illness. So when you're down with bronchitis, eat them in any form, except candy-coated or chocolate-covered. How about a little almond cream to drizzle over your oatmeal in the morning? If you prefer cold cereal, sprinkle some whole or sliced almonds on top. Or sliver some almonds and garnish your veggies. They're good in a citrus fruit salad for a little added crunch or rubbed in a little honey, coated with cinnamon, and roasted in a 325°F oven for 10 to 25 minutes.

COFFEE. The xanthine derivatives in coffee are good bronchodilators. To cut down on mucus problems, add 1 teaspoon apple cider vinegar and 2 drops peppermint oil to a cup of black coffee, either instant or brewed. Drink 1 cup in the morning and evening.

HONEY. To relieve the cough that comes from bronchitis, slice an onion into a bowl, then cover with honey. Allow to stand overnight, then remove the onion. Take 1 teaspoon of the honey four times a day.

SALT. Make a saltwater gargle by mixing 1 teaspoon salt into a glass of warm water. The gargle is soothing, and it can cut down on annoying mucus that's difficult to clear out of the throat. Just be sure not to use more salt, as it can burn your throat, or less salt, as it will be ineffective.

FROM THE REFRIGERATOR

HORSERADISH. The irritating allyl isothiocyanates (mustard derivatives) in horseradish open up the sinuses. Be careful not to use horseradish if you're having stomach problems, though, because it's too potent. Eat it straight, on a salad, or atop meat. Fresh horseradish is the best choice, but commercial products will work, too. Make sure it's straight horseradish, though. Sandwich spreads with horseradish won't work.

LEMONS. These help rid the respiratory system of bacteria and mucus. Make a cup of lemon tea by grating 1 teaspoon lemon rind and adding it to 1 cup boiling water. Steep for five minutes. Or, you can boil a lemon

WHEN TO CALL THE DOCTOR

- If symptoms last more than three to four days
- If your bronchitis keeps returning
- If the person with bronchitis is an infant or an older adult. Complications in these people can become very serious or even deadly.
- If you have a lot of greenish mucus. You may need antibiotics.
- If you have lung or heart disease, or any other debilitating chronic illness or immune problem
- If you cough up blood. Tiny bright red specks normally come from irritation to the airways, so a few specks of blood can be normal. Coughing up larger amounts or blood that is dried and brownish may require treatment.
- If your temperature lingers at 102°F for a couple of days

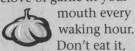
wedge. Strain into a cup and drink. For a sore throat that comes from coughing, add 1 teaspoon lemon juice to 1 cup warm water and gargle. This helps bring up phlegm.

ONIONS. These are expectorants and help the flow of mucus. Use raw, cooked, baked, in soups and stews, as seasoning, or any which way you like them.

FROM THE SINK

WATER. Lots and lots of it. The more you drink, the more your mucus will liquify. This makes it easier to cough out. You can also use water for a steam treatment. Fill the sink with hot water, bend down to it, cover your head with a towel, and breathe in the steam. Add a few drops of eucalyptus, peppermint, or rosemary oil if you have one of them. These help clear and soothe the respiratory passages.

FROM THE SPICE RACK

ANISEED. Here's a bronchitis cough reliever that's also said to bring on breast milk and relieve heartburn. Boil 1 quart water, then add 7 teaspoons aniseed. Simmer until the water is half gone, strain the seeds, and add 4 teaspoons each of honey and glycerine (glycerine is available at the drugstore). Take 2 teaspoons every few hours.

BAY LEAF. Ancient Romans and Greeks believed that this simple herb was the source of happiness, clairvoyance, and artistic inspiration. Whatever the case, it does act as an expectorant and is best taken in tea. To make the tea, tear a leaf (fresh or dried) and steep in 1 cup boiling water.

Warning! Bay leaf tea should not be used during pregnancy, as it may bring on menstruation.

Another bronchitis remedy with bay leaf is to soak some leaves in hot water and apply as a poultice to the chest. Cover with a kitchen towel. As it cools, rewarm.

GINGER. This is a potent expectorant that works well in tea. Steep ½ teaspoon ginger, a pinch of ground cloves, and a pinch of cinnamon in 1 cup boiling water.

MUSTARD. The warmth of an old-fashioned mustard plaster relieves symptoms of many respiratory ailments, including bronchitis. Take 1 tablespoon dry mustard and mix with 4 tablespoons flour. Stir in enough

BRONCHITIS-FRIENDLY FOODS

These won't cure, but studies indicate that foods rich in these nutrients may protect against another bout of bronchitis. The more vegetables you eat, the more protection you have.

BETA-CAROTENE	VITAMIN E	VITAMIN A	OMEGA-3 FATTY ACIDS
carrots	avocados	mackerel	herring
sweet potatoes	green leafy veggies	canned red salmon	kippers
apricots	whole-grain cereal	anchovies	mackerel
mangoes		whole milk	salmon
green veggies		cheese	sardines
		egg yolks	trout
			fresh tuna
			crab

warm water to make a runny paste. Oil the chest with vegetable shortening or olive oil, then spread the mustard mix on a piece of cloth—muslin, gauze, a kitchen washcloth—and cover with an identical piece. Apply to the chest. Keep in place until cool, but check every few minutes to make sure it doesn't burn the skin. Remove the plaster if it causes discomfort or burning.

SAVORY. This potent, peppery herb is said to rid the lungs of mucus. Use it as a tea by adding ½ teaspoon savory to 1 cup boiling water. Drink only once a day.

THYME. This herb helps rid the body of mucus, strengthens the lungs to fight off infection, and acts as a shield against bacteria. Use it dried as a seasoning or make a tea by adding ¼ to ½ tea spoon thyme (it's a very strong herb, so you don't need much) to 1 cup boiling water. Steep for 5 minutes and sweeten with honey. If you have thyme oil on hand, dilute it (2 parts olive or corn oil to 1 part thyme oil) and rub on the chest to cure congestion.

FROM THE STOVE

HUMIDITY. You don't need a humidifier to get moisture into your lungs. In fact, because humidifiers can cause as many problems as they cure (see "About that Humidifier," page 54), this is a better solution. Simmer a pot of water on the stove to send some steam into the atmosphere, which will kill germs and viruses. Or

MUCUS-MAKERS TO AVOID

When you're congested, there are a few simple foods that should be avoided because they produce more mucus. Here's the list:

- Dairy foods
- Sugary products, such as carbonated and noncarbonated soft drinks; sugar-coated cereal; sugary throat lozenges
- Refined cereals, bread, pasta
- Fried and fatty foods
- Red meat, including pork

Here's a handy avoidance reminder: When you're congested, skip the white stuff—milk, flour, sugar.

better yet, use a tea kettle: It's designed to shoot out that warm, moist air. And if you have a few drops of peppermint or eucalyptus oil to add, these can relieve congestion and be quite soothing.

MORE DO'S & DON'TS

- Rest up. Then rest some more. Since bronchitis is usually the second half of a double-illness whammy, your body needs all the rest it can get to build up its strength.

- Don't take a cough suppressant unless your doctor prescribes it. Coughing is your body's way of getting rid of mucus. Mucous buildup can lead to serious respiratory complications such as pneumonia, so when you're congested, that cough is your friend!

- Stay out of harm's way. With bronchitis you're at risk for picking up another infection. Avoid crowds, children with colds, smoky rooms, and contact with anyone who has a cold or flu. Wear gloves or a mask if you have to.

- Wash your hands often—especially after using a pay phone, handling a contaminated tissue, or shaking hands with someone who may have a cold or a virus.

- Pamper yourself. Go to bed, read a book, listen to music, watch an old movie. Don't be tempted to go about business as usual just because bronchitis isn't usually contagious or serious.

ABOUT THAT HUMIDIFIER

More humidity usually is beneficial for a respiratory ailment because it thins out thick mucous secretions. But not all respiratory conditions can tolerate the added moisture—asthma and emphysema are two that can't.

If you're suffering from a simple case of bronchitis, however, steaming those lungs might be soothing. But here's a warning! Warm water quickly breeds bacteria, including Legionnaires' Disease, usually within 8 hours. And you don't want to breathe those bacteria in. So if you're using a home humidifier, here are a few tips:

- Clean it every 8 hours with vinegar, then replace water. This eliminates the bacteria and the mineral buildup from tap water. Using bottled distilled water will prevent the mineral buildup, but it won't stop the growth of bacteria.

- Grab a new copper pot scrubber and stick it in the humidifier. Copper has a bacteriostatic property that slows bacterial growth.

- Add a capful of vinegar to the water in the humidifier. It will slow bacterial growth.

- If you have any chronic respiratory condition, check with your doctor before you use a humidifying treatment.

Burns
PUTTING OUT THE FIRE

The home is one hot place. Just look at all those things heating up in your kitchen: the stove, the oven, the toaster, the microwave, and the waffle iron. Add to that electrical currents and harsh cleaning chemicals and you have plenty of ways to get toasted.

Doctors classify burns by degree. First-degree burns affect the outer layer of skin, called the epidermis. These burns cause pain and redness but no blistering. Most household burns and sunburns are first degree and they can usually be treated at home.

Second-degree burns go deeper, involving the epidermis and the dermis, the underlying skin layer. Fluid leaks from damaged blood vessels and causes blistering. The burns are very painful but usually aren't serious unless they are large or become infected. Some second-degree burns can be treated at home; however, if the burn is large or involves the face, hands, feet, or genitals, seek medical attention.

The most serious of all are third-degree burns, which require immediate medical attention. Deep and damaging, this burn involves the outer and inner layers of skin and leaves a path of destruction. Hair, nerves, blood vessels, glands, fat, and even muscle and bone can be damaged. The burn appears white or black and is generally painless since nerves have been destroyed. Third-degree burns often result in death, especially when they cover large areas of the body.

The following remedies only cover minor household burns. Blistering or infected burns, third-degree burns, or chemical and electrical burns require medical attention.

FROM THE CUPBOARD

HONEY. If you're suffering from a burn, the treatment should at least be sweet. Honey has long been a folk remedy to disinfect wounds and heal burns. Everyone knows bees are attracted to honey, but did you know water is, too? When applied to a burn, honey draws out fluids from the tissues, effectively cleaning the wound. You may also apply the honey to a gauze bandage, which is less sticky than direct application. On a piece

WHEN TO CALL THE DOCTOR

- If someone has experienced a third-degree burn
- If the burn is large or involves the face, hands, feet, or genitals
- If the burn blisters severely
- If someone has suffered an electrical or chemical burn
- If the pain and itching get worse after the first 24 hours
- If the victim develops chills or a fever and feels weak

of sterile gauze, place a dollop of honey and put the bandage directly on the burn, honey-side down. Change the dressing three to four times a day.

OATMEAL. As minor burns heal, they can become itchy. A good way to relieve the itch is by putting this breakfast cereal into the tub. Crumble 1 cup uncooked oatmeal into a bath of lukewarm water as the tub is filling. Soak 15 to 20 minutes, and then air-dry so that a thin coating of oatmeal remains on your skin. Use caution getting in and out of the tub since the oatmeal makes surfaces slippery.

SALT. Mouth burns can be relieved by rinsing with salt water every hour or so. Mix ½ teaspoon salt in 8 ounces warm water.

TEA BAGS. Teatime can be anytime you suffer a minor burn. The tannic acid found in black tea helps draw heat from a burn. Put 2 to 3 tea bags under a spout of cool water and collect the tea in a small bowl. Gently dab the liquid on the burn site.

Another method is to make a concoction using 3 or 4 tea bags, 2 cups fresh mint leaves, and 4 cups boiling water. Strain liquid into a jar and allow to cool. To use, dab the mixture on burned skin with a cotton ball or washcloth.

If you're on the go, you can also make a poultice that will stay in place using 2 or 3 wet tea bags. Simply place cool, wet tea bags directly on the burn and wrap them with a piece of gauze to hold them in place.

VINEGAR. Vinegar works as an astringent and antiseptic on minor burns and helps prevent infection. Dilute the vinegar with an equal amount of water, and rinse the burned area with the solution.

FROM THE FREEZER

ICE CUBE. A tongue burn is best treated with ice rather than cool water. Since it's tricky to stick a burned tongue under the faucet, try sucking on an ice cube. First rinse the cube under water so it doesn't stick to the tongue or lips.

FROM THE REFRIGERATOR

MILK. Got milk? Then you've also got a great way to soothe a burn. For a minor burn, soak the burned area in milk for 15 minutes or so. You may also apply a cloth soaked in milk to the area. Repeat every few hours to relieve pain. Be sure to wash out the cloth after use, as it will sour quickly.

PLANTAIN LEAVES. In the folk medicine of the Seneca Indians, as well as the contemporary writing of New Englanders and the Hispanics of the American Southwest, plantain *(Plantago major)* is a popular remedy for treating burns. The leaves of plantain are primarily used as medicine. The major constituents in plantain are mucilage, iridoid glycosides (particularly aucubin), and tannins. Together these constituents are thought to give plantain mild anti-inflammatory, antimicrobial, antihemorrhagic, and expectorant actions. To get the full effect, crush some fresh plantain leaves and rub the juice directly onto the burn.

FROM THE SINK

COOL WATER. While ice is nice for sore muscles, cool water is best for burned skin. Ice can restrict blood flow to the burn site and further damage delicate tissues. Instead, gently run cool water or place cool compresses over the burn site for ten minutes. Cool water not only feels good but will help stop the burn from spreading.

> ## BUTTER ISN'T BETTER
>
> Many folk remedies have you smearing butter on burns like you would on bread. But butter, or any grease for that matter, should never be applied to burns. First, that butter in the back of your refrigerator isn't sterile. Second, the grease will insulate the burn and hold in the heat. It's best to leave butter for your toast.

MORE DO'S AND DON'TS

Of all the areas in the home, the kitchen is number one for burns. The following are some precautions you can take to prevent an accident.

- Lower the temperature of your hot-water heater to below 120°F. A second-degree burn can happen within seconds when your skin comes in contact water hotter than 120°.
- Turn pot handles in on the stove.
- Keep that steaming cup of java out of a child's reach, which means off the coffee table or other low-lying areas.
- Cover all electrical outlets with specially made caps if children are present.
- Never leave a child unattended in the kitchen.
- Make the stove area off-limits to children.
- Put a childproof lock on the oven.
- Keep oven mitts and pot holders handy when cooking.
- Keep a fire extinguisher and a box of baking soda nearby in case of a grease fire.

Bursitis
FOILING FLARE-UPS

You head out to the backyard after a long winter indoors to turn over your garden. The fresh air smells sweet, and you spend the afternoon pulling weeds. As the sun sets and you head inside, you feel an unfamiliar pain in your shoulder. The dull ache becomes a more intense pain, and you start to think you might be getting arthritis. Because it causes pain and stiffness near the joint, many people mistake bursitis for arthritis. But bursitis is a different problem altogether.

Bursitis goes by many aliases, including "Housemaid's Knee," "Clergyman's Knee," and "Baker's Cyst." Despite its nicknames, bursitis does not only affect the knee. It can hit any major joint, including the shoulder, elbow, hip, ankle, heel, or base of the big toe.

Bursitis Basics

Bursa are tiny sacks of fluid that protect your muscles and tendons from rubbing against the rough edges of your bones. There are 150 bursa in your body, and any one of them can become inflamed. Inflamed bursa are very painful.

Though bursitis is associated with physical activity, you don't have to be an athlete to develop the condition. Anytime you exercise too strenuously, especially after laying off your workout for a while, you can aggravate bursitis. You can also have bursitis problems if your work or hobby requires repetitive physical movements, especially lifting

---

THE ORIGIN OF ASPIRIN

Aspirin, like many pharmaceutical drugs, has a botanical source. It was "discovered" as chemists studied plants such as willow bark, sage, and pennyroyal. Willow bark was the first plant to be studied for its pain-relieving properties. The source of willow bark's pain-alleviating power, salicin, was discovered in the 19th century.

Chemists then began to look at the same properties in other plants and developed aspirin (acetylsalicylic acid) obtained from salicin in the herb meadowsweet. Those original botanical investigations ultimately led to the development of 20th century nonsteroidal anti-inflammatory agents (NSAIDs).

things over your head. A bursitis attack can be triggered when you bump or bruise your bursa. And sometimes bursitis can just flare up for no good reason.

Though most people associate bursitis with the older crowd, the condition is not limited to that age-group. It affects young and old alike. And once you've had one attack of bursitis, it tends to come back again and again.

Bursitis does mimic other conditions, so it's helpful to know what its symptoms are. If you have any of these symptoms, you may indeed have bursitis:

- Pain is specific and localized.
- Pain can be characterized as a dull ache or stiffness.
- Pain is predominantly in joint areas.
- Pain gets worse with movement.
- Affected area feels swollen or warm to the touch.

Most cases of bursitis clear up in a couple weeks if you stop aggravating the area, but there are a few simple things you can do that will speed healing and make the process more comfortable. There are also some nutritional secrets that may help prevent future bursitis flare-ups.

FROM THE FREEZER

ICE. Ice is a must when you're dealing with swelling. Cooling off the area slows down the blood flow and reduces inflammation. Wrap an ice pack in a thin towel and put it on the painful area for about 20 minutes.

FROM THE REFRIGERATOR

ORANGE JUICE. Vitamin C is a wonder nutrient. Its antioxidant properties make it an ideal addition to the diet, especially when you are recovering from an injury. Vitamin C is vital for preventing and repairing injuries. Not getting enough vitamin C has been found to hinder proper formation and maintenance of bursa. Men and women older than 15 years of

WHEN TO CALL THE DOCTOR

Bursitis is not life threatening, and the pain that accompanies a flare-up will usually go away after a couple weeks if you go easy on the joint. However, if this is the first time you suspect you have bursitis, check with your doctor to make sure you do indeed have the condition. Seeing a doctor will also ensure you don't have a more serious problem—bursitis can be caused by an infection, gout, or arthritis. Even though bursitis is common, talk to your doctor if you have these symptoms:

- Your pain is disabling
- Your pain doesn't go away after ten days of treatment at home
- You have excessive swelling or bruising
- You have a rash in the affected area
- Your pain is sharp or shooting

age need at least 60 milligrams a day. Drink just ¾ cup orange juice a day and you've met your daily quota.

PINEAPPLE. Pineapples contain bromelain, an enzyme that studies have shown reduces inflammation in sports injuries, such as bursitis, and reduces swelling.

FROM THE SPICE RACK

TURMERIC. Studies have found that turmeric, specifically the yellow pigment in turmeric called curcumin, is a very effective anti-inflammatory. In animal studies turmeric was as effective as cortisone, and it didn't have any side effects.

MORE DO'S AND DON'TS

- Always warm up and stretch before doing any physical activity.

- Elevate the injured joint above your heart to help reduce swelling.

- When performing repetitive tasks, take frequent breaks.

PRACTICAL WAYS TO EASE BURSITIS PAIN

- Take it easy. Avoid doing the activity that caused the bursitis attack, but don't completely stop using the joint or it could become immobilized with scar tissue.

- Get a new pad. If you have bursitis in your heel, make sure your shoes are well cushioned and well fitted. If your knees or elbows are the culprit, invest in some knee or elbow pads. Leaning on your knees and elbows on hard surfaces can inflame the bursa in those areas.

- Look over the counter. Use nonsteroidal anti-inflammatory drugs (NSAIDs) such as aspirin and ibuprofen to reduce swelling and ease pain. But be careful: NSAIDs can also cause bleeding in the stomach, especially with prolonged use.

- Heat things up. Once you've gotten the swelling under control, applying heat will increase circulation and help get rid of excess fluid. A heating pad or heat pack also feels very good.

- Make a motion. Once you're on the road to healing, start doing low-intensity exercises that will help you regain your range of motion.

Canker Sores

VANQUISHING THE PAIN

That wonderful spaghetti sauce has been simmering on the burner for hours, and you can't wait for the feast to begin. Just one last taste before culinary paradise and... Zap! It got you. It stings and your eyes tear up just a bit. All your well-planned preparations have been con-quered by a painful canker, squelched by stomatitis (an inflammation of the mouth), annihilated by an aphthous ulcer (the medical name for a canker). You get the point. That acidic sauce you've been craving doesn't get along with your canker, so your pasta should be served without the sauce tonight.

Cankers are small white sores with red edges that develop inside your mouth. They hurt like the dickens, but usually they're not serious. The most painful phase lasts about three to four days, and the sores go away in about ten days. More than 80 percent of all mouth sores are cankers, but many people confuse them with cold sores (fever blisters), which they are not (see "Cold Sores," page 70). Canker sores and cold sores are two different problems altogether. The chart on the next page will help you compare them.

Who Gets Them?

Anybody can get a canker sore, and about 20 to 60 percent of the population does at one time or another. Women are more sus-ceptible than men, especially during their menstrual periods. The first canker sore usually occurs between the ages of 10 and 40. Medical evidence also suggests that people taking certain drugs for rheumatoid arthritis may be more prone to developing cankers. And heredity is a factor, too. If both your parents were canker sore sufferers, there's a 90 percent chance you will be, too.

WHEN TO CALL THE DOCTOR

- If you have a fever of 100°F or more, diarrhea, headache, or skin rash
- If you have general physical discomfort or feel slow, sluggish, or lethargic
- If your lymph glands are swollen
- If your canker sore persists for more than three weeks or worsens, even after home treatments
- If you think tooth or denture problems are causing your cankers, call your dentist

CANKER SORES	COLD SORES
Usually inside the mouth: on the gums, tongue, soft palate; inside the lips or cheeks	Usually outside the mouth: on or around the lips or mouth
Small craterlike sores	Blisters
White, gray, or yellowish, with a red halo	Red, often fluid-filled
Not contagious	Contagious
Cause: Injury to the area, stress, exhaustion, hormonal changes, menstrual period, food allergies, dietary deficiencies, medications	Cause: Herpes simplex virus

GOLDTHREAD YOUR CANKER

Goldthread is a flower that blooms in the spring, known by its plant kingdom name, *Coptis trifolia*. The first clue that it might cure your canker is its nickname, Canker Root. The remedy is to boil the root and rinse your mouth with the water after it cools. Some people prefer to chew the root. To find it, check a specialty market that sells herbs and natural cures.

Canker sores, unfortunately, can be repeaters, and some people are simply predisposed to getting them over and over again. Most of the time the sores are not a major concern. They usually don't get infected, spread, or bleed if you don't bite them. But they're definitely a major pain.

You can find over-the-counter antiseptic creams, lozenges, and mouthwashes at your local pharmacy to help relieve canker sore pain. But you can also find some relief over the kitchen counter. Here's how.

FROM THE CUPBOARD

BAKING SODA. Make a baking soda and water paste and apply to the canker. Baking soda is also a component of a canker sore mouth rinse (see "Salt" below).

CRANBERRY JUICE. Drink this juice between meals: It's both a pain reliever and canker healer.

HONEY. Mix 1 teaspoon honey with ¼ teaspoon turmeric and dab it on your canker. This one may sting a bit.

SALT. Combine 1 teaspoon salt, 1 teaspoon baking soda, and 2 ounces hydrogen peroxide. Mix and rinse your mouth with it four times daily. If the taste is too strong or the tingle uncomfortable, dilute with 2 ounces water. You can also just rinse your mouth with lukewarm salt water. Or, if you're brave, just apply a little salt directly to your wound.

TEA. Moisten a regular tea bag and apply it directly to the canker. The tannic acid will help dry it out.

EDIBLE NO-NOS

Some of canker's prevailing causes are said to be spicy, sour, or acidic foods. If you develop a canker after eating pineapple or a mild sandwich that you spiced up with mustard or barbecue sauce, these could be trigger foods. Only you know what you eat before cankers pop up, so if you're plagued and can't figure out why, keep a canker sore diary. Note the foods you eat before a canker erupts, and also record other facts in your life such as menstrual cycle or hormonal fluctuations, medications you took, and undue stress. You may see a pattern. In the meantime, here are a few of the foods to avoid when that canker comes calling:

- Carbonated soft drinks
- Tomatoes and tomato-based products
- Citrus fruits
- Pineapple
- Spicy foods
- Foods at a hot temperature
- Chocolate
- Foods with sharp edges: crackers, chips
- Alcoholic beverages

FROM THE FREEZER

ICE. This won't make the canker disappear, but it will sure make it feel better. Simply apply ice or rinse your mouth with ice water.

FROM THE SPICE RACK

CAYENNE PEPPER. Cayenne contains capsaicin, which temporarily desensitizes the nerves that cause pain. That's why it's in a candy recipe that will relieve canker sore pain. Melt 1 pound caramels. Add ½ teaspoon cayenne pepper. Mix well and drop by teaspoonfuls onto waxed paper. Be careful, though, as this may be too irritating for some people.

SAGE. Used most often to spice up turkey stuffing, this herb is one that can be used to calm an angry canker. Simply add 3 teaspoons sage leaves to 1 pint boiling water. Steep, covered, for 15 minutes. Rinse your mouth with the liquid several times a day. You can also rub sage leaves into a powder and apply them directly to your sore.

FROM THE SUPPLEMENT SHELF

MINERALS. A mineral deficiency is a suspected cause of canker sores. Make sure you get enough of these minerals in your diet by checking out the food chart on the next page, or consider a supplement that contains the RDAs of both.

HERBAL REMEDIES

Herbal teas can help relieve canker sore pain and help them heal faster. Steep a little myrrh in warm water, then swish around your mouth.

Or rinse with these other herbal teas: calendula, dandelion, or goldenseal.

VITAMINS. A vitamin deficiency is suspected of being a cause of canker sores. Make sure you get enough vitamins in your diet by checking out the food chart below, or consider a supplement.

FROM THE WINDOWSILL

ALOE. That beautiful aloe plant sitting on your sill has some quite potent curative powers. A little aloe juice from the juicy inner portion of the leaf rinsed over the canker several times daily could be just what you need.

MORE DO'S AND DON'TS

• Check your toothpaste ingredients. If you see sodium lauryl sulfate in the lineup, buy something else. It's a harsh detergent that can leave you with dry mouth, making your mouth vulnerable to sores. Or better yet, go to the kitchen pantry and grab that box of baking soda. Sprinkle a little into your palm, dip your damp toothbrush into it, and brush. Its salty flavor can be sweetened with saccharine or aspartame.

• Use a soft toothbrush and be gentle on your gums, as injury from overzealous brushing can cause canker sores.

• Do not try to remove the canker by any method. Removal can cause an infection.

• Try not to aggravate it. Biting down on a canker is sometimes unavoidable, but that prolongs pain and delays healing. Chew on the opposite side of your mouth.

CANKER CRUSADING FOODS

Because a nutritional deficiency, particularly in vitamin B_{12} and minerals iron and zinc, is suspected as a cause of canker sores, it's a good plan to eat foods that are rich in those vitamins and minerals. Try to include some of each of these foods in your diet to help ward off canker sores.

IRON	B_{12}	FOLIC ACID	ZINC
• Meat	• Liver	• Beets	• Oysters
• Fish	• Meat	• Green leafy	• Other shellfish
• Poultry	• Poultry	vegetables	• Red meats
• Nuts	• Fish	• Black-eyed peas &	• Whole-grain cereals
• Seeds	• Dairy products	other legumes	
• Green leafy	* See note	• Brussels sprouts	
vegetables		• Whole-grain foods	

Note: Vegetables are rarely a source of B_{12}.

Colds

SNUFFING OUT THE SNIFFLES

Every year Americans will suffer through
more than one billion colds. That's one
billion runny noses, coughs, sneezes, aches,
and sore throats. Colds make such frequent
appearances that the infection has
come to be known as the "common cold."

Small children are the most
likely to catch a cold: Most
kids will have six to ten colds a
year. That's because their young immune systems combined with the
germy confines of school and day-care situations make them prime
targets for the virus. The upside of having so many colds as a child is
that you develop immunities to some of the 200 viruses that cause colds.
As a result, adults get an average of only two to four colds a year. By age
60, most people are down to about one cold per year. Women, however,
especially women between 20 and 30 years old, tend to get more colds
than men.

How Do Colds Beat a Path to Your Door?

Viruses are like the bully that torments all the kids on the playground.
After entering the mucous layer of your nose and throat, the cold virus
strong-arms your cells until they let the virus take over, forcing the cells
to produce thousands of new virus particles.

But the virus is not the reason your throat begins throbbing and your
nose starts flowing like Niagara Falls. Your immune system is responsible
for that. As the virus begins replicating, the body gets the message that
it's time to go into battle. The little soldiers of the body, the white blood
cells, run to the body's rescue. One of the weapons the white blood cells
use in their virus war are immune system chemicals called kinins. During
the battle the kinins tell the body to go into defensive mode. So that
runny nose is really your body fighting back against the cursed virus.
That should make you feel a little better while you lie on the couch
surrounded by tissues.

Because there are so many viruses that cause colds, the exact virus
that you contracted is not easily pinned down. The most likely culprit in
most colds is a rhinovirus (rhino is a Greek word meaning "nose"). There

WHEN TO CALL THE DOCTOR

Colds generally have to run their course, typically 2 to 14 days. In rare cases, they can lead to a more serious infection. Call your doctor if you have

- High fever
- Severe pain in the chest, ears, head, or stomach
- Enlarged lymph nodes
- A fever, sore throat, or severe runny nose that doesn't get any better in a week
- A headache and stiff neck but no other symptoms (could be meningitis)
- A headache and sore throat but no other symptoms (could be strep throat)
- Typical cold symptoms and pain across your nose and face that sticks around (could be a sinus infection)
- Lessening severity of cold symptoms but a sudden onset of fever (could be pneumonia)

are more than 110 specific rhinoviruses, and they are behind 30 to 35 percent of most colds. The second most common reason for that aching head is a coronavirus. These are especially common in adults. An unknown viral assailant causes 30 to 50 percent of colds, and about 10 to 15 percent of colds are caused by a virus that will probably lead to something more serious, such as the flu.

How Colds Are Spread

The cold virus can take many routes to its ultimate destination—your cells. Most people are contagious a day before and two to four days after their symptoms start. There are typically three ways a cold virus is spread:

- Touching someone who has the virus on them. The virus can live for three hours on skin.

- Touching something that contains the virus. Cold viruses can live three hours on objects.

- Inhaling the virus through airborne transmission. It may sound implausible, but if someone sitting next to you sneezes while you are inhaling, voilà! It's likely you'll get a cold.

One study found that kids tend to get colds from more direct contact while adults tend to get colds from airborne viruses (parents of young children can expect to get colds both ways). Research has also found that emotional stress, allergies that affect the nasal passages or throat, and menstrual cycles may make you more susceptible to catching a cold.

Where's the Cold Vaccine?

Good question! One of the main reasons we don't yet have a vaccine for the cold is that cold viruses are just too hard to pin down. Viruses live inside cells, which means they are protected from most medicines in the bloodstream. So even if you took an antiviral drug, chances are your body wouldn't allow it to penetrate the cells. Another reason viruses are so difficult to kill is that they don't grow well in a laboratory setting. Their ultimate playground is a warm, dry place, just like the inside of your nose.

Don't give up hope, though. Researchers are still on the job. Scientists have discovered the receptor sites that the rhinovirus attaches to when it invades a cell. They tested an antibody that blocked these receptor sites and helped slow down the time the virus actually took to develop into a cold. It also reduced the severity of its symptoms.

While colds are here to stay for now, you don't have to be totally at their mercy. Thankfully, there are some things you can do to fend off the germs that cause colds, as well as techniques to ease your symptoms once you're sick.

FROM THE CUPBOARD

CHICKEN SOUP. Science actually backs up what your mom knew all along—chicken soup does help a cold. Scientists believe it's the fumes in the soup that release the mucus in your nose and help your body better fight against its viral invaders. Chicken soup also contains cysteines, which are good at thinning mucus. And the soup provides easily absorbed nutrients.

CORN SYRUP. You can make a sugar-water gargle to ease your throat. Use 1 tablespoon syrup per 8 ounces warm water, mix together, and gargle.

HONEY. Make your own cough syrup by mixing together ¼ cup honey and ¼ cup apple cider vinegar. Pour the mixture into a jar or bottle and seal tightly. Shake well before using. Take 1 tablespoon every four hours.

SALT. Make your own saline drops by adding ¼ teaspoon salt to 8 ounces water. You can also make a saltwater gargle for your sore throat with the same ratio of salt to water. Salt is an astringent and helps relieve a painful throat.

SESAME OIL. Dry nasal passages are prime breeding grounds for the cold virus. Although doctors typically recommend saline nose drops during

WATCH THE MEDICINES

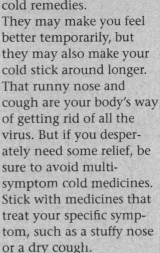

During cold season, you'll find tons of commercials for over-the-counter cold remedies. They may make you feel better temporarily, but they may also make your cold stick around longer. That runny nose and cough are your body's way of getting rid of all the virus. But if you desperately need some relief, be sure to avoid multi-symptom cold medicines. Stick with medicines that treat your specific symptom, such as a stuffy nose or a dry cough.

PRIME TIME FOR COLDS

Most colds happen in the fall and winter in the United States. The cold countdown starts in late August or early September, about the time kids start school, and stays high until March or April.

YOU CAN'T CATCH A COLD FROM THE COLD

Cold weather may make you uncomfortable, but it doesn't make you more susceptible to getting a cold. There are two reasons colds tend to make more of an impact in cold weather. Number one, most people are indoors a lot more in the winter, so you've got a lot more opportunities to share the wealth of cold viruses. And number two, the heat in your house dries out the air, and cold viruses like it warm and dry. So if you throw a little wintertime soiree in your well-heated home, you've got the ideal climate for a cold virus. Scientists have done numerous tests in which they've exposed people to the cold virus in 86°F and 40°F temperatures, and much to the participants' chagrin, both groups ended up with a cold.

the winter to keep nasal passages moist, a recent study compared saline drops to sesame oil. The people who used sesame oil had an 80 percent improvement in their nasal dryness, while the people who used traditional saline drops had a 30 percent improvement. While it may not be a good idea to shoot sesame oil up your nose (it could get into the lungs), try rubbing a drop around the inside of your nostrils.

TEA. A cup of hot tea with honey does the same trick as chicken soup; it loosens up your nasal passages and makes that stuffy nose feel better. Folk healers have known this secret for centuries. They often suggest drinking tea with spices and herbs that contain aromatic oils with antiviral properties. Try tea with elder, ginger, yarrow, mint, thyme, horsemint, bee balm, lemon balm, catnip, garlic, onions, or mustard.

FROM THE REFRIGERATOR

PEPPERS. Hot and spicy foods are notorious for making your nose run and your eyes water. The hot stuff in peppers is called capsaicin and is pharmacologically similar to guaifenesin, an expectorant found in some over-the-counter cough syrups. This similarity leads some experts to believe that eating hot foods can clear up mucus and ease that stuffy nose.

YOGURT. One study found that participants who ate ¾ cup yogurt a day before and during cold season had 25 percent fewer colds. But you've got to start early and maintain your yogurt eating throughout the peak cold season.

FROM THE SUPPLEMENT SHELF

VITAMIN C. Vitamin C won't prevent a cold, but research shows that it can help reduce the length and severity of symptoms. But to reap the benefits, you've got to take a lot of "C." The RDA for men and women age 15 and older is 60 mg, but studies show that you'd need to take upward of 1,000 mg to 3,000 mg to get the cold-symptom-sparing

HOW TO WIN THE COLD WAR

- Washing your hands is the most effective way to keep a cold at bay as well as to keep one from spreading. Antibacterial soaps don't necessarily do any more good than regular soap, and some researchers believe the prevalence of antibacterial products is contributing to the increase in resistant bacteria strains. Experts suggest washing your hands for at least 15 seconds—long enough to say the alphabet. So next time you're scrubbing, just say those ABCs.

- Always sneeze or cough into a tissue and throw it away immediately. Sounds like a no-brainer, but how many tissues have you left sitting around the house?

- Clean any potentially virus-carrying surface of your home either with a heavy-duty cleanser or disinfectant.

- Try not to hang around people who have colds, and try to limit your exposure to others if you have a cold.

rewards of vitamin C. For the short term, experts believe that wouldn't be harmful, but taking too much vitamin C for too long can cause severe diarrhea. Before loading up on vitamin C, check with your doctor.

ZINC. Studies have found that zinc may help immune cells fight a cold and may ease cold symptoms. The most effective zinc lozenges are those that contain 15 to 25 mg of zinc gluconate or zinc gluconate-glycine per lozenge. You can get the most out of your zinc lozenges if you start using them at the first sign of a cold and continue taking them for several days.

MORE DO'S AND DON'TS

- Don't fix yourself a hot toddy; they don't work. Alcohol can make you more stuffy. Best to avoid it while you've got a cold.

- Don't smoke. Smokers tend to have longer colds, and they're more likely to end up with complications, such as bronchitis.

- Don't take antibiotics. Antibiotics don't fight viral infections, so they aren't effective against colds. And taking too many antibiotics can build up your immunity to them, so when you truly need an antibiotic your body will be resistant to its healing properties.

Cold Sores
MINIMIZING THE MISERY

You know it's coming when you feel that notorious tingling on your lip and the accompanying itching and burning. You can't help stressing out about it; all you can think about is the pain and embarrassment those ugly cold sores cause. But there's not a darned thing you can do to stop a cold sore, also known as a fever blister, from erupting.

Many people get confused about whether they have a cold sore or a canker sore. But that confusion is easily cleared up. (See Canker Sores/Cold Sores chart, page 62.) If the sore is on your external lip or near your mouth or nose and looks like a fluid-filled blister, chances are it's a cold sore. Caused by a virus called herpes simplex type 1, herpes blisters are very contagious. They also love company, so where there's one there are usually many. Within a few days to a week, the blisters break, ooze, and form an ugly yellow crust that can stay around for weeks. When it finally sloughs off, though, there's nice, healthy, pink skin underneath. Best of all, cold sores leave no scars.

You can't cure cold sores, and they like to keep coming back, usually to the scene of a previous visit. When a cold sore's not making itself a huge lip ache, it's snoozing in the nerves below your skin, just waiting for a reason to wake up. And what sets off its alarm clock?

- Fever
- Infection, colds, flu
- Ultraviolet radiation, such as a sunburn
- Stress
- Fatigue
- Changes in the immune system
- Trauma
- Food allergies

WHEN TO CALL THE DOCTOR

- If your eyes hurt or you have vision problems while you have the cold sore
- If you have a fever of 100°F or more
- If you develop chills
- If the sores don't heal on their own within 7 to 10 days
- If sores come back frequently
- If you suspect you may have infected your genitals

- Menstruation
- Dental work

Who's Prone?

Anyone who comes in contact with the herpes simplex virus can catch it. It is spread in air droplets and by direct contact with fluid from the blister. Those at highest risk have a weakened immune system and a family history of cold sores.

Conventional medicine does have a few tricks in its little black bag, including antiviral lotions and creams. But they don't cure, just treat. So take a look in your kitchen. You might just find some useful treatments there, too.

FROM THE CANDY JAR

LICORICE. Studies show that glycyrrhizic acid, an ingredient in licorice, stops the cold sore virus cells dead in their tracks. So try chewing a licorice whip. Just be sure it's made from real licorice, as most candy in the United States today is flavored with anise. If the ingredient list says "licorice mass," the product contains real licorice. You could also try buying some licorice powder and sprinkling it on the sore. Or mix up a cream with a pinch of licorice power and a smidgen of pure vegetable shortening, then apply to the sore.

FROM THE FREEZER

ICE PACKS. If you ice a cold sore when it first arrives, you may cut down on the amount of time it hangs around. Ice packs and cold compresses will also provide some temporary relief. A tasty Popsicle will feel good, too, but skip the juice bars. Their acid content may irritate that major irritation even more. Super-cold drinks such as slushes or smoothies are another tasty way to provide comfort.

FROM THE REFRIGERATOR

MILK. This remedy doesn't involve drinking. Soak a cotton ball in milk and apply it to the sore to relieve pain. Better yet, if you feel the tell-tale tingling before the cold sore surfaces, go straight to the cold milk. It can

FOODS TO AVOID

During a herpes simplex episode, anything with arginine, an amino acid, is on the no-no list. Arginine causes the herpes virus to multiply. Foods that contain arginine include:

- Chocolate
- Peanuts and other nuts
- Raisins
- Seeds
- Wheat and wheat products
- Oats
- Coconut
- Soybeans

Several foods that don't contain arginine can also make the episode worse. Stay away from sugar, coffee, fried foods, alcohol, and hot spices. And if you're prone to cold sores, stay away from tobacco, too, as it suppresses the immune system.

FOODS THAT FIGHT COLD SORES

There's a good amino acid, lysine, that helps block the herpes virus. So try these foods high in this cold-sore warrior:

- Meats
- Milk
- Fish
- Chicken
- Eggs
- Beans & bean sprouts
- Cheese

Foods rich in bioflavonoids can help prevent or speed up the course of the blisters that flare up, too. These include

- Onions
- Apples
- Grapes
- Tea

Foods packed with vitamin C are also valiant in their quest to rid you of your herpes foe. Eat a lot of these foods that are rich in vitamin C:

- Oranges, grapefruits, seedless berries (they all make great smoothies)
- Peppers
- Green leafy vegetables
- Sweet potatoes and potatoes

help speed the healing right from the beginning.

MORE DO'S AND DON'TS

- Change toothbrushes: once when the blister has formed and once when the attack has cleared up. Toothbrushes can harbor the virus.

- Don't kiss. Whether you're the one with the cold sore or it's your partner, don't give any smooches. In fact, don't even make skin contact when blisters are present.

- Reduce your stress. Exercise, meditate, try yoga, read a good book.

- Don't share drinks, foods, utensils, towels, or anything that may have come in contact with a moist secretion from the blister.

- Don't touch other parts of your body (or anybody else's body) without first washing your hands. Cold sores can spread to your eyes and your genitals, so wash those hands frequently or that little lip sore could turn into something much worse.

- Use a strong sunblocking lip protectant.

- Don't hide your boo-boo with makeup. The chemicals can make the sore worse. And don't share your lipstick or other makeup either.

- Don't squeeze, pinch, or pick a blister. These actions can cause a bacterial infection.

- Suck on zinc lozenges. During stressful times they can boost the immune system.

- Carry hand sanitizer in case you accidentally scratch and there's no wash basin handy.

Constipation
GETTING A MOVE ON

Nothing's moving, even though you know you have to move your bowels. Everything in your body is sending you that signal. You feel bloated and uncomfortable pressure, but when you try to go, nothing happens. Or, if you do finally go, it hurts.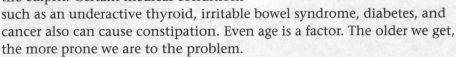

Constipation occurs for many different reasons. Stress, lack of exercise, certain medications, artificial sweeteners, and a diet that's lacking fiber or fluids can each be the culprit. Certain medical conditions such as an underactive thyroid, irritable bowel syndrome, diabetes, and cancer also can cause constipation. Even age is a factor. The older we get, the more prone we are to the problem.

And constipation is a problem, although it's not an illness. It's simply what happens when bowel movements are delayed, compacted, and difficult to pass.

What's Normal?

Some people mistakenly believe they must have a certain number of bowel movements a day or a week or else they are constipated. That couldn't be further from the truth, although it's a common misconception. What constitutes "normal" is individual and can vary from three bowel movements a day to three a week. You'll know if you're constipated because you'll be straining a lot in the bathroom, you'll produce unusually hard stools, and you'll feel gassy and bloated.

Laxatives Aren't Number One

It's not a good idea to use laxatives as the first line of attack when you're constipated. They can become habit-forming to the point that they damage your colon. Some laxatives inhibit the effectiveness of medications you're already taking, and there are laxatives that cause inflammation to the lining of the intestine.

Conventional thinking on laxatives is that if you must take one, find one that's psyllium- or fiber-based. Psyllium is a natural fiber that's much more gentle on the system than ingredients in many of the other products available today. Or, simply look in the kitchen for relief.

WHEN TO CALL THE DOCTOR

- If you have a fever or lower abdominal pain with constipation
- If you have blood in your stools
- If constipation develops after you start taking a new medication, including vitamins and minerals
- If you're elderly or disabled and have been constipated for more than a week
- If you experience sudden weight loss with constipation
- If the problem persists, off and on, for more than two weeks
- If you have gone so long without a bowel movement that you're experiencing extreme pain and discomfort
- If constipation is causing a problem with normal daily activities
- If there is a marked change in your bowel habits

FROM THE CUPBOARD

BARLEY. It can relieve constipation as well as keep you regular, and it has cholesterol-lowering properties, too. What more could you ask of a simple grain? Buy some barley flour, flakes, and grits. Add some barley grain to vegetable soup or stew.

BLACKSTRAP MOLASSES. Take 2 tablespoons before going to bed. It has a pretty strong taste, so you may want to add it to milk, fruit juice, or for an extra-powerful laxative punch, prune juice.

GARLIC. In the raw, it has a laxative effect for many. Eat it mixed with onion, raw or cooked, and with milk or yogurt for best results.

HONEY. This is a very mild laxative. Try taking 1 tablespoon three times a day, either by itself or mixed into warm water. If it doesn't work on its own, you may have to pep it up by mixing it half and half with blackstrap molasses.

OIL. Safflower, soybean, or other vegetable oil can be just the cure you need, as they have a lubricating action in the intestines. Take 2 to 3 tablespoons a day until the problem is gone. If you don't like taking it straight, mix the oil with herbs and lemon juice or vinegar to use as salad dressing. The combination of the oil and the fiber from the salad ought to fix you right up.

VINEGAR. Mix 1 teaspoon apple cider vinegar and 1 teaspoon honey in a glass of water and drink.

WALNUTS. Fresh from the shell, they may be just the laxative you need.

FROM THE REFRIGERATOR

APPLE CIDER, APPLE JUICE. These are natural laxatives for many people. Drink up and enjoy!

APPLES. Eat an hour after a meal to prevent constipation.

BANANAS. These may relieve constipation. Try eating two ripe bananas between meals. Avoid green bananas because they're constipating.

PRUNES. Yep, they work! And here's a great-tasting way to cure constipation. Cover several prunes with boiling water. If you want to sweeten the prunes, stir 1 or 2 teaspoons honey into the boiling water before you pour it over the fruit. Let the prunes stand in the water overnight, and eat them the next day. Drink the prune juice, too.

RAISINS. Eat a handful daily, an hour after a meal.

RHUBARB. This is a natural laxative. Cook it and eat it sweetened with honey or bake it in a pie. Or, create a drink with cooked, pureed rhubarb, apple juice, and honey.

FROM THE SPICE RACK

SESAME SEEDS. These provide roughage and bulk, and they soften the contents of the intestines, which makes elimination easier. Eat no more than ½ ounce daily, and drink lots of water as you take the seeds. You may also sprinkle them on salads and other foods, but again, no more than ½ ounce. Sesame is also available in a butter or paste and in Middle Eastern dips, such as tahini.

MORE DO'S AND DON'TS

- Exercise. A nice, brisk 30-minute walk can lead to regularity.

- Drink at least 8 glasses of water a day.

- Don't rush things. It takes time for your bowels to move, so allow sufficient time.

- Don't take mineral oil unless prescribed by your physician.

- If you suffer frequent bouts of constipation, keep a food diary to discover which foods are clogging you up.

- Cut back on refined foods, such as processed cereals, white flour, and sugar.

- A movement delayed can result in constipation. In other words, when it's time, it's time. Go when nature calls.

- A daily routine is best. Train yourself. Pick a time, possibly after a meal, and retire to the bathroom. Follow that routine every day, whether you have to go or not, and soon it may very well become your time.

THE SCOOP ON CASTOR OIL

Castor oil is a constipation cure that's been used for 5,000 years. And it was so popular fifty years ago that some people were even dosed on a regular basis just for the sake of regularity. Castor oil works quickly, in 4 to 5 hours. However, it's generally not recommended any longer because it's a very strong laxative that can interfere with the body's ability to absorb certain vitamins and minerals. As with other laxatives, your intestinal muscles may be weakened and your body may become dependent on the oil, only making matters worse.

Children under twelve and women who are pregnant should never take castor oil.

Cough
HAMPERING THE HACK

Annoying, loud, and disruptive, a persistent cough can put a damper on your daily routine. Coughs can be defined by how long they last. A brief cough is caused by such factors as cold air, irritating fumes, breathing dust, or drawing food into the airways. A persistent cough, however, typically results from mucus and other secretions brought on by respiratory disorders such as a cold, the flu, pneumonia, or tuberculosis.

Moisture content also differentiates coughs. Some are dry, accompanied by a ticklish or sore throat. Others are accompanied by a thick phlegm and are called wet coughs.

A Beneficial Reflex

Regardless of time and moisture content, a cough is produced when viruses, bacteria, dust, pollen, or other foreign substances irritate respiratory passages in the throat and lungs. The cough reflex is the body's effort to rid the passageways of such intruders, and it spares no power in the expulsion. A cough can expel a foreign substance at velocities as high as 100 miles per hour.

Determine what kind of cough you have and search for cures specific to that type. Some remedies aim to moisten dry throats, while others are expectorants, helping you cough up and get rid of mucus and irritants. Most of these kitchen cures battle both coughs unless otherwise noted.

FROM THE CANDY JAR

LICORICE. If you love licorice, you're in for a treat with this remedy. Many folk remedies use licorice root to treat coughs and bronchial problems. It serves not only as a flavoring agent but also as a demulcent (a substance that soothes inflamed or irritated throats) and an expectorant. Real licorice or candy that's actually made with real licorice (look for licorice mass on the label) works best. Reach into your candy jar and slice up 1 ounce licorice sticks. Add 1 quart boiling water and steep for 24 hours. Drink throughout the day, adding a teaspoon of honey for sweetness.

FROM THE CUPBOARD

GARLIC. Eating garlic won't have you winning any kissing contests, but who wants to kiss you when you sound like a seal? Since kissing isn't on your agenda, you can indulge in one of nature's best cures for coughs: garlic. It's full of antibiotic and antiviral properties, plus garlic is also an expectorant, so it helps you cough up stubborn bacteria and/or mucus that are languishing in your lungs.

Some experts advise that to reap garlic's full cold- and flu-fighting benefits, you have to eat it raw. Yet swallowing 4 to 8 raw garlic cloves a day (the recommended amount) is hard for most people to stomach. Cheat a little by mixing the cloves into plain yogurt and putting a dollop on your soup. If you make a pasta sauce, put the garlic in at the last moment, or toss garlic slices into your salad.

A cup of garlic broth may do the trick for your cough, too, and it is easy to prepare. Smash 1 to 3 cloves garlic (depending on how strong you like your garlic), add 2 quarts water, and boil on low heat for one hour. Strain and sip slowly.

You can also chop up some garlic cloves and toss them into that pot of chicken soup (see "From the Stove," page 79).

HONEY. Honey has long been used in traditional Chinese medicine for coughs because it's a natural expectorant, promoting the flow of mucus. This is the simple recipe: Mix 1 tablespoon honey into 1 cup hot water and enjoy. Now how sweet is that? Squeeze some lemon juice in if you want a little tartness. Before bedtime, adults may add 1 tablespoon brandy or whiskey to aid in sleep.

WHEN TO CALL THE DOCTOR

- If you have a persistent cough that doesn't improve after ten days of treatment, especially an unexplained cough or one that's dry and hacking
- If you have a cough that produces thick, foul-smelling, rusty or greenish phlegm
- If you experience chest pain when you breathe
- If you cough up blood

A WORD OF WARNING

A hacking, violent cough does more than just irritate your airways. Violent coughing can lead to fractured ribs, especially in people with osteoporosis.

FROM THE REFRIGERATOR

GINGER. Ginger, which has antiviral properties, shares the limelight with licorice in this cough remedy. To make ginger-licorice (anise) tea, combine 2 teaspoons freshly chopped gingerroot, 2 teaspoons aniseed, and if available, 1 teaspoon dried licorice root in 2 cups boiling water. Cover and steep for ten minutes. Strain and sweeten with 1 or 2 teaspoons honey. Drink ½ cup every one to two hours, but don't have more than 3 cups a day.

A SOOTHING CHEST RUB

When the chest hurts from coughing fits and breathing is congested, a soothing remedy to loosen and lighten things up is a home-made eucalyptus-lavender chest rub. Eucalyptus, a common ingredient in store-bought vapor balms, opens congested airways and acts as an antimicrobial. Lavender, long regarded as a soothing herb that eases anxiety, also aids slightly in the battle against bad germs and microorganisms. To make a chest rub, combine 10 drops lavender essential oil, 15 drops eucalyptus essential oil, and ¼ cup olive oil or vegetable oil. Mix and massage on your upper chest before getting into bed.

If you'd rather not have an oily chest but want the same benefits, try taking a bath instead. Add 3 drops eucalyptus oil and 3 drops lavender oil to a full warm bath. Soak for ten minutes.

FROM THE SPICE RACK

MUSTARD SEED. An irritating but useful spice for wet coughs, mustard seed has sulfur-containing compounds that stimulate the flow of mucus. To get the full effect of the expectorant compounds, the mustard seeds must be broken and allowed to sit in water for 15 minutes. Crush 1 teaspoon mustard seeds or grind them in a coffee grinder. Place the seeds in a cup of warm water. Steep for 15 minutes. This concoction might be a little hard to swallow, so take it in ¼-cup doses throughout the day.

PEPPER. Pepper is a bit of an irritant (try sniffling some), but this characteristic is a plus for those suffering from coughs accompanied by thick mucus. The irritating property of pepper stimulates circulation and the flow of mucus in the airways and sinuses. Place 1 teaspoon black pepper into a cup and sweeten things up with the addition of 1 tablespoon honey. Fill with boiling water, steep for 10 to 15 minutes, stir, and sip.

SALT. A saltwater gargle is a simple solution to a cough, although you have to remain devoted to gargling to get results. Mix ¼ teaspoon salt into 4 ounces warm water. Mix and gargle. Repeat this every one to two hours each day for best results. The salt, combined with soothing warm water, acts as an astringent to help ease irritated and inflamed throat tissues and loosen mucus.

THYME. Store-bought cough syrups are often so medicinal tasting that it's hard to get them down without gagging. Here's a sweet, herbal version, made of thyme, peppermint, mullein, licorice, and honey, that's guaranteed to go down the hatch easily. Thyme and peppermint help clear congested air passages and have antimicrobial and antispasmodic properties to relieve the hacking. Mullein and licorice soothe irritated membranes and help reduce inflammation.

To make the syrup, combine 2 teaspoons each dried thyme, peppermint, mullein, and licorice root into 1 cup boiling water. Cover and steep for half an hour. Strain and add ½ cup honey. If the honey doesn't dissolve, heat the tea gently and stir. Store in the refrigerator in a covered container for up to three months. Take 1 teaspoon as needed.

FROM THE STOVE

CHICKEN SOUP. Take some advice from your grandma: Sip a bowl of chicken soup. It doesn't matter if it's homemade or canned. Chicken soup is calming for coughs associated with colds. While scientists can't put a finger on why this comfort food benefits the cold sufferer, they do believe chicken soup contains anti-inflammatory properties that help prevent a cold's miserable side effects, one being the cough. Plus, chicken soup contains cysteine, which thins phlegm. The broth, chock-full of electrolytes, keeps you hydrated, and the steam helps soothe irritated mucous membranes and air passageways. Last, but not least, it tastes yummy.

STEAM. One of the kitchen's best remedies for a cough is also one of the easiest. Inhaling steam helps flush out mucus, and it moisturizes dry, irritated air passageways. Fill a cooking pot one-quarter full with water. Boil, turn off the heat, and if available, add a couple drops essential oil of eucalyptus or a scoop of Mentholatum or Vicks VapoRub. (These work as decongestants and expectorants.) Carefully remove the pot from the stove, and place it on a protected counter or table. Drape a towel over your head, lean over the pot, and breathe gently for 10 to 15 minutes. Don't stick your face too far into the pot or you'll get a poached nose.

THE GOODS ON GARLIC

One of the oldest cultivated plants, garlic's virtues have long been extolled. It has been used for centuries to treat everything from the plague to toothaches. The ancient Egyptians valued the little white orb for its medicinal qualities, Greek Olympians chewed on it before competing, and Louis Pasteur acknowledged it as an effective bacteria fighter. Even today, entire Western towns celebrate the garlic harvest with lavish festivals.

Cuts, Scrapes, and Sores

OVERCOMING "OWIES"

It could be a scene in a National Lampoon movie. One balmy afternoon on the way back to work, you're trying to juggle a large coffee and your purse while navigating the stone pathway that leads to your office. As you're slipping your keys into your purse, a stone you've never seen before jumps up and trips you. As you fall to the ground, you catch yourself with your hands and knees. And before you can say "bloody mess," you've got your belongings thrown back into the purse and are headed for the nearest bathroom. Once you reach the bathroom, you look down to see a trickle of blood heading down your leg from cuts on your knee and dirt-engraved scrapes on your hands. If it's any consolation to your bruised ego and skin, you've just had one of the most common accidents. Americans have almost 18 million lacerations a year. Now your biggest concern is figuring out how to take care of yourself without alerting the whole office to your fiasco.

GUNG HO FOR GARLIC

Galen, the noted Roman doctor, used flour infused with garlic to stop the bleeding in gladiators with serious sword wounds. Roman soldiers showed the British how to dress wounds with a garlic-soaked moss. This method of treating serious wounds was used until the early 20th century.

Accidents Happen

The sidewalk scenario is replayed thousands of different ways every day. Especially if you take care of small children, cuts and scrapes are so common you probably have a stockpile of supplies to treat them. Both cuts and scrapes can hurt like the dickens, even if they are usually only minor injuries. But they hurt for different reasons. Cuts are incisions in the skin, made accidentally, say from the jagged edge of an aluminum can, or surgically.

Although cuts may be bloody, they don't affect as many nerves as scrapes do, and so they actually hurt less. Scrapes hurt so badly because they basically slough away a layer of skin on a rough surface, such as the pavement, and leave raw nerve endings hanging underneath. Scrapes often damage some blood vessels, so they are prone to bleed but usually not as heavily as cuts do.

Cuts and scrapes should be attended to immediately because of the risk of infection. Skin is the body's shield against germs. When a foreign body invades the skin, germs have an open invitation to raid healthy cells. Left untreated, cuts and scrapes can become painful sores, which are wounds that are slow to heal. Sores can also come from acute or chronic bacterial or fungal infections or from diseases that affect the body's ability to heal, such as diabetes or AIDS.

FROM THE CUPBOARD

GARLIC. Garlic is an old folk remedy for healing cuts, scrapes, and sores. It contains an antimicrobial agent called allicin that protects against infection. But be careful, as fresh garlic can be irritating to the skin and should never be left on the skin for more than 20 to 25 minutes. Mix 3 cloves garlic with 1 cup wine in a blender. Let it stand for two to three hours, then strain. Apply to the well-cleaned wound with a clean cloth one to two times a day. Discontinue if the treatment is irritating.

HONEY. If you think bees are attracted to honey, you should see germs flock to the stuff when it's applied to a cut, scrape, or sore. Honey dehydrates the bacteria in a wound, making it clean and free from infection. Place honey on sterile gauze and apply it directly to the cleaned wound area.

WHITE VINEGAR. Use a mixture of 1 tablespoon white vinegar to 1 pint water to soak off scabs. This will help kill bacteria and get rid of the scab gently without picking. Just remember: Vinegar stings!

FROM THE DRAWER

KITCHEN TOWEL. If you're bleeding, clean the wound and then put firm pressure on it with a clean cloth (not a used dish towel!).

WHEN TO CALL THE DOCTOR

- If there are signs of infection, such as redness, red streaks, swelling, pus, fever, or enlarged lymph nodes
- If you haven't had a tetanus shot in ten years and a dirty object was responsible for your injury
- If your face is the site of injury
- If your cut or scrape is too dirty or too deep to clean properly at home
- If your cut is wider than ¼ inch or has ragged edges that can't be closed evenly
- If you cut yourself in an area full of tendons and nerves and you can't feel or move the area
- If bleeding is severe. If blood is spurting out of the cut, cover it with a cloth, elevate it above heart level, and get to an emergency room, pronto.

TO BANDAGE OR NOT TO BANDAGE?

Letting a scab form is not the best way for a cut or scrape to heal. Scabs interfere with the body's ability to make new skin cells. The new skin cells are what heals the injury. Just as important, the new cells reduce the risk of scarring while a scab actually increases the chances of a scar forming. A bandage can prevent further damage (especially if you tend to be a magnet for accidents). A basic generic bandage will do fine. Avoid bandages with antibiotic creams, aloe, or vitamin E on the pads. They won't help with healing and may cause allergic reactions in some people.

MAKE YOUR OWN DISINFECTANT

Rosemary is known in folk medicine for its disinfectant properties. To make a disinfectant, put 1 ounce rosemary leaves in a 1-pint jar and fill with boiling water. Cover tightly and let stand until the tea reaches room temperature. Wet a cloth with the solution and apply to the wound three to four times a day.

FROM THE FAUCET

WATER. The first step to treating a cut or scrape is cleaning it. So rinse the injury thoroughly with water. Clean it with soap, then rinse it again.

FROM THE REFRIGERATOR

ONION. Allicin, an antimicrobial component of garlic, is also found in onions. And onions don't irritate the skin like garlic does. Crush half an onion in a blender. Mix with honey and apply to a sore. Do not leave in place more than one hour. Repeat three times a day.

PLANTAIN LEAVES. The leaves of this plant (*Plantago major*) are well-known in folk medicine for their cleansing and anti-inflammatory properties. Crush the leaves to get the potent juice. Apply the leaves to the cleaned wound.

FROM THE WINDOWSILL

ALOE. In addition to healing burns, the sap from an aloe vera plant can be used to treat sores. Break off an aloe vera leaf and apply the sap to the sore. Repeat every few hours.

MORE DO'S AND DON'TS

- Wash the wound every day with soap and water to keep it clean and prevent infection.

- Lick the wound if you can't wash it. That's not a misprint! Research has found that saliva can help kill bacteria.

- Check how long it's been since you last had a tetanus booster if you've been injured by a rusty object or have a puncture wound or animal bite. Adults need to be reimmunized every ten years.

- Use tincture of iodine or povidone-iodine for minor cuts and bruises. Iodine kills bacteria and viruses effectively.

Dehydration
GETTING FLUSH AGAIN

Every cell in your body needs water to function properly. In fact, an adult's body weight is 60 percent water while an infant's is up to 80 percent water. Other than oxygen, there's nothing that your body needs more than water. Water is so important because it has many critical functions in the body. Among other activities, water

- lubricates your joints and connective tissues
- helps digest food
- liquifies mucus when you've got a cold. This makes it easy to blow and cough it out.
- eliminates body heat through sweat
- carries oxygen, carbohydrates, and fats to working muscles, then carries away wastes such as carbon dioxide and lactic acid
- flushes wastes from the body through urine
- boosts endurance during prolonged exercise
- dilutes and disperses medications and vitamins so they won't give you a bellyache
- fights flight fatigue, often caused by dehydration from the dry air on the plane
- wards off bladder infections by washing out harmful bacteria
- helps curb your appetite
- plumps up wrinkles. We have water in and around every cell in our bodies, and when water around those cells decreases, wrinkles happen.
- quenches thirst. Thirst is our body's mechanism to alert us to insufficient fluids. If you're thirsty, it's time to restock.

The Great Escape

Each and every time you exhale, water escapes your body—up to as much as 2 cups per day. It evaporates invisibly from your skin—another 2 cups a day. And you urinate approximately 2½ pints every 24 hours.

WHEN TO CALL THE DOCTOR

- If you're experiencing excessive thirst, no matter how much you drink. This can be a sign of diabetes. (See Diabetes, page 99.)
- If you can't stop the diarrhea flow. Diarrhea causes dehydration. Ride it out for a couple days and be sure to drink plenty of fluids, but if it doesn't stop, dial the doc. (See Diarrhea, page 105.)
- If you suffer chronic constipation
- If mild fever, which can cause dehydration, lasts more than a couple of days. Also, if fever spikes above 104°F. (See Fever, page 116.)

FASCINATING FACT

By the time you feel thirsty, you've already lost one percent of your body's total water.

Add it up, and you could be losing up to 10 cups of water every day, and that's before you break a sweat.

Because water has so many life-sustaining functions, dehydration isn't just a matter of being a little thirsty. The effects depend on the degree of dehydration, but a water shortage causes your kidneys to conserve water, which in turn can affect other body systems. You'll urinate less and can become constipated. As you become increasingly more dehydrated, these symptoms will develop:

- Diminished muscular endurance
- Dizziness
- Lack of energy
- Decreased concentration
- Drowsiness
- Irritability
- Headache
- Tachycardia (galloping heart rate)
- Increased body temperature
- Collapse
- Permanent organ damage or death

How Much Is Enough?

Obviously, you don't want to develop the problems listed above, so how much water do you need each day? Under normal conditions, 64 ounces a day is sufficient. That includes water from sources other than the tap. If you're an athlete or someone who spends a lot of time out in the sun sweating, you'll probably need more. A good way to tell if you're adequately hydrated is by observing the color of your urine. If it's dark yellow or amber, it's concentrated and there's not enough water in the wastes that are being eliminated. If it's light, the color of lemon juice, that's normal.

Here are more facts about your urine:

- Some medications change the color, so you can't keep an eye on your hydration level. Ask your physician about the medications you take,

including over-the-counter drugs, vitamins, and minerals, that could change the
color of your urine.

- Urine is normally darker and more concentrated in the morning, but with adequate
hydration it lightens to lemon juice color
and remains that way throughout the day.

- Bathroom breaks should be necessary every
two to three hours. If you don't need to
urinate for longer periods of time, you're
not drinking enough water.

The simplest cure for dehydration comes
from the tap. Turn it on and take a drink. But
there are other kitchen helpers that will also
help keep you hydrated.

FROM THE CUPBOARD

BLAND FOODS. If you've experienced dehydration, stick to foods that are easily digested for
the next 24 hours because stomach cramps
are a symptom and can recur. Try soda crackers, rice, bananas, potatoes, and flavored
gelatins. Gelatins are especially good since
they are primarily made of water.

DECAFFEINATED TEA. Just another tasty way
to get fluids in your body. Don't drink caffeinated tea, however, as caffeine is a mild
diuretic.

RAISINS. They're packed with potassium, a body salt lost during dehydration.

SALT. If you're experiencing symptoms of mild dehydration or heat
injury, or you're just plain sweating a lot, make sure you replace your
salt. Don't just chug salt straight from the box, however. Try eating salty
nuts, salted pretzels, or salted crackers.

And, to slough off the dry, flaky skin that comes from dehydration,
try this: After you bathe and while your skin is still wet, sprinkle salt
onto your hands and rub it all over your skin. This salt massage will
remove dry skin and make your skin smoother to the touch. It will also
invigorate your skin and get your circulation moving.

Also, if your skin is itchy as a result of dehydration, soaking in a tub
of salt water can be a great itchy skin reliever. Just add 1 cup table salt or
sea salt to bathwater. This solution will also soften skin and relax you.

DEHYDRATION IN SENIORS

Older adults have a decreased sense of thirst, so they are even less able to tell when they need to drink than younger people. Indicators of dehydration in older adults include:

- Decreased urination
- Dry tongue
- Dry gums, or the inside cheeks are dry
- Upper-body weakness that's out of the ordinary
- Mental confusion
- Difficulty speaking
- Sunken eyes

FASCINATING FACT

About 45 percent of all Americans are always mildly dehydrated.

VINEGAR. Since achy muscles are a side effect of dehydration, this can bring relief. Add 8 ounces apple cider vinegar to a bathtub of warm water. Soak in the tub for at least 15 minutes.

FROM THE FREEZER

ICE. Suck on it, or rub it on your body when you're overheated. This will help cool you down and prevent excess evaporation, which may lead to dehydration.

POPSICLE. A great way to restore water to your body. It's an easy way to get fluids into kids, too.

WATER BOTTLE. If you drink bottled water, freeze some in the bottom of an empty bottle, then top if off with cold water when you're ready to go. You'll have cold water ready to drink for hours. If you know you'll need more than one bottle of cold water, grab another full bottle, drain about an inch from the top and freeze the whole thing. By the time the first bottle is empty, you'll have plenty of cold water in the second.

FROM THE REFRIGERATOR

BANANAS. They have great water content and are especially good for restoring potassium that has vanished with dehydration. (See "Banana Basics," page 13.)

BOTTLED WATER. Easy to take along.

FRUIT JUICE. It's liquid and has essential vitamins and minerals that need to be replenished.

JET LAG CURE

Some experts believe jet lag is caused by dehydration. But even if dehydration isn't the main cause of jet lag, it certainly is part of the jet-lag package. The air on board a plane is desert-dry, and you don't have access to fluids the way you do on land, unless you plan ahead. Those who are worried about making trips to the cramped airplane bathroom may consciously or subconsciously cut down on liquids.

If you're going to be traveling, here's how to avoid that jet lag:

- One hour before flying, drink a cup of ginger tea to soothe your nerves and provide last-minute hydration.

- On the plane, drink 2 to 3 cups water every couple of hours. Airlines may provide sufficient water, but to be sure you have a supply when you want it, take bottled water along. And skip the caffeinated drinks and alcohol. They are diuretics, which cause the body to lose water.

- After you arrive, don't stop hydrating. Be sure to continue drinking fluids.

LIME JUICE. Add 1 teaspoon lime juice, a pinch of salt, and 1 teaspoon sugar to a pint of water. Sip the beverage throughout the day to cure mild dehydration.

SPORTS DRINKS. Not only will they add water back into your system, they'll restore potassium and other essential electrolytes (a salt substance, such as potassium, sodium, and chlorine found in blood, tissue fluids, and cells that carry electrical impulses). For children, these adult drinks may be too harsh, so talk to your pharmacist about pediatric rehydration drinks now on the market.

WATERY FRUITS. Bananas are the number one fruit for rehydration, but watery fruits are another delicious and nutritious way to restore fluids. Try cantaloupe, watermelon, and strawberries. Watery vegetables such as cucumbers are good, too.

YOGURT. Or, cottage cheese. These have both sodium and potassium for replacing electrolytes.

FROM THE SINK

WATER. Drink your daily requirement at home or on the go. Start your day with 16 ounces, and end your day with 16 ounces. That's a great way to prevent mild dehydration.

MORE DO'S & DON'TS

WATER-LOSS FORMULA

Here's how to tell how much you've lost and how much you'll need to drink to replace it.

- Weigh yourself nude before activity.
- Weigh yourself nude after the activity.
- Every one-pound weight loss equals a half-liter (about 16 ounces) of water that must be replaced.

SALTY FACTS

We always hear that we need to cut back on salt consumption, but salt hangs on to essential body water and is vital to these:

- Nerve impulse transmission
- Muscle contraction
- Heart muscle contraction

- Don't cut back if you're retaining fluids. Water retention that's caused by salt needs to be addressed by increasing water consumption to flush salt from the body.

- Drink even when you're not thirsty. You're losing body fluids every second of the day, and they must be replaced.

- Don't depend on sport drinks or soft drinks for all your fluid requirements. They can come with side effects and calories. Plain old water is the best choice.

- Don't skip water if what comes from the tap tastes terrible. Bottled brands are available everywhere.

- Humidify your home in the winter. It will help keep your body hydrated.

Dental Decay
CHERISHING YOUR CHOPPERS

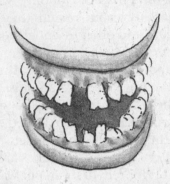

We take those choppers for granted, don't we? Except for that first year or two of life, they've always been there, ready to take on the grueling task of chewing. We douse them with sugar that erodes their enamel, require them to work overtime on foods hard enough to be called petrified, and then we forget the basics our parents taught us: Brush after every meal, and don't eat so many sweets.

Our teeth serve us well when they're in good order, but when something goes wrong, ouch! First comes that off-and-on-again little twinge, the one we ignore and hope will disappear. Next comes the sensitivity to hot and cold. And finally the full-out throb that hurts so bad that pulling the tooth out with a piece of string tied to a doorknob doesn't seem like such a bad way out.

Tooth problems hurt like a... toothache, and ultimately the solution comes in a dentist's chair, the drill screaming in your ear, your teeth clenching against the needle being jabbed into your mouth.

Yes, we do abuse our teeth. And what's amazing about that is that overall, we're not neglecting our dental health. On average, 65 percent of all Americans visit their dentist regularly. So what's the deal? Why the toothache?

- Poor food choices
- Bacteria
- Bad brushing technique
- Not enough flossing
- Heredity
- Lack of professional care

Take your pick, the list is long. But there's also a kitchen list that can remedy some of your dental dilemmas, from toothache to tooth care.

FROM THE CUPBOARD
BAKING SODA. Pack it into a sore tooth for relief. To whiten your smile, mix 1 teaspoon baking soda and ½ teaspoon hydrogen peroxide (the 3 percent solution found over-the-counter at the pharmacy) together into

a paste, then swab onto your teeth. For a better antibacterial effect, allow the paste to remain on your teeth for several minutes before you rinse. This can be a bit harsh on the enamel, however, so only do this once or twice a week. **COCONUT OIL.** Massage this into sore gums for relief.

SALSA. The spicier the better. Foods that make your mouth water actually fight dental decay. They stimulate the salivary glands, and all the extra saliva cleans your teeth and gums. And if that salsa is too hot, the water you'll drink to cool the burn will clean your mouth, too.

SALT. Dissolve 1 teaspoon salt in 1 cup warm water, and rinse your mouth with it to help treat bleeding gums, canker sores, and toothache. Salt makes a great whitening toothpaste, too. Pulverize salt in a blender, food processor, or coffee grinder, or spread some on a cutting board and roll it with a pastry rolling pin to crush it into a fine sandlike texture. Mix 1 part crushed salt with 2 parts baking soda, then dip a dampened toothbrush into the mixture and brush your teeth. Keep the powder in an airtight container in your bathroom. This mixture also helps remove plaque.

SESAME OIL. Gargling with warm sesame oil is an Ayurvedic treatment for gum disease. Take a mouthful and swish it around twice a day, then rinse. It's also said that this simple gargle can reduce cheek wrinkles. What a great bonus!

VINEGAR. Here's an easy but temporary toothache fix. Try rinsing your mouth with a mixture of 4 ounces warm water, 2 tablespoons vinegar, and 1 tablespoon salt.

WHEN TO CALL THE DENTIST

- When the tooth feels sensitive to heat, cold, or pressure from eating
- When gingivitis or periodontitis might be present
- If pain is severe
- If you see pus or symptoms of an abscess

FROM THE DRAWER

SPOON. Brushing or scraping your tongue is an important part of your oral hygiene routine. It rids your mouth of bacteria and food particles, and it stimulates your salivary glands to wake up and get to work. Use a spoon to scrape from the back of the tongue to the front, repeating until you've covered the entire area.

FROM THE FREEZER

ICE. That's the last thing you want to stick on an aching tooth, isn't it? Well, don't stick it on your tooth. Rub an ice cube in the soft spot between your thumb and first finger. This acupressure treatment may stop tooth pain. If your jaw is really throbbing and swollen, though, an ice pack to the face for about ten minutes every hour will help relieve

MORE BAKING SODA TIPS

- To clean your tooth-brush, soak it overnight in a solution of baking soda and water.
- Clean your dentures by scrubbing or soaking them in baking soda and water.

ENAMEL BUSTERS

Fruits containing citric acid, such as oranges and grapefruit, can erode the enamel in teeth, so eat them only with meals.

If you do eat citrus fruits as a snack or drink fresh citrus fruit juice, swish your mouth out with water afterward. Do the same when you drink colas and other carbonated beverages.

both the pain and the swelling. Just be careful, as rapid cooling can increase pain. If that does not work, try moist heat.

FROM THE REFRIGERATOR

APPLES. Munching on a raw apple an hour after a meal cleans the teeth and helps heal the gums.

CARROTS. They're hard and crunchy, and like apples, they stimulate saliva production, which washes away food particles. Also, they have lots of beta-carotene, which may help prevent gum disease caused by dry mouth. Sweet potatoes, also loaded with beta-carotene, are another good choice.

CHEESE. You know that nasty bacteria that's just waiting to take a whack at your tooth enamel? Cheese is its sworn enemy. First, it stimulates the salivary glands to clean the mouth. According to studies, just a few ounces of hard cheese eaten after a meal may protect against decay. There's also evidence to suggest that fatty acids in cheese may have antibacterial properties. And finally, cheese proteins may actually coat and protect tooth enamel. So, here's another reason to "say cheese"!

FIGS. To "strengthen" your teeth, eat 4 figs in one sitting, once a day. Chew well and slowly. This stimulates the saliva flow and cleanses the mouth.

LEMON JUICE. Squeeze the juice of half a lemon into a cup full of water and drink to staunch bleeding gums and gingivitis. Don't take lemon juice full strength, as it can erode tooth enamel.

MELON. Any melon will do. One hour after eating, chew some melon slowly. It will help stop gums from bleeding.

MILK. Milk is alkaline, which doesn't erode tooth enamel like acidic fruit juices and soft drinks do. It's also calcium-rich, which is vital for strong teeth and bones. Check your fridge for these other calcium-packed foods while you're there: yogurt, broccoli, Swiss chard, and salmon.

ORANGE JUICE. Add ½ teaspoon natural sugar and a pinch of cumin to 1 cup fresh orange juice to help bleeding gums. Rinse your mouth with water afterward.

RHUBARB. It's high in potassium and calcium, which are both tooth protectors. But don't eat it. Instead, crush fresh rhubarb to extract the juice, then rub your teeth with the juice to protect the enamel. Apply the juice once every other day.

STRAWBERRIES. They're a wonderful tooth whitener. Rub the juice on the teeth and leave for five minutes. Then rinse off with warm water that has a pinch of baking soda dissolved in it.

TEA BAG. Black tea contains fluoride that can suppress the growth of bacteria that cause decay and dental plaque, the sticky white film that forms on your teeth. (When it hardens, it's called tartar.) Drop a tea bag of black tea into a cup of hot water, and let it brew for six minutes. This will allow the maximum amount of fluoride to escape into the water. Squeeze the tea bag into the water before discarding it to get that last little bit of fluoride. Use the tea as a rinse to prevent plaque buildup after you eat sweets.

WATERCRESS. Chew fresh watercress several times a day to treat sore or bleeding gums.

FROM THE SPICE RACK

ALLSPICE. It helps relieve toothache. Wet your finger and dip it into the spice, then rub it along the gum line near the aching tooth. You can also steep some in a glass of warm water, then rinse your mouth with it. Not only does this rinse relieve pain, it also freshens your breath.

CLOVES. Cloves contain eugenol, a chemical with natural antiseptic and anesthetic properties. That explains why ground cloves have been used to relieve toothaches for thousands of years. Moisten 1 teaspoon powdered cloves in olive oil and pack it into an aching cavity. Dentists still use a mixture of eugenol and zinc oxide before applying amalgam when filling teeth.

CORIANDER. This spice, as well as thyme and green tea, has antibacterial properties. Brew a tea from your choice of the three and use as a mouth rinse after meals.

A DENTAL MARVEL

Who would have guessed that something as common as sugarless gum could work dental wonders? Sugar-free gum with a sweetener called xylitol may prevent plaque buildup by helping remineralize teeth. But it offers other key benefits, too. Xylitol increases the production of saliva, cutting down on the number of bacteria in the mouth, and it seems to increase the efficiency of fluoride toothpastes. Other sweeteners, such as sorbitol and mannitol, do not support the growth of oral bacteria either.

FASCINATING FACT

Tooth enamel is the strongest substance in the body, but unlike bone, it will not heal or regenerate when it is broken.

THE ANATOMY OF A TOOTHACHE

Most toothaches result from dental decay, which is a destruction of the tooth enamel. The destruction process is simple. You consume carbohydrates such as candy or soft drinks and don't clean your mouth of the leftover particles immediately. The bacteria that normally live in your mouth jump on this feast you've left behind and have a party. What they leave behind for you is acid that will, over time, eat right through the enamel, causing a cavity and, when the acid invades the nerve-filled and very sensitive pulp inside your tooth, a great big pain in the mouth. Be aware, too, that all the dental preventatives won't stop those annoying little bacteria from invading your tooth if it's cracked or a filling is loose. To them, these are open invitations to go on in and party.

SAGE. Add 2 teaspoons sage to 2 cups water, then boil. Cool for 15 minutes, then swish in your mouth for several minutes. Sage has an antibacterial property that may reduce decay. **SESAME SEEDS.** Chew a handful slowly but don't swallow. Brush your teeth with a dry toothbrush, using the chewed seeds as you would a toothpaste. They will both clean and polish.

MORE DO'S & DON'TS

• Try an over-the-counter pain reliever, such as acetaminophen or ibuprofen.

• Keep your head upright to decrease pressure in the painful area.

• Floss regularly. If you develop sudden pain, it may be food lodged in tight. Try to floss that pain away first.

• Keep the air out if your tooth is sensitive. Cover it with gauze or sugarless gum until you can get professional treatment.

• Use a few drops of clove oil or eugenol from your pharmacy to help deaden pain temporarily. Follow the directions on the bottle.

Denture Discomfort
MAKING THE ADJUSTMENT

Anyone who has donned a set of dentures knows discomfort is part of the process. There are two periods when discomfort is at its peak: the initial days of wearing the new device and several years later when the dentures may no longer fit properly.

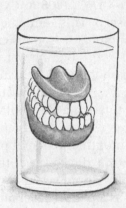

The cause of the discomfort isn't a mystery. After the teeth are extracted, the dentures sit on the bony ridge that's left over. Without the stability of permanent teeth, this bony ridge changes and shrinks over the years while the dentures remain fixed. Slipping and sliding dentures cause sore spots, which is the reason for much of the discomfort.

Dentures may not fit like a glove, but you shouldn't suffer. There are a variety of ways to prevent and resolve denture discomfort.

FROM THE REFRIGERATOR

FIGS. The fig remedy for mouth sores requires some time, coordination, and a fresh fig. Cut the fruit in half and set one half between your cheek and the sore spot on your gum. The open side of the fig should touch the gum. This is a bit tricky to keep in place, so plan on watching TV or keeping still while you fig out.

SOFT FOODS. Eat like a baby during the adjustment period. You don't have to mash peas in a blender, but you should stick to soft, easy-to-chew foods such as soups, stews, and pastas (macaroni and cheese). If you chew on hard foods, such as carrots and pretzels, you'll risk damaging tender gum tissues that are still reeling from the shock of losing their natural teeth. For dessert, enjoy puddings, gelatin, and applesauce.

FROM THE SINK

SOAP. After teeth are extracted and new dentures fitted, it's of prime importance to keep

---

WHEN TO CALL A DENTIST

- If you develop soreness that doesn't improve within a week
- If an area on your gum bleeds spontaneously or is filled with pus
- If you notice extra tissue growing, particularly between the upper lip and the gum
- If a white sore persists for more than a week
- If you have a mouth sore that doesn't heal completely within 10 to 14 days

your new choppers sparkling clean. Excess bacteria buildup on dentures can retard the gum's healing process. Plain old soap, warm water, and a hand brush do a grand job at cleaning. Scrub at least twice a day and rinse well.

FROM THE SPICE RACK

ANISEED. This gentle herbal mouth rinse is perfect for sensitive mouths. Combine 2 teaspoons crushed aniseed, 1 tablespoon peppermint leaves, and 2 cups boiling water. Cover and steep for eight hours. Strain and add 1 teaspoon myrrh tincture, which acts as an antiseptic and preservative. Use 2 tablespoons twice a day for rinsing. The remainder of the rinse can be stored in a glass bottle. Shake before using.

CLOVE. By the third century B.C., the clove was the universal folk remedy for mouth and dental pain in the Mediterranean. Clove's medicinal use continued into the 19th century, when dentists used clove oil to relieve dental pain. Even today dentists use eugenol, a major ingredient in clove oil, as a pain reliever and to disinfect dental abscesses. To tap into these healing properties, blend 1 teaspoon cloves into a powder using a coffee grinder or use ½ teaspoon prepackaged ground cloves. Moisten with olive oil and dab around a mouth or gum sore.

SALT. Gargling with warm salt water may help denture wearers breeze through the adjustment phase sans mouth sores. Prevent sore spots from becoming infected or inflamed by rinsing every three to four hours. The salt water cleans out bacteria, shrinks swollen tissue, and helps toughen the tender tissue. Make a saltwater rinse by adding ½ teaspoon salt to 4 ounces warm water. Gargle and spit. Do this twice daily.

MORE DO'S AND DON'TS

- Give your mouth a rest. Always remove your false teeth at night. You may also want to remove dentures for 24 hours should you develop a red spot on the gums.

- Have your dentures checked yearly.

- Have your dentures relined every two to three years.

- Replace dentures every five to six years, depending on the amount of wear and tear and the shrinkage of the gums.

Depression
BATTLING THE BLUES

There are many times in the course of life that you may feel overwhelmed and distraught. If you didn't feel like singing the blues now and again you wouldn't be human. It's actually very healthy to get down from time to time. It's when that down-in-the-dumps feeling begins to stick around longer than a couple of weeks that you might be suffering from a more serious condition, such as clinical depression. If you are experiencing a bout of depression, don't feel alone. Mental health experts say at least 30 million people deal with mild depression every year, and 18.8 million Americans are diagnosed with a more serious form of depression annually.

Major or Minor?

Though it'd be nice to go through life pretending like you're in a *Brady Bunch* episode, it's not realistic. There are going to be times when life throws you a few curveballs. Perhaps you suddenly lose a parent or your spouse is diagnosed with a major illness. Feeling depressed during tough times is normal. Mild depression is something everyone encounters. But sometimes stressful situations can cause more than a few days of sadness.

If your hopeless feelings begin to become more intense and last more than a couple of weeks, you could be experiencing clinical depression. Major depression, one form of clinical depression, may only happen once in your lifetime, or it may come back several times. Major depression usually lasts weeks or months and is disabling. It can cause you to lose interest in work, sleep, eating, or going out to dinner with a friend. A less severe form of clinical depression is dysthymia. Dysthymia isn't as emotionally crippling as major depression. With dysthymia you go

FASCINATING FACT

Women are twice as likely to suffer from depression as men. About 12.4 million women and 6.4 million men are diagnosed with clinical depression each year.

WHEN TO CALL THE DOCTOR

If you've felt several of these symptoms for more than two weeks, call a doctor.

- You feel sad, anxious, numb, or empty
- You have become pessimistic and hopeless
- You feel helpless, guilty, or worthless
- You've lost interest in things you enjoyed
- You have less energy and feel tired
- You can't concentrate or remember things
- You have trouble making decisions
- You can't sleep or you sleep too much
- You don't have any appetite or you eat too much
- You are increasingly restless and irritable
- You dwell on death and think about suicide. Call a medical professional immediately!

about your life, attending soccer games and birthday parties, but it feels as though there's a gray cloud hanging over your life. Dysthymia is a chronic condition. And people with dysthymia may suffer bouts of major depression throughout their lives.

Causes of Depression

Researchers have discovered that depression can run in the family. That doesn't mean that you'll definitely suffer bouts of depression if your mother did. But if you encounter a stressful situation, such as losing your job, you will be more likely to slip into a major depression than someone who doesn't have a genetic link to the condition.

Physiologically most types of depression are related to a malfunction in neurotransmitters in the brain. Researchers have discovered that if there is a glitch in the way neurotransmitters communicate, you can experience problems with mood, sleeping, and eating. Also, people who are more susceptible to depression physiologically tend to overreact to stress.

Other causes of depression include:

- Major stresses, such as going through a serious illness or losing someone close to you.

- Hormonal changes. As hormones fluctuate—after having a baby, before and during menstruation, and during menopause—women have a tendency to suffer more depression.

- Medications. Check with your doctor if you've recently started a new medication and are feeling symptoms of depression.

FROM THE CUPBOARD

BRAZIL NUTS. Selenium, a trace mineral found abundantly in Brazil nuts (100 mcg in one nut), can help ease depression. Studies have shown that people who had low levels of selenium tended to be more anxious, depressed, and tired. Once they ate foods containing selenium, however, they felt better. Other selenium-rich foods are tuna, swordfish, oysters, and sunflower seeds.

COFFEE. If you're a regular morning coffee drinker, you know what life can be like if you don't have your morning cup. You get a headache, you're cranky, and you feel bad. Well, researchers are finding that caffeine can indeed alter your mood. It makes you less irritable and helps you feel better. Experts do think that having a cup or two of coffee a day may indeed help ease mild depression. But don't go overboard. Downing too much caffeine can make you jittery and may even make you more anxious.

GARLIC. German researchers studying garlic's effect on cholesterol discovered that participants being treated with garlic experience an elevation in mood. So try a little garlic therapy if you're feeling down.

THE HAPPY HERB

St. John's wort may make a difference if you're suffering from mild depression. This plant with pretty yellow flowers has been used for medicinal purposes for centuries. It's commonly prescribed for depression in Germany and has become quite popular as a natural antidepressant in the United States. There have been dozens of studies on the herb and most of those studies found the herb to be effective in treating mild depression.

FROM THE REFRIGERATOR

CHICKEN. Low levels of vitamin B_6 may be an instigator of depression, especially in women on birth control pills. Vitamin B_6 is necessary for the body to make serotonin, a neurotransmitter. The RDA for vitamin B_6 is 1.3 mg for men and women up to age 50; after age 50 the amount increases to 1.7 mg. There are 0.5 mg of vitamin B_6 in 3 ounces of chicken.

SPINACH. Studies are finding that a folic acid deficiency is a major cause of depression. Scientists began to suspect a link between this B vitamin and the brain when they discovered that people diagnosed with depression have lower levels of folic acid than the general population. It seems that folic acid deficiency causes serotonin levels to fall, which can lead to feelings of depression. Ironically enough, folic acid deficiency is one of the most common nutrient deficiencies in women. But the good news is you need only about 200 mcg a day to meet your folic acid needs. That's about ¾ cup of cooked spinach.

TUNA. The brain is one of the richest sources of fatty acids in the body. And research is finding that depressed people have lower levels of omega-3 fatty acids. This polyunsaturated fat is found mostly in fatty fish. Researchers believe that getting enough omega-3 fatty acids is essential to ensure the brain is at its healthiest. And a healthy brain is less likely to become seriously depressed.

EAT TO LIVE, HAPPILY

What you eat affects how you feel, but what you don't eat may do the same. Depression has been linked to low levels of many nutrients, such as biotin, calcium, copper, iron, magnesium, pantothenic acid, potassium, pyridoxine, riboflavin, thiamin, vitamin C, vitamin E, and zinc. So if you are dealing with a mild depression, take a look at what you're eating. Changes in your diet may make a difference in your mood.

MORE DO'S AND DON'TS

If you're dealing with mild depression, there are some practical things you can do to lift your mood.

• Get some R & R. Be sure you are getting plenty of sleep and are taking time to stop and smell the flowers.

• Junk the junk food. Sure that sugar high feels good, but when you go through detox a couple of hours after that cupcake, you can feel terrible. Try skipping the sugary stuff and eating something more nutritious.

• Abstain from alcohol. Alcohol is known to aggravate a depressed mood.

• Energize with exercise. Runner's high is caused by an increase in endorphins—the feel-good brain chemicals. But you don't have to run a marathon to get the same mood-lifting feeling. Try taking a walk around the block or walking the dog for 10 or 15 minutes. You'll feel good the rest of the day.

• Focus on friends and family. Leaning on others is one of the healthiest things you can do to get through a tough time in your life.

• Learn to laugh. Laughing actually triggers the same endorphins that are affected by exercise. Read a little Dilbert, watch your favorite Three Stooges movie, and if possible, try to find humor in your situation.

• Think happy thoughts. A recent study found that people who learn to have a more optimistic attitude are less likely to become depressed—even if they were naturally pessimists. Changing the way you perceive life can have a dramatic effect on your mental health.

Diabetes

CONTROLLING BLOOD SUGAR

Diabetes is a disease that reduces, or stops, the
body's ability to produce or respond to insulin, a
hormone produced in the pancreas. Insulin's
role is to open the door for glucose, a form of
sugar, to enter the body's cells so that it can
be used for energy. When the body has a
problem metabolizing glucose, it builds up in
the blood, and the body's cells starve.

There are two major types of diabetes:

Type 1. The body produces no
insulin at all, and daily insulin shots
are required. This disease used to be
called juvenile diabetes because there is a higher
rate among children ages 10 to 14. It is also referred to as insulin-
dependent diabetes because insulin injections are required to control
blood glucose. The cause isn't known, but Type 1 tends to run in families.
A much smaller number of people with diabetes—only five percent—have
Type 1.

Type 2. This is the most common form of diabetes, and it occurs when
the body is insulin resistant. That could be either because the body fails
to make enough insulin or because it doesn't properly use the insulin it
does produce. The cause is often poor dietary habits, sedentary lifestyle,
and obesity. Those with Type 2 may or may not need oral medication or
insulin, depending on how their body responds to changes in diet and
exercise.

Here's the risk list for diabetes. Do any of these describe you?

• More than 45 years old

• Family history of diabetes

• Overweight

• Don't exercise regularly

• Low HDL cholesterol (see High Cholesterol, page 180) or high
  triglycerides

• Member of an at-risk ethnic group (see "Top Ten Diabetes Stats,"
  page 103)

WHEN TO CALL THE DOCTOR

If you have not been diagnosed with diabetes, call if one or more of the symptoms outlined on this page are present. Otherwise call if:

- You've been vomiting or have diarrhea for more than 24 hours
- You can't eat or drink
- Your blood sugar is more than 240 or less than 80 for more than 48 hours
- You run a fever of 101°F or more for two days
- Your vision becomes blurry
- You experience other unusual physical symptoms such as weakness or difficulty when speaking
- You have an open sore on your legs or feet

FASCINATING FACT

As fruits are dehydrated, the sugar in them becomes concentrated. Limit your intake of dried fruit to two or three times a week or less.

Symptoms

In children, the symptoms of the onset of Type 1 diabetes may be similar to flu symptoms. They may also include these:

- Frequent urination
- Unusual thirst
- Extreme hunger
- Unexplained weight loss
- Extreme fatigue
- Irritability

Symptoms of Type 2 diabetes include:
- Any of the Type 1 symptoms
- Frequent infections, including those of the skin, gums, and bladder
- Blurred vision
- Sores that are slow to heal
- Tingling or numbness in hands or feet
- In women, recurring vaginitis

Treatment

There is no cure for diabetes, but it can be controlled. And control is essential because diabetes can lead to heart disease, stroke, kidney disease and failure, blindness, and amputation if not treated. This profile will not address diabetic medical treatment, including prescribed diabetic diets. Those specifics must be left up to your physician and dietitian. But this profile will cover the go-alongs—things from your kitchen that can make the diabetic experience easier, as well as alternative practices that might help. Before you try any alternative practice, consult your physician. Nothing contained in this profile is intended to stop or replace your prescribed diabetic care!

Diabetes is a complex disease, affecting many parts of the body. Some of the problems of the disease can be relieved with simple things right from the kitchen, though. And for a person with diabetes, a little relief never hurts.

FROM THE CUPBOARD

GARLIC. Eating a combination of garlic, parsley, and watercress may shave a few points off the blood sugar. Try combining these herbs in a vegetable stir-fry or salad.

OLIVE OIL. Studies indicate this may reduce blood sugar levels. Use it in salad dressing or wherever cooking oils are indicated. For an inexpensive and easy no-stick olive oil spray-on coating, buy an oil mister in any department store kitchen supply area and use it to spray your pans before cooking.

PEANUT BUTTER. After you've experienced an episode of low blood sugar and corrected it, follow up with a protein and carbohydrate snack. Peanut butter on a couple of crackers supplies both, and it's easy to fix when you may still feel a little jittery. Just avoid brands that contain added sugar, glucose, or jelly.

PLASTIC CONTAINER. If you're on insulin, keep your extra vials in the refrigerator. Designate a spot where your insulin bottle won't freeze yet is away from the food. Then keep the vial in a plastic container, preferably one that shields it from light, in that spot to keep it from rolling around or getting knocked aside or misplaced. If the insulin bottle is frosted or the insulin clumps, do not use it. Consult your pharmacist and the package insert for information about proper storage.

SALT. Dry, itchy skin is a side effect of diabetes, and soaking in a tub of salt water can be a great itchy skin reliever. Just add 1 cup table salt or sea salt to your bathwater. This solution will also soften skin and relax you. To exfoliate, after you take a shower or bath and while your skin is still wet, sprinkle salt onto your hands, rub it all over your skin, then rinse. This salt massage will remove dry skin and make your skin smoother to the touch. It will also invigorate your skin and get your circulation moving.

AN INFORMATIVE TEST

A simple blood test called hemoglobin A1C (also called HbA1C) can measure your cumulative average blood sugar levels for the past three months. It's the best test to find out whether your blood sugar is under control. People with diabetes should have a hemoglobin A1C test at least every six months. The goal is a finding of 7 percent. That's because a major diabetes study shows that those whose results were 7 percent or lower had a much better chance of delaying or preventing diabetes complications related to the eyes, kidneys, and nerves than those whose levels were 8 percent or higher.

FASCINATING FACT

If your blood sugar level drops to the point that you need a quick pick-me-up, candy's fine, but skip the chocolate. Its high fat content slows the absorption of sugar, so it doesn't work quickly enough.

FASCINATING FACT

According to a Dutch study, fish eaters are half as likely to get Type 2 diabetes as people who don't eat fish. The amount consumed was small—1 ounce a day. Most likely the omega-3 oil found in fish helps the pancreas handle glucose.

FASCINATING FACT

The "fight or flight" response doesn't always work in people with diabetes. Insulin normally lets extra energy, in the form of sugar, into the cells when the body readies itself for its fight or flight. But in people with diabetes, the insulin isn't always capable of getting this energy boost into the cells, and the sugar accumulates in the blood.

SALTSHAKER. Set it aside, put it back in the cupboard, hide it. High blood pressure is a side effect of diabetes, and that salt's a no-no. So don't cook with it, and don't make it handy to grab when you eat a meal or snack. Instead, reach for a nice herb or spice blend that's sodium free. Make one yourself with your favorite spices or buy one at the store.

SUGAR. Yes, even people with diabetes need it occasionally, when their blood sugar goes too low. A spoonful of straight sugar will work, as will a piece of hard candy. Just be sure it's not sugarless.

VINEGAR. Muscle cramps, especially in the legs, can affect people with diabetes. For relief from the ache, add 8 ounces apple cider vinegar to a bathtub of warm water. Soak for at least 15 minutes.

FROM THE DRAWER

FORK. This is how you should apply salad dressing and sauces to limit your intake of sugar, as well as fat and cholesterol. Instead of dumping the dressing or sauce all over your food, have it served "on the side" and dip your fork into it, then pick up your food. You'll get the flavor without the extra goop.

NOTEBOOK. Use this to keep track of glucose readings, medication schedules, and symptoms.

FROM THE REFRIGERATOR

ASPARAGUS. This vegetable is a mild diuretic that's said to be beneficial in the control of diabetes. Eat it steamed and drizzled with olive oil and lemon juice.

BEANS. They've been known to reduce blood sugar in some people. Kidney beans are the best, fresh in the pod. Boil 2 ounces of sliced pods in 4 quarts of water. Simmer four hours. Strain and cool the liquid for eight hours. Strain again. Drink 1 glassful every two hours. In the absence of kidney bean pods, fresh green beans will work, too. Beans eaten with a meal, just as they are, have been known to lessen the rise in blood sugar that comes after the meal.

LEMON. A tasty substitute for salt. It's great squeezed into a diet cola, too. It cuts the aftertaste.

TOP TEN DIABETES STATS

According to the American Diabetes Association:

1. 18.2 million people in the United States have it, or about 6.3% of the population
2. 5.2 million of those who have diabetes are not aware they have it
3. About 2,200 people are newly diagnosed every day, totaling about 798,000 people a year
4. 5 to 10 percent of those with diabetes have Type 1 diabetes
5. 90 to 95 percent of those with diabetes have Type 2 diabetes
6. Diabetes is the 6th leading cause of death in the United States, averaging more than 200,000 deaths per year
7. An estimated 10.8 percent of the African American population have Type 2
8. An estimated 10.6 percent of the Mexican American population have Type 2
9. An estimated 12.2 percent of the Native American population have Type 2
10. An estimated 5.2 percent of the general population (minus the above three groups) have Type 2

PARSLEY. Steep into a tea and drink. This may act as a diuretic as well as lower blood sugar.

WATERCRESS. This is said to strengthen the natural defense systems of people who have diabetes. It's also a mild diuretic. Wash the leaves thoroughly, and add them to a salad. Or smear a little cream cheese on a slice of bread, then top with watercress for a delicious open-faced sandwich.

MORE DO'S AND DON'TS

- Monitor your glucose levels regularly via finger sticks. That's the only way you can accurately gauge how you're doing. Record the results for your doctor and dietician.

- Maintain a regular eating schedule.

- Lose weight if you carry extra pounds.

- Exercise. It lowers blood sugar and, combined with weight loss, can minimize the disease to easily manageable levels.

- See your eye doctor at least once a year. Diabetes is the leading cause of blindness.

- Don't despair. Diabetes is treatable. Seek emotional support from friends and family, or call a counselor if necessary.

- Eat foods with a low glycemic index, as they release sugar slowly into the bloodstream.

THE DIABETIC FOOT

Even though it looks much the same as any other foot, the diabetic foot requires special attention. Why? Nerve damage is common with diabetes, especially in the lower extremities. Blood vessels are damaged as a result of the disease and circulation is decreased. When this happens, feet and legs tend to be cold and sores heal slowly, in some cases taking years to heal. This can easily lead to infection. Nerve damage can also decrease your ability to feel sensations in your feet, such as pain, heat, and cold. That means you may not notice a foot injury until you have a major infection.

Here are some general guidelines for diabetic foot care:

- Don't think a foot injury will heal on its own. It may not. If you develop a sore—even a blister—call your doctor immediately.

- Don't be tempted to warm your cold feet with a heating pad or hot water bottle. If you have neuropathy, you may burn yourself without even feeling it. Instead, wear warm socks, or indulge yourself in a gentle foot massage with olive oil. Make sure that after the massage you clean away any remaining oil from between your toes. A mild solution of vinegar and water will do it.

- Wear good shoes. Specialty diabetic shoes are available.

- Always wear socks with your shoes to prevent blisters.

- Inspect your feet daily.

- Don't let your physician overlook your feet during a physical. Take off your shoes and socks, and remind the doctor to take a look.

- Expect dry skin. The nerves that control sweating in your feet may no longer work. So, after a bath, dry your feet and coat them with a thin layer of moisturizer. DO NOT use oils or creams between your toes. Moisture there can cause an infection such as athlete's foot.

- DO NOT soak your feet. The more you do, the more you put yourself at risk for infection.

- If you have a callus, don't cut it off. Use a pumice stone to rub it off. Oil down the callus with olive oil before you begin, then dab a little more on the spot when you've finished. If the callus becomes thick and too difficult to care for, it can cause an ulcer. Before it gets to this stage, call your podiatrist.

- Keep your toenails trimmed. Carefully cut them straight across to prevent an ingrown toenail, and file off the rough edges.

Diarrhea

RIDING OUT THE RUNS

It's got all kinds of colorful nicknames, including "Greased Lightning," "Turkey Trots," and "Montezuma's Revenge." You may have even heard your 11-year-old singing a catchy little ditty about it. But just saying the word diarrhea gets a reaction from most people—they either giggle or turn pale. Diarrhea is probably one of the most unpleasant problems that plagues us. And it's a common malady. Americans usually suffer from diarrhea a couple times a year. For most adults, diarrhea isn't serious. And it does give you a chance to ponder some redecorating ideas for the bathroom.

The Rundown on Diarrhea

On a typical day, you eat a hoagie and drink an iced tea and your meal makes its way through the digestive system without any problems. By the time it reaches the intestines, your food is mostly fluid with bits of solid material. The intestines reabsorb most of the fluid, and the solid stuff is excreted in the usual fashion. But when you've got diarrhea, something blocks the intestine's ability to absorb fluid. You've got loads of watery fluids mixed in with your stool, and you get that "gotta go" feeling.

There are essentially two types of diarrhea: acute and chronic. Thankfully, the vast majority of diarrhea is acute, or short-term. This type of diarrhea keeps you on the toilet for a couple of days but doesn't stick around long. Acute diarrhea is also known as noninflammatory diarrhea. Its symptoms are what most people associate with the condition: watery, frequent stools accompanied by stomach cramps, gas, and nausea.

Acute diarrhea usually has a bacterial or viral culprit. Gastroenteritis, mistakenly called the "stomach flu," is one of the most common infections that cause diarrhea.

MILK'S NOT ALWAYS GOOD FOR YOU

Between 70 and 90 percent of Asian, African American, Native American, and Mediterranean adults lack the enzyme lactase, which is responsible for digesting lactose, a sugar found in milk. Lactose intolerance is the most common reason for chronic diarrhea.

WHEN TO CALL THE DOCTOR

Most diarrhea has to run its course. However, diarrhea can be a sign of a more serious problem. If you're concerned, here are some symptoms that warrant a trip to the emergency room or a call to your family physician.

- Your diarrhea symptoms last more than 48 hours
- You have severe stomach cramps
- You have blood or pus in your stool
- You start showing any signs of severe dehydration such as dizziness when you stand, urinating less frequently or in very small amounts, dark yellow urine, increased thirst, and dry skin
- You have fever or chills

Gastroenteritis can be caused by many different viruses. Eating or drinking foods contaminated with bacteria can also cause diarrhea. Other causes of acute diarrhea are lactose intolerance, sweeteners such as sorbitol, over-the-counter antacids that contain magnesium, too much vitamin C, and some antibiotics.

If you have chronic, or long-term, diarrhea that comes on suddenly and stays for weeks, you may have a more serious condition such as irritable bowel syndrome or a severe food allergy.

Dehydration Dangers

With any kind of diarrhea, you lose a lot of fluids. One of the quickest ways you can end up going from the bathroom to the emergency room is to take a pass on liquids while you're sick. Fluids not only keep things running smoothly in your body, they also keep electrolyte levels balanced. Electrolytes are sodium, potassium, and chloride salts that your body needs for proper organ function. An electrolyte imbalance can cause your heart to beat irregularly, causing life-threatening problems. Though drinking or eating anything while you're running back and forth to the bathroom might sound unpleasant, it will help make you more comfortable and get you back on your feet more quickly.

Though experts don't see eye to eye on which fluids are best during a bout with diarrhea, they do agree that getting two to three quarts of fluid a day is a good idea. When you drink, it's easier on the tummy if you sip instead of gulp and if you drink cool, not cold or hot, fluids. Here are some tried-and-true fluids that should get you through the rough days.

- Decaffeinated tea with a little sugar
- Sports drinks
- Commercially available electrolyte replacement drinks for children
- Bouillon
- Chicken broth
- Orange juice

Though it may not sound logical to put diarrhea and food in the same sentence, if you don't put something in your body while you're enduring tummy troubles, you might end up getting sicker. There are loads of good things from the kitchen that will ease your grumbling stomach, and there are even a few things that will prevent those diarrhea-causing agents from coming back for a return engagement.

FROM THE CUPBOARD

BLUEBERRIES. Blueberry root is a long-time folk remedy for diarrhea. In Sweden, doctors prescribe a soup made with dried blueberries for tummy problems. Blueberries are rich in anthocyanosides, which have antioxidant and antibacterial properties, as well as tannins, which combat diarrhea.

CHAMOMILE TEA. Chamomile is good for treating intestinal inflammation, and it has antispasmodic properties as well. You can brew yourself a cup of chamomile tea from packaged tea bags, or you can buy chamomile flowers and steep 1 teaspoon of them and 1 teaspoon of peppermint leaves in a cup of boiling water for fifteen minutes. Drink 3 cups a day.

COOKED CEREALS. Starchy foods, such as precooked rice or tapioca cereals, can help ease your tummy. Prepare the cereal according to the directions on the box, making it as thick as you can stomach it. Just avoid adding too much sugar or salt, as these can aggravate diarrhea. It's probably a good idea to avoid oatmeal since it's high in fiber and your intestines can't tolerate the added bulk during a bout with diarrhea.

POTATOES. This is another starchy food that can help restore nutrients and comfort your stomach. But eating french fries won't help. Fried foods tend to aggravate an aching tummy. Other root vegetables such as carrots (cooked, of course) are also easy on an upset stomach, and they are loaded with nutrients.

FOODS TO AVOID WHEN YOU'VE GOT TUMMY TROUBLE

- Caffeine. It stimulates the nervous system, including the intestines.
- Sweeteners such as sorbitol, xylitol, and mannitol. These are mostly found in fruit juices and sugarless candy.
- Milk and cheese. The intestines work extra hard to digest the enzymes in these dairy products. While your body is down for the count, and even a few days after you're better, you might want to avoid dairy of any kind except for yogurt.
- Fiber. Now is not the time to bulk up. Fiber is simply too hard for an aching tummy to digest.
- Sugar. Some sugar is good during a case of diarrhea— it can help you absorb electrolytes needed for rehydration—but too much can make things worse.

No More Excuses to Be a BRAT

Although the classic BRAT (bananas, rice, applesauce, and toast) diet is touted as the best for refeeding after a bout with diarrhea, The American Academy of Pediatrics considers that diet too low in energy density, protein, and fat for children. While those foods can be tolerated, the Academy suggests introducing complex carbohydrates (rice, wheat, potatoes, bread, and cereals), lean meats, yogurt, fruits, and vegetables. Research shows these foods, too, are well-tolerated. Foods to avoid giving your children include those that are high in fat, salt, or sugar (including juice and soft drinks).

Rice. Cooked white rice is another starchy food that can be handled by someone recovering from diarrhea.

Sugar. To make your own fluid replacement, mix 4 teaspoons sugar and ½ teaspoon salt with 1 quart water. Mixing electrolytes (such as salt) with a form of glucose (sugar) helps the body to better absorb the nutrients.

From the Fruit Basket

Banana. Long known as a soother for tummy trouble, this potassium-rich fruit can restore nutrients and is easy to digest.

Orange peel. Orange peel tea is a folk remedy that is believed to aid in digestion. Place a chopped orange peel (preferably from an organic orange, as peels otherwise may contain pesticides and dyes) into a pot and cover with 1 pint boiling water. Let it stand until the water is cooled. You can sweeten it with sugar or honey.

From the Refrigerator

Yogurt. Look for yogurt with live cultures. These "cultures" are friendly bacteria that can go in and line your intestines, providing you protection from the bad guys. If you've already got diarrhea, yogurt can help produce lactic acid in your intestines, which can kill off the nasty bacteria and get you feeling better, faster.

From the Spice Rack

Fenugreek seeds. Science has given the nod to this folk remedy. But this one is for adults only. Mix ½ teaspoon fenugreek seeds with water and drink it up.

More Do's and Don'ts

• To ease stomach pain, try resting with a heating pad on your belly.

• Don't take antidiarrheal medications at the onset of your illness. Let your body rid itself of whatever's causing the problem first.

• Wash your hands thoroughly before preparing food. You don't want to pass your illness to everyone in the household.

Diverticular Disease

PREVENTING PROBLEMS

Diverticulosis is a common condition in which small pouches, called diverticula, develop in the colon. It happens when the inner lining of the large intestine is forced, under pressure, through weak spots in the outer layer of the colon. No one is sure what causes diverticulosis, but a low-fiber diet and lack of exercise have been shown to put you at greater risk. The diverticular pouches are present in about 50 percent of people more than 60 years of age, and the pouches themselves are not much of a problem. However, when a food particle or piece of waste material lodges in the pouches, it can become inflamed and cause a more serious illness called diverticulitis. Diverticulitis can range from a mild infection to a severe one requiring hospitalization and even surgery.

WHEN TO CALL THE DOCTOR

- If you experience severe abdominal pain along with fever, swelling, chills, and nausea or vomiting, go to the emergency room immediately. Your symptoms can't wait for a call to the doctor.
- If there's blood in the stool or your stool is black and tarlike. You may be bleeding internally.
- If pain persists in spite of treatment

Symptoms

Diverticulosis usually causes no symptoms. Most people won't even know they have the condition unless it shows up on a routine colonoscopy or develops into diverticulitis. But diverticulitis does have symptoms, including

- Abdominal cramping, usually more severe on the lower-left side
- Abdominal pain triggered by touch
- Nausea
- Gas, belching, bloating
- Fever
- Diarrhea, constipation, or very thin stools
- Blood in the stools
- General feeling of being tired or run-down

If you have any of these symptoms, don't self-diagnose. Call a doctor or, if the symp-

FABULOUS FIBER (BULK)

Fiber, also known as bulk, is essential to alleviating problems associated with diverticulitis and for having a healthy colon. Everyone needs 25 to 30 grams a day. The problem is, even though we think we're getting plenty of fiber, most of us are getting only half of what we need.

Remember, though, to add fiber to your diet slowly at first. Try a little one day, skip a day, then add a little more the next. Too much too soon can lead to constipation. And be sure to drink plenty of water as you're adding fiber—at least 8 glasses a day. That helps push all that added fiber on through the digestive system. The faster it's gone, the less likely the chances of it, or any other foods, getting lodged in one of the diverticula and causing a problem.

toms are severe, get yourself to the doctor's office or an emergency room. Diverticulitis that's untreated can lead to perforation of the colon, formation of an abscess, or peritonitis, a life-threatening infection.

Diverticula don't go away. Once you have them, you're stuck with them. It's a good idea to adjust your lifestyle to avoid flare-ups, and for mild symptoms there's relief to be found in the kitchen.

Warning! The following are to help prevent the development of diverticulitis or to ease the mildest of symptoms. For all other symptoms, see a doctor!

FROM THE CUPBOARD

BARLEY. This grain is a digestive anti-inflammatory. Add some to vegetable soup or stew. Or buy some barley flour, flakes, and grits.

BROWN RICE. It's easy on the digestive system, rich in fiber, and calms inflammation and spasms in the colon. Eat it plain or as a dessert with a little honey, mix it with vegetables for a stir-fry, try it in the morning as a breakfast food instead of oatmeal, or boil it for a tea and drink the liquid in addition to eating the rice. There are no limits to the ways you can serve up brown rice.

GARLIC. Eating garlic can help prevent infection. Eat 1 clove, three times a day. You don't have to eat it plain, though. Try mincing it and adding it to a salad or to a soup or stew. Don't eat pasta sauce, however, because tomato-based, spicy, and acidic foods can exacerbate symptoms.

FROM THE REFRIGERATOR

PAPAYA. This soothes diverticulitis. Find a nice, ripe, red-tinged papaya, cut it open, toss away the seeds, and eat. Use it in a fruit salad; it's especially good with melons. Or put it in the blender and make juice. Add a little honey to sweeten it up, if necessary. Papaya has an unusual but enjoyable flavor.

PEAR. Another fruit that can soothe inflammation, pears don't need any doctoring to eat. Simply find one that's ripe and enjoy.

POTATOES. They're tasty and nourishing, and they have soothing, anti-inflammatory properties that are especially good for digestive woes. Because grease can aggravate diverticulitis, avoid fried potatoes of any sort. But any other cooking method will do: baking, broiling, or boiling.

MORE DO'S & DON'TS

- Exercise. Everything in your body works better, including your digestive tract, when you exercise.

- Skip the caffeine. It can cause digestive upset.

- Don't rush things. It takes time for your bowels to move, so allow sufficient time.

- Cut back on red meats. They weaken the wall of the colon, which is where the pouches in diverticulosis start.

FACTS ABOUT DIVERTICULOSIS

- 10 percent of people over age 40 have diverticulosis
- 50 percent over age 60 have diverticulosis
- Almost everyone over age 80 has diverticulosis
- About 20 percent of those with diverticulosis will develop diverticulitis

OLD WIVES' TALE OR NOT?

One of the traditional warnings that used to come with a diagnosis of diverticulosis was to avoid nuts, popcorn, and seeds. Why? Because they can lodge in the diverticula and cause inflammation. The truth is, some doctors still say to avoid these, but there's no evidence that these foods cause diverticulitis, according to the National Institutes of Health. What should you do? Listen to your gut. If you love popcorn, for example, try a small amount and see what happens. If it causes problems, don't eat it again. If it doesn't, enjoy it in moderation. Just be sure to chew those seeds and nuts well. And don't forget to drink plenty of water to wash them down the diverticular obstacle course.

Fatigue
RESTORING VITALITY

Americans are all too familiar with being tired. A poll conducted by the National Sleep Foundation discovered that Americans are sleeping and playing less and spending more time tied to the job than they did five years ago. Sixty-three percent of adults don't get eight hours of sleep a night, the amount that's recommended for good health and safety. And almost one-third get less than seven hours a night during the work week.

Not getting enough sleep is sure to contribute to fatigue, but what people are doing while they're awake is another problem. The same poll showed one-third of Americans are working more than 50 hours a week. People are spending less time taking care of themselves—sitting down to read a good book, going for a bike ride with the kids, eating a healthy meal. The bottom line: Most people are exhausted. In fact, ten million Americans will visit their doctors this year and ask the same question, "Why am I so tired?"

What Type of Tired Are You?

There are two types of fatigue: emotional and physical. Emotional fatigue is a tiredness of the mind. It happens when stress piles up, such as having to meet multiple deadlines at work or dealing with the unexpected death of a parent. Physical fatigue happens when you physically exert yourself, such as when you spend the day working in the garden. Both types of tiredness can cause you to feel lethargic. And they both require rest and relaxation.

How do you know what type of tired you're experiencing? If you wake up tired in the morning but start feeling better as the day goes on, take a look at what's going on in your life emotionally. The key to your fatigue may be in your head. If the morning finds you energized and raring to go, but you start to lose your spark as the afternoon appears, you're probably dealing with a physical problem.

> ### WHEN TO CALL THE DOCTOR
>
> • When you have ongoing, unresolved fatigue that lifestyle changes, such as eating a balanced diet, getting more rest and exercise, and reducing stress, haven't helped improve

Reasons for emotional fatigue:

- Doing too much. You're a room mother, a Girl Scout leader, and now you've decided to take on the school's annual fund drive. And you wonder why you're wiped out?

- Doing too little. Sounds strange, but boredom makes you tired. Being motivated to accomplish goals adds a spark to your life. The secret is finding the right balance.

- Stressful situations. Major turmoil such as changing jobs or moving to a new city can make you feel exhausted.

- Mental maladies. People who are lonely or depressed are prone to tiredness.

Reasons for physical fatigue:

- Skipping needed nutrients. Low-calorie diets, fasting, or just missing meals because of meetings or busy schedules can wipe you out.

- Not sleeping enough. There's no perfect number of hours you should sleep. Different people have different sleep needs. But if you wake up feeling exhausted morning after morning, you might need to add a few more sleeping hours in your day.

- Getting no exercise. Exercise is essential to feeling better—physically and mentally.

- Dodging drinks. Dehydration is an energy zapper. Drinking and eating go hand-in-hand in giving your body the fuel it needs to feel good.

UNCOVERING CHRONIC FATIGUE SYNDROME

Occasional fatigue is normal, ongoing fatigue is not. Chronic fatigue syndrome (CFS) has gotten a load of press lately, mostly because it is such a mystery. Unlike normal tiredness, chronic fatigue syndrome starts out feeling like the flu. Sufferers feel extreme fatigue, and they have muscle and joint aches, sore throat, low-grade fever, memory impairment, and swollen lymph nodes. The problem is these symptoms don't go away after a few days or even a few weeks.

No one knows what causes CFS, and a doctor can't tell you for sure that's what's ailing you. The verdict of chronic fatigue syndrome is given after the doctor has eliminated other conditions that may have the same symptoms.

The good news is that with increased numbers of CFS, doctors are finding out more keys to understanding and treating the disease. Though there is no cure, there are ways you can learn to deal with your symptoms and get on the road to feeling better. Your first destination if you think you have CFS is your doctor's office.

SAY "SI" TO SIESTAS

Many cultures have long known the benefits of grabbing an afternoon nap. The Amish are fond of saying that a half-hour nap in the afternoon is worth two hours of sleep at night. And scientific studies are confirming what the Amish have known all along. One study found that nodding off for as little as ten minutes can make you more alert and energized.

Fatigue as a Symptom of Disease

Fatigue that is brought on by an unexpected loss of sleep, such as being a new parent, or a stressful situation, such as a deadline at work, is usually easily remedied simply by taking good care of yourself. But ongoing fatigue can be the signal that something more serious is going on in your body. It can often be a symptom of

• anemia

• arthritis

• a slower-than-usual thyroid (hypothyroidism)

• an underlying sleep disorder

• cancer

• chronic fatigue syndrome

• diabetes

• heart disease

FROM THE CABINET

COFFEE AND TEA. Caffeine is a known pick-me-up. And the American Dietetic Association says there's no harm in drinking the stimulating stuff, as long as you do so in moderation. Studies confirm that caffeine does perk up the brain and get those mental faculties humming. But be careful—the ADA says a couple of cups a day should do you fine. More than that and you risk anxiety and insomnia.

FROM THE REFRIGERATOR

EGGS. This is a folk remedy that is backed by sound nutrition. One of the most important ways you can battle fatigue is to eat a well-balanced diet, and eggs are loaded with good things such as protein, iron, vitamin A, folic acid, riboflavin, and pantothenic acid. Eat one egg a day, however you like it, and you may be feeling better in no time.

FLUIDS. Drink plenty of water, juice, milk, or other beverages to keep yourself hydrated. Dehydration can contribute to fatigue.

SKIM MILK. Mixing a little protein with your carbohydrates can keep you energized. Eating only carbohydrates, such as a doughnut or a pancake slathered in syrup, can cause serotonin, a neurotransmitter, to build up in the brain, making you feel drowsy. Eating protein with your carbohydrates can block that sleepy feeling and leave you feeling energized. A good meal to start your day: cereal and skim milk.

FROM THE SPICE RACK

GINSENG. Ginseng is an age-old energy booster. This root has a sweet licorice taste and has been used for thousands of years to treat weakness and exhaustion. Be cautious: Don't take ginseng unless you are really fatigued. It can be too stimulating if you're feeling fine. In America you're probably wise to buy Asian ginseng. Another variety, Siberian ginseng, may not be as potent as the Asian variety. Both Asian and Siberian ginseng varieties of the herb have been labeled "adaptogens." That means they help you adapt to stresses in your environment. You can buy ginseng powder at a reputable herb shop. Take 2 grams of ginseng powder a day for a six-week stint. Then take at least a two-week break before using the energizing herb again.

MORE DO'S AND DON'TS

- Take some time for yourself. Try taking a prayer walk or simply sitting in the garden and meditating on your blessings. Play some soothing music. Focusing on what's important can restore your energy.

- Get moving. Exercise at least 30 minutes, three days a week. Walk up and down the stairs in your office building or take a dance class at your local gym. Exercise releases endorphins in your brain that make you feel better and give you more strength mentally and physically to face anything that life throws at you.

- Take off a few pounds. If you're carrying around a spare tire or two, you can get tired faster. Taking off the weight slowly and nutritiously can restore your energy.

- Nix the television. Instead of turning into a vegetable, choose something that will keep those brain cells stimulated, such as playing a game with your sweetie or picking up that novel you keep meaning to finish.

COMBING CENTURIES OF CAFFEINE

Caffeine is a mild stimulant and is found naturally in foods such as chocolate, coffee, and tea. It's been around for thousands of years and was once so valuable that coffee beans were used as currency in Africa. Many early physicians wanted caffeine banned from common use because they were afraid the stimulant would be too powerful for your average Joe. Around the 15th century, coffee finally made its debut in Europe, both pharmaceutically and in coffeehouses (the Starbucks of the Middle Ages). And coffee is now the number one source of caffeine in the United States.

Fever
FEELING THE HEAT

Fever is a good thing. It's your body's attempt to kill off invading bacteria and other nasty organisms that can't survive the heat. The hypothalamus, which is the body's thermostat, senses the assault on the body and turns up the heat much the way you turn up the thermostat when you feel cold. It's a simple defense mechanism, and the sweat that comes with a fever is merely a way to cool the body down.

It used to be standard medical practice to knock that fever out as quickly as possible. Not so anymore. The value of fever is recognized, and since a fever will usually subside when the infection that's causing it runs its course, modern thinking is to ride out that fever, especially if it stays under 102°F in adults. However, if a fever is making you uncomfortable or interfering with your ability to eat, drink, or sleep, treat it. Your body needs adequate nutrition, hydration, and rest to fight the underlying cause of the fever.

Fever is a symptom, not an illness, and so there's no specific cure. But there are some fever-relievers in the kitchen that may make you feel better for the duration. Be aware that the most significant side effect of fever is dehydration. Specific ways to deal with it can be found in the Dehydration profile, pages 83–87.

FROM THE CUPBOARD

CREAM OF TARTAR. Try this fever tea. Combine 1½ teaspoons cream of tartar, ½ teaspoon lemon juice, 2½ cups warm water, and ½ teaspoon honey. Drink 4 to 6 ounces at a time.

PINEAPPLE. Fresh is best. It's one of nature's anti-inflammatory agents that can fight fever. Pineapple is also packed with juice that can prevent dehydration.

WHEN TO CALL THE DOCTOR

- In infants under 3 months, 100°F or above
- Infants 3 to 6 months, 101°F or above
- In children and adults under 60, 104°F
- In adults over 60, 102°F
- In adults and children, 101°F for more than three days
- In children, if febrile seizures develop
- If pain, diarrhea, swollen joints, rash, or stiff neck occur with fever

RAISINS. Drink a little of this several times a day to keep yourself hydrated during a fever. Put ¾ cup chopped raisins in 7½ cups water. Bring to a boil, then simmer until the water has been reduced by one-third. Strain out raisins and drink.

SALT. An Ayurvedic remedy for fever is to mix 1 teaspoon salt into a bowl of cool water. Take two clean dishcloths, dip them in water, then place one on the forehead and one over the belly button.

FROM THE FREEZER

POPSICLE. These can reduce the risk of dehydration and are particularly good at keeping fluids in small children. Fruit juice bars work, too.

FROM THE REFRIGERATOR

APPLE WATER. It tastes good, relieves the miseries of fever, and keeps the body hydrated. To make it, peel, core, and slice 3 sweet apples. Put them in a pan with 3¾ cups water. Bring to a boil, then simmer until the apples are barely mushy. Remove, strain without pressing apple puree into the liquid, and add 2 tablespoons honey. Drink and enjoy.

BLACKBERRY VINEGAR. This is a great fever elixir, but it takes several days to prepare. Pour cider vinegar over a pound or two of blackberries, then cover the container and store it in a cool, dark place for three days. Strain for a day, since it takes time for all the liquid to drain from the berries, and collect the liquid in another container. Then add 2 cups sugar to each 2½ cups juice. Bring to a boil, then simmer for 5 minutes while you skim the scum off the top. Cool and store in an airtight jar in a cool place. Mix 1 teaspoonful with water to quench the thirst caused by a fever.

CILANTRO (CORIANDER LEAVES). Fresh cilantro can be turned into a simple fever remedy. Wash thoroughly and place a handful of leaves in a blender with ⅓ cup water. Blend thoroughly, then strain, reserving the liquid. Take 2 teaspoons of the liquid three times a day.

FASCINATING FACT

Shivering increases the amount of heat your body produces by up to five times.

FEVER FACTS

You say your temperature's not 98.6°F? Don't sweat it. That number is just the average normal temperature reported in 1868 by Carl Wunderlich. Wunderlich took 1 million temperature readings from 25,000 people and determined the average to be 98.6.

Recently, researchers in a smaller study found that the average adult's body temperature is closer to 98.2.

More about fever:

- Body temperature varies according to time of day. The lowest usually occurs around 6 A.M. and the highest at 4 P.M.
- Women's temperatures average .3 degree higher than men's.
- For each degree that body temperature rises, heart rate increases almost 2½ beats per minute.

FRUIT JUICE. It will replace the fluids lost through sweating. Lemonade is a good choice, too.

GINGER. This can help break a high fever. Grate 2 tablespoons fresh ginger and add to 2 cups boiling water. Steep 30 minutes. Add a little honey to sweeten, and drink a cup of the warm beverage every two to three hours.

LETTUCE. Pour a pint of boiling water over an entire head of lettuce and let it steep, covered, for 15 minutes. Strain, sweeten the liquid to taste, and drink. In addition to keeping you hydrated, this may help you sleep better.

FROM THE SINK

WATER. Drink lots of it to prevent dehydration. Sponging the body with lukewarm water can relieve fever symptoms, but use fever-reducing medication first to decrease the possibility of chills and shivering. Do not use cold water or ice on the body.

FROM THE SPICE RACK

BASIL. Mix 1 teaspoon basil with ¼ teaspoon black pepper. Steep in 1 cup hot water to make a tea. Add 1 teaspoon honey. Drink two to three times a day.

OREGANO. A tea made from a mixture of some spice-rack staples can help reduce fever. Steep 1 teaspoon each of oregano and marjoram in a pint of boiling water for 30 minutes. Strain, and drink warm a couple times a day. Refrigerate unused portion until needed, then gently warm.

SAGE. Mix 2 teaspoons dried sage with 1 teaspoon dried peppermint. Pour 1 cup boiling water over these and steep 15 minutes. Strain and sweeten with honey. Drink 2 to 3 cups per day, rewarmed. Add a little honey to sweeten the taste.

MORE DO'S & DON'TS

- Do not sponge alcohol on the body to reduce fever. It can cause chills and increased fever.

- Use analgesics if necessary. Acetaminophen will reduce a fever, as will aspirin. However, NEVER give aspirin to children under 18 without first consulting the doctor. The result can be Reye's syndrome, a potentially fatal disease.

- Skip the alcohol and caffeine. They're diuretics, and you don't need to lose more fluid.

- Use only light clothing and blankets. Heavy clothing and blankets will only make the fever go higher.

- If you don't feel like eating, just make sure you get sufficient fluids. Reintroduce foods gradually if you haven't been eating very much.

Fibrocystic Breast Disease
DECREASING DISCOMFORT

Although the term fibrocystic breast disease may sound ominous, it actually describes a benign condition of the breasts that more than 60 percent of all women experience. If your breasts feel lumpy and you have intermittent breast discomfort, such as tenderness, swelling, and pain, you may have fibrocystic breast disease.

How can you tell? Symptoms include a dense, irregular, and bumpy consistency of the breast tissue. During a self-exam, you may feel a thick area of irregularly shaped tissue with a lumpy or ridgelike surface, or you may encounter a beadlike texture to your breast tissue. Fibrocystic breasts typically become swollen, tender, heavy, and lumpier a week or two before the menstrual period. There also may be changes in nipple sensation, and the nipples may itch. These symptoms can range from mild to severe, and they usually improve after menstruation. Some women, however, have persistent rather than intermittent symptoms. The condition tends to subside with menopause.

What's Behind the Pain...and What's Not

No one understands the causes of this condition, but some researchers believe that breast lumps are inherited. What we do know is that the condition is related to how the breast responds to hormonal changes during the monthly cycle. Hormonal stimulation causes milk glands and ducts to swell and the breast to retain water. The condition is more common in women aged 30 to 50, most likely because of years of repeated hormonal stimulation, which can harden lumps.

What's usually not behind the pain is breast cancer. Only five percent of fibrocystic conditions have the type of changes that would be considered a risk factor for developing breast cancer, according to the American Cancer Society. Unlike the lumps associated with fibrocystic breast disease, which are tender and move freely, cancerous lumps most often are not tender and don't move freely.

If you think you have fibrocystic breast disease, be sure to check it out with your physician, who should always examine any lump(s) in the

WHEN TO CALL THE DOCTOR

- Anytime you detect a new lump in your breast. A physician can determine if the lump is benign.
- If an existing lump increases in size or doesn't go away with menstruation
- If you feel a distinct lump, rather than a lumpy area
- If you think your birth control pills or hormone replacement therapies are aggravating your condition. Your doctor can recommend alternatives if these are part of your problem.
- If you experience a change in the size of one breast that's not related to your menstrual period or if your breast doesn't return to normal after menstruation

breast. You'll be pleased to discover that breast tenderness and other symptoms can usually be managed through diet.

FROM THE CUPBOARD

DRINKS. Coffee, tea, soft drinks, wine, and beer all contain methylxanthines—chemicals that trigger the body to increase production of stress hormones. Such hormones are linked to breast lumps and tenderness. Studies have shown that reducing or eliminating such liquids from the diet can diminish symptoms in up to 80 percent of women.

FROM THE FREEZER

COLD COMPRESSES. Ice packs may be a bit of a shock to delicate breasts. However, a cold compress can give breasts some relief from tenderness and inflammation. To make this initially shocking but ultimately soothing remedy, fill a plastic, reclosable bag with crushed ice or use a bag of frozen peas and wrap in a towel. Lie down and place on the sore breast(s) for ten minutes. Note: Some women find alternating heat and cold, applying heat first for 30 minutes then cold for 10 minutes, helps minimize pain.

FROM THE REFRIGERATOR

FISH. The best fish for female health include those high in the omega-3 fatty acids such as salmon, trout, and mackerel. These fish are also high in iodine, a deficiency of which may be a factor in the development of breast lumps. Eating moderate amounts of fish may help prevent lumps.

MEATS. Cut back on meat consumption. Before heading to the butcher's block, cows, chicken, and other livestock are often pumped full of hormones. Your body doesn't need the additional influx, especially during the hormone high time of your period. If meat needs to be on the menu, purchase hormone-free meats and poultry.

VEGETABLES. Diuretics help flush excess fluids from the body and reduce breast swelling. Unfortunately, many store-bought diuretics can also deplete your potassium reserves, unbalance your electrolyte count, and interfere with glucose production. Turn to natural diuretics instead. Parsley, cucumbers, and cabbage are healthy for you and will keep you naturally flushed.

WHOLE-GRAIN FOODS. Increasing your intake of fiber can help control the hormonal fluctuations behind fibrocystic breast disease. Eat whole-wheat bread, brown rice, beans, and fruits.

FROM THE SPICE RACK

KELP. Kelp and other sea vegetables, such as nori and dulse, are good sources of iodine. Studies suggest that an iodine deficiency can predispose women to having breast lumps. While you can find these vegetables in some food markets, kelp and dulse are also available in powdered form and can be used in cooking as a salt substitute.

SALT. Two weeks before your period, hide the saltshaker. During the menstrual cycle, women tend to retain water, which in turn causes their breasts to feel heavy and become sensitive. Salt only increases this uncomfortable bloating. Be aware of hidden salts in processed foods, and don't order pizza until after your period.

FROM THE STOVE

HOT COMPRESSES. Less shocking than ice packs, but equally soothing to swollen breasts, is the hot compress. Run hot water over face towels and place on your chest for a few minutes. Rewarm when necessary. A heating pad or a homemade rice bag holds the heat longer. To make a rice bag, fill a clean, thick sock with a cup of rice, close the opening with a knot, and place in the microwave for 30 seconds or so. (Watch it carefully, so the rice doesn't pop!) Remove, test the temperature, and place on your breasts. Note: Some women find alternating heat and cold, applying heat first for 30 minutes, then cold for 10 minutes, minimizes pain.

FROM THE SUPPLEMENT SHELF

ESSENTIAL FATTY ACIDS. Several studies have looked at the beneficial effects of evening primrose oil on fibrocystic breast disease. Evening primrose oil is an excellent source of the essential fatty acid linolenic acid and its chemical derivative, gamma linolenic acid (GLA). Typical dosages used in the studies were 1,500 mg twice a day. (This would amount to taking 6 of the 500 mg capsules commonly available at health food stores.) Borage oil and black currant oil are more concentrated sources of GLA, so you need to take fewer capsules. For example, 3 or 4 capsules per day of borage oil may be sufficient. However, always discuss dosages with your physician before taking any of these oils.

VITAMIN A/BETA-CAROTENE. Some studies have shown that vitamin A can reduce breast pain in women with moderate to severe symptoms. High doses of vitamin A can be toxic, though. It's safer to eat a diet high in beta-carotene, the precursor to vitamin A, with yellow, orange, red, and dark green vegetables and fruits.

VITAMIN E. In several controlled studies, vitamin E was found to be quite helpful in reducing the pain, tenderness, and size of breast lumps. Vitamin E is found in vegetable oils, nuts, green leafy vegetables, and some fortified cereals. Or take a daily supplement of 400 IU.

MORE DO'S AND DON'TS

- Wear a well-fitting, supportive bra. It eases tenderness by immobilizing the breasts and eliminating the feeling of heaviness. If your breasts swell considerably before your period, don't squeeze into your regular size. Buy the next size up.

- Exercise regularly, eat a low-fat diet, and maintain an ideal weight. Body fat produces and stores estrogen, the hormone partially responsible for changes in the breasts. Being excessively overweight can predispose you to breast discomfort.

- Don't smoke.

- Stop using herbal cosmetics and remedies, especially those made with ginseng. These can have steroidal effects similar to estrogen.

THE BREAST SELF-EXAM

Only by getting to know your breasts through regular monthly breast self-exams will you be able to learn what's normal for you and what's not. Familiarity will allow you to discover a new lump or suspicious area and get it checked out by your doctor.

The best time in your cycle to do a breast exam is one week after your period. (Try marking your calendar or programming your e-mail to send you a message each month.) The exam is best performed in the shower, since the water allows for less friction and easier movement for your hand across breast tissue.

Here's how:

- Use the opposite hand for the opposite breast; i.e., left hand for the right breast.

- Press firmly with your fingers and move the fingers in a circle covering the entire breast and the armpit.

- Check the other breast in the same manner.

- After your shower, check your breasts in a mirror for any dimpling, discharge, or other changes.

- Immediately report any lumps, knots, or changes to your physician.

Flatulence
Taking a Pass on Gas

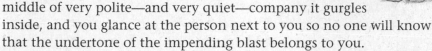

Who is the most glamorous person you know? Well, guess what. That person's not exempt from this particular problem. No one is. And it happens at the most awkward times, doesn't it? You feel that rumble way down deep in your belly, and it's traveling even lower. In the middle of very polite—and very quiet—company it gurgles inside, and you glance at the person next to you so no one will know that the undertone of the impending blast belongs to you.

Well, gas happens. Called flatus, or flatulence when it finally does escape, it's normal. Its beginnings are in the foods we eat. We eat, therefore we pass gas. Why? Our stomach acids are breaking down last night's pasta primavera into elements that will either be absorbed into the body or eliminated. And that breakdown causes... You guessed it: Gas!

Bodily gas originates in the stomach and travels down to the intestines (unless it comes back up as a belch). Its construction is pretty simple: carbon dioxide, hydrogen, nitrogen, and methane. Well, those gases make up about 99 percent of the gas we pass. The other 1 percent is divided among up to 250 different gases, all of which occur naturally when carbohydrates are broken down. If you swallow air, you add oxygen to the mix.

Here are some other interesting flatus facts:

- Normal flatus production is 6 to 64 ounces each day.

- There are 400 different kinds of bacteria living in your colon, and they're just waiting to mix and mingle with your food and give you gas.

When to Call the Doctor

- If you're experiencing sharp pain that starts near the naval and moves to the lower right side of the abdomen. Actually, call 9-1-1 for this one. It could be appendicitis.

- If you're experiencing pain in the upper right side of your abdomen

- If bloating and unexplained gas continues for more than three days

- If you're losing weight in addition to being unusually gassy

- If bowel movements smell worse than usual

FLATULOGENIC FOODS

Here are some foods that are definitely on the top of the flatus-maker list:

Beer
Bran
Broccoli
Brussels sprouts
Cabbage
Carbonated drinks
Cauliflower
Corn
Legumes (beans, lentils, dried peas)
Milk
Onions
Rutabaga

These are also gas-making culprits:

Apples
Apricots
Bananas
Carrots
Citrus fruits
Coffee
Eggplant
Lettuce
Melon
Potatoes
Radishes
Raisins
Soybeans
Spinach
Wheat products

• We pass gas, on average, 14 to 23 times every day.

Gas normally has no odor, unless you're squeezed into the elevator with the people who ate beans for dinner last night. Then the eye-watering "squeakers" they're responsible for are enough to make you haul out the old gas mask. The reason: Some foods simply hang around in the intestines too long and begin to ferment. Fermentation causes the offensive odor. And the more food that's fermenting, the more volume of gas building up for its grand exit.

Who's Prone

There are a few factors that make you more prone to passing gas. See if you're on the list:

• Anyone who dines regularly on the flatulogenic food list. See "Flatulogenic Foods" on this page.

• Those with certain stomach or intestinal ailments, such as lactose intolerance or irritable bowel syndrome

• Air-swallowers

• Those with gassy relatives. The tendency can be inherited.

• Anyone with food allergies that manifest in flatus after certain foods are eaten

Gas is a side effect or symptom, not an illness in itself. And it's a symptom that can be treated several different ways with things you find in the kitchen.

FROM THE CUPBOARD

BEANO. Keep it sitting right next to that bag of dry beans to remind you it's a gas-busting enzyme that breaks down hard-to-digest disaccharides, thereby avoiding the formation of gas. Use this product as you eat the gassy foods, not afterward. It's available at groceries and pharmacies.

CARAWAY CRACKERS. Caraway seeds and their oils are carminatives (they get rid of gas), but who wants to eat just the seeds? Caraway seed crackers and breads with caraway seeds are a tasty way to make your system gas-unfriendly.

PRESSURE COOKER. Beans that are undercooked are more likely to cause gas than beans that are well-cooked. To ensure that your beans are cooked thoroughly, pull out the pressure cooker and follow the manufacturer's advice for cooking beans. Or, cook them up to pressure for 30 minutes at 15 pounds per square inch on the gauge.

FROM THE DRAWER

PAPER. And a pen. List the foods that are causing your gas. Include such information as the type of food, when you ate it, and how much you ate. Do you get gassy after gulping down cucumbers or cola? Or maybe it happens after eating ice cream? (See Lactose Intolerance, page 207.) The truth about most gas is that, in some way, you're causing it. If you want to find out how, a food diary is one of the easiest ways to re-create the events leading up to the noxious crime.

FROM THE REFRIGERATOR

CITRUS FRUITS. Vitamin C in tablet form may cause gas, especially amounts in excess of 500 milligrams. So, reduce the dosage and replace the C with high-in-C fruits. Also try eating potatoes and sweet peppers, which are high in vitamin C.

PUMPKIN. It soothes the tummy, and best of all, it cuts down on flatulence. Try some baked, steamed, or broiled. Or, make yourself a simple pumpkin soup.

YOGURT WITH ACIDOPHILUS. It alleviates digestive woes, including gas. But the yogurt must have live acidophilus, a bacteria that helps with digestion.

SUGAR-FREE MISERY

Sorbitol, an artificial sweetener made of sugar alcohol that's used in many diet drinks and products, is often difficult to digest. Even a small amount, 10 grams, can cause bloating and gas. Double that amount and you may have cramping or diarrhea.

How do you know if you have sorbitol intolerance? That's easy. In mild cases, symptoms (normally gas) start 30 to 90 minutes after ingestion and go away after several hours. When diarrhea is present, it may take up to 24 hours for sorbitol to clear the system. If symptoms last longer, call the doctor and explain that you've eaten something with sorbitol.

So, if you get gassy after you've eaten a sugar-free food or drunk a sugar-free beverage, check the ingredients list. If sorbitol's there, chances are you can't handle it. And neither can your friends!

THINKING ABOUT GIVING THOSE BEANS THE BOOT?

Don't do it! Beans are loaded with cholesterol-lowering fiber and bone-saving calcium, and they have a hand in protecting against colon cancer and heart disease. So instead of bagging the beans, find out which ones cause you the most trouble and boot those out of your diet. Pintos, black beans, and Great Northerns are generally the biggest gas-makers. What's gassy for some, though, may not be gassy for others. It's all a matter of how your body digests them. Also see "De-Gas Those Beautiful Beans," page 127, for a great way to de-gas your favorite beans.

FROM THE SPICE RACK

CARDAMOM SEEDS. These speed digestion. Add them to sautéed vegetables or to rice or lentils before cooking. You can also chew whole pods or steep pods in boiling water for several minutes to make a tea.

CLOVES. They pep up digestion and eliminate gas. Add 2 to 3 whole cloves to rice before cooking. Sprinkle on apples and pears when baking. Or steep 2 to 3 whole cloves in a cup of boiling water for ten minutes, sweeten to taste, and drink.

CORIANDER. This helps in the downward movement of foods being digested and can ease cramps, hiccups, bloating, and flatulence. Crush the seeds into powder and add to foods such as vegetable stir-fry. Its flavor really enhances curry and Middle Eastern dishes, too.

FENNEL SEEDS. It's an acquired taste, but it may be one well worth acquiring if you're plagued by gas. Fennel's digestive powers are so good that in India fennel is customarily eaten after a meal to help digestion and freshen the breath. For gas, drink it as a tea by steeping ½ teaspoon seeds in 1 cup boiling water for ten minutes. Or, sprinkle them over those gassy vegetables during cooking or add to stir-fries.

GINGER. Combine 1 teaspoon fresh grated ginger with 1 teaspoon lime juice. Take after eating.

LEMON. Stir 1 teaspoon lemon juice and ½ teaspoon baking soda into 1 cup cool water. (Don't use cold water, as it can bring on gas.) Drink after meals.

MASSAGE HERBS. Add any of these to massage oil and rub over the abdomen to relieve gas: cardamom, clove, cinnamon, fennel, ginger. Warmed olive and sesame oils are wonderful for massages.

ROSEMARY. If you're eating a gassy food, sprinkle on a little rosemary to cut down the effect. You can do the same with sage and thyme, too.

TEA HERBS. Steep and drink a tea made from any of these: aniseed, basil leaves, chamomile, cloves, cinnamon, ginger, peppermint, sage. Steep about ½ teaspoon in 1 cup boiling water, then add honey or lemon to taste. Drink one to three times each day.

TURMERIC. This may stop a gas problem. Turmeric is one of the many flavorful and curative spices found in curry powder. You can add turmeric itself to rice or season a bland dish with curry powder, which contains turmeric. However you use it, it helps alleviate gas.

MORE DO'S & DON'TS

- Try cutting back some on fiber, especially from legumes. Fiber is good for you, but increasing fiber intake too quickly can cause gas.

- Reduce the amount of fermented foods you eat, such as cheese, soy sauce, and alcohol.

- Cut back on carbonated beverages. Those bubbles aren't just in your drink!

- Exercise. It stimulates digestion and the expulsion of gas. Do not exercise within two hours of eating, though. This can disrupt the normal digestive processes. A nice leisurely walk right after a meal is good, though.

- Sit down at the kitchen table and take off your shoes. On each foot, apply pressure to the sole for about one minute, halfway above midline and below the ball, right in the middle. This is the stomach point in acupressure.

- Stay calm. The digestive system is sensitive to emotional upset, stress, anxiety, and other strong emotions. When you're under stress, abdominal muscles tighten, causing painful spasms. This leads to gas, as well as swallowing air that can cause gas.

- Do try some over-the-counter aids. Activated charcoal products can help relieve gas. So can antigas medications. Check with your pharmacist to make sure they will work with medications you might already be taking. And if you have a condition in which salt intake can be detrimental, check with your doctor before taking any over-the-counter gas reliever.

- Don't stuff yourself when you eat. The more food in the gut, the more the gas builds up. And take your time—you'll swallow less air.

- Don't sip drinks through a straw. You'll suck in air, which causes gas.

DE-GAS THOSE BEAUTIFUL BEANS

If you love them but they don't love you back, there's a simple solution to eliminate most of the gas-causing effects.

1. Soak beans in water overnight.
2. Replace the water with fresh water and cook the beans for 30 minutes. Drain the water again.
3. Add fresh water and cook for another 30 minutes. Drain the water one more time.
4. Add fresh water and cook until done.

And, if you like the flavor of onion in those beans, skip the fresh onions. They share their gassy juices with everything that's in the bean pot. Instead, opt for dehydrated onions that will absorb the liquid already there instead of adding to it.

Flu (Influenza)
SURVIVING THE SIEGE

Boo hoo if you've got the flu. Unlike the common cold, which causes a stuffy nose, sore throat, and sneezing, the flu is a viral infection that strikes the entire body with a vengeance. The misery starts suddenly with chills and fever and spirals into more unpleasant symptoms that will take you out of commission: a sore throat, dry cough, stuffy or runny nose, headache, nausea, vomiting, severe muscle aches and pains, weakness, backache, and loss of appetite. Some people even experience pain and stiffness in the joints.

The worst of your symptoms will probably last about three to five days, but others, such as cough and fatigue, can linger for weeks. And a bout with the flu can deliver a double whammy if you develop a secondary infection, such as an ear or sinus infection or bronchitis. Even pneumonia can be a complication—and a potentially serious one—of influenza.

Flu viruses strike like clockwork in the United States. Every year they begin to show up in October and exit in April. Peak flu season is December and January.

Flu is a highly contagious illness, spread by droplets from the respiratory tract of an infected person. They can be airborne, such as those released after a person coughs or sneezes, or they can be transferred via an infected person's hands.

Taking a yearly flu shot can help you ward off infection, and this is particularly recommended for senior citizens, people with compromised immune systems, or people with asthma. Flu shots won't give you 100 percent protection, but they will significantly increase your chances of avoiding the flu.

If you do get the flu, there are kitchen remedies to help ease your suffering.

FROM THE CUPBOARD
BROTH. Drinking canned broth, whether it's beef, chicken, or vegetable, will help keep you hydrated and also help liquefy any mucous secretions. Broth is an easy food to eat and to keep down, even when you have no

appetite, and it will provide at least some nutrients.

HONEY. A hacking cough can keep you and every other household member up all night. Keep the peace with honey. Honey has long been used in traditional Chinese medicine for coughs. It's a simple enough recipe: Mix 1 tablespoon honey into 1 cup hot water, stir well, and enjoy. Honey acts as a natural expectorant, promoting the flow of mucus. Squeeze some lemon in if you want a little tartness.

MUSTARD. Not to discredit dear old Grandma, but she didn't come up with the mustard plaster, although by the way she touts its virtues, you might believe so. Actually, this remedy for the flu, chest colds, and bronchitis dates back to the ancient Romans, who understood early on the healing properties of mustard. Mustard is loaded with antimicrobial and anti-inflammatory properties, many of which can be inhaled through the vapors. Impress Grandma by making a mustard plaster with 1 tablespoon dry mustard and 2 to 4 tablespoons flour. Mix both with 1 egg white (optional) and warm water to form a paste. Next, find a clean handkerchief or square of muslin large enough to cover the upper chest. Smear the cloth the same way you'd smear mustard on a sandwich, then plop another cloth over it. Dab olive oil on the patient's skin and apply the mustard plaster to the upper chest. Check the patient every few minutes since mustard plaster can burn. Remove after a few minutes. Afterward, wash off any traces of mustard from the skin.

TEA. A cup of hot tea is just another way to take your fluids, which are so essential when you have the flu. Just be sure to choose one of the decaffeinated varieties. Caffeine is a mild diuretic, which is counterproductive when you have the flu, and you certainly don't want to be awakened with the need to use the bathroom when you need your rest!

WHEN TO CALL THE DOCTOR

- If flu symptoms are accompanied by a high fever that lasts more than three days
- If a cough persists, becomes worse, or is associated with chest pains and shortness of breath
- If the flu drags on and you don't get better
- If you have lung or heart disease, consult your physician at the first sign of flu. The elderly and the very young should also be taken to a doctor at the first sign of flu.

TAKE FLU SERIOUSLY

In the average year, influenza is associated with more than 20,000 deaths and 100,000 hospitalizations nationwide.

Myths About the Dreaded Flu

Myth #1: The 24-hour flu.

Fact: There is no such thing as a 24-hour flu, although we wish it were so. The sudden onslaught of vomiting, diarrhea, and a general feeling of malaise that is intense for a few hours, but subsides after 24 hours, is indeed caused by a viral agent, but not the one that causes influenza. The correct term should be "the 24-hour attack of gastroenteritis," which is an infection that affects the gastrointestinal tract.

Myth #2: Going outside without a hat or catching a chill causes the flu.

Fact: Venturing outside ill-prepared for the elements may not be the brightest idea, but it doesn't directly cause the flu. Several scientific studies have shown that people exposed to cold temperatures for several hours fare no worse than those kept toasty warm. This myth grows from the observation that a severe chill is one of the first flu symptoms. Thus, people conclude that being chilled leads to the flu.

From the Refrigerator

Juice. Any flavor or kind will do. Just drink lots of juice both to keep yourself hydrated and to give yourself some extra vitamins.

Lemon. The lovely lemon may cause a puckered face if eaten raw, but in a hot beverage lemons will have you smiling. Hot lemonade has been used as a flu remedy since Roman times and is still highly regarded in the folk traditions of New England. Lemons, being highly acidic, help make mucous membranes distasteful to bacteria and viruses. Lemon oil, which gives the juice its fragrance, is like a wonder drug containing antibacterial, antiviral, antifungal, and anti-inflammatory constituents. The oil also acts as an expectorant. To make this flu-fighting fruit drink, place 1 chopped lemon—skin, pulp, and all—into 1 cup boiling water. While the lemon steeps for 5 minutes, inhale the steam. Strain, add honey (to taste), and enjoy. Drink hot lemonade three to four times a day throughout your illness.

From the Spice Rack

Pepper. Pepper is an irritant (try sniffling some), yet this annoying characteristic is a plus for those suffering from coughs with thick mucus. The irritating property of pepper stimulates circulation and the flow of mucus. Place 1 teaspoon black pepper into a cup and sweeten things up with the addition of 1 tablespoon honey. Fill with boiling water, let steep for 10 to 15 minutes, stir, and sip.

Thyme. Wonderfully fragrant, thyme delights the senses (if you can smell when sick) and works as a powerful expectorant and antiseptic, thanks to its constituent oil, thymol. By cupping your hands around a mug of thyme tea and breathing in the steam, the thymol sets to work through your upper respiratory tract, loosening mucus and inhibiting bacteria from settling down to stay. Make thyme tea in a snap by adding 1 teaspoon dried thyme leaves to 1 cup boiling water. Let steep for five minutes while inhaling the steam. Strain the tea, sweeten with honey (to taste), and slowly sip.

More Do's and Don'ts

- Get plenty of rest. Okay, you may not need to be told this, at least when the flu first hits. But rest is essential to allow your body to fight the virus. So indulge yourself, you've got a good reason to.

- Drink lots of fluids. Water's good, as are teas, juice, and soups. Off-limits are coffee and soda pop, as they may contain caffeine and have no nutritional benefits whatsoever.

- If you have lots of aches and pains and just can't get comfortable, use an over-the-counter pain reliever. But don't give aspirin to anyone under age 18 because of the risk of Reye's syndrome, a potentially fatal illness that is linked with aspirin use and the flu in young people.

Herbal Remedies

You may not ordinarily keep these herbs in your kitchen, but it's a good idea to stock up on them before flu seasons starts. Then you can put together some soothing remedies for influenza symptoms.

Lemon Balm. For adults who can't catch their ZZZs while coping with the flu, lemon balm acts as a mild sedative. It also contains antiviral compounds to help disinfect mucous membranes. To make this relaxing potion, place 1 teaspoon dried lemon balm in 1 cup boiling water. Cover and let steep for 10 minutes. Strain, sweeten with honey (to taste), and drink up to 4 cups a day. (Note: Lemon balm is also known as balm mint, bee balm, blue balm, garden balm, Melissa, and sweet balm.)

Peppermint. If you're running a fever, cool your hot head, via sweating, with a cup of peppermint tea. As a bonus, peppermint contains menthol, which works as a decongestant to help unstuff sinuses. And peppermint has antispasmodic properties to help that hack. To make this fever fighter, place ½ ounce peppermint leaves in a 1-quart jar of boiling water. Cover and let steep 20 minutes. Strain, add a cube of sugar if you'd like, and enjoy 2 to 3 cups a day.

Thyme and Peppermint. Combine thyme and peppermint to make an herbal steam broth that will deliver healing aromas to your aching nose and throat. Combine 1½ quarts boiling water and 2 tablespoons each of dried thyme and peppermint in a large pot. Cover and steep for 5 minutes. Place the pot on a table and remove the lid. Lean in and cover both your head and the pot of steaming herbs with a large towel. Slowly breathe the herbal broth for 15 minutes. (*Warning:* Don't stick your nose too close to the broth or you'll risk a burn.)

Food Poisoning

BEATING THE BUG

The company's annual 4th of July barbecue started out a huge success. The ribs were superb. The potato salad was excellent. Even Helen's famous coleslaw got rave reviews. But about the time the sun went down, people started sprinting in all directions, and they weren't running in the three-legged race. Most of them were headed for the nearest bathroom. Food poisoning claims another round of victims.

The Centers for Disease Control and Prevention estimates that there will be about 76 million cases of food poisoning this year. It's an estimate because most cases of food poisoning go unreported, chalked up to the stomach flu or another bug. Even though the United States has strict guidelines when it comes to processing and handling food, there is always a risk of some food becoming contaminated. Ironically, though many cases of food poisoning do happen in restaurants, the most common place for foodborne illnesses to strike is your kitchen.

How Spoiled Food Makes You Feel

The symptoms you have after eating a pork chop laden with bad bacteria can range from mild (a few stomach cramps) to severe (you spend a couple of days camped out on the bathroom floor). Many people describe food poisoning as akin to being hit by a very large truck. The most common symptoms are diarrhea, stomach pain, cramping, nausea, and vomiting.

Because most of the symptoms of food poisoning are similar to those of other illnesses, such as a stomach virus, people aren't always sure food is the problem. If you think you've got food poisoning but aren't sure, take note: Most people get sick about 4 to 48 hours after eating the suspect food. And if you got sick, chances are everyone else who ate a contaminated chop will be sick, too.

Foiling Food Poisoning

You've had some potato salad that's been sitting in the sun too long. Your stomach starts to cramp, and you make your first trip to the bath-

room. Now what? There's not really anything you can do to stop the symptoms of
food poisoning once they start, and you
shouldn't try. As awful as it is, the diarrhea
and vomiting that happen when you contract a foodborne illness help your body get
rid of the poison. Taking over-the-counter
medications that halt the process can make
you sicker. The best thing you can do is take
care of yourself while you're sick. These
kitchen remedies can at least make dealing
with the symptoms more bearable and get
you feeling better faster. There are also some
things in your kitchen that will help prevent
food poisoning from visiting your house.

FROM THE CUPBOARD

BLEACH. Scrubbing your counter with warm
soapy water and bleach is one of your best
defenses against bacteria that tend to hover
on countertops. It's a good idea to clean
your cutting boards in a bleach and water
solution: Try soaking them in a mixture of
2 teaspoons bleach to 1 quart water. Let the
boards air dry.

CHICKEN SOUP. Once you start feeling a bit
better, start your stomach out with bland
foods. Chicken soup is tasty and easy to
digest.

SUGAR. Sugar helps your body hold onto
fluid, and adding a spoonful of sugar to a
glass of water or a cup of decaffeinated tea
may be more palatable if you find sports
drinks too sugary.

FROM THE FRUIT BOWL

BANANA. As you spend more time embracing the porcelain throne, your
body is losing essential elements such as potassium. Losing these vital
nutrients can make that I've-been-hit-by-a-truck feeling worse. Once
you've come to a lull in the bathroom visitations, usually after the first
24 hours, try eating a banana. It's easy on your stomach and can make
you feel a bit better.

WHEN TO CALL THE DOCTOR

Food poison-
ing can be
debilitating
for a day or
two, but you'll
start feeling better after
the poison leaves your
system. Sometimes,
though, food poisoning
can be very dangerous. If
you have any of these
symptoms, see a doctor
immediately:

- Diarrhea and vomiting
  that last more than
  48 hours
- A fever over 101°F
- Stomach cramps that
  keep getting worse
- Blood in your stool
- Dehydration
- Stiff neck, severe
  headache, and fever

An important note: If
the person poisoned is a
young child, an elderly
person, or someone with
an impaired immune
system, see the doctor at
the first sign of food
poisoning.

FROM THE REFRIGERATOR

SPORTS DRINKS. Losing all that fluid means you're losing electrolytes (salts that keep your body functioning properly) and water. Replacing that fluid with a sports drink will help replace needed electrolytes, and the sugar in the drink will help your body better absorb the fluid it needs. If the sugar is too much for your tummy, tone the drink down by diluting it with water.

♂ BACTERIA'S BAD BOYS

About 100 bacteria can cause food poisoning. But these are on the "Most Wanted" list:

Campylobacter jejuni. A common cause of foodborne illness, this bacteria is found in raw and undercooked poultry and meat, unpasteurized milk, and untreated water. Cook food properly and clean hands and utensils to kill it.

Clostridium perfringens. Known as the "buffet germ," this bacteria grows fastest in casseroles, stews, and gravies that are held at low or room temperature. Make sure hot foods are kept hot and cold foods cold.

Escherichia coli (E. coli) 0157:H7. Found mostly in raw or undercooked ground beef or unpasteurized milk, this bacteria is killed by cooking food properly.

Salmonella. Found mostly in raw or undercooked meat, poultry, eggs, and fish, and in unpasteurized milk, salmonella is easy to get rid of. Cook foods thoroughly and drink only pasteurized milk.

Staphylococcus aureus. Staph bacteria is found on people (skin, nose, throat) but is spread through contaminated foods. It can't be killed by cooking; avoid this one by keeping hands and kitchen utensils clean.

Vibrio vulnificus. This bacteria is found in raw oysters and raw or undercooked mussels, clams, and whole scallops.

WATER. You may not feel like having anything pass your lips, but you've got to stay hydrated, especially when you are losing fluids from both ends. Start off with a few sips of this easy-to-swallow liquid and work your way up to more substantial stuff.

MORE DO'S AND DON'TS

• Use a hot water bottle or a heating pad to ease your stomach cramps.

• Get lots of rest. Not that you'd feel like running a marathon or even attempting to go to the office, but take it easy at home. Stick to the bed or the couch, and let time do its magic.

• Don't start back on foods that are hard to digest. Give your stomach and your intestines time to recuperate. Stay away from spicy, smoked, fried, or salty foods. Stay away from raw vegetables or rich pastries or candies, and don't drink alcohol.

• Tell the health department about your woes. Telling your story may keep others from experiencing the same problems, especially if you experienced food poisoning after eating at a restaurant or other food establishment.

• Once you're sick, get someone else to go to the kitchen for you. You could be spreading more harmful bacteria and inviting others to share in your suffering.

• Wash your hands thoroughly before preparing food. You don't want to pass your illness to everyone in the household.

KEEPING BACTERIA AT BAY

Food that's very hot or very cold won't allow bacteria to grow. Here are the important numbers to know:

160°F: The food temperature at which you can begin saying "sayonara" to bacteria.

140°F: Foods cooked and held at this temperature won't be free of bacteria, but bacteria will not be able to spread.

125°F: At this temperature, bacteria can survive and a few will grow.

60°F: If risky food is left at this temperature for too long, bacteria will begin to take over.

40°F: The magic temperature at which potentially dangerous bacteria begin to grow.

32°F: Though most bacteria are halted at this temp, some bacteria will grow.

0°F: Bacteria don't die at this frigid temperature, but you can keep them from spreading.

Foot Discomfort
TLC for Tootsies

Overworked and taken for granted; that's the lot of the lowly foot. But feet are a marvelous work of nature and an absolute architectural wonder. Each one of your feet is made up of 26 bones, 33 joints, 107 ligaments, and 31 tendons. Together, they comprise one-quarter of all the bones in your body.

Every day, on average, we take about 10,000 steps. That adds up to four hikes around the planet during a lifetime. And each time a step is taken, the impact of hitting the ground is about four times your body weight. No wonder, then, that 70 percent of us experience foot and ankle problems at some time.

Here are some common problems that cause foot pain, most often due to an overuse injury.

Plantar fasciitis. A heel injury, affecting the area where the arch meets the heel. Plantar fascitis is marked by heel pain with first steps in the morning, possible swelling, and heel pain as you rest. It can usually be worked out with activity. What to do: Wear better shoes, or try orthopedic shoes prescribed by a podiatrist. Don't walk barefoot. Use ice unless you have circulatory problems or are diabetic. Try heel cups in your shoes for shock absorption. If the pain is persistent, see a podiatrist.

Heel spurs. A little outgrowth of the bone, a result of the bone's attempt to heal after repetitive stress and inflammation in the *plantar fascia*. What to do: If it causes foot pain, a simple surgery to shave the spur away may be required.

Neuroma. A pinched nerve, causing pain between the third and fourth toes. It can feel like a tooth that needs a root canal. One of the most common causes is a poor shoe fit. What to do: Buy a shoe with a wider toe area.

> ### WHEN TO CALL THE DOCTOR
> - If numbness or tingling is present
> - If you can't cure your cold feet with simple measures
> - If the pain gets worse
> - If an open sore on your foot does not heal
> - If walking becomes difficult
> - If fever and general achiness is associated with your achy feet
> - If the swelling does not diminish

Tendinitis. An inflammatory process in the tendons, common in athletes. It can be a serious, painful, and persistent problem. What to do: Rest, ice, use anti-inflammatory drugs, and change exercise technique and shoe gear.

Stress fracture. A break in the bone usually resulting from repetitive pounding. Common to athletes. What to do: Limit weight-bearing activities, and stick to low-impact exercise. An orthotic device may be necessary to reduce pressure at the fracture site. Be sure to confirm and locate the stress fracture via X ray for proper treatment.

> ## IF THE SHOE FITS
> Shoe models change, even though their names may stay the same. Even if that last pair of shoes was the perfect fit, have a proper fitting each time you purchase new ones because they may not be quite the same.

Ankle sprains. A ligament that is stretched or torn. It is the most common athletic injury. What to do: Ice, compression with an elastic bandage or splint to eliminate motion, and elevation to decrease swelling. Limit weight-bearing activities, and stay off feet for a few days. In cases of a severe sprain, your podiatrist may recommend a brace or surgery.

Here are a few more foot aches that aren't attributed to overuse. Instead, these are caused by simple everyday wear and tear, as well as poorly fitting shoes.

Black toenail. A hematoma (bruising) under the nail. What to do: Wear proper-fitting shoes that aren't too tight or too loose, clip toenails short so they won't rub against the shoe, soak foot in salt water.

Bunions. A misaligned big toe joint in which the toe slants outward causing inflammation and swelling. The most common cause is tight-fitting shoes. What to do: Wear proper-fitting shoes and padding, and rest and soak the foot. Bunions must be treated by a podiatrist.

Hammertoe. When a toe, usually the second toe, bends up to look like a claw. It frequently accompanies a bunion, and while the actual cause is a muscle imbalance, the underlying cause of that imbalance is usually an ill-fitting shoe that cramps the toes. What to do: Wear proper-fitting shoes and padding. Hammertoes must be treated by a podiatrist.

Ingrown toenail. This happens when the side of your toenail cuts into your skin. The cause is usually a bad toenail clip job, but pressure from a bad shoe fit can cause it, too. A mild ingrown nail can be removed with careful clipping, but if it is deep or painful, consider a trip to the podiatrist.

Bad Shoes, Good Shoes

Bad shoes are what many foot injuries have in common. Bad shoes, according to the American College of Foot and Ankle Surgeons, are to blame for about 90 percent of all foot problems.

No matter what type of shoe you're wearing, a bad shoe is one that does not fit properly, has lost its shape, causes pain or rubbing, or is worn unevenly. Bad shoes cause foot and ankle problems. But they can cause leg and back problems, too.

To get a good fit for any type of shoe:

- Buy shoes at the end of the day, after work or exercise, when your feet are at their largest. If you buy shoes earlier in the day, they may be too tight.

- Measure both feet and fit your shoe to the largest one, since your feet aren't the same size.

- Make sure you can wiggle your toes. If you can't, the fit is too tight. Also make sure the widest part of your foot is comfortable but secure.

- Walk around the store to see if the shoes are comfortable. Never buy shoes without first trying them on, and don't assume they will get comfortable with wear. If they don't feel good when you try them on, don't buy them.

- Try on shoes with the socks you plan to wear with them.

- When the shoe is on and you're standing up, make sure you can fit the width of your little finger between your heel and the back of the shoe—no more and no less.

- If your heel slides in the shoe as you walk, the shoe doesn't fit.

- Don't let anyone tell you the shoe will stretch. Good shoes fit properly when you buy them.

TOENAIL TIPS

- Soak your feet in equal parts vinegar and water to soften and clean the nail before you clip.

- Clip the toenail straight across with nail clippers. Leave enough nail so that there's a little white showing at the end of your nail.

- Remove rough edges with a nail file.

- For an ingrown toenail: Trim excess nail, then put cotton under the corner to separate it from the skin. Change cotton daily. If the area is red, apply hydrogen peroxide, then coat with an over-the-counter antibacterial cream. Cover with a bandage. Repeat daily.

- For a toe ache, soak in warm water.

  Call the doctor or podiatrist about that ingrown toenail if you experience severe pain or discharge around or under the nail, if you can't trim the nail yourself, or if you have diabetes and the ingrown nail becomes infected.

- And, no matter how much you're attached to your closet full of comfortable old shoes, toss them in the trash when they are worn out and get new ones.

Now that you know what that foot pain might be, as well as possible treatment options, here are a few kitchen remedies to help heal those tired, aching dogs.

FROM THE CUPBOARD

BEANS. Spread a few dried navy beans on the floor and practice picking them up with your toes. This is an exercise that will help keep your feet strong and flexible.

CARBONATED WATER. Soaking your feet in sugarless carbonated water can be refreshing.

CIDER VINEGAR. Swollen feet can be annoying when your favorite shoes don't fit. Here's an easy fix to reduce the swelling, which is a buildup of fluid in the tissues called edema. Mix 4 teaspoons cider vinegar in a large glass of water. Drink three times a day. (*Warning!* If you are taking a diuretic medication, consult your doctor before trying this remedy.)

EPSOM SALTS. For plain old tired feet, put 2 tablespoons Epsom salts into a basin of warm water. Soak for 15 minutes. Epsom salts can be drying, so moisturize your feet afterward.

FLOUR. This simple paste may speed up the healing of a sprain or strain: gardenia, flour, and wine. Mix and apply.

FOODS. For bloated, uncomfortable feet, here are some foods to eat to help balance your fluid levels: Bananas are high in potassium, which helps relieve fluid retention. Coffee and tea are both diuretics. (See also "From the Refrigerator" on the next page for other helpful foods.)

OLIVE OIL. Use as a massage oil for tired feet.

POSTUM. Got cold feet? Brew up a cup of Postum (a coffee substitute), add a pinch of cayenne pepper, and drink. Your toes will feel toasty warm fast. This is also good for cold hands.

VINEGAR. To soothe tendinitis, sprains, strains, and general foot aches, alternate hot and cold vinegar wraps. First, heat equal amounts of vinegar and water. Soak a towel in the mixture, wring it out, and wrap it around your foot. Leave it wrapped for five minutes. Then mix equal parts vinegar and cold water and follow the same procedure. Repeat this entire sequence three times.

FOODS THAT CAUSE FLUID RETENTION

Sometimes a simple dietary change is all it takes to get rid of those aching swollen feet. Avoid these foods, which can make your feet puff right up:

- Bacon and other cured meats. Curing is done with salt, which causes fluid retention.
- Lunch meats. These, too, have lots of salt.
- Canned foods. Salt is added to most canned foods, including vegetables.

DIABETES CAUTION

Foot problems can result in serious illness and even amputation for people with diabetes. To learn more about the care of diabetic feet, see page 104. ·

FROM THE FAUCET

WATER. Sometimes plain water is the best cure of all. If you have varicose veins in your feet or ankles, this remedy will alleviate the ache and may even slow the development of varicose veins. Dip your feet in hot water for 2 minutes, then in cold for 15 seconds. Repeat, and continue alternating hot and cold for 15 minutes.

FROM THE FREEZER

ICE. An ice pack (or a bag of frozen vegetables) will reduce the inflammation of tendinitis.

FROM THE REFRIGERATOR

ASPARAGUS. For swollen feet, steam and eat some asparagus. Asparagus acts as a natural diuretic, flushing the excess fluid out of your system.
FOODS. For bloated, uncomfortable feet, here are some foods that can help balance your fluid levels: poultry and fresh fish, both of which are low in sodium, and yogurt, which can reduce histamine-producing bacteria. Histamine causes fluid retention.

FROM THE SPICE RACK

CAYENNE PEPPER. To warm cold feet, sprinkle a little cayenne pepper in your socks. Cayenne peppers have a chemical called capsaicin that warms, and it also relieves pain. However, this can be irritating to the skin after a while, so carry some spare socks in case you need to change.
CINNAMON. For cold feet, stir a gram of powdered cinnamon into a glass of hot water and steep for 15 minutes. Drink three times a day.
CUMIN. For swollen feet, mix ¼ teaspoon each of cumin, coriander, and fennel into a cup of hot water and drink two to three times a day.
SAGE. Take a handful of sage leaves and rub them in your palm. Put them in a saucepan with ⅔ cup cider vinegar. Boil, then simmer for five minutes. Remove from the heat, soak a cloth in the solution, and apply it to a sprain or sore foot, as hot as tolerable.
SALT. To ease the pain of tendinitis, make a paste of equal amounts of salt and turmeric powder. Apply to the achy area.

MORE DO'S AND DON'TS

- Don't stand too long, and don't stand on hard surfaces if you can avoid it. Foot pain is often muscle fatigue from standing.
- Don't ignore foot pain, tired legs, aching knees, lower-back problems, or sore hips. They could all be symptoms of serious conditions.
- Maintain your ideal weight. The more weight you put on those puppies, the more pain they'll cause you.

Foot Odor

STANCHING THE STENCH

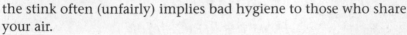

When you kick off your shoes, do you clear a room? That's one sure sign that your feet reek like week-old garbage. Your olfactory region may be blissfully unaware of the odors emitted from down below, but others' noses aren't so immune. Foot odor may leave you friendless, too, as the stink often (unfairly) implies bad hygiene to those who share your air.

Foot odor, known in the medical profession as bromhidrosis, can be traced to bacteria that find your moist and warm feet, socks, and shoes the perfect place to breed and multiply. Thousands of sweat glands on the soles of the feet produce perspiration composed of water, sodium chloride, fat, minerals, and various acids that are the end products of your body's metabolism. In the presence of certain bacteria (namely those found in dark, damp shoes), these sweaty secretions break down, generating the stench that turns people green.

Foot odor is only a temporary curse and can easily be cured. Kick off your shoes without worry after trying some of these refreshing remedies.

FROM THE CUPBOARD

BAKING SODA. Don't just let those shoes sit there without odor support! Bring on the baking soda! Deodorize shoes by sprinkling 1 or 2 teaspoons baking soda inside to absorb moisture and hide odors. For added fragrance, combine 3 tablespoons baking soda with 3 tablespoons ground, dried sage leaves. Combine the sage and baking soda and place into an airtight glass jar. After removing your shoes for the day, sprinkle 1 tablespoon of the mixture into each shoe. Shake and leave overnight. The following day, keep the sage-soda in the shoes. In the evening remove excess sage-soda mix, and replace it with a fresh supply. Repeat nightly.

WHEN TO CALL THE DOCTOR

- If home remedies and frequent washings of feet and socks have failed to eradicate odor in a few weeks
- If you suspect you have a zinc deficiency. Foot odor may be caused by a zinc deficiency, so talk to your doctor about trying a zinc supplement.

Another way to use baking soda is in a footbath. Add 2 tablespoons baking soda to a bowl of warm water. Soak feet every night for a month.

CORNSTARCH. A less fancy solution to keeping shoes deodorized and dry is to sprinkle the inside with 1 to 2 teaspoons cornstarch.

SALT. Add table salt or Epsom salts to water for a foot soak. Pour a few teaspoons of salt into a tub of warm water. Soak for ten minutes.

VINEGAR. Soak your feet several times a week in an apple cider or plain vinegar bath. Mix ⅓ cup vinegar into a bowl of warm water. Soak for 10 to 15 minutes.

FROM THE REFRIGERATOR

GINGER. Mash a 1- or 2-inch piece of ginger into a pulp, put it into a handkerchief or piece of gauze, and soak it in some hot water for a few minutes. Rub the ginger liquid onto each foot nightly after taking a shower. Try for two weeks.

RADISH. You can't squeeze blood from a turnip, but you can squeeze an anti-stink solution from a radish. Juice about two dozen radishes, add ¼ teaspoon glycerine, and pour in a squirt or spray-top bottle. Spritz on toes to reduce foot odor.

FROM THE SINK

BLACK TEA. Soak tootsies in black tea. Tannic acid, a component of tea, is thought to have astringent properties that prevent feet from perspiring. To make a foot-tea soak, brew 5 bags black tea in 1 quart boiling water. Let cool, add ice cubes (during the summertime), and soak in this "iced tea for the toes" bath for 20 to 30 minutes.

WATER. A remedy for sweaty feet involves alternating footbaths of hot and cold water to help reduce blood flow to your feet and reduce perspiration. After luxuriating in a hot footbath, shock those toes by dipping them into a second footbath containing cool water, ice cubes, and 1 to 2 teaspoons lemon juice (if available). Rub your feet with alcohol following the bath. Try this dual treatment once a day, especially in warmer months.

MORE DO'S AND DON'TS

- Give your feet a rest...from your shoes, that is. Everyone has a favorite pair of shoes. The secret to keeping that pair in first place is to let them air out at least 24 hours between wearings. If not, the sweat buildup keeps them moist and makes bacteria happy.

- Wear socks designed to wick moisture away. Look for such fabrics as orlon, polypropylene, and brand name patented fabrics such as Cool Max. If possible, change socks at least twice a day.

- Watch what foods you eat in abundance. Strong, pungent foods such as garlic, onions, scallions, peppers, and curry spices can cause foot odor. The odoriferous products in each pass through the bloodstream and concentrate in the perspiration.

- When the shoe fits, wear it. When it starts to stink, throw it out with the garbage.

- Don't step into solid rubber or synthetically lined shoes. Neither lets your feet breathe easily, allowing odor-producing bacteria to take over.

- Once a month toss those tennis shoes into the washing machine. Let them air dry.

- Go barefoot or wear sandals when possible.

- Try dusting some activated charcoal in your shoes. It's an effective (but messy) odor absorbent. Or, you can purchase inexpensive foot pads that contain it.

A BIT ABOUT BAKING SODA

Baking soda, or sodium bicarbonate, is a mild base that can neutralize acidic environments (in this case, smelly shoes and feet). The white powder works by balancing the pH, bringing acidic and basic odors back to a neutral, odorless state.

PEE-U

An unorthodox home remedy that we can't recommend, but many swear by, is to pee on your feet. That's right...miss deliberately. This begs the question: If foot odor is viewed as unhygienic, then what do you call this remedy?

Gallbladder Problems
AVERTING AN ATTACK

Unless you've had problems with your gallbladder, you probably don't know much about it. Be thankful. If you do know the specifics of your gallbladder, you're probably one of the 10 to 15 percent of Americans who have gallstones. While half of those with gallstones experience no symptoms, the other half can have chronic problems, including discomfort and pain in the upper abdomen, indigestion, nausea, and intolerance of fatty foods. A gallbladder attack, which occurs when a gallstone gets stuck in the bile duct, can double you over in pain for hours and leave you wishing something, anything, could make you feel better.

Casting Stones

The gallbladder is a little pear-shaped pouch tucked behind the lobes of the liver. Its main job is to store up the cholesterol-rich bile that's secreted by the liver. Bile helps your body digest fatty foods. So when that piece of prime rib reaches the intestines, they send a message up to the gallbladder to send some bile their way. Once the bile saturates your steak, it becomes more digestible and easily makes its way through the rest of the digestive process.

At least that's the way things should work. But the reality is that many people, especially older people and women, will have some gallbladder trouble. Ninety percent of the time that trouble is in the form of gallstones. Gallstones form when the bile contains excessive amounts of cholesterol. When there isn't enough bile to saturate the cholesterol, the cholesterol begins to crystallize, and you get a gallstone. These tough bits can be as tiny as a grain of sand or as large as a golf ball. You may not even know you have gallstones unless you happen to have an ultrasound or X ray of your tummy. But the 20 percent of the time that gallstones do cause problems, it's excruciatingly painful.

WHEN TO CALL THE DOCTOR

- If you have a fever
- If your skin or eyes have a yellowish tinge
- If you have persistent pain
- If you are sweating
- If you have chills
- If you have clay-colored stools

Gallstones become a problem when they get pushed out of the gallbladder and into the tube that connects the liver and the small intestine. The tube gets blocked, and you get 20 minutes to 4 hours of indescribable agony. Pain usually radiates from your upper right abdominal area to your lower right chest, and it can even leave your shoulder and back in agony. Gallstones typically fall back into the gallbladder or make their way through the duct, leaving you feeling better. After you have an attack, you'll probably be sore and wonder what in the world happened.

Sometimes, though, the gallstones can get stuck in the bile duct. Symptoms of a stuck gallstone include chills, vomiting, and possibly jaundice in addition to the pain described above.

Who's at Risk?

Pregnancy, obesity, diabetes, liver disease, a sedentary lifestyle, a high fat diet, and certain forms of anemia can all increase the risk of gallstones. People who are overweight and lose and gain weight repeatedly are more susceptible to gallstones, as are women who have had two or more children. Lack of exercise is a significant contributor to the development of gallstones. In fact, according to the Nurses' Health Study, inactivity can actually account for more than half of the risk of developing gallstones. Women are twice as likely as men to develop gallstones. And people older than 60 years of age have a greater risk of gallstones.

Other risk factors include a family history of gallstones and taking hormones, such as birth control pills or estrogen.

Take heart. There are some specific things you can find in your kitchen to help you avoid a gallstone attack and even prevent gallstones from forming in the first place. What you eat has a great effect on whether or not you develop gallstones. And research is finding that certain foods can help you avert a painful attack or, better yet, avoid gallstones altogether.

FROM THE CUPBOARD

COFFEE. New studies are finding that drinking a couple cups of java a day can prevent gallstones. One study discovered that men who drank 2 to 3 cups of regular coffee a day cut their risk of developing gallstones

---

SURVIVING WITHOUT A GALLBLADDER

Believe it or not, you actually can get along just fine without your gallbladder. Instead of being stored in the gallbladder, bile flows directly from the liver into the small intestine. Diarrhea may be a side effect, and you may have higher blood cholesterol levels. You may also risk stomach upset if you eat too much fat at one time. But aside from that, life will continue as normal—that is, minus the chronic pain from gallbladder attacks.

GOOD-BYE GALLBLADDER

Every year 500,000 people will have their gallbladder removed.

ETHNIC GALS AND GALLSTONES

Seventy percent of Native American women over age 30 have gallstones. Ten percent of African American women in the same age-group have gallstones.

by 40 percent. Four cups a day reduced the risk by 45 percent. Researchers are not sure what it is about coffee that helps reduce the risk of forming gallstones, but the effect was the same whether it was cheap, store-bought instant coffee or high-priced espresso. It might be the caffeine; however, teas and soft drinks containing caffeine did not produce the same effect— and neither did decaffeinated coffee.

HIGH-FIBER CEREAL. People who eat a sugary, high-fat diet probably will have more problems with their gallstones. But adding in some fiber-rich foods and avoiding the sugary snacks and fatty foods can help you keep your gallbladder healthy. Grabbing some cereal in the morning will also get something in your tummy. Studies have shown that going for long periods without eating, such as skipping breakfast, can make you more prone to getting a gallstone.

LENTILS. An interesting study found that women who ate loads of lentils, nuts, beans, peas, lima beans, and oranges were more resistant to gallbladder attacks than women who didn't eat much of the stuff.

FROM THE REFRIGERATOR

RED BELL PEPPER. Getting loads of vitamin C in your diet can help you avoid gallstones, and one red bell pepper has 95 mg of the helpful vitamin—more than the 60 mg a day the government recommends for men and women older than age 15. A recent study found that people who had more vitamin C in their blood were less likely to get the painful stones.

SALMON. Research is finding that omega-3 fatty acids, found in fatty fish such as salmon, may help prevent gallstones.

VEGETABLES. Eating your veggies is a good way to ward off gallstones. One study found that vegetarian women were only half as likely to have gallstones as their carnivore counterparts. Researchers aren't sure exactly how vegetables counteract gallstones, but they believe vegetables help reduce the amount of cholesterol in bile.

WINE. Half a glass of wine a day can avert gallstone attacks. Scientists discovered that drinking half a glass of wine or beer cut the number of gallstone attacks by 40 percent. But don't go overboard. The study didn't find that drinking more than half a glass would offer any more protection.

MORE DO'S AND DON'TS

- Exercise! Staying active can cut your risk of developing gallstones in half.

- Lose some weight. Being overweight, even as little as 10 pounds, can double your risk of getting gallstones.

- Diet sensibly. If you are overweight, plan on shedding pounds slowly. Losing weight too fast can increase your chances of developing gallstones.

- Reduce your saturated fat intake. Too much fat in the diet increases your risk of gallstones. But don't cut back too drastically. You need some fat to give the gallbladder the message to empty bile. If you're trying to lose weight, don't go below 20 percent calories from fat.

- Eat a low fat, low-cholesterol, high-fiber diet. Multiple studies show this is your best bet for a healthy body and a healthy gallbladder.

SHOCKING THOSE STONES: THE WAVE OF THE FUTURE

Until recently, most people who had recurring painful bouts with gallstones had one choice—get rid of the gallbladder. But there's a new procedure that may allow people to get rid of their gallstones without losing any body parts. The procedure is based on the same shock-wave theory that demolishes kidney stones. But this time the shock waves are more specific, delivered directly to the gallstones. It is an invasive procedure. The doctor inserts a tube into the gallbladder via a small puncture hole, and the electric shock is delivered directly to the gallstones. Then the fragments of the stones are scooped up and removed from the body. The whole process takes about an hour and leaves you on R & R for a few days. But compared to the major surgery required to remove your gallbladder, this procedure is a breeze.

Genital Herpes

COUNTERACTING RECURRENCES

Genital herpes is a sexually transmitted disease (STD) caused by the
herpes simplex virus type 1 (HSV-1)
and type 2 (HSV-2). The type 1
virus is the same one that causes
cold sores on the mouth, face, and
lips (see Cold Sores, page 70),
although it can also cause sores on
the genitals. The type 2 virus, however, most often causes sores on the genitals.

How You Get Genital Herpes

Herpes can spread to the genitals from a cold sore if hand washing
and other hygiene precautions are not taken. Or, it can be spread though
oral or genital sexual contact. And be warned: The virus does not have to
be in an active state—that is, blisters do not have to be present—for a
partner to become infected. The virus can also be passed during the
preactive state, when there is itching or tingling in the area in which the
sores generally appear. Sometimes, the virus can be passed along before
the infected person is even aware that the virus is being shed. What's
more, saliva also carries the virus!

Symptoms

The first episode usually starts within a couple weeks of exposure, and
the initial onset can be pretty bad, including an initial round and then a
second round of painful sores, flulike symptoms, fever, and swollen
glands. Sometimes the symptoms are mild, however, and appear as little
more than insect bites or a rash.

> **WHEN TO CALL THE DOCTOR**
> • The minute you suspect you are infected!

Once you have genital herpes, you have it
for life. Luckily, it spends most of its life, and
yours, dormant. But like cold sores, genital herpes recurs, often up to four or five times a year.
Check the cold sore triggers list (pages 70–71) to
see some of the reasons why these demons
return.

There are a few kitchen remedies that can
help you through an episode, however.

FROM THE CUPBOARD

BAKING SODA. Using a cotton ball, pat baking soda on the sores to dry them out and decrease itching. Just be careful not to double dip: You don't want to contaminate the unused baking soda.

CORNSTARCH. This also can help dry out the sores and help alleviate itching. Use a cotton ball that's been dipped in cornstarch and dust it onto the sores.

FOOD. Eat well to boost your immune system. For some immune-boosting foods, see pages 214–215.

PEPPERMINT TEA. A nice cup of peppermint tea may help reduce pain and fever.

TEA. Place a cold wet tea bag right on the sores. Tannic acid can soothe genital tissues. Throw away the tea bag afterward.

FROM THE FREEZER

ICE. To reduce pain and itching, apply ice to the sores. Fill a plastic bag with crushed ice or use a bag of frozen peas. Wrap the bag in material the thickness of a sheet. Apply for 10 or 15 minutes, and repeat several times a day. Be careful about the time because prolonged exposure to ice can cause tissue damage.

FROM THE REFRIGERATOR

MILK. For pain relief and to promote healing, soak cotton balls in milk and apply to the area.

MORE DO'S AND DON'TS

- Don't depend on a condom to protect you or your partner. They help, but they may not cover the entire area. Viral shedding may also occur in the infected area, making the spread of the disease to a sexual partner easy, even if protection is used. Be sure to use a latex or vinyl condom between outbreaks.

- Don't wear tight-fitting pants or underwear.

- Shower, don't soak in the tub. Shedding virus can escape into the water.

FACTS ABOUT GENITAL HERPES

Here are some staggering facts. In the United States

- 45 million people age 12 and older are infected, translating into 1 out of 5 of the total adolescent and adult population.

- HSV-2 is more common in women (approximately 1 out of 4) than men (approximately 1 out of 5).

- Since the 1970s, the spread of genital herpes has increased 30 percent.

- Teens and young adults aged 20 to 29 are developing genital herpes at the fastest rate.

Gout
AVOIDING EXCESS

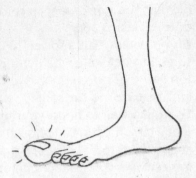

The word gout may make you think of kings and medieval history. But gout isn't a disease of the past. That's because gout is an inflammatory joint disease and a form of arthritis, not some mysterious illness of the rich and powerful.

Gout, which occurs in about five percent of people with arthritis, results from the buildup of uric acid in the blood. Uric acid is the result of the breakdown of waste substances, called purines, in the body. Usually it is dissolved in the blood, processed by the kidneys, and passed out of the body in the urine. But in some people there is an excess amount of uric acid, too much for the kidneys to eliminate quickly. When there is too much uric acid in the blood, it crystallizes and collects in the joint spaces, causing gout. Occasionally, these deposits become so large that they push against the skin in lumpy patches, called tophi, that can actually be seen.

A gout attack usually lasts five to ten days, and the most common area under siege is the big toe. In fact, 75 percent of people with gout will be affected in the big toe at some time. Gout in the big toe can become so painful that even a bedsheet draped over it will cause intolerable pain. Besides the big toe, gout may also develop in the ankles, heels, knees, wrists, fingers, and elbows.

Who Gets Gout?

Though anyone can get gout, it's primarily a man's disease. Women have the good fortune of being more efficient in the way they excrete uric acid. And children rarely get it.

Other risk factors include:

- Middle age. Men in their 40s and 50s are at greatest risk.
- Family history of gout. Up to 18 percent of all people with gout have family members with gout.

WHEN TO CALL THE DOCTOR

- If you experience any of the symptoms described on page 151
- If, with your gout attack, you experience fever or other unusual physical symptoms
- If you notice joint deformity
- If the pain is unmanageable with over-the-counter remedies

- Overweight. Excessive eating steps up the production of uric acid.

- Eating too many foods with purines, such as organ meats (liver, kidney, brains, sweetbreads), sardines, anchovies, meat extracts, dried peas, lentils, and legumes.

- An enzyme defect that prevents the breakdown of uric acid.

- Heavy alcohol use.

- Exposure to environmental lead.

- Using certain medications, including diuretics, salicylates, and lev-odopa.

- Taking niacin, a vitamin that's also called nicotinic acid.

Gout symptoms come on quickly the first time, often overnight. You can go to bed feeling fine and wake up later in excruciating pain. You may also experience joint swelling and shiny red or purple skin around the joint. If you're already predisposed to gout, you can trigger an episode by

- Drinking too much alcohol

- Overeating, especially high-purine foods

- Having surgery

- Experiencing a sudden severe illness or trauma

- Going on a crash diet

- Injuring a joint

- Having chemotherapy

- Being under stress. The link isn't the stress but the comfort eating or drinking that accompanies it.

If you have gout, professional medical treatment is required. There are several prescription medications that are very effective at eliminating excess uric acid.

GOOD FOODS, BAD FOODS

Diet plays an important role in gout prevention. Here are some foods that will help to keep gout under control:

Whole-grain cereals and whole-wheat bread. These are loaded with zinc that may be depleted during a gout attack.

Breakfast cereals and breads fortified with folic acid. These foods can slow the production of uric acid.

Bread, pasta, low fat milk and dairy products, eggs, lettuce, tomatoes. These foods are low in purines.

Citrus fruits. They have vitamin C that may assist the kidneys in ridding the body of uric acid.

And if you have gout and don't want it to come back, avoid these foods:

- Asparagus, spinach, cauliflower, mushrooms. They have purines.

- Shrimp and crabs. They also contain purines.

- Alcohol. That means beer, too! Alcohol increases uric acid production in foods.

- Dried fruit and fruit sugar. If you eat it, do so in moderation. The fructose in it produces uric acid.

GOUT FACTS

- It's not contagious, it doesn't spread from joint to joint, and there is no cure.
- 2.1 million people in the United States suffer from gout.
- 70 percent of those who have gout experience a second attack within a year.
- 95 percent of those with gout experience a second attack within five years.

Untreated, gout may progress to serious joint damage and disability. Also, excess uric acid can cause kidney stones. For gout, though, there are several kitchen remedies that can be effective along with medication to alleviate the pain and symptoms.

FROM THE REFRIGERATOR

APPLE PRESERVES. This may neutralize the acid that causes gout. Take as many apples as you wish, then peel, core, and slice. Simmer in a little water for three hours or more, until they turn thick, brown, and sweet. Refrigerate. Use as you would any preserve.

CHERRIES. Cherries may remove toxins from the body, clean the kidneys, and yes, even help give you a rosy complexion. Because of their cleansing power, they're at the top of the gout-relief list. If you can bake a cherry pie, you may be making a gout treatment. Actually, cherry anything works: cherry compote, cherry juice, cherry jam, cherry tea.

FIGS. Crush and boil 4 figs in 1 pint water. Cook until half the water is gone. Cool, then drink.

FROM THE SINK

WATER. To rid yourself of uric acid, you absolutely must keep your body flushed out. Drink at least 2 quarts of water a day—more, if you can manage it.

FROM THE SPICE RACK

CELERY SEED. It neutralizes acid in the body, including the uric acid that builds up to cause gout. Crush 1 to 2 teaspoons celery seeds and place in a cup of boiling water. Steep 20 minutes, strain, then sweeten to cover the bitter taste. Drink 1 cup three times a day.

CHICORY. If you've been to New Orleans, you know the flavor. It's in the coffee, and it's definitely an acquired taste. Chicory is an old herb, its first use recorded around the first century A.D., and over the past 2,000 years it's seen many medicinal uses. Gout is one of them. Here's a recipe said to relieve symptoms. Mix 1 ounce chicory root to 1 pint boiling water, and take as much of it as you want. This can work as a poultice, too, when it is applied to the skin in the area affected by gout.

MUSTARD POWDER. Make a mustard plaster and apply to the achy joint. Mix 1 part mustard powder (or crushed mustard seeds) to 1 part whole-wheat flour and add enough water to form a thick paste. Slather petroleum jelly, vegetable shortening, or lard on the affected area. Spread a thick coat of mustard paste on a piece of gauze or cloth, then apply over the greased-up area. Tape down and leave in place for several hours or overnight.

THYME. Drink as a tea. Add 1 to 2 teaspoons to a cup of boiling water. Sweeten, and drink.

ONION IT AWAY

An Amish remedy for gout calls for chopping up an onion and applying it as a poultice to the affected toe joint.
Leave it on for one day.

MORE DO'S & DON'TS

- Take fish oil supplements to ease the inflammation that comes with gout.

- Lose weight. Uric acid levels increase as weight increases.

- Don't put weight on the joint until the episode subsides.

- Keep the joint elevated to reduce pain, and immobilize it to reduce pain and prevent joint damage.

- Take ibuprofen for pain and swelling. Don't take aspirin; it can make the problem worse.

- Don't ice or heat the achy area. Either can cause further damage and pain.

- Wear comfortable shoes that allow plenty of room for your big toe.

- Don't take nonprescription diuretics. They can keep you from properly excreting uric acid.

- Remind your doctor that you're on diuretics or medication for blood pressure or heart disease if you are prescribed gout medication. They may have bad interactions.

- Do keep your toes warm enough. Gout seems to rear up more often when it's chilly.

- Avoid turkey meat, organ meats, herring, anchovies, meat gravies, beer, and red wine. These are high in purines, which are metabolized to uric acid.

Hangovers
MORNING-AFTER MISERY

Well, you partied from sundown to sunup, and now you're paying the price. You've got the pounding headache, the queasiness, the dizziness, the sensitivity to light and sound, the muscle aches, and the irritability that comes from overconsumption of alcoholic beverages. How quickly last night's fun turns into this morning's nightmare when you have a hangover!

Why Such Suffering?

Although we don't like to think of it as such, especially when we're having such a good time, alcohol is actually a drug. It's a depressant, and when taken in excess, it fills your body with toxins. Your body reacts as it would to any drug overdose: It tries to metabolize and get rid of the offending substances.

Researchers aren't sure what in the alcohol causes a hangover. But they do know that the debilitating symptoms you experience are a result of the body's inability to get rid of the toxins quickly enough, and they build up in your bloodstream.

Your body's attempts to flush out the alcohol puts a strain on the liver, which madly draws on the body's water reserves to get the job done. Since alcohol is a major diuretic, causing you to urinate more frequently, you lose more water than your body takes in with the beverage. As strange as it may sound, the more alcohol you drink, the more vital fluids you lose. The considerable water loss associated with drinking alcohol increases the liver's burden to get ahold of water anywhere it can. It will take water from the brain and from other vital organs. The resulting dehydration is what's behind many of the worst symptoms of a hangover.

The process of metabolizing the alcohol and excreting large quantities of water also robs the body of glucose and other vital nutrients. Being malnourished further contributes to the unpleasant hangover symptoms.

In addition to dehydration, fatigue is also behind some of your hangover pain. Excessive drinking and late nights usually go hand-in-hand.

But more than that, alcohol interferes with a normal sleep pattern, robbing you of the dream state, which is essential to feeling rested. You may pass out on the floor and sleep for hours, but it won't be the kind of sleep that will allow you to restart your engine in the morning. Lack of proper rest contributes to the malaise a hangover brings.

Prevention

The best way to prevent a hangover is, of course, drinking in moderation or abstaining from alcohol. But keeping yourself well-hydrated and well-nourished when you're drinking can go a long way toward minimizing the morning-after symptoms. Try drinking a glass of water or other noncaffeinated beverage for each alcoholic beverage you drink. And don't drink on an empty stomach. Food helps slow the absorption of alcohol, giving your body time to metabolize it and decreasing the chances of a hangover.

The best cure for a hangover: time. Of course, people ignore the prevention and don't have "time" for the cure. So, here are some remedies to ease the suffering for those who have had one drink too many.

FROM THE COUNTER

BANANA. Bananas are your best friend! While you were drunk and peeing like a racehorse, lots of potassium drained from your body. Eating a banana bursting with potassium will give you some giddyap and go. All you have to do is peel and eat.

FROM THE CUPBOARD

GINGER. Ginger has long been used to treat nausea and seasickness. And, since having a hangover is much like being seasick, this easy remedy works wonders. If you're really green, the best bet is to drink ginger ale (no preparation required). If you can remain vertical for ten minutes, brew some ginger tea. Cut 10 to 12 slices of fresh gingerroot and combine with 4 cups water. Boil for ten minutes. Strain and add the juice of 1 orange, the juice of ½ lemon, and ½ cup honey. Drink to your relief.

WHEN TO CALL THE DOCTOR

- If a person passes out from too much alcohol
- If you are severely dehydrated
- If symptoms don't improve after a few days' rest
- If drinking in excess becomes a habit. Seek professional help.

FACTS ABOUT HANGOVERS

According to the Alka-Seltzer Morning Relief Hangover Survey of 900 Americans aged 21 or older:

- The average number of drinks that cause a hangover is 3.2.
- About 1 in 10 people more than 21 years of age get hangovers after 1 or 2 drinks.
- 55 percent of Americans of legal drinking age consume alcoholic beverages at least once a week.

PICK YOUR POISON CAREFULLY

If you do drink, know that your beverage choice may determine your hangover fate. Keep these recommendations in mind when seated at the bar.

- Mixing different types of alcohol makes for a difficult recovery.
- Darker-colored liquors (such as bourbon or rum) will give you worse hangovers than light-colored liquors (gin or vodka). Darker liquors have more impurities called congeners, which are by-products of fermentation and make for horrific hangovers.
- Red wine can cause a worse hangover because of an amino acid it contains called tyramine.
- Carbonation in drinks speeds up the absorption of alcohol.
- Don't choose quantity over quality. Cheap liquors make you sicker, quicker.
- Tropical drinks with creams and sugars (such as piña coladas) mask the taste of alcohol, sing a siren song to your sweet tooth, and make you want "just one more."

HONEY AND LEMON. The classic hot toddy (nonalcoholic, of course) is honey, lemon, and hot water. Easy to swallow, this beverage replenishes fluids and sugars lost to a hangover. It is vital, however, to use honey instead of white sugar. Honey contains fructose, which competes for the metabolism of alcohol. Some healthy competition is needed, since it prevents the rapid change in alcohol levels that results in headaches. Plain sugar contains sucrose, which isn't absorbed as quickly. To make a toddy, boil 1 cup water and mix in honey and lemon juice to taste. Enjoy a toddy several times a day.

RICE, SOUP, OR TOAST. Food is probably the last thing you want to look at while recovering, but you do need some substance for energy. Stay with clear liquids until you can tolerate something solid. Then start off slowly with mild, easy-to-digest foods such as plain toast, rice, or clear soup.

SPORTS DRINKS. These are a good way to replace fluids as well as electrolytes and glucose.

FROM THE FREEZER

ICE. Put an ice compress on your aching head. Place crushed ice in a plastic bag, wrap in a dry towel, and apply it to where it hurts. Or just rinse a washcloth under cold water, place it on your forehead, and rest.

FROM THE REFRIGERATOR

JUICE. Juice, especially freshly squeezed orange juice, will help raise your blood sugar levels and help ease some of your hangover symptoms. However, if your stomach is upset, skip acidic juices such as orange juice and stick with apple juice instead.

FROM THE SINK

WATER. Next to time, drinking water is the best cure for a hangover. Dehydration does a doozy on your body and causes much of the discomfort associated with a hangover. Stick to water, be it tap, bottled, or carbonated. Drink more than 8 glasses a day while recovering.

MORE DO'S AND DON'TS

• Drink to the night. If you can remember one thing while intoxicated, remember this: Guzzle plenty of water before going to bed. It will help nip dehydration, and you'll feel much better in the morning.

• Stick to 1 drink (or less) per hour, and sip it slowly. One hour is about the time it takes for the average adult body to process an alcoholic beverage. One drink is a 5-ounce glass of wine, a 12-ounce beer, or 1.5 ounces of hard liquor.

• Rest. Pull the shades down, unplug the telephone, and go to sleep.

• Never drink and drive.

• Try Pepto-Bismol or an antacid to relieve queasiness and settle your stomach.

• Take a multivitamin with B vitamins to replace those lost during your night of carousing.

Headaches
THWARTING THE THROBBING

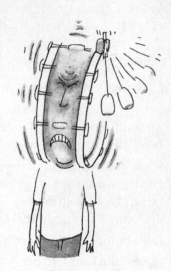

The day starts with screaming kids, continues slowly onward with stop 'n' go traffic,
and ends on a sour note with an angry boss.
By this point, you are ready to chop your
head off to relieve the pounding pain.
You can take a little comfort in knowing
that almost everyone has had such a
day...and such a headache. Yet some people fare worse than others do. An estimated
45 million Americans get chronic, recurring
headaches, while as many as 18 million of
those suffer from painful, debilitating
migraines.

The Three Kinds of Headaches

Although there are nearly two dozen types of headaches, they all fall
into three basic categories: tension, vascular, and organic.

Tension headaches, the most common of the trio, cause a dull, non-
throbbing pain, usually accompanied by tightness in the scalp or neck.
Triggers range from depression to everyday stresses such as screaming
kids and traffic jams.

Vascular headaches are more intense, severe, throbbing, and piercing:
Cluster and migraine headaches fall into this category. Triggers for cluster headaches are unknown, although excessive smoking and alcohol
consumption can ignite them. Migraines are thought to be caused by
heredity, diet, stress, menstruation, and environmental factors such as
cigarette smoke.

Less common are organic headaches, in which pain becomes increasingly worse and is accompanied by other symptoms, such as vomiting,
coordination problems, visual disturbances, or speech or personality
changes. Triggers include tumors, infections, or diseases of the brain,
eyes, ears, and nose.

If you are prone to the usual tension headache, head to the kitchen
for a variety of remedies that can help your throbbing head.

FROM THE FREEZER

ICE. A washcloth dipped in ice-cold water and placed over the pain site is
an easy way to relieve a headache. An ice compress works well, too. Place

a handful of crushed ice cubes into a zipper-type plastic bag and cover it with a dry washcloth. (A bag of frozen vegetables is a good substitute.) Apply where needed. Whatever method you use, try to apply the cold compress as soon as possible after the headache develops. Relief typically starts within 20 minutes of use.

FROM THE REFRIGERATOR

PEACH JUICE. Drinking peach juice or apricot nectar can help alleviate the nausea that sometimes accompanies a bad headache.

FROM THE SINK

HOT WATER. If snow is falling and the last thing you want on your head is an ice pack, turn to heat for soothing relief. Dip a washcloth into hot but not scalding water. Squeeze out and apply over your eyes or on the pain site. Leave the compress on for 30 minutes, rewarming as necessary.

FROM THE SPICE RACK

CLOVES AND OTHER SPICES. Here's a remedy that includes the whole kitchen sink...or should we say the whole spice rack? A blend of scented herbs eases away tension headaches. Look into your spice rack. Do you have dried marjoram, rosemary, and mint? They work well together. And if you have dried lavender and rose petals, they make wonderful additions to the mix. Put 4 tablespoons of each (or whichever you have) into a cloth sachet bag. Add 1 tablespoon cloves. Close up the sachet bag, and whenever you have a headache or feel one coming on, hold the bag to your nose and inhale deeply until you feel it subsiding. (If you don't have a sachet bag, a clean handkerchief works fine.) You can also apply this bundle of herbs to your head when you rest.

PEPPERMINT. A dab of peppermint oil rubbed on the temples can ease a tension headache. Don't try this with children or if you have sensitive skin as the oil can have a burning effect.

ROSEMARY. Rosemary is a well-recognized folk cure for easing pain in the United States, China, and Europe. One of its constituents, rosmarinic acid, is an anti-inflammatory similar to aspirin and ibuprofen. Since

---

WHEN TO CALL THE DOCTOR

- If you get daily headaches
- If you get headaches after intense coughing or sneezing
- If you have pain in the ear or eyes
- If you experience nausea or vomiting
- If you experience vision changes
- If you have hallucinations
- If you experience sensitivity to light and sound
- If you have weakness or dizziness
- If you experience loss of consciousness
- If you have a severe, debilitating headache

rosmarinic acid is also an important constituent in sage, the two herbs are often combined to make a pain-relieving tea. Place 1 teaspoon crushed rosemary leaves and 1 teaspoon crushed sage leaves in a cup. Fill with boiling water. Cover to prevent the volatile oils from escaping, and steep until the tea reaches room temperature. Take ½-cup doses two to three times a day. You don't have to mix the two herbs to benefit from rosmarinic acid, however. If you only have one, make a tea of it alone.

MORE DO'S AND DON'TS

- Lie down. Sometimes the best headache treatment is to go to bed and sleep. For some headaches, sleep interrupts the pain cycle.

- Keep it dark. Bright light, whether it's sunlight or the glare of a computer screen, can bring on a headache or make one you already have worse. If you're sensitive to light, wear sunglasses outdoors and adjust your blinds so that intense light doesn't hit your eyes. If you've already got a headache, darken the room where you're resting.

- Distract yourself from stress. Try to concentrate on pleasant thoughts only, and shut out tension-producing ones. Stress can bring on a headache or make one you already have much worse.

- Check for tension. Many people unconsciously clench their jaw muscles, grip the steering wheel tightly, furrow their brows, or make fists when they're tense. All of these can lead to a headache. If you notice you're in the grip of tension, force yourself to breathe slowly and deeply, and gently relax your tense muscles.

- Don't smoke. Aside from the fact that it's unhealthful, smoking can give you a headache or make one worse.

PLEASURE AND PAIN

Ice cream, that summertime delight, can truly make you scream—or at least writhe in agony. Eating ice cream can cause an ice-cream headache, and anyone who has eaten an icy treat too fast knows the pain well. What sparks this headache is a change in mouth temperature. As the icy dessert touches the top of your mouth (or back of your throat), it causes a nerve reaction that swells blood vessels in the head. The result: an intense, shooting pain that lasts for 30 to 60 seconds. The cure: Spend more time licking your ice cream cone and less time gulping it down—and keep icy cold foods to the side of your mouth.

Heartburn
PUTTING OUT THE FIRE

Boy, oh boy, did you do it this time. You added that heaping second helping to all the platter pickings you just couldn't resist, and what do you have? Indigestion (an incomplete or imperfect digestion), that's what. And it may be accompanied by pain, nausea, vomiting, heartburn, gas, and belching. All this because you couldn't resist temptation. But don't worry. It happens to everybody, and it goes away.

So, now that you've eaten until you're about ready to burst, what's next? The couch, maybe? Stretch out, let your digestive system do its thing, take a nap?

Wrong! The worst thing you can do after a binge is to lie down. That can cause heartburn, also known as acid indigestion. Whatever you call it, it's the feeling you get when digestive acid escapes your stomach and irritates the esophagus, the tube that leads from your throat to your stomach. After you eat, heartburn can also fire up when you:

• Bend forward

• Exercise

• Strain muscles

Why Acid Backs Up

Occasionally the acid keeps on coming until you have a mouthful of something bitter. You may have some pain in your gut, too, or in your chest. Along with that acid may come a belch, one that may bring even more of that stomach acid with it.

The purpose of stomach acid is to break down the foods we eat so our body can digest them. Our stomachs have a protective lining that shields it from those acids, but the esophagus does not have that protection. Normally that's not a problem, because after we swallow food, it passes down the esophagus, through a sphincter, and into the stomach. The sphincter then closes.

WHEN TO CALL THE DOCTOR

- If you've tried home remedies or over-the-counter medications and they're not working. Your heartburn could be a symptom of another ailment, such as an ulcer, gallbladder disease, or hiatal hernia.

- If heartburn happens on a prolonged or regular basis, even if home treatments are working

- Call 9-1-1 or go to the nearest emergency room if your chest pain spreads into your arm, jaw, or shoulder, especially if you have any of these symptoms: sweating, nausea, dizziness, shortness of breath, fainting. This could be a heart attack.

FASCINATING FACT

Cold beverages may help cause heartburn. They cool down your stomach, which requires a certain amount of heat in order to function at its best.

Occasionally, though, the muscles of that sphincter are weakened and it doesn't close properly or it doesn't close all the way. Scarring from an ulcer or frequent episodes of acid reflux (when the acid comes back up), stomach pressure from overeating, obesity, and pregnancy can all cause this glitch in the lower esophageal sphincter (LES). And when the LES gets a glitch and allows the gastric acid to splash out of the stomach, you will get a case of heartburn.

Generally, heartburn isn't serious. In fact, small amounts of reflux are normal and most people don't even notice it because the swallowing we do causes saliva to wash the acids right back down into the stomach where they belong. When the stomach starts shooting back amounts that are larger than normal, especially on a regular basis or over a prolonged period of time, that's when the real trouble begins and simple heartburn can turn into esophageal inflammation or bleeding.

Who's prone to heartburn? Just about anybody. According to the National Digestive Diseases Clearinghouse, 25 million adults suffer from heartburn daily and about 60 million Americans get gastroesophageal reflux and heartburn at least once a month.

There are several prescription medicines available for the treatment of long-term or serious heartburn or acid reflux, and over-the-counter remedies are available at your pharmacy, too. But there are several remedies right in your own kitchen that can fight the fire of heartburn.

FROM THE CUPBOARD

ALMONDS. Chewing 6 or 8 blanched almonds during an episode of heartburn may relieve the symptoms. Chew them well, though, to avoid swallowing air and causing yourself more discomfort.

BAKING SODA. Take ½ teaspoon in ½ glass water. Check the antacid use information on the box before using this remedy, however.

Warning! If you're on a salt-restricted diet, do not use baking soda. It's loaded with sodium. And do not use it if you're experiencing nausea, stomachache, gas, cramps, or stomach distention from overeating.

BROWN RICE. Plain or with a little sweetening, rice can help relieve discomfort. Rice is a complex carbohydrate and is a bland food, which is less likely to increase acidity or relax the sphincter muscle.

CREAM OF TARTAR. For an acid neutralizer, mix ½ teaspoon with ½ teaspoon baking soda in a glass of water. Take 1 teaspoon of the solution as needed.

SODA CRACKERS. This is an old folk cure that actually works. Soda crackers (preferably unsalted) are bland, they digest easily, and they absorb stomach acid. They also contain bicarbonate of soda and cream of tartar, which neutralize the acid. Tip: You know that package of soda crackers they always give you at the restaurant that you leave on the table? From now on, take them with you. These come in handy when you're plagued by heartburn and can't seek immediate relief.

VINEGAR. Mix 1 tablespoon apple cider vinegar, 1 tablespoon honey, and 1 cup warm water. Drink at the first sign of heartburn.

FROM THE DRAWER

PAPER AND PEN. Keep a food diary. This can tell you which foods or food combinations cause that heartburn.

FROM THE FAUCET

WATER. Drink water in between meals, not with meals. If you drink fluids with meals, you increase the volume of stomach contents, which makes it easier for heartburn to happen.

OLD WIVES' TALE (OR NOT?)

Cabbage's ability to heal the digestive system has been known for 450 years, since 1557 when a Dutch doctor by the name of Drodens recorded the benefits of cabbage, especially in juice form. Taken a step further, there are many hearty Germans who swear by the internal healing properties of sauerkraut juice. If you have a taste for it, you can find it in your grocery store if you look hard enough.

FIRE-FIGHTING FOODS

Proteins may strengthen the sphincter that allows the stomach acid to escape. Make sure all your meals contain some protein in order to keep that valve in good working order. These top the sphincter-friendly list:

- Lean meats
- Fish
- Poultry
- Low fat dairy products

GUMMY FACTS

Gum-chewers are notorious air-swallowers. And air-swallowers are prone to indigestion. So if you're a gum-chewer who gets frequent indigestion, skip the gum for a while to see if there's a connection.

If you already are suffering with a bout of heartburn, however, chewing sugarless gum can bring relief. It increases the flow of saliva, which washes down the acid. Skip the mint flavors and don't chew too much because 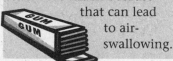 that can lead to air-swallowing.

FROM THE REFRIGERATOR

APPLE HONEY. This is a simple remedy that will neutralize stomach acids. Peel, core, and slice several sweet apples. Simmer with a little water over low heat for three hours until the mixture is thick, brown, and sweet to the taste. Refrigerate in an airtight container and take a few spoonfuls whenever you have the need.

APPLES. Fresh or cooked, they cool the burn of stomach acid.

BUTTERMILK. This is an acid-reliever, but don't confuse it with regular milk, which can be an acid-maker, especially if you are bothered by lactose intolerance.

CABBAGE. Like apples, cabbage is a natural fire extinguisher. For the best relief, put the cabbage through a juicer, then drink it down.

FRUIT JUICES. Skip juices from citrus fruits, but try these stomach-cooling juices for heartburn relief: papaya, mango, guava, pear.

LIME JUICE. Mix 10 drops lime juice with ½ teaspoon sugar and ¼ teaspoon baking soda, in that order. When the baking soda is added it will fizz, and that's when you need to drink it down. The fizz will neutralize stomach acid.

PAPAYA. Eat it straight to reap the benefit of its natural, indigestion-fighting enzyme papain. Or drink 1 cup papaya juice combined with 1 teaspoon sugar and 2 pinches cardamom to relieve acid.

Warning! Pregnant women should not eat papayas; they're a source of natural estrogen that can cause miscarriage.

POTATO. Mix ½ cup raw potato juice with ½ cup water, and drink after meals. To make raw potato juice, simply put a peeled raw potato through a juicer or blender.

PUMPKIN. Eat it baked as a squash to get rid of heartburn. Fresh is best. Spice it up with cinnamon, which is another heartburn cure. Or, make a compote of baked pumpkin and apples, spiced with cinnamon and honey, for a dessert that's both curative and tasty.

YOGURT. Make sure the yogurt you eat has live cultures in it. It's because of the helpful and digestive-friendly microorganisms in yogurt that this food may soothe the acid-forming imbalances that can lead to heartburn.

FROM THE SPICE RACK

CARDAMOM. This old-time digestive aid may help relieve the burn of acid indigestion. Add it to baked goodies such as sweet rolls or fruit cake, or sprinkle, with a pinch of cinnamon, on toast. It works well in cooked cereals, too.

CINNAMON. Cinnamon is a traditional remedy for acid relief. Brew a cup of cinnamon tea from a cinnamon stick. Or try a commercial brand, but be sure to check the label. Cinnamon tea often has black tea in it, which is a cause of heartburn, so make sure your commercial brand doesn't contain black tea. For another acid-busting treat, make cinnamon toast.

GINGER. A tea from this root can soothe that burning belly. Add 1½ teaspoons gingerroot to 1 cup water; let steep, then simmer for ten minutes. Drink this tasty tea as needed.

MORE DO'S & DON'TS

- If you're carrying extra pounds, lose them. All that baggage pushing in on the abdomen increases pressure on the stomach, which causes heartburn.

- Eat smaller meals. The more food in your belly, the more likely that bulk will push stomach acid right back up.

- Eat slowly, chew thoroughly. Sometimes heartburn will

THE USUAL SUSPECTS

Here's the food list that's commonly associated with heartburn. Cut back on these, or cut them out altogether, and see what happens:

Fried and fatty foods, pies, cakes, cookies, butter, margarine, oils, cream: These may weaken your LES. Also, fatty foods take longer to digest, meaning the gastric juices are working overtime and have more opportunity to cause a backup.

Peppermint in any form*: It relaxes the stomach muscle and valve, allowing the release of acids back up into the esophagus.

Caffeinated beverages, such as coffee, tea, cola: Caffeine causes extra acid production.

Chocolate: It contains methylxanthines, a second cousin to caffeine, and can weaken the stomach valve.

Fruit and vegetable juices, especially tomato and citrus juice: They can irritate the throat and cause pain if heartburn has already caused irritation. Pineapple juice has an especially potent punch.

Garlic and onions: May weaken the LES.

Spicy, pickled, or fermented foods: These are heartburn-makers, too.

Alcohol: It causes the LES to relax.

Smoking and certain drugs such as aspirin, ibuprofen, and some antibiotics: These also relax the LES, causing acid reflux.

Warning! Peppermint is often prescribed for other symptoms of indigestion but should never be used when heartburn is present.

flare because the food is simply too large to get through the digestive tract and it, along with the acids, is forced back up.

- Don't eat right before bedtime. Give your stomach a two- or three-hour break before you sleep. And if you're plagued by the burn at night, sleep with your head elevated on pillows.

- Let the gravity be with you. Stay upright so the gastric contents are forced to stay down. In other words, don't head for the couch after you eat. If you must snooze, try the recliner, but don't recline too steeply.

- Loosen the belt. Tight clothing and belts can create enough pressure to cause heartburn.

- Stay in shape. Heartburn hates people who are fit. However, skip strenuous exercise for a couple hours after a meal. Instead, go for a nice leisurely walk. This helps keep the stomach acid in its place.

- Stay calm. Stress increases acid production.

CONSIDER YOUR OVER-THE-COUNTER ANTACID CHOICES

Choosing an over-the-counter (OTC) antacid is not always as simple as grabbing the first box or bottle you come to on the shelf. Antacids come with their own unique qualities as well as risks. If a simple OTC is your choice, talk with your doctor or pharmacist about which is best for you. People with high blood pressure, for instance, should NOT take over-the-counter antacids without first checking with the doctor. And ask your pharmacist about possible interactions with other drugs you're taking. Most pharmacies have readily available printouts about drug interactions that are free for the asking. In the meantime, here are some common antacid ingredients and their possible side effects.

- Aluminum hydroxide. Can cause constipation. Because there may be a link between Alzheimer's disease and aluminum, antacids with aluminum hydroxide are not recommended for people with, or who are at risk for, AD.

- Magnesium salts. May cause diarrhea. However, choosing an antacid containing both aluminum hydroxide and magnesium salts may balance out the constipation/diarrhea side effects.

- Alginic acid. May prevent reflux.

Heart Disease

Tending Your Ticker

The heart is an amazing structure, tough yet fragile. A muscle, its network of arteries and veins transport blood through your body, nourishing organs and tissues. When the heart is working as it should, you barely notice it. But when your heart starts acting strangely, you have cause to worry. Thankfully, you live in an age when heart disease can be treated very successfully, and in some cases, the condition can even be reversed.

Heart Trouble

Heart disease is any condition that keeps your heart from functioning at its best or causes a deterioration of the heart's arteries and vessels. Coronary heart disease (CHD), also known as coronary artery disease, is the most common form of heart disease, affecting 12.6 million people in America. If you are diagnosed with CHD, it means you have atherosclerosis, or hardening of the arteries on the heart's surface. Arteries become hard when plaque accumulates on artery walls. This plaque develops gradually as an overabundance of low-density lipoprotein (LDL) cholesterol (the bad stuff) makes itself at home in your arteries. The plaque builds and narrows the artery walls, making it more and more difficult for blood to pass through the heart and increasing the opportunity for a blood clot to form. If the heart doesn't get enough blood, it can cause chest pain (angina) or a heart attack.

Not treating coronary heart disease can also lead to congestive heart failure (CHF). CHF happens when your heart isn't strong enough to pump blood throughout the body—it fails to meet the body's need for oxygen. This often causes congestion in the lungs and a variety of other problems for your heart and the rest of your body.

Honing In on Heart Disease

There are many risk factors for heart disease. A family history of heart disease, for instance, puts you at much greater risk. While you can't do anything about your genes, there are many risk factors you can control. These are the ones you can do something about:

WHEN TO CALL THE DOCTOR

- If you have any symptoms in "How To Know If You Have Heart Disease," page 170. However, if you have any of the following symptoms, go to the nearest emergency room or call 9-1-1 immediately.
- Painful pressure or squeezing in the chest that lasts for a few minutes or goes away and returns
- Pain that radiates to the shoulders, neck, or arms
- Light-headedness, fainting, sweating, nausea, or shortness of breath along with chest pain

- High levels of low-density lipoprotein (LDL) cholesterol (the bad stuff), and low levels of high-density lipoprotein (the good stuff) (see High Cholesterol, page 180)
- High levels of triglycerides. Triglyceride levels increase when you eat too many fatty foods or when you eat too much—excess calories are made into triglycerides and stored as fat in cells. Having an abundance of triglycerides has been linked to coronary heart disease.
- High blood pressure (see High Blood Pressure, page 175)
- Smoking
- Lack of regular exercise
- A high fat diet
- Being overweight or obese
- Diabetes (see Diabetes, page 99)
- Ongoing stress or depression

FROM THE CUPBOARD

BRAN. Bran cereal is a high-fiber food that will help keep your cholesterol levels in check. Other high-fiber foods in your cupboard include barley, oats, whole grains such as brown rice and lentils, and beans, such as kidney beans and black beans.

OLIVE OIL. The American Heart Association and the American Dietetic Association recommend getting most of your fat from monounsaturated sources. Olive oil is a prime candidate. Try using it instead of other vegetable oils when sautéing your veggies.

PEANUT BUTTER. Eat 2 tablespoons of this comforting food and you can get ⅓ of your daily intake of vitamin E. Because vitamin E is a fat-soluble vitamin (other antioxidant vitamins are water soluble), it is found more abundantly in fattier foods such as vegetable oils and nuts. If you're watching your weight, don't go overboard on the peanut butter.

PECANS. These tasty nuts are full of magnesium, another heart-friendly nutrient. One ounce of pecans can give you ⅓ of your recommended daily allowance of this vital mineral.

WHOLE-WHEAT BREAD. One slice of whole-wheat bread has 11 mcg of selenium, an antioxidant mineral that works with vitamin E to protect your heart.

WINE. Health experts are quick to note that alcohol in moderate amounts is helpful in the battle against heart disease. They define moderate as one glass a day for women and two glasses of alcohol a day for men. What's in one drink? Twelve ounces of beer, 5 ounces of wine, or 1.5 ounces of whiskey.

FROM THE REFRIGERATOR

BROCCOLI. Calcium is another heart-healthy nutrient, and there are lots of nondairy foods that are rich in it. One cup of broccoli can supply you with 90 mg of calcium.

CHICKEN. Eating three ounces of chicken will give you ⅓ of your daily requirement for vitamin B_6, which is a nutrient that's necessary for maintaining heart health.

SALMON. Adding fatty fish to your diet is a good idea if you're at risk for heart disease. Three ounces of salmon meets your daily requirement for vitamin B_{12}, a vitamin that helps keep your heart healthy, and it's a good source of omega-3 fatty acids, which have been proven to lower triglycerides and reduce blood clots that could potentially block arteries in the heart.

SPINACH. Make yourself a salad using spinach instead of the usual iceberg lettuce and get a good start on meeting your folic acid needs (½ cup has 130 mcg of folic acid). Along with the other B vitamins, B_6 and B_{12}, folic acid can help prevent heart disease.

STRAWBERRIES. You can fill up on 45 mg of the heart-healthy vitamin with ½ cup of summer's sweet berry. Vitamin C is an antioxidant vital to maintaining a happy heart. Strawberries are also a good source of fiber and potassium, both important to heart health.

SWEET POTATOES. With double your daily requirements for vitamin A, a heart-protecting nutrient, sweet potatoes are a smart choice for fending off heart disease.

FROM THE SPICE RACK

GARLIC. Chock-full of antioxidants, garlic seems to be able to lessen plaque buildup, reduce the incidence of chest pain, and keep the heart

THE HEART OF A WOMAN

Heart disease isn't a subject that comes up much in discussions of women's health. But 1 out of every 2 women will die of heart disease or stroke. Compared to the 1 in 27 who will die of breast cancer, it seems heart disease needs a little more attention by the gentler gender. Estrogen helps reduce the risk of coronary heart disease (CHD), which is why younger women are less prone to heart attacks than men. But after menopause, when estrogen levels drop, women are on equal footing with men in their risk for getting CHD.

THE AMAZING BLOOD MOVER

Every minute, your heart pumps about 1.5 gallons of blood through your body.

generally healthy. It is also a mild anticoagulant, helping to thin the blood. The advantages may take some time: One study found that it took a couple of years of eating garlic daily to get its heart-healthy benefits.

FROM THE SUPPLEMENT SHELF

COENZYME Q10. This nutrient, found in fatty fish, is not classified as a vitamin or a mineral. But studies have found that it is necessary for heart health. It seems coenzyme Q10 re-energizes heart cells, especially in people who have already been diagnosed with heart failure. It blocks the process that creates plaque buildup in the arteries and helps lower blood pressure. Coenzyme Q10 has been used to treat congestive heart failure in Japan for decades. Talk to your doctor before trying the supplement. If you get the go-ahead, buy supplements from Japanese manufacturers.

MORE DO'S AND DON'TS

- Don't smoke. People who smoke are twice as likely to have a heart attack.
- Get moving. Your heart is a muscle, and if you don't exercise it, it will get weaker and be less able to rebound from heart troubles.
- Lose weight. The American Heart Association (AHA) says that if you're overweight, losing as little as 10 to 20 pounds is a boon to your heart.
- Eat healthy. The AHA suggests getting less than 30 percent of your calories from fat, less than 10 percent of which should be the saturated kind. You should get no more than 300 mg of cholesterol a day.

HOW TO KNOW IF YOU HAVE HEART DISEASE

About 25 to 30 percent of people who have heart disease don't know it until something serious happens. That's why it's a good idea to see your doctor for a regular checkup and to have your cholesterol and triglyceride levels and your blood pressure checked and monitored. If you have any of these symptoms, schedule a checkup as soon as you can:

- Chest pain (angina). If you feel like you have an elephant sitting on your chest after climbing the stairs, your body could be giving you a warning signal.
- Shortness of breath. This is especially noticeable after a game of one-on-one with your daughter or an intense meeting with your boss.
- Nausea or stomach upset. This could be more than what you ate at dinner, especially if you have recurrent bouts of tummy trouble.
- Sweating. This is a symptom when you can't blame it on exercising.
- Feeling weak or tired.

How What You Eat Affects Your Heart

Recent research shows that some specific nutrients help keep your heart healthy and can even reverse the effects of heart disease.

Antioxidants

Sources: Vitamins A, C, and E, and selenium

What they do: They keep LDL ("bad") cholesterol from oxidizing and block oxygen-free radicals, both of which keep plaque from building up in the arteries. Bottom line: They reduce the risk of atherosclerosis, or hardening of the arteries, which can lead to heart disease, heart attack, and stroke.

How much you need:

- Vitamin A: After age 11, men need 1,000 REs a day; women need 800 REs a day. (RE is retinol equivalent—it's the way scientists measure amounts of the vitamin).
- Vitamin C: After age 15, men and women need 60 mg a day.
- Vitamin E: After age 11, men need 10 mg a day; women, 8 mg a day.
- Selenium: Men need 70 mcg a day; women need 55 mcg.

B Vitamins

Sources: Vitamins B_6, B_{12}, and folic acid

What they do: When your body digests meat, it raises the homocysteine levels in your blood. High levels of homocysteine put you at risk for clogged arteries and blood clots. Eating a sufficient amount of B vitamins can help turn homocysteine into something harmless to your body, lessening your chances of developing plaque in your arteries.

How much you need:

- Vitamin B_6: Up to age 50 you need 1.3 mg a day; after 50 men's needs rise to 1.7 mg a day. After age 50, women need 1.4 mg daily.
- Vitamin B_{12}: All adults need 2.4 mcg a day.
- Folic Acid: Men and women older than 14 need 400 mcg daily.

Minerals

Sources: Calcium and magnesium

What they do: Calcium reduces the risk of death from heart disease, lowers blood pressure, and lowers cholesterol. Magnesium is vital to keeping your heart healthy. It helps prevent plaque buildup and strengthens artery walls. And if you have a heart attack, having adequate amounts of magnesium in your body can increase your chances of surviving.

How much you need:

- Calcium: Adults up to age 50 need 1,000 mg a day. After 50 you need 1,200 mg daily.
- Magnesium: From 18 to 30, men need 400 mg a day. After age 30, men need 420 mg. From ages 18 to 30, women need 310 mg; after 30, they need 320 mg daily.

Hemorrhoids
DEALING WITH DISCOMFORT

Hemorrhoids are a sore subject, and not one that is brought up at the dinner table. Yet privately, millions of people suffer from these painful protrusions. Also known as "piles," hemorrhoids are swollen, stretched out veins that line the anal canal and lower rectum. Internal hemorrhoids may either bulge into the anal canal or protrude out through the anus (these are called prolapsed). External hemorrhoids occur under the surface of the skin near the anal opening. Both types hurt, burn, itch, irritate, and bleed.

About one-half to three-fourths of Americans will develop hemorrhoids in their lifetime. Most cases are caused by constipation or physical strain while making a bowel movement. Other causes include heredity, age, a low fiber diet resulting in constipation, obesity, the improper use of laxatives, pregnancy, anal intercourse, prolonged sitting, and prolonged standing.

Fortunately, most hemorrhoids respond well to home treatments and changes in the diet, so you can keep this sore point under wraps.

FROM THE CUPBOARD

WHEN TO CALL THE DOCTOR

- If you have rectal bleeding. Although rectal bleeding is associated with hemorrhoids, it can also be a warning sign of colon and rectal cancer.
- If you are pregnant and develop hemorrhoids
- If you are in pain

POTATO. A poultice made from grated potato works as an astringent and soothes pain. Take 2 washed potatoes, cut them into small chunks, and put them into a blender. Process until the potatoes are in liquid form. Add a few teaspoons water if they look dry. Spread the mashed 'taters into a thin gauze bandage or clean handkerchief, fold in half, and apply to the hemorrhoids for five to ten minutes.

Warning! Some folk remedies will have you placing raw potato pieces in places that don't see the light of day. Using potatoes or any other food as a suppository to help hemorrhoids should first be discussed with your physician.

PRUNES. If you haven't eaten a prune since your mother tried to force one down your throat at age five, then it's time to try again. As Mama knew, prunes have a laxative effect and help soften stools. Try to eat 1 to 3 a day, and look at it as pleasure, not punishment.

VINEGAR. Applying a dab of apple cider or plain vinegar to hemorrhoids stops itching and burning. The vinegar has astringent properties that help shrink swollen blood vessels. After dry wiping, dip a cottonball in vinegar and apply.

FROM THE FREEZER

ICE. Now here's a remedy guaranteed to wake you up and soothe hemorrhoid pain. Sit on a cold compress. That's right, literally freeze your rear end. Break ice into small cubes (easier for the ice to shape itself around certain regions), and place it in a plastic, reclosable bag. Cover with a thick paper towel and sit on it! The cooling works to relieve pain in two ways: First, it numbs the region, and second, it reduces blood flow to those distended veins.

FROM THE REFRIGERATOR

ORANGES. Vitamin C plays a role in strengthening and toning blood vessels, so eat lots of vitamin C-rich fruits and vegetables.

FROM THE SINK

WATER. Think of water as the plumber of the digestive tract, without the $85-an-hour fee. Water keeps the digestive process moving along without block ups—one of the main causes of hemorrhoids. Reaping the benefits requires drinking a minimum of 8 large glasses of water each day. Drinking other fluids, such as juice, and eating plenty of water-loaded fruits and vegetables can help the flow of things, too.

FROM THE WINDOWSILL

ALOE VERA. Versatile aloe vera comes to the rescue once again as a hemorrhoid healer. The very same anti-inflammatory constituents that reduce blistering and inflammation in burns also help reduce the irritation of hemorrhoids. Break off a piece of the aloe vera leaf and apply only the clear gel to the hemorrhoids.

AN HERBAL REMEDY

German folk medicine uses chamomile as a hemorrhoid treatment. Chamomile contains strong anti-inflammatory substances that may reduce the pain or itching associated with hemorrhoids. To reap the benefits of chamomile, use it in a bath. Combine 1 ounce dried chamomile with 2 quarts boiling water to make a tea. Let steep until warm. Pour the tea into a tub deep enough to sit in and soak for 15 minutes. If possible, bathe two to three times a day for acute hemorrhoids. Or, you can make the tea and apply it to the hemorrhoids with a cotton ball after having a bowel movement. Do not use chamomile if you have pollen allergies.

THE HEALING BENEFITS OF WITCH HAZEL

Witch hazel has long been used as a soothing, cooling astringent for hemorrhoid pain, itching, and bleeding. It has anti-inflammatory properties and, when applied to hemorrhoids, tightens up the tissues and stanches bleeding. A dab of witch hazel applied to the outer rectum with a cotton ball (after dry wiping) is one of the best and easiest remedies available for external hemorrhoids. Give your hemorrhoids a cool treat by keeping a bottle of witch hazel refrigerated. You can also make a compress soaked in witch hazel and leave it on your bottom while resting.

MORE DO'S AND DON'TS

- Be kind to your posterior by taking a nice soak in the tub. A bath does much to soothe inflamed tissues and ease pain. If you have hemorrhoids, it's recommended that you take a sitz bath three to four times a day for 30 minutes. Since this time commitment is often an impossibility for active people and working adults, try a mini-soak. Apply a washcloth moistened with warm water to the hemorrhoids for a few minutes a few times a day.

- Don't burst a blood vessel. Try to make a bowel movement without straining. If you don't have the urge to go, get off the pot. Along those same lines, don't be a bathroom reader and sit on the throne all day in anticipation.

- Exercise. Regular aerobic exercise helps the digestive system work more efficiently.

- Easy does it. After a bowel movement, don't vigorously clean yourself with dry toilet paper. Buy premoistened wipes designed for anal care or, after gently wiping with toilet paper, apply the witch hazel or vinegar remedy (mentioned previously) to clean yourself.

High Blood Pressure
REVERSING THE TREND

Sometimes what you don't know can hurt you. Such is the case with high blood pressure, or hypertension. Although one in four adults has high blood pressure, according to the American Heart Association (AHA), almost a third of them don't know they have it.

That's because high blood pressure often has no symptoms. It's not as if you feel the pressure of your blood coursing through your circulatory system. When the heart beats, it pumps blood to the arteries, creating pressure within them. That pressure can be normal or it can be excessive. High blood pressure is defined as a persistently elevated pressure of blood within the arteries.

Over time, the excessive force exerted against the arteries damages and scars them. It can also damage organs, such as the heart, kidneys, and brain. High blood pressure can lead to strokes, blindness, kidney failure, and heart failure.

In 90 to 95 percent of all cases, the cause of high blood pressure isn't known. In such cases, when there is no underlying cause, the disease is known as primary, or essential, hypertension. Sometimes the high blood pressure is caused by another disease, such as an endocrine disorder. In such cases the disease is called secondary hypertension.

Who's at Risk?

While no one knows the exact cause of hypertension, there are specific factors that put you at risk of developing it. These include:

Age. The older you are, the greater the likelihood of developing hypertension.

Weight. The heavier you are, the greater your risk of hypertension.

Race. African Americans are more prone to high blood pressure than Caucasians.

WHEN TO CALL THE DOCTOR

- If you have a sudden weight change
- If you have palpitations
- If you have swelling in your extremities
- If you become dizzy or unsteady
- If you have sudden, severe headaches
- If you develop chest pain or a cough that does not go away

MILLIONS OF MILLIGRAMS OF SODIUM

(These are approximations since each brand may differ.)
10 olives=820 mg
10 soda crackers=310 mg
1 cup vegetable bouillon= 900 mg
1 cup vegetable soup= 820 mg
1 cup tomato sauce= 730 mg
(Remember, the maximum recommended daily allowance of salt is 2,400 mg)

Heredity. If high blood pressure runs in your family, then you have an increased chance of developing it.

Alcohol use. Heavy drinking increases blood pressure.

Sodium consumption. Too much salt in your diet will do you in if you're sodium sensitive.

A sedentary lifestyle. Couch potatoes are at an increased risk for hypertension.

Pregnancy. Some expectant mothers experience elevated blood pressure.

Oral contraceptives. Some women who take birth control pills develop hypertension, especially if other risk factors are also present.

What to Look For

Hypertension is known as "the silent killer" because it has no or few obvious symptoms. The symptoms that it does present are shared by other diseases and conditions. But if you have any of these symptoms, be sure to have your blood pressure checked to rule out high blood pressure:

• Frequent or severe headaches

• Unexplained fatigue

• Dizziness

• Flushing of the face

• Ringing in the ears

• Thumping in the chest

• Frequent nosebleeds

Diagnosis

Finding out whether you have high blood pressure is simple. You just need to have your blood pressure checked by a doctor, nurse, or other health professional. Oftentimes you can even find blood-pressure-check booths at your local mall or at the pharmacy. The blood pressure test is simple, quick, and painless, but the results can save your life.

A blood pressure reading is given in two numbers, one over the other. The higher (systolic) number represents the pressure while the heart is beating, indicating how hard your heart has to beat to get that blood moving. The lower (diastolic) number represents the pressure when the heart is resting between beats.

AMERICAN HEART ASSOCIATION RECOMMENDED BLOOD PRESSURE LEVELS			
BLOOD PRESSURE CATEGORY	SYSTOLIC (MM HG)	DIASTOLIC (MM HG)	FOLLOW-UP RECOMMENDED
Optimal	less than 120*	and less than 80*	Recheck in 2 years
Normal	less than 130	and less than 85	Recheck in 2 years
High normal	130–139	or 85–89	Recheck in 1 year
High			
Stage 1 (mild)	140–159	or 90–99	Confirm within 2 months
Stage 2 (moderate)	160–179	or 100–109	Evaluate within 1 month
Stage 3 (severe)	180 or higher	or 110 or higher	Evaluate immediately

*Your doctor should evaluate unusually low readings.

Blood pressure of less than 140 (systolic) over 90 (diastolic) is considered a normal reading for adults, according to the AHA, while a reading equal to or greater than 140 over 90 is considered elevated (high). A systolic pressure of 130 to 139 or a diastolic pressure of 85 to 89 needs to be watched carefully.

The key to controlling high blood pressure is knowing you have it. Under the guidance of a physician, you can battle hypertension through diet, exercise, lifestyle changes, and medication, if necessary. The kitchen holds several blood pressure helpers.

FROM THE COUNTER

BANANA. The banana has been proved to help reduce blood pressure. The average person needs three to four servings of potassium-rich fruits and vegetables each day. Some experts believe doubling this amount may benefit your blood pressure. If bananas aren't your favorite bunch of fruit, try dried apricots, raisins, currants, orange juice, spinach, boiled potatoes with skin, baked sweet potatoes, cantaloupe, and winter squash.

TASTY, NOT SALTY

Americans nearly preserve themselves with salt. The average American consumes between 3,000 and 6,000 mg of sodium each day. (The maximum intake suggested is 2,400 mg, which is about the amount in a level teaspoon of salt.)

A diet high in salt, or sodium chloride, is directly linked to high blood pressure in salt-sensitive individuals, so start on the road to lower blood pressure by waving bye-bye to the saltshaker. There are several salt-free substitutes you can purchase, or you can make your own salt-free substitute that will spice up your meals without compromising your health. See the Recipe Box on page 178.

FROM THE CUPBOARD

BREADS. Be good to your blood with a bit more "B," as in the B vitamin folate. Swimming around the blood is a substance called homocysteine,

SALT-FREE HERB BLEND

5 teaspoons onion powder

2½ teaspoons sweet paprika

2½ teaspoons garlic powder

2½ teaspoons dry mustard

1½ teaspoons dried thyme

1 teaspoon black pepper

¼ teaspoon celery seed

1 teaspoon cayenne pepper (optional)

Combine ingredients and mix well. Spoon into a shaker.

Makes ⅓ cup

which at high levels is thought to reduce the stretching ability of the arteries. If the arteries are stiff as a board, the heart pumps extra hard to move the blood around. Folate helps reduce the levels of homocysteine, in turn helping arteries become pliable. You'll find folate in fortified breads and cereals, asparagus, brussels sprouts, and beans.

CANOLA, MUSTARD SEED, OR SAFFLOWER OILS. Switching to polyunsaturated oils can make a big difference in your blood pressure readings. Switching to them will also reduce your blood cholesterol level.

FROM THE REFRIGERATOR

BROCCOLI. This vegetable is high in fiber, and a high-fiber diet is known to help reduce blood pressure. So indulge in this and other fruits and vegetables that are high in fiber.

CELERY. Because it contains high levels of 3-N-butylphthalide, a phytochemical that helps lower blood pressure, celery is in a class by itself. This phytochemical is not found in most other vegetables. Celery may also reduce stress hormones that constrict blood vessels, so it may be most effective in those whose high blood pressure is the result of mental stress.

MILK. The calcium in milk does more than build strong bones; it plays a modest role in preventing high blood pressure. Be sure to drink skim milk or eat low fat yogurt. Leafy green vegetables also provide calcium.

FROM THE SPICE RACK

CAYENNE PEPPER. This fiery spice is a popular home treatment for mild high blood pressure. Cayenne pepper allows smooth blood flow by preventing platelets from clumping together and accumulating in the blood. Add some cayenne pepper to the salt-free seasonings listed in the

Recipe Box, opposite, or add a dash to a salad or in salt-free soups.

FROM THE SUPPLEMENT SHELF

VITAMIN C. An antioxidant, vitamin C helps prevent free radicals from damaging artery walls, and it may help improve high blood pressure. Take a supplement or eat vitamin C-rich foods.

MORE DO'S AND DON'TS

- Do aerobic exercise. Aerobic exercise that elevates your pulse and sustains the elevation for at least 20 minutes will help reduce your blood pressure if you do it several times a week. It will also help you lose weight, which will help lower your blood pressure. Check with your doctor before starting an exercise program if you've been sedentary.

- Avoid strength-training exercise, such as weight lifting, unless you first consult with your doctor. This kind of exercise can be dangerous for people with hypertension.

- Lose the saltshaker. Although there is some debate about salt's role in high blood pressure, most experts agree that cutting back on salt intake can reduce blood pressure.

- Quit smoking. Smoking causes blood pressure to rise, and it increases your risk of stroke.

- Skip processed foods. Not only are they loaded with sodium (salt) but they are also high in saturated (read: artery-clogging) fat.

SALT WEARS MANY DISGUISES

Sodium chloride isn't the only name for salt. Soda or sodium also indicate the presence of salt. Look closely at labels for these sources of salt:

- Monosodium glutamate (MSG) is a popular flavor enhancer in restaurant cooking and in packaged and canned foods and seasoning mixes.
- Baking soda (sodium bicarbonate or bicarbonate of soda) and baking powder are often used to leaven breads and cakes.
- Disodium phosphate is found in some quick-cooking cereals and processed cheeses.
- Sodium alginate is what makes ice cream smooth.
- Sodium benzoate is used as a preservative in many condiments.
- Sodium hydroxide is used to soften and loosen the skins of ripe olives and certain fruits and vegetables.
- Sodium nitrate is used to cure meats and sausages.
- Sodium propionate helps inhibit the growth of molds in baked goods.
- Sodium sulfite is used to bleach foods that will then be colored or glazed. It's also used as a preservative in some dried fruits.

High Cholesterol

LOWERING THE NUMBERS

Cholesterol is that waxy, soft stuff that floats around in your bloodstream as well as in all the cells in your body. It takes a bad rap these days because the word cholesterol strikes fear in the hearts of even the healthiest of people.

Having cholesterol in your blood is normal and even healthy because it's used in the formation of cell membranes, tissues, and essential hormones. So, in proper amounts, cholesterol is good. In excessive amounts, though, it can clog the arteries leading to your heart and cause coronary disease, heart attack, or stroke.

Cholesterol comes from two sources: the foods you eat and your very own liver. And the truth of the matter is, your liver can produce all the cholesterol your body will ever need. This means that what you get in your food isn't necessary. Some people get rid of extra cholesterol easily through normal bodily waste mechanisms, but others hang on to it because their bodies just aren't as efficient in removing it, which puts them at risk.

So, what makes people prone to high blood cholesterol?

• Family history

• Eating too many foods high in saturated fats

• Diabetes

• Kidney and liver disorders

• Alcoholism

• Obesity

• Smoking

• Stress

FASCINATING FACT
Every one-percent reduction in cholesterol levels produces a two-percent reduction in heart disease risk.

Good and Bad Cholesterol?

There are two different kinds of cholesterol, and yes, one's good and one's bad. Cholesterol can't get around on its own, so it hitches a ride from lipoproteins to get to the body's cells. Problem is, there are two different rigs picking it up: One is called HDL, or high-density lipoprotein; the other is called LDL, or low-density lipoprotein. HDL is the good ride; it travels away from your arteries. LDL is the bad ride; it heads straight to your arteries. Bottom line: HDL is what you want more of; you want less of LDL.

High cholesterol can be cured two ways: by medication and/or by diet. There are numerous effective drugs on the market that will make drastic reductions in cholesterol levels, but they all come with side effects and require frequent blood tests to monitor for possible problems. But there are kitchen cures, and they may work on their own or along with conventional treatment. Whatever your cure, it must come with advice from your doctor since your heart is at risk.

FROM THE COUNTER

GARLIC. Studies show that garlic may not only reduce LDL but raise HDL and decrease the amount of fat in your blood. Add some fresh garlic regularly to your cooking to keep your heart healthy.

FROM THE CUPBOARD

ALMONDS. Studies indicate that snacking on almonds regularly for as little as three weeks may decrease LDL by up to ten percent.

HONEY. Add 1 teaspoon honey to 1 cup hot water in the morning, and you may rid your system of excess fat and cholesterol, according to Ayurvedic medicine. Add 1 teaspoon lime juice or 10 drops cider vinegar to give that drink a more powerful cholesterol-fighting punch.

OATS. In any pure form, oats are a traditional cholesterol buster. Eating only

WHEN TO CALL THE DOCTOR

Call 9-1-1 for:

- Crushing chest pain, possibly accompanied by nausea, vomiting, shortness of breath, sweating, weakness
- Dull chest pain or a feeling of tightness or heavy pressure
- Pain that starts in the chest, possibly radiating to the arms and jaw
- Symptoms of stroke: loss of speech, balance or coordination problems, sudden weakness or paralysis on one side of the body, sudden vision problems, numbness in your extremities

Call the doctor for:

- Weakness or pain in the buttocks, legs, or feet during exertion
- Cold feet that never warm up
- Leg or foot sores that won't heal
- Discolored skin on legs and feet
- Sharp, sudden leg or foot pain during rest

FASCINATING FACT

The egg yolk has 213 mg of cholesterol, but the white has 0. In recipes that call for an egg, cut out the cholesterol by using 2 egg whites in place of 1 whole egg.

CHOLESTEROL COUNTER

- The average American male gets 337 mg cholesterol a day from the food he eats.
- The average American female gets 217 mg cholesterol a day from the food she eats.
- The American Heart Association recommends limiting cholesterol from food to no more than 300 mg. For people with coronary disease, that recommendation drops to less than 200 mg of cholesterol a day.

FASCINATING FACT

- 20 percent of all Americans have high blood cholesterol.
- 33 percent have borderline high levels.

½ cup oatmeal a day, along with a low fat diet, may reduce cholesterol levels by nine percent.

RICE. The oil that comes from the bran of rice lowers cholesterol. And brown rice is particularly high in fiber, which is essential in a cholesterol-lowering diet. One cup provides 11 percent of the daily fiber requirement.

SOYBEANS. These may reduce LDL by as much as 20 percent when 25 to 50 grams of soy protein are eaten daily for as short a time as a month. Soy may also fend off a rise in LDL in people with normal levels and improve the ability of arteries to dilate, which allows the unimpeded passage of fats and other substances that otherwise might cause a blockage.

WALNUTS. A cholesterol-lowering diet that includes walnuts eaten at least four times a week may lower LDL by as much as 16 percent. And studies indicate that those who munch on these nuts regularly cut their risk of death by heart attack in half when compared to non-walnut munchers.

FROM THE DRAWER

CALCULATOR. Add up those cholesterol milligrams daily to see how you're doing.

NOTEBOOK. Chart your daily diet.

NUTRITION & FOOD GUIDE. Use it to gauge the cholesterol content of the foods you eat. Record the results.

FROM THE REFRIGERATOR

ALFALFA SPROUTS. These may improve or normalize cholesterol levels.

Warning! Sprouts are not clean or washed when you buy them in the store and may be a source of *E. coli* bacteria. Wash them thoroughly before using them or use a veggie-cleaning product on them.

APPLES. Apples are high in pectin, which can lower cholesterol levels.

ARTICHOKES. These veggies can actually lower cholesterol levels. Early studies pointed to their cholesterol-busting properties, but recent studies have shown that artichokes may be even more effective than first thought.

BEETS. Full of carotenoids and flavonoids, beets help lower—and may even prevent—the formation of LDL, the bad cholesterol.

CARROTS. They're full of pectin and good at lowering cholesterol levels.

OLIVE OIL. It protects your heart by lowering LDL, raising HDL, and preventing your blood from forming clots.

PEARS. These are high in soluble fiber, which helps regulate cholesterol levels.

RHUBARB. Yep, this is a cholesterol-buster. Consume it after a meal that's heavy in fats. You can cook it in a double boiler, with a little honey or maple syrup for added sweetness, until done. Add cardamom or vanilla if you like.

YOGURT. Eating 1 cup plain yogurt with active cultures a day may reduce LDL by 4 percent or more and total cholesterol by at least 3 percent. Some scientists believe that eating yogurt regularly may even reduce the overall risk of heart disease by as much as 10 percent.

CHOLESTEROL BY THE NUMBERS

The numbers can be confusing, especially if your doctor rushes you through the explanation, so here are the numbers you need to know, and what they mean:

TOTAL BLOOD CHOLESTEROL LEVEL

Desirable level: Less than 200 mg/dL. Your heart attack risk from cholesterol-related problems is relatively low.

Borderline high risk: 200–239 mg/dL. You have twice the risk of heart attack as people whose levels fall under 200 mg/dL.

High risk: 240 mg/dL. Your risk of both heart attack and stroke is greater.

LDL CHOLESTEROL LEVEL (THE BAD STUFF)

129 mg/dL or less: Desirable.

130–159 mg/dL: Borderline high risk.

160 mg/dL or higher: High risk.

HDL CHOLESTEROL LEVEL (THE GOOD STUFF)

In men: 40–50 mg/dL is average.

In women: 50–60 mg/dL is average.

Less than 40 mg/dL: too low. The lower the HDL the more you are at risk.

CHOLESTEROL RATIO:

Some doctors prefer to tell you the absolute numbers for total blood cholesterol. Others prefer to tell you the ratio, which is dividing the HDL into the total cholesterol count. The goal is to keep the ratio below 5:1. The best ratio is 3.5:1.

TRIGLYCERIDES (FATS) Note: Triglycerides and cholesterol are not the same thing, but people with high triglycerides often have high cholesterol.

Less than 150 mg/dL: normal

150–199 mg/dL: borderline high

200–499 mg/dL: high

500 mg/dL or higher: very high

FAT FACT

The more liquid the margarine (tub, liquid form), the less hydrogenated it is and the less trans fatty acid it contains. Trans fatty acids raise total blood cholesterol levels, so the less of them you eat, the better off you are.

FROM THE SPICE RACK

TURMERIC. This may lower blood cholesterol.

MORE DO'S & DON'TS

- Don't grease those pans. Use a nonstick olive oil spray or buy an inexpensive oil mister in a kitchenwares store and make your own spray.

- Bulk up. Whole grains are high in fiber. Stick to complex carbohydrates, too, because they fill you up faster and leave you feeling satisfied. Try eating more fruits, veggies, pasta, rice.

- Exercise. Regular exercise can boost your HDL.

- Read the food labels. They list the cholesterol content, so keep your cholesterol goal in mind: less than 300 mg a day.

- Eat small meals. Instead of 3 big meals a day, go for 5 or 6 small meals. The body deals with cholesterol intake more efficiently when it comes in small amounts.

KNOW YOUR FATS

Good fats, bad fats, it's all so confusing. But if you're concerned about your cholesterol levels, you've got to know your fats.

Saturated fat. This is the main dietary cause of high blood cholesterol. It is found in animal foods, including beef, beef fat, veal, pork, lard, poultry fat, butter, cream, cheese, and whole-milk dairy products. And it is also found in plant foods, including coconut oil, palm oil, palm kernel oil, and cocoa butter. This is a bad fat, so limit your saturated fat intake to 7 to 10 percent (or less) of your total calories per day.

Hydrogenated fat. This fat is the result of chemical processing that some fats undergo. It is found in margarine and shortening. A bad fat, it may raise blood cholesterol. Use it only if it contains no more than 2 g/tablespoon of saturated fat.

Polyunsaturated fat. This is an unsaturated fat. It is found in safflower, sunflower, and sesame seeds; corn; soybeans, nuts; seeds—and oils from these seeds. It's a good fat and may help you lower blood cholesterol levels when used instead of saturated fats.

Monounsaturated fat. This is an unsaturated fat that's found in canola, olive, and peanut oils, and in avocados. A good fat, it may help lower your blood cholesterol level if eaten in place of saturated fats.

Trans fatty acids (TFA). These fats are either the result of a chemical process that allows foods to stay fresh longer or one that produces a solid fat product. They are found in margarine and in commercial products: fried foods, baked goods, and commercial shortening. These are bad fats! They raise total blood cholesterol and LDL, and they lower HDL. Limit your daily intake of fats and oils to 5 to 8 teaspoons to avoid excess trans fatty acids.

Hives
CATCHING THE CULPRIT

You decide to make two special batches of
birthday brownies for your office—one
with nuts and one without because one of
your coworkers has a nut allergy. But to
save on dishwashing, you bake both
batches in the same pan. Big mistake!
About an hour after eating your nut-free
brownies, red spots begin radiating up the
arm and neck of your nut-sensitive
coworker. The essence of walnuts left in the
unwashed baking pan was enough to spark
a mild allergic reaction. You remind yourself to fix cheesecake next time there's a
birthday bash.

Hives, Histamine, and You

When you eat a food that you're allergic to, your body reacts by producing histamine. Histamine can do all sorts of things in the body in
response to an allergen, such as making your eyes water or your tongue
or throat swell. But in the case of hives, histamine causes blood vessels to
leak blood plasma into the skin. This blood leakage comes to the surface,
causing inflammation and itching, and lucky you, you've got a case of
hives.

Hives, whose technical name is urticaria, can be as tiny as a dot or as
big as a dinner plate. They have very defined edges and are usually irregularly shaped. If you've ever had hives, you know that though the
swelling can be uncomfortable, it's the itching that drives you bonkers.
The good news is hives usually run their course in a couple of hours.
Sometimes, though, they can last as long as a couple of days. If they last
longer than that, you should contact your doctor.

Those Annoying Allergens

Because hives are an allergic reaction, your best bet in preventing
future flare-ups is finding the source of the problem. You'll need to do a
little detective work to figure out what caused your itchy bumps. But if
you can't put your finger on the culprit, you're not alone: About 50
percent of the time the trigger is undetermined. To help your investiga-
tion along, here's a look at the primary causes of hives. Perhaps you'll be

WHEN TO CALL THE DOCTOR

Most hives run their course within a couple of days. But if you have any of the following symptoms, head to your doctor's office or the closest emergency room:

- Significant swelling around your face and throat
- Nausea or dizziness
- Difficulty breathing
- Fever
- Weight loss
- Fatigue and lethargy
- Hives that come and go for six weeks or more

lucky and discover the source of your itchy bumps below:

Foods. Certain foods are more likely to cause a heaping helping of hives. Strawberries are a problem for many people because they promote the production of histamine in the body. Other well-known hive producers are nuts, chocolate, fish, tomatoes, eggs, fresh berries, and milk. If you're going to have an itchy reaction to food, it will probably happen within 30 minutes of eating it.

Food additives. Food colorings, flavorings, preservatives, and emulsifiers or stabilizers can cause a hive outbreak. If you think food additives might be the reason your skin's so red, look for ingredients such as salicylates, sulfites, and polysorbate on the label of any processed foods you've eaten.

Medications. Penicillin and aspirin are the two most common drug offenders. Penicillin and other antibiotics are the number one cause of drug-related hives.

Heat. Getting too hot by spending too much time outside on a summer day or by exercising are two causes of heat-induced hives. Sometimes known as "prickly heat," these heat-related hives calm down as your body temperature returns to normal.

Cold. Sticking your arm in ice-cold water may cause cold-induced hives. These hives happen when you're exposed to cold objects or water, or even when you step outside on a cold, blustery day. Like heat-related hives, these will disappear once your body temperature normalizes.

Insect bites or stings. Components of insect venom are allergenic. Some people have a systemic (bodywide) reaction to these components that produces hives.

Infections. Bacterial, viral, and yeast infections can cause an outbreak of hives. Fever is also related to hive production.

Everyday objects. Sometimes hives simply happen from pressure on the skin; from contact with everyday objects such as furniture, towels, watch bands, or bedsheets; or from wearing clothing that's too tight.

Stress. Many people find that stress triggers an episode of hives.

Diseases. Hives can be a symptom of thyroid disease, hepatitis, lupus, and even some cancers. That's why you shouldn't ignore a lingering case of the hives.

What Are Your Chances of Bumping Into Hives?

If you've never had a run-in with the itchy inflammation, you've got a 20 percent chance that you'll end up with it at some time in your life. Young adults are most likely to get hives. Children and adults are at the same risk for getting the itchy red patches, but from different sources. Kids seem to get hives from food allergies or infections, while adults tend to break out in hives in reaction to a medication.

Whether or not you can uncover the source of your hives, there are some items in your kitchen that can help relieve your symptoms while you're investigating.

FROM THE CUPBOARD

BAKING SODA. Add ½ to 1 cup baking soda to a warm bath to soothe your itching.

HERBAL TEA. De-stress yourself by relaxing with a soothing cup of herbal tea.

OATMEAL. Add 1 to 2 cups finely ground oatmeal to a warm bath (not hot or you might have breakfast for the next month in your tub) to ease your itches.

FROM THE DRAWER

OVEN MITTS. Putting something on your hands can keep you from scratching. Cotton gloves are a good option, as are oven mitts. Tape them at the wrist, and you'll be less tempted to remove them to start scratching. If you wear the gloves to bed at night, you won't do damage if you scratch your itches unconsciously.

FROM THE FREEZER

ICE. An ice pack helps shrink blood vessels, which alleviates swelling. Put the compress, wrapped in a thin towel, on your skin for five minutes, three or four times a day.

FROM THE REFRIGERATOR

MILK. Calm your hives with a milk compress. Wet a cloth with cold milk and put it on your skin for 10 to 15 minutes.

FROM THE SPICE RACK

ASAFOETIDA. This cousin of onions and garlic may help relieve your hives. Look for asafoetida powder in the spice section of your grocery

---

FASCINATING FACT

Hives are usually worse at night.

BRING OUT HIVES

Hives in a young baby are considered to be a good sign in traditional African American folk medicine. The hives, according to this tradition, are a sign that impurities are being released.

PLAYING DETECTIVE

Many allergists recommend keeping a journal to help uncover the source of your hives. Every day, record the foods you eat, your activities, the places you go, medications you've taken, and any exposure to animals and insects. If you break out in hives, be sure to write down the time of day and where you are as well as a description of them (how many, how large, where on your body, and how long they last). After keeping your daily journal for a week or two, you may be able to pinpoint the cause of your hives.

store. Add ¼ teaspoon asafoetida powder to 4 tablespoons castor oil and mix well. Apply the solution directly to your hives. Be sure to do this when you won't be seeing anyone for a few hours. Asafoetida makes you smell like a piece of garlic.

BASIL. The Chinese believe bathing in basil tea is a good antidote for hives. Put 1 ounce dried basil in a 1-quart jar and fill the jar with boiling water. Let cool to room temperature and use it as a wash.

FROM THE SUPPLEMENT SHELF

VITAMIN C. High doses of vitamin C have been found to lower histamine levels. This may ward off an attack of the hives. Taking at least 2,000 mg a day is necessary to alter histamine levels. Check with your doctor before loading up on vitamin C. Too much of this valuable nutrient can cause kidney stones and diarrhea.

MORE DO'S AND DON'TS

• Calm down. Emotional stress has been known to spark a case of hives. But even if stress isn't the cause, worrying about your hives can make the pain and itching worse. Relax: Your hives will heal shortly.

• Take an over-the-counter antihistamine. It can keep your hives from spreading and lessen the severity of itching and swelling. Since most antihistamines make you very, very sleepy, take one of the newer nondrowsy antihistamine products if you're planning on dosing and driving.

• Ignore the itch. Sure that's easier said than done, but scratching can increase swelling and may cause your hives to spread.

• Consider cortisone. Using an over-the-counter 1 percent cortisone preparation may help.

• Leave the lotions alone. Nonprescription anti-itch lotions can cause an allergic reaction, making your itching more irritating.

• Get loose. Wearing clothes that are too tight can induce a case of hives. Try loosening up waistbands, bra straps, or other clothing that is snug.

Incontinence
CHECKING THE FLOW

Laughter is the best medicine, unless, of course, it causes you to wet your pants. Then it's no laughing matter. The leaking of urine that occurs when laughing, exercising, coughing, sneezing, or lifting heavy objects is called incontinence and varies by degree. No matter if it is a small leak or a major plumbing disaster, incontinence is an embarrassing problem to an estimated 12 to 20 million Americans, the majority of them women.

What Causes the Leak?
The causes of incontinence may be as minor as an infection triggered by a cold, bladder irritation, constipation, or the use of certain medications. In women, incontinence is often the result of sagging pelvic-floor muscles. These muscles at the bottom of the pelvis support the lower internal organs and help them maintain their shape and proper function. Childbirth and certain types of surgery, such as a hysterectomy, can cause these muscles to weaken, allowing urine to squeeze out at the most inappropriate times.

WHEN TO CALL THE DOCTOR
• If you experience frequent leakage

There are four main types of incontinence. They are:

Stress incontinence. This type occurs from rigorous or spontaneous activity such as jumping, running, coughing, laughing, or sneezing.

Urge incontinence. This type is marked by a sudden need to urinate. The person loses urine as soon as there is a strong need to use the toilet. Often the bathroom is one step too far away.

Overflow incontinence. This is a full bladder that starts leaking.

Reflex incontinence. This type is marked by lack of awareness of the need to urinate, resulting in leakage.

Fortunately, most types of incontinence can be solved, especially by doing pelvic-floor exercises recommended by your doctor. In addition, there are several home remedies to help you remain dry and free from embarrassment.

FROM THE CUPBOARD

VINEGAR. A person prone to leakage is also at risk for developing irritated skin from the wetness. Always clean damp areas with plain soap and water, followed by a rinse of diluted vinegar to disinfect and control odors. For a quick cleanup, keep a bottle of diluted vinegar and cotton balls close to the toilet.

FROM THE REFRIGERATOR

JUICE. Grape, cranberry, cherry, and apple juices are not irritating to the bladder and may help control the odor of your urine. They may also help diminish urinary tract infections.

FROM THE SINK

WATER. Drink to your bladder! Cozy on up to the sink and down a glass of water. Sounds strange, considering the bladder is leaking, but being well hydrated actually helps. If you cut back on fluid intake, you may become dehydrated, resulting in constipation. This, in turn, irritates nerves that may trigger the bladder to let loose. Schedule water consumption so you can regulate the fullness of your bladder. Stick to the recommended eight 8-ounce glasses of water each day.

MORE DO'S AND DON'TS

- Stop smoking. Nicotine irritates the bladder, and a smoker's hack only increases problems with leakage.

- Maintain your normal weight. Adding more pounds puts more pressure on the pelvic-floor muscles, causing them to sag or weaken.

- Keep pelvic-floor muscles in shape by regularly doing strengthening exercises.

- Empty your bladder before going on long trips or watching long movies.

- Wear clothing that is easy to take off.

HOW TO CURE URINE STAINS

Urine accidents on clothing should be cleaned immediately. First rinse the clothing with warm water. Then mix 3 tablespoons white vinegar and 1 teaspoon liquid soap. Apply the mixture to the stained area, and leave it on for 15 minutes. Rinse the clothing well and dry.

THE EVER-EXPANDING BLADDER

The normal bladder holds about 2 cups of fluid. Normal bladder function is considered to be urinating every 2 to 5 hours during the day (seven to nine times per day) and up to one time at night before 65 years of age and one to two times a night after 65.

Insomnia/Sleep Disorders
Reclaiming Your Rest

The house is completely quiet. The kids are in bed. Your hubby is sawing logs. But you are staring at the ceiling listening to the fan hum. You've tried everything: counting sheep, counting dots on the ceiling, reading *War and Peace,* watching old sitcoms. But nothing is working. So you resign yourself to another dreary day of being a poster child for the walking dead.

Thirty to forty million Americans have some sort of trouble sleeping. There are more than 60 sleep disorders that plague men and women, from sleep apnea to restless legs syndrome. The number one sleep problem for men and women is insomnia. The National Sleep Foundation reports that 48 percent of Americans have insomnia occasionally, and 22 percent deal with sleeplessness almost every night. This wouldn't be such an unsettling statistic if lack of sleep was no big deal. But your body and mind need to shut down for a while at the end of the day.

Insufferable Insomnia

Insomnia can be classified in one of three ways—trouble falling asleep (called sleep-onset insomnia), trouble staying asleep (called sleep-maintenance insomnia), or waking up feeling groggy and sleepy after what should have been a full night's sleep. Most episodes of insomnia last anywhere from a couple of nights to a few weeks. There are myriad causes, including stress, anxiety, depression, disease, pain, medications, or simply not creating a relaxing sleep routine.

There's no magic number when it comes to how many hours you should sleep. Some people get by just fine on a few hours, and some

> ### WHEN TO CALL THE DOCTOR
> - If your sleep problems last for three weeks
> - If your sleep problems impact your ability to function during the day
> - If you continually have to get up several times a night to urinate
> - If you can't stay in bed because you need to keep moving your legs

WHEN YOUR LEGS WANT TO DO SOME WALKING . . . BUT YOU WANT TO SLEEP

Restless legs syndrome is a frustrating condition. The name of the problem explains it all. When you finally get into bed, your legs decide it's time to get up and move. The symptoms of restless legs syndrome have been described as tingling, crawling, or prickling sensations that peak during times of inactivity, such as when you're trying to go to sleep. Walking, massaging your legs, or taking a hot shower can help relieve the problem for a bit, but it'll come back, leaving you with a sleep-deprived night. Restless legs syndrome has been connected with a deficiency in iron and folic acid. The problem worsens with age and is more frequently diagnosed in people over 65. It can be treated with prescription medicines.

people need more than eight. But it won't be a mystery to you if you're not getting enough sleep. Waking up exhausted and being sleepy most of the day are signs that you're not well-rested.

Suffering Through Sleepless Nights

Women are 1.3 times more likely to experience insomnia than men. And if you're more than 65 years of age, you're 1.5 times more likely to have trouble sleeping than someone younger. Having problems in your marriage makes you more likely to have insomnia, as do hormonal changes such as those that occur during menopause, menstruation, and pregnancy.

Insomnia's Ill Effects

Insomnia can have a significant impact on your health and well-being. If you don't get enough sleep, you're setting yourself up for some serious problems. People with insomnia are

• Four times more likely to be diagnosed with depression.

• More likely to have a serious illness, including heart disease.

• More likely to have an accident on the job, at home, or on the road.

• More likely to miss work and accomplish less on the job than well-rested coworkers.

FROM THE CUPBOARD

COOKIES. Yes, that comforting nighttime snack of milk and cookies may be just what the doctor ordered. Sugary foods eaten about 30 minutes before bedtime can actually act as a sedative, and you can wake up without the morning fuzziness that accompanies synthetic sleeping pills. Be careful to eat only a few cookies, though; eating too much sugar can keep the sandman at bay.

EPSOM SALTS. Naturopathic practitioners recommend this remedy for sleepless nights. Add 1 to 2 cups Epsom salts to a hot bath and soak for about 15 to 20 minutes before hitting the hay.

HONEY. Folk remedies often advise people with sleeping difficulty to eat a little honey. It has the same sedative effect as sugar and may get you to bed more quickly. Try adding 1 tablespoon honey to some decaffeinated herbal tea or even to your warm milk for a relaxing pre-sleep drink.

TOAST. High-carbohydrate, low-protein bedtime snacks tend to be easy on the tummy and can ease the brain into blissful slumber.

FROM THE REFRIGERATOR

MILK. Drinking a glass of milk, especially a glass of warm milk, before bedtime is an age-old treatment for sleeping troubles. There is some debate, however, about what it is in milk—if anything—that helps cause slumber. Some scientists believe it's the presence of tryptophan, a chemical that helps the brain ease into sleep mode, that does the trick. Others believe it may be another ingredient, a soothing group of opiatelike chemicals called casomorphins. Whatever the reason, milk seems to help some people hit the sack more easily. And warm milk seems to be more effective at relaxing body and mind. Other foods that are high on the

HERBS THAT HELP YOU SLEEP

Sleep problems have been around since biblical times, so it's no wonder that there are many, many botanical remedies for insomnia.

Here are a few of the most common.

Chamomile. Chamomile tea is one of the most popular sleep-inducing drinks on the market. It's best used for sleep problems due to upset stomach. To brew your own chamomile tea: Put 1 heaping tablespoon chamomile flowers in a cup. Add boiling water, cover, and let steep for ten minutes.

Ginseng. Drinking a ginseng wine may help sleepless nights, especially if they're related to stress or a fever-producing illness. Chop 3½ ounces ginseng (use only American ginseng) and place in 1 quart liquor, such as vodka. Let it stand for five to six weeks in a cool, dark place. Turn the container frequently. Take 1 ounce before bed.

Lavender. Lavender's scent is so calming that in one study it was actually as potent as a tranquilizer. In Germany, where herbs are prescribed for medical conditions, doctors often give lavender for insomnia. Buy lavender essential oil at natural food stores.

Valerian. In the United States, this herb was listed as a sedative until the late 19th century. Studies have found it's as effective as Valium in some people, but it can act as a stimulant in others. Use cautiously. Valerian is often combined with another herb, such as hops, to avoid overstimulating effects.

Other herbs that might help you catch some ZZZs are catnip, cinnamon, clove, hops, juniper, pine, passionflower, peppermint, sage, and skullcap. For the most relaxing effect, drink them in warm teas. Drink ½ cup an hour before bedtime and a second dose right before you hit the sack.

SELLING SLEEP

Over-the-counter (OTC) sleep aids can be helpful for occasional sleeplessness, but be sure to use them properly. Many OTC sleep aids contain antihistamines, which are medications typically used to clear up stuffy noses. Sleepiness is a side effect of antihistamines, which is why they are included in sleep aids. Just because these medications are available over the counter doesn't mean they're safe. They can have side effects, and adverse reactions do occur. Here are some safety recommendations:

- Don't combine OTC sleep aids with alcohol or other prescription or nonprescription drugs containing sedatives.
- Be cautious if you are older and want to take an OTC sleep aid. Slower metabolism could mean the effect lasts longer than you want it to.
- Certain medical conditions may not mix well with a sedative. If you have breathing problems, glaucoma, chronic bronchitis, or an enlarged prostate, or if you're pregnant or nursing, skip the OTC sleep helpers.

tryptophan scale include cottage cheese, cashews, chicken, turkey, soybeans, and tuna.

FROM THE SPICE RACK

DILL SEED. Though scientists haven't proved its worth, this herb is often used as a folk cure for insomnia in China. Its essential oil has the most sedative-producing properties.

FROM THE SUPPLEMENT SHELF

5-HTP. Some experts believe a tryptophan deficiency can cause problems with sleep. Made from tryptophan, 5-HTP helps the body make serotonin. Low levels of serotonin are a known factor in sleepless nights. Taking a 5-HTP supplement may be a benefit if your body has low levels of tryptophan. How do you know if you're low? Low levels of tryptophan are most common in people who are depressed. If your insomnia is associated with depression, it might be a good question to ask your doctor. In one study, 100 mg of the supplement was enough to make sleep longer and better.

MELATONIN. Melatonin is a hormone that regulates your biological clock. As you get older you make less melatonin, which experts believe is probably why older folks have more trouble sleeping. Research is showing that taking a melatonin supplement can help you sleep. Ask your doctor about taking 1 to 3 mg of melatonin 1½ to 2 hours before bedtime.

MORE DO'S AND DON'TS

- Nix the nap. People who have trouble falling asleep or staying asleep shouldn't try to sleep during the day. If you simply must have some rest, take a nap for no longer than 30 minutes early in the afternoon.
- Cut out the caffeine. Caffeine, by its nature, stimulates your brain. When you're trying to snooze, caffeine can cause problems. Having a couple of

cups of coffee or a soda early in the day is fine, but switch to decaf after you eat lunch.

• Avoid alcohol. Yes, alcohol is a sedative, but the effects soon wear off and you'll end up tossing and turning.

• Get physical. Exercise does help you sleep better, but watch when you do it. Exercise too close to bedtime and you may be too keyed up to rest. Try that early afternoon salsa class.

• Take it easy on yourself. Don't try so hard to get to sleep. If the sandman doesn't come 30 minutes after hitting the sack, get up and go to another room. Read a book or watch TV, do something relaxing, and try again when you're feeling tired.

• Create bedtime bliss. Make your bedroom as dark, quiet, and peaceful as you can, and reserve the bed for sleep and sex only.

• Maintain a relaxing routine. Try to do the same things before turning in. Take a hot bath or read a book, whatever relaxes you. This will help your brain prepare for a peaceful night's sleep.

PAY ATTENTION TO APNEA

Your husband is having a Fred Flintstone moment. His snoring is so loud you keep waiting for the neighbors to complain. But just when you're about to elbow him into more peaceful slumber, you hear a gap in the noise. For a scary few seconds you notice he's not breathing at all. Your sweetie may have sleep apnea, a sleep disorder that affects more than 10 million Americans.

Sleep apnea literally takes your breath away. It's a condition in which there is prolonged lack of breathing or irregular breathing during sleep. The National Sleep Foundation divides sleep apnea into three categories: obstructive apnea, central apnea, and mixed apnea. Obstructive apnea happens when the back of the throat relaxes so much that it blocks the upper airway. Breathing stops for a few seconds, and catching that breath causes you to wake up (though you probably wouldn't remember waking up). This is the most common apnea and is the kind associated with obnoxious snoring. Central apnea happens when the diaphragm and chest muscles stop working. Again, you wake to catch a breath, but you probably wouldn't remember it either. You have mixed apnea if you experience both central and obstructive apnea at different times.

Middle-aged men and people who are overweight are more likely to have sleep apnea. Untreated, the condition can cause sleepiness during the day because of the constant awakening during the night. But sleep apnea can also cause high blood pressure and increase the risk of heart attacks and stroke.

Not everyone who snores has sleep apnea, but if you think you or your spouse might have it, see your doctor immediately.

Irritable Bowel Syndrome

CONQUERING CRAMPING

Does this sound familiar? You're enjoying the evening, having a nice meal at a nice restaurant, feeling pretty good. Coffee and dessert come and you're lingering over pleasant conversation, then all of a sudden wham! Out of the blue you've got a belly cramp, a gut gurgle that registers a 3.5 on the Richter scale. And suddenly you're off to find the nearest facility. There was no warning, no nothing. It just hit, and now your evening is on hold, changed, or canceled until you see how this latest attack resolves itself.

Irritable Bowel Syndrome (IBS) is a real condition, with real symptoms. (A decade ago it was one of those things doctors thought was just "in your head.") But it's a mysterious one to medical experts, who still don't know what it is or what causes it exactly. What they do know is that it's common—about 15 percent of all adults are afflicted with it sometime in their lives—and that it is a malfunction of the digestive tract.

Symptoms of irritable bowel syndrome include

• diarrhea or constipation, or alternate bouts of each

• abdominal pain or cramping

• gas and bloating

• nausea, especially after eating

• headache

• fatigue

• depression or anxiety

• mucus-covered stools

• the urge to have another bowel movement after you've just had one

What We Know

Irritable bowel syndrome is also called spastic colon. It's an apt name that describes the abnormal digestive function that's typical of IBS. Normally, food is pushed through the intestine by synchronized muscle contractions. They are all dancing the same dance. But then something happens and one of those dancers steps out of the chorus line, does its own dance, and messes up everybody else's rhythm. As a result, the food that's being passed down that chorus line is suddenly disrupted in its travel.

Why does the muscle contraction become unsynchronized? No one knows for sure. Stress and poor diet are at the top of the suspected culprit list, since the majority of people with IBS seem either to be stressed-out or to have poor dietary habits. But that's only a guess. The other triggers most likely to cause it are: food intolerance, abdominal operations, medications, and hormonal changes during menstruation.

IBS is frustrating and inconvenient, but it's not serious, even though it does stand shoulder to shoulder with the common cold as a major reason for people to miss work. But the good news is, IBS doesn't lead to other more serious intestinal conditions. And it can be treated with medications that relieve the symptoms. However, treatment isn't always easy, since the cause isn't known.

Regardless of the source of the problem, it does seem that there are some remedies for IBS symptoms right in your own kitchen.

> ### WHEN TO CALL THE DOCTOR
> - If you're experiencing pain in the left lower abdomen with fever
> - If bowel habits change in consistency, color, or frequency
> - If you're losing weight
> - If you find blood or mucus in your stools
> - If IBS symptoms interfere with your normal daily activities
> - If symptoms have just started

FROM THE CUPBOARD

OAT BRAN. Increasing fiber is a cure for almost every intestinal ill, and oat bran is especially good for IBS because it's mild and usually colon-friendly. So use some every day: a bowl of oatmeal, oat bran bread, oatmeal cookies. But don't expect immediate results. It may take up to a month to get any IBS relief.

FROM THE DRAWER

NOTEBOOK. Keep a food diary and track the foods that seem to trigger the attacks. Eliminate a specific food for a couple of weeks to see if that makes a difference. If it does, you may have isolated the cause. If not, go back to your food diary, then choose another food you've eaten around the time of an attack and eliminate it. This is called an exclusion diet, and if what you're eating is a trigger for IBS, this is the best way to find out what it is. Also make note of anxiety or stress you're feeling and what you think is causing it. If you notice that your attacks seem to come during stressful events, you may need to consider ways to eliminate them.

No-No Foods

You may have your own personal list of foods that cause your IBS flare-ups, but these are a common cause, too:

- Dairy products
- Cereals, especially wheat cereals
- Red kidney beans
- Lentils
- Peas
- Apples
- Grapes
- Raisins
- Brussels sprouts
- Broccoli
- Cauliflower
- Preserved, processed, or cured meats

From the Fridge

Cabbage. Juice of the cabbage soothes the symptoms of intestinal ills. To turn this veggie into juice, simply wash and put through a juicer or blender. If these are not available to you, cook the cabbage in a very small amount of water—just enough to keep it from scorching or burning—until very mushy. Then pulverize with a fork or mixer.

Carrots. These little gems help prevent the symptoms of IBS as well as regulate diarrhea and constipation. Eat them raw, by themselves or in salads, or eat them cooked—steamed and tossed with a little melted butter and brown sugar for a sweet treat. You can put raw carrots through the juicer, too. Since they're not a juicy veggie to begin with, add a little pure apricot nectar when you make carrot juice. Any way you eat a carrot is fine, just don't overcook them so much that you boil out all the goodness.

Lettuce. You can eat it raw to relieve symptoms of IBS, but it's especially helpful if lightly steamed. And when you're picking out your lettuce, go for the darker varieties. The darker the color, the more nutrients it contains.

Pears. Fresh, ripe, sweet pears are nutritious fruits that also help relieve the symptoms of IBS. Buy them when they're still hard and let them ripen at room temperature for a few days. Pure pear juice and dried pears are also helpful in treating this intestinal woe.

Yogurt. Yogurt with active cultures will supply your digestive tract with the helpful kind of bacteria, which can ease IBS symptoms. You can also try mixing 1 cup yogurt with ½ teaspoon psyllium husks (or psyllium bulk you can buy in any pharmacy) and eating the mixture one hour after meals.

From the Spice Rack

Fennel seeds. These can relieve the intestinal spasms associated with IBS. They may also aid in the elimination of fats from the digestive system, inhibiting the over-production of mucus in the intestine, which is a symptom of the ailment. Steep the seeds into a tea by adding ½ teaspoon fennel to 1 cup boiling water. Or add them to veggies such as carrots or cabbage, both of which soothe IBS symptoms. You can also sprinkle the seeds on salads or roast them and snack on them after a meal to reduce the symptoms of IBS and freshen your breath. To roast, spritz a baking sheet with olive oil, then cover with fennel seeds. Bake at 325°F for 10 to 15 minutes.

FLAXSEED. Make a tea using 1 teaspoon flaxseed per cup of water, and drink at bedtime for relief of symptoms.

PEPPERMINT. Steeped into a nice, relaxing tea, this can relieve intestinal spasms. Use 1 heaping teaspoon dried peppermint, and steep in 1 cup boiling water for ten minutes. Drink as often as necessary.

FASCINATING FACTS

- One-third of all people who have IBS claim that stress exacerbates the problem.
- Half of all people who have digestive complaints have IBS.
- More women have IBS than men, and they are especially prone to symptoms around the time of their menstrual period.

MORE DO'S & DON'TS

- Make sure you get enough fiber. It helps maintain good bowel function. You need about 35 grams a day. Chances are you're only getting about half of what you need.

- Limit alcohol and caffeine. They irritate your stomach lining, which can lead to IBS symptoms.

- Nix the tobacco. It can cause stomach cramps, among other deadly things.

- Skip the gassy foods. And try to eliminate air swallowing. The more gas you introduce into your intestine, the more likely you'll have a flare-up of IBS.

- Drink between meals, not with meals. Drinking when you eat dilutes digestive juices and frustrates digestion.

- Avoid anything that causes stress. Relax during mealtimes. Give yourself plenty of time to complete your tasks. Avoid the morning rush-rush hassle by getting up a few minutes earlier. Spend a few minutes alone, working on progressive relaxation.

- For cramping, try a hot bath. Or, apply hot compresses or a heating pad to your abdomen.

- Forget the artificial sweetener called sorbitol. It can cause bowel problems, including constipation.

- Exercise moderately. This will make the entire digestive system work better, but don't overdo it. In people with IBS, strenuous exercise can lead to symptoms.

Itching
SOOTHING WITHOUT SCRATCHING

To scratch or not to scratch, that is the question. When confronted with an itch, most of us tend to throw self-discipline out the door and scratch to our skin's content. While that may prove momentarily satisfying, scratching exces-

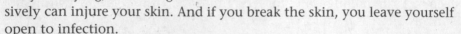

sively can injure your skin. And if you break the skin, you leave yourself open to infection.

Itching, medically known as pruritus, is caused by stimuli bugging some part of our skin. There are a lot of places to bother on the body, too. The average adult has 20 square feet (2 square meters) of skin, all open to the world of irritants. When something bothers our skin, an itch is a built-in defense mechanism that alerts the body that someone is knocking. We respond to an itch with a scratch, as most people want to remove the problem. But the scratching can also set you up for the "itch-scratch" cycle, where one leads to the other endlessly.

An itch can range from a mild nuisance to a disrupting, damaging, and sleep-depriving fiasco. Itches happen for many reasons, including allergic reactions; sunburns; insect bites; poison ivy; reactions to chemicals, soaps, and detergents; medication; dry weather; skin infections; and even aging. More serious itches, such as those caused by psoriasis or other diseases, are not covered here.

Scratching isn't the only solution to an itch. The kitchen cupboards hold a few more.

WHEN TO CALL THE DOCTOR

- If the itching is severe and lasts more than 24 hours
- If the skin is broken, blistered, or damaged by scratching
- If you are experiencing other symptoms with the itch, such as difficulty breathing, nausea, faintness

FROM THE CUPBOARD

BAKING SODA. Baking soda battles itches of all kinds. For widespread or hard-to-reach itches, soak in a baking soda bath. Add 1 cup baking soda to a tub of warm water. Soak for 30 to 60 minutes and air dry. Localized itches can be treated with a baking soda paste. Mix 3 parts baking soda and 1 part water. Apply to the itch, but do not use if the skin is broken.

OATMEAL. Add 1 to 2 cups finely ground oatmeal to a warm bath to ease your itches.

FROM THE REFRIGERATOR

LEMON. Many American folk remedy recipes call for using a lemon to treat itchy skin—and rightly so. The aromatic substances in a lemon contain anesthetic and anti-inflammatory properties, which may help reduce itching. If nothing else, you'll smell good. Squeeze undiluted lemon juice on itchy skin and allow to dry.

FROM THE SPICE RACK

BASIL. Splash your skin with refreshing basil tea. Like cloves, basil contains high amounts of eugenol, a topical anesthetic. Place ½ ounce dried basil leaves in a 1-pint jar of boiling water. Keep it covered to prevent the escape of the aromatic eugenol from the tea. Allow to cool. Dip a clean cloth into the tea and apply to itchy skin as often as necessary.

CLOVES AND JUNIPER BERRIES. The American Indians of the Paiute, Shoshone, and Cherokee tribes knew how to stop an itch in its tracks. They used what nature provided, namely juniper berries. (No need to run out in the wilderness to gather berries. They are available in some grocery stores.) These berries contain anti-inflammatory, volatile substances. When combined with cloves, which contain eugenol to numb nerve endings, the result is no more itch. To make a salve of both spices, melt 3 ounces unsalted butter in a saucepan. In a separate pan, melt a lump of beeswax—about the amount of 2 tablespoons. When the beeswax has melted, combine with butter and stir well. Add 5 tablespoons ground juniper berries and 3 teaspoons ground cloves to the mixture and stir. Allow to cool and apply to itchy skin. Note: It is best to grind the spices at home because the volatile substances are preserved better in whole berries and cloves.

MINT. If you're saving that basil for spaghetti sauce, try a mint tea rinse instead. Chinese folk medicine values mint as a treatment for itchy skin and hives. Mint contains significant amounts of menthol, which has anesthetic and anti-inflammatory properties when applied topically. In general, mint also contains high amounts of the anti-inflammatory rosmarinic acid, which is readily absorbed into the skin. To make a mint tea rinse, place 1 ounce dried mint leaves in 1 pint boiling water. Cover and allow to cool. Strain, dip a clean cloth in the tea, and apply to the itchy area when necessary.

THYME. If you're saving that mint for a glass of lemonade, there is one more spice on the rack that makes a good anti-itch rinse: thyme. This fragrant herb contains large amounts of the volatile constituent thymol, which has anesthetic and anti-inflammatory properties. In other words, it numbs that darn itch while reducing inflammation caused by all your scratching. To make a thyme rinse, place ½ ounce dried thyme leaves in a 1-pint jar of boiling water. Cover and allow to cool. Strain and dip a clean cloth into the tea, then apply to affected areas. Note: In Chinese folk medicine, dandelion root, easily plucked from most yards, is added to this rinse. If in season, place 1 ounce dried dandelion root and ½ ounce dried thyme leaves into 1 quart boiling water and proceed as directed.

FROM THE WINDOWSILL

ALOE VERA. Aloe vera is a must for burns, but how about itches? The same constituents that reduce blistering and inflammation in burns also work to reduce itching. Snap off a leaf, slice it down the middle, and rub the gel only on the itch.

MORE DO'S AND DON'TS

• Try not to scratch!

• Wear gloves, if need be, to keep yourself from opening your skin by scratching with your nails.

ITCHES IN NETHER REGIONS

Some types of itches are just not socially acceptable, especially when it comes to those around the derriere. *Pruritus ani* is the medical term for an "itchy bottom," and it's one itch that isn't discussed in polite company.

For those who silently suffer, the itching is often unbearable and without relief in a public setting. The causes of an itchy bottom are many:

• Tight clothing and underwear

• Allergic reaction to perfumed or rough toilet paper

• Offending condiments such as hot sauces and acidic foods such as tomatoes, citrus drinks, coffee, and alcohol

• Pinworm infestation

• Infections by viruses, yeast, or bacteria

For the less-serious causes, there are some cures that can be used in the privacy of your home.

• Be free. If you want to make your own petri dish, wear tight-fitting underwear! With no airflow, combined with moist, warm conditions, your underwear and skin become a science experiment with itchy results. Throw out any snug underwear. Men should switch to boxer shorts, too.

• Splurge on softness. Plush, soft toilet paper may provide some relief to your itchy bottom. If you're really willing to splurge, purchase alcohol-free, pre-moistened wipes designed for anal care.

• Clean it up. During the day, sweat and fecal material can gather down below and cause irritation and itch. Clean your rectal area every night with warm water and non-irritating, fragrance-free soap. Air dry and apply witch hazel or vinegar as needed.

Kidney Stones
CLEARING THE PATH

In one episode of a famous sitcom, one of the characters is in labor with triplets. As she screams during a contraction, her (male) friend doubles over in pain. Thinking he's having sympathy pains, he shouts, "I didn't know I cared so much!" Alas, he soon discovers his agony isn't because he's such a sympathetic guy. He has a kidney stone. The rest of the show examines the parallels between having a baby and passing a stone, a comparison many kidney-stone sufferers would echo. And since four out of five people who get kidney stones are men, there are many husbands gaining new respect for their spouses. (And many wives of kidney-stone sufferers believing that justice has finally been served!)

The Stone Source

Each about the size of your fist, your kidneys are located in your back, just below your rib cage. The main function of kidneys is to get rid of extra waste and fluid, clear the blood of impurities, and keep your blood pressure under control. The majority of kidney stones form when there's not enough fluid passing through the kidneys. Certain minerals, namely calcium, magnesium, and phosphate, along with oxalate, a substance found in some foods, begin to crystallize on the sides of the kidneys. When the stones break loose, these little calcified pebbles make a path through your ureter, the tube that connects your kidneys with your bladder. The majority of kidney stones are small—ninety percent are less than five millimeters, about the size of a tiny pea—and usually pass without notice. Occasionally, however, kidney stones can grow quite large, some even as big as golf balls. As these grainy, rough rounds pass through your ureter, you experience the legendary anguish of passing a stone.

What causes stones? Scientists don't know for sure. But there are some factors that put you at greater risk. These include:

• Inadequate fluid intake

• Heredity. If your mom or dad battled the stones, you probably will, too.

• Frequent urinary tract infections

• Some diuretics

WHEN TO CALL THE DOCTOR

Pain that starts in the back, in the general vicinity of your kidneys, and moves to the groin could be kidney stones. The pain generally follows the path of your ureter and can last up to three days. While agonizing, the pain will go away once you pass the stone. However, some stones are simply too big to pass through the body and may need medical attention. According to the National Institute of Diabetes and Digestive and Kidney Diseases, call your doctor if you experience any of these symptoms:

• Extreme pain in your back or side that will not go away
• Blood in your urine
• Fever and chills
• Vomiting
• Urine that smells bad or looks cloudy
• A burning feeling when you urinate

• Taking calcium-based antacids
• Some metabolic disorders, such as hyperparathyroidism
• Gout
• Excessive intake of vitamin D

Stone Stats

The National Kidney Foundation estimates that one million Americans will be treated for kidney stones this year. This doesn't account for the brave souls who pass stones without visiting a doctor. The majority of those with kidney stones will be men, although the number of women with kidney stones is increasing. Experts blame that growing statistic on high-protein diets. Too much animal protein in the diet can spark kidney stone formation. Most people have their first attack between ages 20 and 40. And if you have one attack, odds are you'll have another. Fifty percent of people who have kidney stones will have another attack within five years.

If you've ever had a kidney stone, there's some good news. Turns out even those at higher risk for kidney stones can prevent another attack simply by watching what they eat. Here are some suggestions for staying free of kidney stones.

FROM THE CUPBOARD

BRAN FLAKES. Fiber helps get rid of calcium and oxalate in your urine, which cuts the risk of kidney stones. A bowl of bran flakes can give you 8 mg of fiber.

MESH STRAINER. If you are passing a kidney stone, doctors recommend catching it. Urinating through a mesh strainer is one of the easiest ways to trap your stone. Allowing your doctor to analyze the stone's content can offer clues about what caused your stones to form and give you more success in treating your stone problem.

TWO-LITER BOTTLE. Many doctors recommend measuring your urine output if you are at risk for kidney stones. You should be urinating at least the equivalent of a two-liter bottle every day. Carrying a bottle to the bathroom with you may seem odd, but if you're having kidney stone trouble, knowing that your kidneys are functioning fluidly will ease your mind.

WHOLE-WHEAT BREAD. A couple slices of whole-wheat bread contain a good amount of magnesium, a mineral known for averting stones. One study found that people who got an adequate amount of magnesium stopped getting kidney stones altogether.

FROM THE REFRIGERATOR

CARROTS. Vitamin A is an essential ingredient for healthy kidneys. One carrot can give you twice your daily requirement for this kidney-friendly nutrient.

CHICKEN. The B vitamins, specifically vitamin B6, are well-known stone fighters. Vitamin B6 keeps the body from building up excess oxalate. Too much oxalate is a major factor in kidney stone formation. Three ounces of chicken provide more than one-third of your daily needs.

MILK. Something to put in your strange but true file. Though calcium is one of the major minerals in kidney stones, recent evidence shows that not getting enough calcium can actually increase chances of getting a stone. The reason: When you have lower levels of calcium, your body produces more oxalate, which makes you more at risk for kidney stones. One study found that men who ate the most calcium had a 34 percent less chance of developing stones than those who ate the least amount of calcium. How much is enough? Meeting your recommended daily allowance, which for most adults is between 1,000 and 1,200 mg a day (the amount in about 3 glasses of milk) should do the trick.

WATER. Hippocrates was the first person to recognize the benefits of drinking water to avert kidney stones. Most modern-day docs recommend drinking about a gallon of water a day if you're at risk for kidney stones. And drinking fluids at night is more beneficial—though you may want to leave the bathroom light on. If you've never had a stone, stick with the recommended 8 glasses a day.

WHEN YOU'VE GOT TO GO

The average adult can hold 24 ounces in the bladder, which is equivalent to three glasses of water. But most people feel the urge to go when their bladder contains between 10 and 16 ounces of fluid.

THE YOUNGEST STONE

Joshua Price, of Jacksonville, Texas, holds the distinction of being the youngest person to ever have a kidney stone removed. A couple of months shy of seven years old, Joshua had a stone removed from his left kidney on October 5, 1993. A painful claim to fame, Joshua now resides in *Guinness World Records.*

ROLL THOSE STONES AWAY

Too much oxalate- or calcium-rich food may be to blame for some kidney stones. If you're at risk for kidney stones, check with your doctor about cutting back on these foods:

Apples
Beer
Berries
Broccoli
Cheese
Chocolate
Cocoa
Coffee
Grapes
Ice cream
Milk
Oranges
Peanuts and peanut butter
Rhubarb
Spinach
Swiss chard
Yogurt

MORE DO'S AND DON'TS

Though what you eat is a major factor in preventing kidney stones, what you don't eat is equally important. These tips will help you give your stones the old heave-ho.

• Minimize the meat. Animal protein tends to increase levels of stone-forming minerals. Try to keep your intake under 7 ounces a day.

• Skimp on the sodium. Less salt means less calcium buildup in your urine. This means less chance of developing a stone. Experts recommend consuming only 2,500 mg a day.

• Observe those oxalates. A buildup of oxalate in your urine is a major factor for forming a painful stone. Certain foods are rich in oxalates, and too much of them can make you more at risk for a stone. See "Roll Those Stones Away," on this page, for a list of foods to avoid.

• Watch the "C." Taking vitamin C supplements, more than 500 mg a day regularly, can increase the oxalate in your urine. Too much oxalate combines with calcium and can create a stone. Getting adequate amounts in your diet should be fine, but skip the supplements.

• Forgo fad diets. High-protein diets can increase the amount of calcium in your urine, which can make you more likely to get a stone.

• Watch what you drink. Increasing your fluid intake is vital to kicking out your stones, and though water is the best option, almost any fluid, including tea, can be part of your daily fluid fill-up. However, some beverages, such as grapefruit juice and soda pop, may contribute to kidney stone formation. If you're at risk, you may want to stick to the basics.

Lactose Intolerance
MANAGING MILK

Lactose, the milk sugar in dairy products, can be pretty rough to digest on a good day. But our bodies manage to do it with the help of an enzyme called lactase that breaks down those tough milk sugars and converts them into glucose, or blood sugar.

When there is an insufficient amount of lactase, your condition is called lactose intolerance, and it can cause some pretty miserable symptoms. Instead of being broken down, lactose instead stays intact in the intestines, absorbing fluids. When this happens, gas, cramping, heartburn, and diarrhea can result one by one or all together.

To add insult to injury, certain bacteria that call the colon home ferment the undigested lactose, causing more gas, cramping, and diarrhea.

A Common Problem

Lactose intolerance is so common that about two-thirds of the world's population suffers from it in some form. This includes:

- About 50 million Americans
- 75 percent of African American, Jewish, Native American, and Mexican American adults
- 90 percent of Asian Americans

Globally, Native Americans, Africans, and people of Mediterranean, Asian, and Middle Eastern descent have the highest incidence of lactose intolerance. However, only 10 to 15 percent of non-Jewish Caucasian American adults suffer from it.

Most adults who are lactose intolerant usually tolerated small amounts of lactose when they were children. With aging, however, the ability to digest lactose diminishes, even for those who aren't lactose intolerant. To some degree, lactose intolerance develops in virtually everyone as they age. In other words, the

WHEN TO CALL THE DOCTOR

- If unexplained weight loss occurs
- If the techniques you've been using to control it no longer work
- If symptoms cause problems in the way you live your life
- If symptoms persist for more than a few days
- If you experience unusual pain or severity of symptoms
- If blood is present in diarrhea

UNMASKING THE MILK

These all may contain milk that you are not aware of:

- bread
- cereals
- pancakes
- chocolate
- soups, especially cream-based
- pudding
- salad dressing
- sherbet
- instant cocoa mix
- soft candy
- frozen dinners
- cookie mix
- hot dogs

The amounts may be negligible, but if you're very sensitive to lactose, even the tiny amounts of milk can cause symptoms.

FASCINATING FACT

Many women are unaware that they have lactose intolerance until they hit menopause and start consuming more milk to obtain the additional calcium they need.

body's production of lactase slows down, or ages, too.

Many people don't realize they're lactose intolerant, especially if they don't consume many milk products. Since the degree of intolerance varies with each individual, some may experience symptoms only after consuming a large amount of dairy. Others will have symptoms from a very small amount.

One way to get some idea of whether you're lactose intolerant is simply to avoid all dairy products for several weeks and see if your symptoms resolve. This isn't a conclusive method, as there may be other reasons that your symptoms don't entirely disappear. But if your symptoms do ease, decrease dairy in your diet, use a dietary aid that replaces lactase, or use a lactose-free milk product.

For a more conclusive diagnosis, schedule a doctor's appointment. The doctor may want to order a lactose intolerance test.

But before you get too discouraged, here are some easy remedies you can try to get some relief.

FROM THE CUPBOARD

COCOA POWDER. Studies indicate that cocoa powder and sugar, or chocolate powders, may help the body digest lactose by slowing the rate at which the stomach empties. The slower it empties, the less lactose that enters your system at once and the fewer symptoms. **FOOD.** People with any degree of lactose intolerance should never drink milk by itself. **SARDINES.** They're high in calcium, which might be lacking in your diet if you're not consuming calcium-rich milk products. Other foods high in calcium include canned salmon with bones; tofu; dark green, leafy vegetables; nuts; cooked dried beans; dried apricots; and sesame seed products.

FROM THE DRAWER

MAGNIFYING GLASS. Check the product content listed on the label for hidden milk. The print may be tiny, but looking for milk could save you from misery. These are the buzzwords to look for: whey, curds, milk by-products, dry milk solids, nonfat dry milk, milk powder, milk sugar, casein, galactose, skim whey protein concentrate.

MEASURING CUP. Most people who suffer lactose intolerance do produce an amount of lactase. So, if that 8-ounce glass of milk you drink in the morning backfires, divide it up. Measure out ⅓ cup three times a day and see if you can handle the smaller amount.

NOTEBOOK. Keep a food diary. First, cut out all milk products for 3 to 4 weeks. Then, add back small amounts of milk at a meal, ¼ to ½ cup at a time, to see what you can tolerate. Gradually increase or decrease the amount according to your symptoms.

FROM THE REFRIGERATOR

BUTTERMILK. It's more digestible than regular cow's milk. So is goat's milk.

HARD CHEESE. Cheddar and Colby are good: The harder the cheese, the lower its lactose content. Skip the soft cheese, including cream cheese, cottage cheese, and any product that's processed or spreadable.

SOY MILK. Soy milk won't cause lactose intolerance. If you can't get used to the taste, try using it in recipes and products such as pudding where adding milk is required.

YOGURT. Research shows that yogurt with active cultures may be a good source of calcium for many people with lactose intolerance, even though it is fairly high in lactose. The bacterial cultures used in making yogurt produce some of the lactase enzyme required for proper digestion.

MORE DO'S & DON'TS

- Check with your pharmacist about the medications you take. Twenty percent of prescription and 6 percent of nonprescription medications contain lactose as a filler.

- Don't forget the calcium. You can incorporate it in your foods, but supplements are also available. Check with your doctor before you take a calcium supplement.

ADDING THE ENZYME

Lactase enzyme supplements are available in either tablet or liquid form, without prescription, and they may be the simple solution to your lactose intolerance. Chew pills with, or right after, you've consumed a milk product. They come in handy carry-along rolls. If you choose the liquid form, just add it directly into the milk.

FASCINATING FACT

Some infants are born with congenital lactase deficiency. A lactose-free formula will be necessary, and a doctor must prescribe a suitable calcium supplement to ensure proper growth and development.

Laryngitis
HANDLING HOARSENESS

Have you been verbally abusing your voice? Too much vocal enthusiasm at a sports event can set you up for swollen vocal cords and no voice the next day. But that's not the only way to cause laryngitis—the result of inflammation of the voice box and voice folds. More often, laryngitis is caused by an upper respiratory infection, usually viral, such as the common cold. Surprisingly, some cases of laryngitis are caused by heartburn, especially in the elderly. During the night, the acid-rich contents of the stomach come back up the throat and cause irritation.

Sounds and Symptoms

When we speak, two membranes, known as the vocal cords, vibrate to produce sounds. Hoarseness, the main sign of laryngitis, is an indicator that something with the vocal cords is wrong, swollen, irritated, or infected. Besides hoarseness, symptoms of acute, or short-term, laryngitis also include a painful or scratchy feeling in the throat, a loss of range in the voice, and fatigue. You may also have the annoying feeling that you must constantly clear your throat. In heartburn-induced laryngitis, symptoms include waking up with a bad taste in the mouth, feeling like something is sticking in the throat, constant throat clearing, and hoarseness that gradually improves during the day.

FROM THE CUPBOARD

SALT. A saltwater gargle helps heal infected and inflamed vocal cords and sore throats. Add ½ teaspoon salt to 1 cup warm water and gargle several times a day as needed. Be careful to use the correct amount of salt. Gargling with a solution as salty as the sea will only increase the irritation.

VINEGAR. Viruses and bacteria dread an acidic environment, so why not make your mouth one big, albeit weak, acid bath? Gargling with vinegar, a weak acid, can help wipe out many infectious organisms. Pour equal amounts of vinegar and water into a cup, mix, and gargle two to four times a day. You can also gargle with straight vinegar, but some people find it too strong, especially at first.

FROM THE REFRIGERATOR

LEMON. Some folk remedies require you to suck on a lemon to cure a sore throat. An impossible task, indeed! Spare yourself the face-contorting agony and try a lemon juice and salt gargle instead. Lemon is naturally acidic and helps stimulate saliva flow. The salt increases the lemon's acidity, which in turn helps kill many microorganisms prone to weak acids. To make this gargle, juice a whole lemon into a bowl and add a pinch of sea salt (or regular salt). Mix well. Add 1 teaspoon of the concentrated lemon-salt mixture to 1 cup warm water. Gargle three to four times a day as needed.

FROM THE SINK

SOAP AND WATER. Laryngitis can be caused by a viral infection and is easily spread by hand-to-hand contact or by touching contaminated surfaces. Avoiding such germs is one of the best ways to prevent laryngitis. If you or someone around you has a cold, be extra vigilant about washing your hands with warm water and soap. Clean common surfaces, such as the telephone and door handles, with vinegar and a clean cloth.

WATER. Keep the throat moistened and stay hydrated by drinking your daily amount of water (eight 8-ounce glasses per day). Fruit juices also fit the bill, as do hot, noncaffeinated drinks, which may feel extra soothing on sore throat tissues.

FROM THE SPICE RACK

GARLIC. Should you have a strong stomach and no social events to attend, try what the Amish and Seventh-day Adventists suggest for treating sore throats and viral infections: Suck on a slice of garlic. Garlic, when sliced or crushed, releases the antimicrobial substance allicin. Allicin kills bacteria, including strep and some viruses. Slice a garlic clove down the middle and place half a clove on each side of the mouth. Pretend the cloves are lozenges and suck on them. Use as often as necessary, or as often as you can handle garlic breath.

GINGER. Fragrant, fresh ginger can help soothe inflamed mucous membranes of the larynx. Try sucking on candied ginger if available or drink a cup of ginger tea. To prepare the tea, cut a fresh 1- to 2-inch gingerroot into thin slices and place in 1 quart boiling water. Cover the pot and

WHEN TO CALL THE DOCTOR

- If pain is present with hoarseness
- If the hoarseness continues for more than 72 hours
- If you have an upper-respiratory infection with fever that lasts more than a couple of days
- If you have trouble breathing
- If you notice a permanent change in the pitch of your voice, especially if you are a smoker
- If you cough up blood

simmer on the lowest heat for 30 minutes. Let cool for 30 more minutes, strain, and drink ½ to 1 cup three to five times a day. Sweeten with honey if needed.

FROM THE STOVE

STEAM. Dry indoor air, so common in the wintertime, combined with an irritated throat can make you extra miserable. Start the day off steamy. Bring half a pot of water to boil, remove from stove, and place on a protected surface. Drape a towel over your head, lean forward over the pot, and breathe gently for 10 to 15 minutes. Be careful not to stick your face too close. Repeat in the evening before bedtime.

MORE DO'S AND DON'TS

- Don't smoke, and stay out of smoky environments. Smoking and breathing secondhand smoke irritate the larynx and cause coughing, which only adds more pain to the picture. Smoking, by the way, is one of the most common causes of chronic laryngitis.
- Avoid alcohol, since it dehydrates the body and can cause long-term vocal problems if abused.
- Cut back on coffee. Same goes for caffeinated teas and soft drinks. Caffeine, like alcohol, sucks moisture from the body, so it's a big no-no if you suffer from heartburn-induced laryngitis. Caffeine relaxes the muscles and valves that control the stomach's entrance (the lower esophageal sphincter).
- Avoid whispering, as it can further irritate the throat. Soothe your vocal cords by speaking in a soft, modulated voice. Better yet, don't talk!
- Don't constantly clear your throat. This only bothers the vocal cords—and the person next to you. If your throat feels like it needs clearing, try gargling with warm water or salt water.
- At night, run a humidifier in your room.
- Be kind to your voice. Use a noisemaker at pep rallies instead of screaming. Use a whistle to call your kids in from play.
- Save dusting for another day. Dust particles aren't friendly to a sore throat.
- In an ultra-dry environment, such as an airplane, stay extra hydrated. Drink more water than usual, and eat waterlogged fruits or vegetables, such as grapes or celery sticks.

Low Immunity
MARSHALING YOUR DEFENSES

In medical terms, having
immunity means that you
have resistance to infection or
a specified disease. So if you
have low immunity, it means
your immune system isn't up
to par and that you have a

greater chance of getting the germ-du-jour. Many factors affect your
body's response to an invader, including how you're feeling at the
moment you're introduced to a suspect germ. But if you consistently end
up with the latest flu bug or stomach virus, your immune system may be
running on empty.

The Battle for Your Body

Imagine your immune system as the front line in your body's war
against foreign invaders. The vast network of glands, tissues, and cells are
all soldiers working together to get rid of bacteria, viruses, parasites, and
anything that invades their turf. The major troops in this war are the
lymphatic system, made of the lymph nodes, thymus, spleen, and tonsils; white blood cells; and other specialized cells such as macrophages
and mast cells. Each of these troops has a specialized job in enhancing
the body's ability to fight off infection.

Lymph nodes are responsible for filtering out waste products from
tissues throughout the body. Under the lymph nodes' command are cells
that overtake bacteria and other potentially harmful foreign bodies and
crush them like ants. That's why your lymph nodes swell up like golf
balls when you are actively fighting off an infection.

The thymus is your immune system's stealth warfare command center. You may not have heard of the thymus, but without it you would be
one sick puppy. The thymus is a gland that produces many of those
disease-fighting foot soldiers—the white blood cells that come to your
defense against many types of infections. And the thymus produces
hormones that enhance your immune function overall. So if your thymus isn't working as it should, your body may have trouble fighting off
infection.

The spleen is vital to your immune defense. It produces white blood
cells, kills bacteria, and enhances the immune system overall. White

blood cells are your body's main defense in the battle against infection. White blood cells with names such as neutrophils, eosinophils, basophils, T cells, B cells, and natural killer cells, are all part of the vast army of disease assaulters.

When the Enemy Strikes

When something enters your body that is viewed by the immune system as harmful, your body goes into a state of heightened alert. When your immune system is healthy and all systems are go, these foreign invaders, or antigens, are typically met by a barrage of antibodies, which are produced by white blood cells. These antibodies latch on to antigens and set into action all the events that lead to the invader's eventual demise.

If things in your immune system are not working properly, you become less able to fight off those foreign invaders. Eventually they set up shop in your body and you get sick. An impaired immune system can make you more susceptible to colds and other merely frustrating illnesses, but it can also make you more at risk for developing cancer.

Science is proving that getting enough of the right nutrients can help you build your immune system. Scientific studies are discovering that avoiding something as simple as a cold or something as life threatening as cancer may all be affected by what you stock in your kitchen.

FROM THE CUPBOARD

ALMONDS. Eat a handful of almonds for your daily dose of vitamin E. An immune-strengthening antioxidant, studies have found that vitamin E deficiency causes major problems in the integrity of the immune system.

CRAB. A zinc deficiency can zap your immune system. Zinc acts as a catalyst in the immune system's killer response to foreign bodies, and it protects the body from damage from invading cells. Zinc also is a necessary ingredient for white blood cell function. Nosh on 3 ounces fresh or canned crab and you've got one-third of your recommended daily allowance (RDA) of this immune-enhancing nutrient.

NAVY BEANS. Everybody needs a little folic acid (it's the most common nutrient deficiency in the United States). And not getting enough of this vital nutrient can actually shrink vital immune system fighters like your thymus and lymph nodes. To make sure you're getting your fill of folic acid, try popping open a can of navy beans with dinner. One cup gets you half of your recommended daily allowance (RDA) of folic acid.

FROM THE FRUIT BASKET

GUAVA. Go a little tropical with this tasty fruit and get more than twice your daily vitamin C needs. Vitamin C acts as an immune enhancer by helping white blood cells perform at their peak and quickening the response time of the immune system.

FROM THE REFRIGERATOR

CHICKEN. Selenium is a trace mineral that is vital to the development and movement of white blood cells in the body. A 3-ounce piece of chicken will give you almost half your daily needs.

PORK. Not getting enough vitamin B6 can keep your immune system from functioning at its best. Eating 3 ounces of lean roast pork will provide you with one-third of most adults' daily requirements for this immune-helping vitamin.

WINE. Have a glass of red wine and you may help your body take out a few potentially harmful foreign bodies. Certain components in wine seem to be helpful in killing infectious bacteria, such as *Salmonella.* But be careful. Drinking too much alcohol can cause your immune system to become depressed, leaving you more open to infection. A glass a day should do the trick.

YOGURT. Yogurt seems to have a marked effect on the immune system. It strengthens white blood cells and helps the immune system produce antibodies. One study found that people who ate 6 ounces of yogurt a day avoided colds, hay fever, and diarrhea. Another study found that yogurt could be an ally in the body's war against cancer.

FROM THE SUPPLEMENT SHELF

ECHINACEA. Research has shown echinacea to boost the body's immune response. It is particularly effective at fighting viral infections, such as the cold and flu, helping your body heal faster. Take 1 or 2 capsules or tablets up to three times a day. You can also buy dried echinacea and brew it into a tea. Simmer 1 to 2 teaspoons in 1 cup boiling water for 10 to 15 minutes; drink up to 3 cups a day.

IS IMMUNITY INHERITED OR ACQUIRED?

The answer is...both. There are two basic types of immunity. Natural immunity is the type you inherit from your parents. If your mom and dad rarely miss a day's work and are the picture of health, chances are that you will be, too. But no matter how good your genes are, if you don't exercise or eat right and are chronically stressed, you could increase your chances of getting sick. The second type of immunity is active immunity. Active immunity means you become immune to a disease because you had it already, like the chicken pox, or because you got a vaccination against the disease, such as your annual flu shot.

CAN MULTIVITAMINS MAKE YOU STRONGER?

Getting enough of essential nutrients is a good start on the road to a healthy immune system. And generally, eating a well-balanced diet will get you on that road. But you may be thinking about taking a multivitamin to help fill in the gaps. Are they worth it? And what should you look for?

Most nutrition experts would tell you to get the majority of your nutrients from food—mostly because there are other good-for-you components in food that a specific vitamin may not offer. Taking a multivitamin is a good backup plan. If you decide to take a multivitamin, follow these tips:

• Look for a vitamin/mineral combination. You need vitamins and minerals to enhance your immune system, so be sure the product you choose has all you need.

• Don't use products that have more than 100 percent of the recommended daily allowance (RDA) or daily value (DV) of a nutrient. You're going to get most of your vitamins and minerals from your diet, so don't go overboard.

• Make sure your multivitamin meets your needs. If you need to boost your immune system, look for a multivitamin that has the vitamins and minerals discussed on the previous pages of this section.

• Check the expiration date. Multivitamins may not start smelling up the place after they expire, but they can lose their potency.

• Only take what is recommended. One a day is exactly what you should take. Don't double up on vitamin pills.

FROM THE VEGETABLE BIN

CARROTS. Carotenes, like the beta-carotene found in carrots and other red, yellow, orange, and dark green, leafy vegetables, are the protectors of the immune system, specifically the thymus gland. Carotenes strengthen white blood cell production, and numerous studies have shown that eating foods rich in beta-carotene helps the body fight off infection more easily.

GARLIC. Garlic is well-known for its antibacterial and antiviral properties. It's even been thought to help prevent cancer. Researchers think these benefits stem from garlic's amazing effect on the immune system. One study found that people who ate more garlic had more of the natural killer white blood cells than those who didn't eat garlic.

KALE. A cup of kale will give you your daily requirement of vitamin A. Vitamin A is an antioxidant that helps your body fight cancer cells and is essential in the formation of white blood cells. Vitamin A also increases the ability of antibodies to respond to invaders.

Shiitake mushrooms. Throw a few shiitake mushrooms in your stir-fry and you may prevent your yearly cold. Scientists have discovered that specific components of shiitake mushrooms boost your immune system and act as antiviral agents.

More Do's and Don'ts

- Skip the sugar. Sugar may keep your white blood cells from being their strongest. Keep the sweet stuff to a minimum if your immune system isn't working like it should.

- Forgo fat. Polyunsaturated fats in vegetable oils such as corn, safflower, and sunflower oil seem to be a deterrent to an efficiently running immune system.

- Lose a few pounds. Being overweight has a major effect on your immune system. One study found that the white blood cells in overweight people weren't as able to fight off infection as those of their healthy-weight peers.

- Try to relax. If stress causes you to lose your cool, you could be impairing your immune system. Chronic stress can even shrink your thymus gland, creating major problems in your body's ability to fight off infection. This is probably why you get a horrible cold after you finish a big project at work.

- Add some activity. Exercise is a proven immune system booster. Don't overdo it, though. Too much exercise can wear you down and create immune system problems.

Give Your Baby a Boost

Science has long told moms that breast-feeding their babies could help them avoid infections, but scientists recently discovered a specific way breast milk boosts tiny immune systems. Breast milk actually triggers growth in the thymus gland—a vital component to fending off infection. One study found that babies who were breast-fed had a thymus gland that was twenty times larger than formula-fed babies.

Memory Problems

Sharpening Your Skills

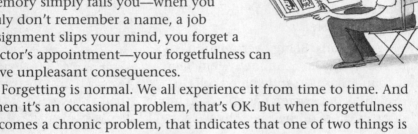

Some events, and some names and faces, definitely should be forgotten. Embarrassing moments, things you wish you hadn't said or done, are memories you can relegate to the memory trash bin. Purposely forgetting is one thing, and we all try to do it on occasion. But on those occasions when memory simply fails you—when you truly don't remember a name, a job assignment slips your mind, you forget a doctor's appointment—your forgetfulness can have unpleasant consequences.

Forgetting is normal. We all experience it from time to time. And when it's an occasional problem, that's OK. But when forgetfulness becomes a chronic problem, that indicates that one of two things is happening:

1. You're not locking in the information you just received. New information will be lost in seven seconds if you don't lock it in right away.

2. You have a physical or mental condition that's preventing you from remembering. For example: Alzheimer's disease, senile dementia, hypoglycemia, severe anemia, depression, anxiety, alcohol or drug abuse, head injury, or severe viral or bacterial illness. Some prescribed medications make remembering a little difficult, too.

Memory is divided into two parts: short-term and long-term. The short-term memory bank holds the memory for only a few seconds, then transfers it to the long-term memory bank. If the transfer doesn't take place, the memory is lost.

If you're affected by the Seven-Second Syndrome, which is failing to lock in information once it's presented to you, there are memory-strengthening techniques that can improve that forgetfulness.

Mnemonics. This is the skill of consciously gathering new memory (information) and connecting it to prior memory (knowledge) for easy recall. For example, if you meet someone named Webster, it might trigger you to think of Webster's dictionary. You've now connected something new, the person's name, with something you already know. The connection itself is the mnemonic.

Acronyms. This is a word formed from a group of letters, each representing the first letter of a word that makes up a phrase. We're such an acronymic society that acronyms are assigned to just about everything, so why not join the crowd and assign your own acronyms to things you want to remember. An easy acronym that comes to mind is ASAP—as soon as possible. Maybe in your cooking ASAP can mean add salt and pepper.

Rhymes. Rhyme and rhythm have always been terrific memory aids.

Lists, mental images, visual prompts. These all can help you forget your forgetfulness.

Sometimes memory problems stem from nutritional deficiencies, stress, and other problems that can be controlled once you know how. Here are some KMBs—kitchen memory boosters—that might just help you remember.

FROM THE CUPBOARD

PISTACHIO NUTS. If your memory loss is the result of a thiamine deficiency, pistachio nuts can help. One of the richest sources of thiamine, ½ cup pistachios supplies 0.54 mg of thiamin. The RDA for thiamine is 1.5 mg for men and 1.1 for women age 50 and younger; slightly less for those older than 50.

WHEAT GERM. Wheat germ is a good source of vitamin E, which may help with age-related memory loss.

FROM THE DRAWER

PAPER. Chart a food plan, then keep a diary. Some foods enhance mental powers, some do not. And some even make mental powers sluggish. So, to find out your best food choices and combinations, chart your choices and reactions.

UTENSILS. You know what's supposed to be there, right? A whisk, a wooden spoon, a rolling pin, measuring cups. Chances are, your utensil drawer hasn't changed for years, so this is a great place to conduct a memory exercise. Take a good look, tidy the drawer to remind you what's there, then ask a friend or loved one to remove an item or two. Tomorrow, take a good look, tidy the drawer again, and see what's missing. This exercise will not only keep your memory on its toes, it will also keep that drawer in perfect order.

WHEN TO CALL THE DOCTOR

- If memory problems develop suddenly
- If memory problems frequently cause difficulty in everyday situations

FASCINATING FACT

The human brain uses more energy than any other organ in the human body. It makes up about 2 percent of total body weight but uses up to 20 percent of the body's total oxygen.

THE ANATOMY OF A MEMORY

- The brain consists of more than ten billion nerve cells, which are called neurons.
- Each neuron has numerous fibers with tiny bulbs on the end.
- These bulbs send out chemicals called neurotransmitters that hit the walls of other brain cells.
- These other brain cells are charged up by the neurotransmitters that hit them, and they send out their own neurotransmitters.
- This happens millions of times each and every minute of our lives.
- Memory is controlled by these neurotransmitters.

FROM THE KITCHEN TABLE

THE MORNING PAPER. Sit, relax, and turn to the crossword puzzle. This is a great way to exercise your brain and jog your memory.

RECIPE BOX. Memory is jogged by familiarity. Sit down at the table, relax, and think about a few favorite and familiar recipes. Try to re-create them from memory, and jot them down. Do the same tomorrow and the following days, with the same recipes, and compare your results.

FROM THE REFRIGERATOR

ARTICHOKES. These are thought to increase your mental acuity. Prepare and eat them as you normally would or follow this recipe for an elixir of artichoke: Pull the artichoke apart, leaf by leaf, then put the pieces into a jar and add enough water to just barely cover. Cover the jar with a lid or saucer, and place in a pan with water. Boil for two hours, adding more water to the pan (not the jar) as necessary. Then strain the contents of the jar and give the artichoke leaves a good squeeze to get out all the juices. Take 3 to 4 tablespoons four times a day.

BLUEBERRIES. These luscious little fruits are the richest source of antioxidants, and recent studies have shown that blueberries may help improve short-term memory.

CARROTS. They contain carotene, which is a memory booster. Eat them raw, cooked, or in casseroles, or make a juice with carrots and apricots. The apricots are used to add a little compatible juice to the dry carrots.

EGGS. These have lecithin, which keeps the memory nerve cells healthy. Lecithin is also found in sunflower and soybean oils and can be purchased in capsule form, too. Studies indicate that taking up to 70 grams a day may improve memory.

OKRA. If not a memorable food, this is at least a memory-enhancing food. So are sweet potatoes, tapioca, and spinach. Fresh fruits—especially oranges—and vegetables, almonds, and milk are also good for stimulating the memory.

HERBS THAT HELP

Frankincense. It's not your everyday herb, but frankincense resin mixed with two common herbs—whole cloves and fresh cardamom—may remedy mild memory loss. Combine 1 teaspoon each and steep in boiling water, then inhale the steam. Do not drink! Do this for 15 minutes, two to three times a day.

Ginkgo. It's the most well-known memory herb of all. It dilates the blood vessels in the brain and increases circulation. Studies have shown a better than 50 percent increase in blood flow with the use of ginkgo, and there are indications that this herb may have properties that will lessen memory problems.

Warning! Gingko is available in capsules in most pharmacies, but before you try any product containing gingko, consult your physician! It comes with powerful side effects when combined with certain medications.

FROM THE SPICE RACK

ANISEED. Some herbalists suggest using aniseed to improve memory. Add 7 teaspoons aniseed to 1 quart boiling water, and let it simmer until it reduces by about half. Strain, and while still warm, add 4 teaspoons honey and 4 teaspoons glycerine, which can be purchased at the drugstore. Take 2 tablespoons three times a day.

HERBAL TEAS. Any of these will help a weak memory: sage, rosemary, marjoram, basil. Use ¼ teaspoon in a cup of boiling water. Steep for five minutes. These herbs, in an essential oil, can be added to olive oil and massaged over the neck and forehead. Add these oils to bathwater, too: 5 drops to a tubful.

FROM THE SUPPLEMENT SHELF

VITAMIN B₆. A deficiency in this vitamin, also called pyridoxine, can cause memory loss. Supplementation may improve memory in older adults.

VITAMIN E. Recent studies have reported improved short-term memory in older adults who took supplemental vitamin E.

MORE DO'S & DON'TS

• Write it down. Post notes. Keep lists. Mark it on the calendar.

• Exercise. This stimulates circulation, which is good for the brain.

• Meditate. The more you worry about memory loss, the more apt you are to suffer from it. Relax and think about other, more pleasant things.

Menopause
MAKING THE CHANGE

Well, "Aunt Flo" won't be making her monthly visit anymore. The baby factory is closed. You won't be indisposed or down with the "flu" or under the weather for those few days every month. Most women look forward to the cessation of menstruation and all its associated annoyances. It happens to every woman sometime between the ages of 40 and 60, and on average at age 51.

But menopause isn't just closing the door on Aunt Flo. It's a process of body changes and a reduction in female hormones, and it occurs over several years.

These are some of the premenopausal changes:

• Estrogen levels begin to drop off around age 30.

• Egg production and release slow down, usually during the 40s.

• Menstrual cycles change. They become longer or shorter, lighter or heavier. Months—or only a week or two—may elapse between periods.

• Whatever happens this month will change next month.

Overall, it takes about four years to get through these changes and cross that menopause threshold, but once menstruation has been absent for a full year, you are considered "postmenopausal."

In the meantime, as menopause is galloping to the finishing line, it's dragging along a lot of symptoms: hot flashes, vaginal dryness, bladder infection, incontinence, heart palpitations, achy joints, dry or itchy skin, headache, insomnia, weight gain, thinning hair, increased facial hair, mood swings, memory problems, and change in sexual drive.

Obviously, this transition requires some medical guidance, since the consequences can be more serious than the profuse sweat-

WHEN TO CALL THE DOCTOR

• If you begin to bleed after your periods have completely stopped

• If periods become extremely long or heavy

• If you experience abdominal pain

• If symptoms interfere with regular activities

ing of a hot flash. But there are ways to curb some menopausal symptoms right in your own kitchen. And since menopause is something to endure rather than cure, curbing those problems so simply can be a big relief.

FROM THE CUPBOARD

OLIVE OIL. Because your face may suffer the effects of dry skin as you go through menopause, mix 1 teaspoon salt and 1 teaspoon olive oil in a small bowl, then use the mixture to gently massage your face and throat to get rid of dead skin cells and replenish lost moisture. Follow by washing with your usual face soap, then rinse.

SALT. Here's what to do to slough off the dry skin that comes with menopause. After you take a shower or bath and while your skin is still wet, sprinkle salt onto your hands and rub it all over your skin. This salt massage will remove dry skin and make your skin smoother to the touch. It will also invigorate your skin and get your circulation moving. Try it first thing in the morning to help you wake up or after a period of physical exertion. And for itchy skin, soaking in a tub of salt water can provide great relief. Just add 1 cup table salt or sea salt to bathwater. This solution will also soften skin and help you relax.

SARDINES. Canned sardines, with bones and oil, are rich in bone-building calcium. Because loss of bone density is a common companion to menopause and can lead to osteoporosis, calcium-rich foods are important. Low fat dairy foods, sesame seeds, nuts, and legumes also should be added to your diet.

SESAME OIL. This can bring relief and comfort for vaginal dryness. Saturate a tampon or a piece of cotton molded into a tampon shape and insert into vagina. Be sure to use regular sesame oil, not dark or blackened sesame oil. Leave in overnight and wear a sanitary pad to catch any oil that might leak out. Remove tampon in the morning. For the best results, you may wish to choose a slim tampon, such as one marketed to teenage girls.

HERBAL CURES

Try some of these herbal remedies for menopause symptoms.

Aloe vera gel. Take 1 teaspoon three times a day to relieve symptoms.

Chamomile. Combine this with valerian to make a tea that can soothe you to sleep when you're experiencing menopausal insomnia. Drink it one hour before bed.

Evening primrose oil. It's known to be helpful in eliminating PMS symptoms, and it may also relieve menopause symptoms. Take up to 1,000 mg a day, in divided doses.

Herbal teas. There are several that are said to reduce symptoms of menopause: red raspberry leaf, dandelion, dong quai, damiana, sarsaparilla, licorice, valerian, and black cohosh.

FASCINATING FACT

Regular alcohol consumption may be linked to an increased risk of breast cancer. It also can exacerbate the weight gain and mood swings that can accompany menopause.

THE CANCER CONNECTION

Female hormones such as estrogen have been linked to many cancers that develop in women. Women at highest risk are premenopausal, because more hormones are being produced; risk drops after menopause, when hormone levels drop off.

VINEGAR. To relieve itchy skin and/or aching muscles, add 8 ounces apple cider vinegar to a bathtub of warm water. Soak for at least 15 minutes. To cleanse and tone your face, use a mixture of half vinegar and half water. Then rinse with vinegar diluted with water, and let face air-dry to seal in moisture. Make a basic skin toner using a 50/50 mixture of apple cider vinegar or white vinegar and water. Keep toner in a small spray bottle and use after your usual wash.

FROM THE DRAWER

PAPER. Something sets off most hot flashes. They can be sparked by spicy food, weather conditions, stress, sweets, clothing, hot drinks, and alcohol, among other things. The list is long and individual to every woman. Each time you experience a hot flash, jot down what you were doing ten minutes prior. Include everything. You may find that your hot flash trigger is that martini you feel you deserve at the end of a long, hard day.

FROM THE FREEZER

FROZEN VEGGIES. Place the bag, wrapped in a thin towel, on the back of your neck during a hot flash.

POPSICLE. Eat one to cool down during a hot flash. Or use ice any way that helps cool you off.

FROM THE REFRIGERATOR

ALFALFA SPROUTS. Their plant estrogen may help prevent thinning of the vaginal walls. Sprinkle on a salad or use in a stir-fry. But first clean raw sprouts because they can be contaminated with the *E. coli* bacteria. Flaxseed is rich in natural estrogen, too.

EGG WHITES. Bring to room temperature and use as a lubricant during sexual intercourse to remedy the vaginal dryness common to menopause.

LIME JUICE. Mix 5 to 10 drops with 1 teaspoon organic sugar and 1 cup pomegranate juice. Drink two to three times a day to relieve hot flashes.

ORANGES. The vitamin C in oranges is a natural immune booster. It also guards your skin against damage. Other C-rich foods include grapefruit, berries, papayas, green leafy veggies, peppers, and sweet potatoes.

SOY. It comes in many forms and they're all great at relieving symptoms such as hot flashes and vaginal dryness, preventing loss of bone density, and lowering cholesterol. Try adding tofu, soy milk, and tempeh to your diet.

FROM THE SPICE RACK

PARSLEY. Joint aches and pains are a common complaint of menopause, and parsley tea may bring relief. Steep a spoonful of parsley in a cup of boiling water for ten minutes, sweeten to taste, and drink two to three times a day. If you can stand the strong taste, add more parsley.

SAGE. This has estrogenlike properties and can help reduce sweating and hot flashes. Steep 1 to 2 fresh leaves or a spoonful of dried sage in 1 cup boiling water for ten minutes. Sweeten with honey, and add lemon if desired. Drink a cup or two every day. Or, use sage as a spice on vegetables or to season meats.

MORE DO'S & DON'TS

- Exercise. Overall health is important in fending off the symptoms of menopause.

- Relax. This can make you feel better both physically and mentally.

- Talk to your doctor about taking a vitamin or mineral supplement, and don't take anything until you have your doctor's recommendation.

HOT FLASH COOLDOWNS!

Since hot flashes are the most common menopausal complaint, here are ten easy ways to cool off.

1. Layer your clothes, then do a safe striptease when the heat surges.
2. Switch your lightbulbs. Fluorescent bulbs put out less heat.
3. Wear cotton. It's the cool fabric that breathes.
4. Try to avoid outdoor activities during the heat of the day.
5. Have sex. Two to four times a week can stimulate hormones and reduce hot flashes.
6. Carry a fan. A small battery-operated one is convenient and portable.
7. Carry cold water. Freeze 3 to 4 inches of water in a take-along bottle, then fill it with cold water when you leave. This way you'll have cold water for hours.
8. Carry a washcloth. You never know when you'll need to pour some cold water on it for a cooling wipe of your face.
9. Sleep in the buff. Hot flashes often happen while you're sleeping. They're called night sweats.
10. Skip the silk sheets. They don't breathe well. Sleep on plain white cotton. And sleep under it, too, without a blanket.

Menstrual Problems
MASTERING THE MONTHLIES

Ah, that time of the month again. It seems as if it rolls around about every other day, doesn't it? When you were young, anticipating your very first period, you were excited by that passage into womanhood. But you didn't anticipate the inconvenience, pain, and all the associated problems: bloat, back-ache, leg aches, headaches, zits, cramps, and mood swings. And those are on a good menstrual day. On a bad day, bleeding is so heavy you can't move without gushing or you're too tired to breathe. When you figure out that it's more of an inconvenience than something to look forward to, you've joined the true menses sisterhood.

Menstruation is the simple process of shedding the old uterine lining to make way for a new one. In other words, it's the body's way of sweeping out the cobwebs at the end of the month in preparation for the arrival of a new egg and a new cycle—all a part of the natural baby-making process with one goal in mind: conception.

Who experiences menstrual problems? At one time or another, every woman who menstruates. But some factors make problems more likely. These include

• Family history of problems

• Being overweight, which is particularly associated with amenorrhea or ogliomenorrhea

• Being severely underweight, also linked with amenorrhea, as is being an athlete

• Taking certain drugs

• Chemotherapy or radiation

Most women will experience in the neighborhood of 400 menstrual cycles in their childbearing lifetime. And that's a lot of cycles that can cause problems. Serious menstrual problems require medical treatment, since many can lead to infertility, infection, and in some cases, death. But some of the milder problems can be relieved with simple kitchen cures. And any menstrual relief, no matter how slight, is welcome!

FROM THE CUPBOARD

BUCKWHEAT. It's high in bioflavonoids and can reduce heavy bleeding when taken with vitamin C. Try it in buckwheat pancakes. Fruits, nuts, and seeds are high in bioflavonoids, too.

FROM THE REFRIGERATOR

CITRUS FRUITS. Eat or drink with your meals to enhance iron absorption into the body, since iron is easily depleted during menstruation.

DRIED APRICOTS. These are high in iron, which is important during menstruation because iron supplies can be depleted with heavy bleeding. Other iron-rich foods are: liver, legumes, shellfish, and fortified breads and cereals.

RED MEAT. It's loaded with iron as well as zinc, which can be depleted during menses, too. Zinc is necessary for healthy bones, and a zinc deficiency may result in amenorrhea. Other iron- and zinc-rich foods: poultry, fish, green leafy vegetables.

FROM THE SINK

HOT WATER. Put it in a hot water bottle and place on the abdomen to relieve cramps. Or, soak a kitchen towel, then wring out excess water, heat in microwave for a minute, and place on abdomen. Be careful not to burn yourself.

WATER. Drink plenty of it. Dehydration can cause the body to produce a hormone called vasopressin that contributes to cramps.

FROM THE SPICE RACK

BASIL. This can relieve some of the normal pain associated with menstruation because it contains caffeic acid, which has an analgesic, or pain-killing, effect. Thyme is also high in caffeic acid. Use it as a spice in cooking. Or steep the herb into tea, adding 2 tablespoons thyme or basil leaves to 1 pint boiling water. Cover tightly and let cool to room temperature. Drink ½ to 1 cup an hour for painful menstruation.

CINNAMON. This has anti-inflammatory and antispasmodic properties that relieve cramps. Use as a tea, or sprinkle on toast or sweet rolls. If you have a heavy period, drinking cinnamon tea the day before or during your period may help.

FENNEL. Another cramp cure, this spice promotes better circulation to the ovaries. Crush 1 teaspoon fennel seeds into a powder. Add to 1 cup

---

WHEN TO CALL THE DOCTOR

- If there are changes in normal menstrual activity
- When menstrual problems affect your daily activities
- If you think that you're pregnant

WHAT IS A MENSTRUAL CRAMP?

It's uterine contractions caused by the release of prostaglandins, which are hormonelike chemicals. Prostaglandins also produce contractions during labor and childbirth.

boiling water, steep five minutes, strain, and drink hot.

GINGER. This is a cramp reliever, and as an added bonus it sometimes can make irregular periods regular. Use in cookies, cake, and candy or as a spice in vegetables and stir-fries. Tea may be the most effective form, however: put ½ teaspoon in 1 cup boiling water, and drink three times a day.

MINT. Either peppermint or wintergreen can relieve cramps. Steep into a tea and drink a cup or two a day. Try sucking on mint candy, too.

MUSTARD. A tablespoon or two of powdered mustard in a basin of nice warm water can relieve cramps, but don't drink it. Soak your feet in it to reap the relaxing effects.

FROM THE SUPPLEMENT SHELF

VITAMIN K. Women who have heavy periods may find relief by taking vitamin K supplements. This is the case even if the blood levels of the vitamin are within the normal range.

MORE DO'S & DON'TS

- Stay warm. Women who stay warm during their period are less prone to cramps.

- Exercise regularly. This increases circulation to the pelvic region and helps clear out prostaglandins.

- Try using sanitary pads. Tampons can cause cramping.

- Do the pelvic tilt to relieve cramps. Lie on your back with your knees bent and your feet flat. Tighten your abdominal muscles and your buttocks and raise your pelvis, angling it toward your head. Press your lower back to the floor, and hold the position for a few seconds. Gently lower your buttocks to the floor. Repeat several times.

- Lie on your back with your knees bent. This position can relieve cramps, too.

- Take a nice hot bath.

- Relax. Listen to soothing music. Read a good book. Invent a pleasant fantasy. Anxiety and stress can make cramps worse.

- Talk to your doctor about your birth control choices. IUDs cause cramps and excessive bleeding. And the Pill can relieve symptoms: It lessens cramps and flow, shortens the length of the period, and makes a menstrual period regular. But some conditions contraindicate the use of the Pill, so have that chat with the doc.

Morning Sickness

QUELLING QUEASINESS

Be it the crack of dawn, high noon, or early evening, the nauseated "I am going to vomit" feeling of the misnamed "morning sickness" can strike anytime. Nausea and the accompanying vomiting associated with early pregnancy have been around since the dawn of motherhood, with little comfort from that day onward. The ancient Egyptians wrote about the condition in 2,000 B.C. but didn't come up with a cure. The same holds true today. There's a lot of literature on the subject, but there is still no cure.

Approximately 50 to 70 percent of American women will suffer from nausea, dry heaves, vomiting, or all three during the first three months of pregnancy. The severity and occurrence varies from woman to woman and pregnancy to pregnancy. Some lucky mothers-to-be feel wonderful from conception on. Other women vomit in the morning but feel fine the remainder of the day. Then there are those expectant mothers who suffer nonstop.

A Hormone High

Morning sickness is usually attributed to hormonal changes during pregnancy. While these hormonal changes do much to maintain the health of mother and baby, they unfortunately come with side effects, notably stomach upset. The hormone that supports your pregnancy, human chorionic gonadotropin or HCG, is the prime suspect, as it runs at an all-time high during the first few months. Other hormones may also play a nauseating role as well, including rising estrogen and progesterone levels.

Luckily, relief is usually just a few months away since symptoms typically subside after the first trimester. In the meantime, you don't need to sit and suffer. While there is no cure for nausea, there are ways to take the edge off that unpleasant feeling. Experiment with a few cures below and find out what works best for you.

WHEN TO CALL THE DOCTOR

- If you are losing weight
- If the vomiting does not let up
- If you are becoming dehydrated. (Signs are infrequent urination and dark urine.)
- If you haven't been able to keep food or drink down for 24 hours
- If you are feeling increasingly tired
- If you feel dizzy or can't focus mentally
- If morning sickness persists past the third month

FROM THE CUPBOARD

CRACKERS. Crackers are a pregnant woman's prize possession (food-wise). They are portable, easy-to-digest, inexpensive, and in many cases, nip nausea in the bud. Plain, whole-wheat crackers, pretzels, plain popcorn, or low-salt soda crackers are your best bets. Nibble on them throughout the day and before going to bed. If morning sickness hits full force in the A.M., stay in bed nibbling on crackers for several minutes. Sudden transitions from the horizontal to the vertical often trigger nausea, so go easy in the morning.

POTATO CHIPS. Perhaps pregnancy is the only time in a woman's life when potato chips offer a cure... and can be consumed without guilt. For many women, munching on a few chips (note the word "few") at the first sign of nausea helps dissipate it. If this cure is for you, stick to regular potato chips and stay away from fat-free varieties that contain Olestra, the fat substitute. Olestra robs yours body of important nutrients and is known to cause diarrhea.

Pregnancy can prompt an over-production of saliva, which can make you sick to your stomach. Nibbling on some salt-and-vinegar chips helps dry up the saliva.

As with any junk food, don't pig out on chips even if they are a cure. Nibble only when needed. Some women in fact may find this remedy distasteful since fat is hard to digest and can cause increased stomach upset.

FROM THE REFRIGERATOR

CITRUS FRUIT. A small slice of lemon, lime, or orange added to your water or herbal tea can help ease nausea.

FRUITS AND VEGETABLES. Water consumption is very important during pregnancy, but all your water doesn't have to come from the tap. Foods high in water content work double time at preventing dehydration and its partner constipation... both of which aggravate nausea. Try snacking on melons, carrots, celery, grapes, apples, pears, and frozen fruit bars.

FROM THE SINK

WATER. Dehydration can bring about nausea. Expectant mothers must drink 8 glasses of water a day.

FROM THE SPICE RACK

FENNEL. Like mint (see below), fennel seed contains anesthetic constituents that may reduce queasiness. Crush 1 tablespoon fennel seeds into a coffee grinder. Place the crushed seeds in a cup and fill with boiling water. Cover and let steep for ten minutes. Drink the tea in sips to treat nausea.

GINGER. Ginger has a well-established track record as a morning sickness remedy. The root of this plant contains chemicals called gingerols and shogaols that relax the intestinal tract, relieving nausea and vomiting. The easiest way to get your ginger is through real ginger ale (noncaffeinated) or ginger tea. For the tea, place ½ teaspoon powdered ginger spice into a cup and fill with boiling water. Cover and let stand ten minutes. Strain and sip. Don't take more than three times daily. If needed, sweeten with a little honey. You can also try ginger candy.

A WORD OF WARNING

Some herbs traditionally used to cure nausea should be avoided during pregnancy because they promote miscarriage or menstruation. Such herbs include catnip, cinnamon, clove, thyme, and yarrow. (The spices, when present in spiced foods, probably present no problem.) Other traditional antinausea herbs, such as mint, ginger, and raspberry, are safe when taken in quantities as directed. It is always best to check with your doctor before taking any herbs during pregnancy.

Warning! Some experts frown upon using ginger during pregnancy, but others say it is OK. Should you have any doubts, consult your doctor.

LAVENDER AND THYME. Smells become more pronounced during pregnancy. Odors that didn't bother you before, like dirty laundry, can now have you reaching for a bucket. Battle smells of any sort by arming yourself with a small satchel stuffed with dried herbs. Lavender and thyme are particularly appealing since both have soothing reputations. A handkerchief scented with fresh-squeezed lemon also makes a handy remedy. Keep the satchel or hanky near the nose and breathe in deeply when odors turn your stomach sour.

MINT. The anesthetic constituents in mint work to minimize nausea by reducing the stomach's gag reflex. Make a cup of mint tea anytime you feel a wave of nausea about to crash ashore. Place 1 tablespoon mint leaves in a 1-pint jar of boiling water. Let stand 20 to 30 minutes, shaking occasionally. Strain and sip as needed.

MORE DO'S AND DON'TS

- Cut out the caffeine. Caffeinated coffee, teas, and soft drinks are diuretics and pull water from your system.
- Graze all day. Eating 6 small meals a day keeps the stomach occupied. An empty stomach and/or low blood sugar can trigger nausea.

Motion Sickness
TAMING TURBULENCE

It can happen almost anywhere—in the backseat of your family van, on the Tilt-a-Whirl at the county fair, on the bumpy airplane ride to Grandma's, on your Alaskan cruise. Anything that moves has the potential to give you a green hue and leave you wishing the world would put on the brakes. Or at least that the plane, train, automobile, amusement park ride, or boat that's making you so ill would stop so you could die in peace. Anyone who has experienced motion sickness would agree that it is a horrible feeling—one they wouldn't want to make a repeat appearance. Thankfully, most people only deal with motion sickness on occasion. And following some simple tips can help avert those rare bouts.

Tummy Turbulence

So why does your tummy do cartwheels every time you sail, fly, or ride? Motion sickness is purely a matter of miscommunication. When you're cruising down the road focused on a book or a person, your eyes tell your brain that you're not moving, but your inner ear tells the brain a different story. For instance, you and your girlfriends are going for a long-awaited women-only weekend. All six of you pile in your friend's minivan. You pop in the passenger seat and as soon as you get on the road, you're turned around chatting with your buddies. You see only your stationary friends sitting in the back of the van, so your eyes tell your brain that you're sitting in a room catching up with old pals. But the fluid in your inner ear is sloshing around with every bump and turn. Your brain is getting mixed signals. And in the confusion, your brain triggers your tummy and you start feeling sick. Next thing you know, you and the girls are forced to make a pit stop.

Symptoms of a Spinning Head

No one can completely avoid motion sickness. Even astronauts have bouts of nausea every now and then. For most people, motion sickness comes on fairly quickly and usually involves one of these symptoms: sweating, hyperventilation, dizziness, paleness, sensation of spinning (even after you're off the Tilt-a-Whirl), loss of appetite, and of course, nausea.

FROM THE CUPBOARD

CRACKERS. Take these easily digestible snacks along and nibble on them every couple of hours to help prevent nausea and vomiting. An empty stomach makes it more likely that you will get sick.

GINGER. Ginger has long been known as an herbal remedy for queasiness, but modern science has proved this spice has merit, especially for motion sickness. One study discovered that ginger was actually better than over-the-counter motion sickness drugs. Make a ginger tea to take along with you when you're traveling by cutting 10 to 12 slices of fresh ginger and placing them in a pot with 1 quart water. Boil for ten minutes. Strain out the ginger, and add ½ cup honey or maple syrup for sweetening if you like. For other ways to take ginger, see "Be Sure to Tote This Herb When You Travel," page 234.

LOW FAT FOODS. If you eat a low fat meal before you head out on your trip, you may avoid getting sick. Eating something before you leave makes your stomach more capable of handling the ups and downs of the road. Experts say not eating destabilizes the stomach's electrical signals, making you susceptible to nausea and vomiting.

PEPPERMINT CANDIES OR LOZENGES. If you start feeling sick, get out the peppermints. Not only will you end up with fresh minty breath when you arrive at your destination, you'll also calm your queasiness. And if you're traveling with little ones, try placing 1 drop peppermint oil on their tongues before the trip. It may quash the queasies.

TEA. Sip on some warm tea if you start feeling sick. Warm beverages tend to be easier on a nauseated tummy than cool or cold ones. Go for the decaf brew; caffeinated drinks aren't a good idea for unstable stomachs.

FROM THE FREEZER

ICE. Sucking on some ice chips may help calm your stomach and help divert your attention from your unsettled tummy.

WHEN TO CALL THE DOCTOR

• If motion sickness becomes a regular occurrence and if it is so extreme it becomes debilitating

TODDLERS AND TRAVEL

Kids ages 2 to 12 are the most likely to suffer from motion sickness. Why is it so common? Kids' nervous systems are still immature, so they are less able to adjust to movement.

BE SURE TO TOTE THIS HERB WHEN YOU TRAVEL

Ginger tea isn't the only way to get the protective and calming benefits of this herb. Studies have found that 250 to 500 mg of dried ginger taken every six hours staves off motion sickness. Your best bet is to take your dose of ginger before you travel. You could also try candied ginger: a one-inch piece should do the trick. And there's also enough ginger in gingersnaps and ginger ale to ease milder bouts of nausea.

FROM THE REFRIGERATOR

APPLE JUICE. Drink a glass of apple juice with your pre-travel low fat meal. Giving your body a bit of sugar with fluids before you start your journey should help you down the road. And if you start feeling ill, sip some noncitrus juice. Citrus juice irritates an already unstable stomach.

MORE DO'S AND DON'TS

- Focus on the horizon. Stay focused on the sunset, a billboard, a tree, anything outside the vehicle that isn't moving. Having a stable object to focus on helps your eyes and inner ear send the same message to your brain.

- Skip the fast food. That hamburger and fries might be quick and convenient, but they won't sit well in your tummy.

- Ax the alcohol. Drinking while traveling will only make you feel worse. Alcohol tends to go through the bloodstream straight to the inner ear, which throws your equilibrium off.

- Put away the book (or laptop or magazine). Looking at these while trees are whipping past your head will only make you sicker.

- Keep busy. Keeping your mind occupied, with music or conversation, will help fend off nausea.

BEST BETS FOR SICKNESS-FREE TRAVEL

Follow these travel tips and you'll be more likely to get where you're going without motion sickness misery.
Airplane. Get a seat near the front edge of a wing. And be sure to get a window seat so you can let your eyes and ears get in sync.
Train. Sit near a window and face forward. Don't face the rear or you're sure to get sick.
Boat. A recent study discovered that where you sleep on a cruise ship isn't all that important. It's where you are when you're awake that can cause problems. Stay on deck when you can so you can spy the horizon at all times, and stay near the middle of the ship if you're sensing some rocking. There's less rocking and swaying in the middle of the ship.
Car. Sit in the front passenger seat so you can see the horizon. Don't turn around if you can help it. If you struggle with sickness every time you ride, try driving. It may take your mind off feeling queasy.

Muscle Soreness/Cramping

EASING THE ACHE

You've made your New Year's resolution: You are going to get in shape. Never mind that the last time you exercised was at a charity walk a few years ago and that the very expensive treadmill you bought is now buried underneath a pile of laundry. Twenty pounds and three kids ago you were an aerobics queen, so you know what it's like to feel, and look, better. So you venture into your local health club and decide to try the low/high aerobics class for people who have been out of circulation for a while. You think you can keep up with the twenty-something girls, so you grapevine and kick and half-jack with the beat for 50 minutes. By the time you get home, though, your muscles have gone on strike. The next day you can barely muster enough strength to make it out of bed, and you spend the day walking like you've been riding the range a bit too long. You'll take it slower next time. But what can you do right now to ease the pain?

Muscle Mayhem

The vast array of muscles in your body is what allows you to do something as simple as picking up a fork or as complicated as a kickboxing routine. Muscles are a complex weave of fibers that work with your brain and skeletal system to give you the agility to return that volley across the tennis court. When you're taking care to stretch and strengthen your muscles, they are your greatest ally. But when they don't work like they should or they get injured, you have a very painful problem on your hands.

Strains are one of the most common reasons for aching muscles. When you strain a muscle, it means you've worked it too hard, causing the muscle fibers to pull and tear. If you haven't worked out for a while and then head back full throttle without preparing your muscles for the trauma they're about to experience, or if you're an experienced exerciser and you don't warm up properly, you risk getting a strained muscle. At best, a strained muscle will leave you sore for a few days; at worst, you could end up with a "pulled" muscle, one whose fibers have been totally torn.

WHEN TO CALL THE DOCTOR

- If you get serious leg cramps often. It could be a signal that there's a problem with the blood flow to your muscle, or it may mean you have a nerve injury.
- If you think you may have a severe strain

Not sure if you have a severe muscle strain? Ask yourself these questions:

1. Did you feel a sharp pain at the moment you injured your muscle?
2. Does moving the muscle cause intense pain?
3. Is there localized swelling and tenderness in the area of the muscle?
4. Are you unable to use the muscle?
5. Do you have bruising or discoloration in the injured area?

If you answered "yes" to any of these questions, you may have a serious strain.

Another common muscle malady is cramps, or spasms. Muscle cramps happen when the muscle isn't getting enough blood, and in response to the restricted blood flow, the muscle shortens and tightens. The slowdown in blood flow can be caused by a variety of problems:

- A deficiency in essential nutrients for maximum muscle power, such as sodium, calcium, and potassium
- Depletion of the muscles' energy supply of glycogen
- Overworked muscles
- Holding the same position for too long

Whatever the reason, when blood doesn't reach your muscles the way it should, your muscles can turn into balls of pain.

Your first priority is to give your muscles some rest. Take a few ideas from the kitchen that will help you feel better, fast.

FROM THE CUPBOARD

BOUILLON. Sipping some warm soup before heading out for a bike ride may not sound appealing, but it may help you skip the muscle cramps. Drink 1 cup beef or chicken bouillon before you ride. It helps replace the sodium you lose when you sweat.

EPSOM SALTS. Jump in a hot bath with Epsom salts to ease the pain of your strain (but wait at least 24 hours before you hit the heat). Epsom salts contain loads of magnesium that is absorbed through the skin. Magnesium helps promote the healing of torn muscles. Add 2 cups Epsom salts to a tub of hot water. It also relieves any swelling.

FROM THE FREEZER

ICE. Immediately after straining a muscle, your first order of business is to allay the swelling. The best way to keep your torn muscle from swelling is to constrict the blood vessels that run to it. The best way to do that: Ice 'em. Some athletes actually take a hop in an ice bath to soothe strained muscles, but if you're not that brave, try an ice pack on the area for 20 to 30 minutes every hour.

FROM THE FRUIT BASKET

BANANA. Eat a banana or two a day and you may cut down your cramping. That's because a potassium deficiency may be to blame for muscle cramps. Though there's no official recommendation for how much potassium you should have per day, the American Dietetic Association suggests adults get about 2,000 mg a day. One banana has 450 mg of the muscle-protecting nutrient.

> ### THIS'LL PUMP YOU UP
> One muscle fiber is thinner than a human hair but can support up to 1,000 times its own weight.

FROM THE REFRIGERATOR

MILK. Getting adequate amounts of calcium in your diet may help curtail cramps. Women especially seem to need plenty of calcium for muscle health. Three glasses of milk a day will meet the calcium needs of most adults.

WATER. Yes, it's the elixir of life as well as your best bet for avoiding a painful muscle cramp while you exercise. When you exercise, you sweat. That sweat depletes your body of needed fluids and can cause your muscles to mutiny. Drink plenty of water before, during, and after you do your activity of choice.

FROM THE SPICE RACK

ROSEMARY. A few leaves of rosemary can help reduce swelling in strained muscles. Use either fresh or dried leaves; fresh has more of the volatile oils. The herb has four anti-inflammatory properties, which can help calm inflamed muscle tissue and speed healing. Because rosemary is easily absorbed through the skin, placing a cloth soaked with a rosemary wash will help ease the pain. Here's how to make a rosemary wash: Put 1 ounce rosemary leaves in a 1-pint jar and fill the jar with boiling water. Cover and let stand for 30 minutes. Apply the wash to the area two or three times a day.

MORE DO'S AND DON'TS

- Stop. If you feel muscle pain or a cramp creeping up on you, stop what you're doing. Don't try to exercise through the pain, you'll only make things worse.

- Stretch and squeeze. When you get a cramp, stretch the offending muscle slowly. As you stretch, use one hand to gently squeeze your ball of painful muscle.

- Try some quinine. Used mostly for treating malaria, some athletes swear by quinine as a treatment for muscle cramps. In the form of tonic water or quinine sulfate pills, these may help alleviate your cramping calves. But be wary: The Food and Drug Administration (FDA) took quinine off the market for a time because it had some potentially harmful side effects.

- Halt the heat. Don't put heat on a strained muscle in the first 24 hours after you exercise. Heat causes blood vessels to dilate and increases swelling and fluid buildup, which means your soreness will last longer than it should.

- Go over the counter. Use an anti-inflammatory drug to ease the pain and stop the swelling.

- Skip the sports drinks. Unless you're running more than an hour every day, you really don't need a sports drink. Water is your best bet for replacing fluids.

- Cancel the creams. Topical sports creams, except those containing capsaicin, won't help your sore muscles because they don't do anything to the tissues underneath. And if you use a cream and place a heating pad over it, you could end up with a serious burn.

- Keep muscles warm. In cold weather, this may help you avoid cramps.

- Don't do too much, too fast. Start slowly and add to your workout. Some experts recommend the ten percent rule: Add ten percent more intensity to your workout every week.

- Keep moving. One of the worst things you can do for sore muscles is to stay still until the pain goes away. Walking around or doing some slow stretches returns blood flow to the muscle, making it much easier for the body to repair itself.

NOCTURNAL NUDGES

There's nothing like a nighttime leg cramp to get you howling at the moon. Pinched nerves are the usual culprit, making your calf muscle knot up and waking you—and the rest of the house—from a peaceful slumber. Or you may simply have rolled and stretched a tendon, which caused some mixed signals to go through your spinal cord and resulted in a cramped calf muscle.

Seventy percent of people older than age 50 find themselves dealing with nighttime muscle cramps. If you find yourself with a cramp, massage the muscle with long strokes, moving toward the heart. Drinking quinine water (tonic water) may also help, as quinine is a skeletal muscle relaxant.

You may be able to avoid muscle cramps by stretching before bed (especially concentrating on the offending muscle), sleeping under a light pile of blankets, and being sure you get enough calcium—which is often deficient in people who get those nocturnal nudges.

Nail Problems

DOCTORING DIGITS

Most people find themselves dealing with
nail problems from time to time. The
American Academy of Dermatology
says that nail disorders make up
ten percent of all skin conditions. So whether you've got
something as frustrating as brittle
nails or something more serious, such
as a fungal infection, taking good care of
your nails will help you put your best foot, or
hand, forward.

Nail Knowledge

Though they may be a source of frustration from time to time (ever
snagged a pair of new pantyhose with a rough nail edge?), your nails are
there for a good reason. They make it much easier to pick up a paper clip
or grip a pencil. They also help support tissues in the fingers and toes
and help protect your body from infection-causing bacteria. Nails are
made of keratin—the same protein in your skin and your hair. Made of
many layers, nails have a unique design that makes them tough and
resilient. Here are their parts:

Nail plate. This is the part you cut and paint and file—the tough part
that is visible on your fingers and toes.

Nail Bed. This is the skin right below the nail. It's best if you only see
that through the translucent nail—if you've ever ripped your nail off
into the nail bed, you understand. (It's painful!)

Matrix. This is a secret place, invisible to the eye, underneath the
cuticle that is essentially the nerve center of nail growth.

Lunula. Look at the bottom of your nail. The whitish, half-moon
shape where your nail disappears into the skin is actually a visible part of
the matrix.

Cuticle. This is the skin that wraps around the sides and base of the
nail.

Nail folds. The skin that frames the nail.

Notorious Nail Offenders

Not paying much attention to your nails can cause you problems in
the long run. And dealing with nail problems can be a painful, and

WHEN TO CALL THE DOCTOR

- If a fungal infection does not respond to over-the-counter antifungal medications
- If your ingrown toenail becomes very painful and pus develops or you notice redness that seems to be spreading
- If you have diabetes and any toenail problems
- If the bruise under your hammer-hit nail puts too much pressure on the nail; the doctor may need to drain it

These may signal a more serious problem:

- Pale or bluish nails can mean anemia.
- Yellowish nails may mean diabetes.
- White nails can indicate liver disease.
- Half-pink, half-white nails can mean kidney disease.
- Thick yellow nails that are growing slower than usual can indicate lung disease.
- Nails shaped like the back of a spoon may signal cardiopulmonary disease or asthma.
- Nails that dip inward may signal anemia.
- A dark spot in the nails may be a sign of skin cancer.

yucky, business. Here is a rundown of the most common nail problems.

Brittle nails. Brittle nails are less painful than many nail problems but they're no less annoying. If you're battling brittle nails, you've most likely got one of two conditions—hard, brittle nails or soft, brittle nails. Both make you more likely to have nails that split and break easily. Hard nails can be caused by using nail polish removers too often, being in a too-dry environment (like indoor heat), or not wearing gloves while dealing with harsh chemicals or detergents. And as you get older, your skin gets drier and you encounter more problems with brittle nails. If you have hard, dry nails, you need to moisturize them, just as you would dry skin. Soft, brittle nails, on the other hand, are caused by exposing the nails to too much moisture—either using too much hand lotion or keeping your hands in water too long. Soft nails need to be kept dry.

Fungus. Fungal infections make up 50 percent of all nail disorders. Toenails are more susceptible than fingernails because toenails are usually enclosed in a warm, moist, fungus-loving environment. Fungal infections may cause the nail plate to separate from the nail bed (ouch!) and cause very unpleasant-looking debris, usually white, green, yellow, or black, to build under the nail plate.

Ingrown nails. A nail becomes ingrown when the corner of the nail curves downward into the skin, causing a very painful condition. Not properly trimming your nails can make you more likely to get an ingrown nail, but wearing too-snug shoes can also be a contributing factor. Ingrown nails are more common on toenails, but fingernails can have the problem, too.

Nail trauma. You slam the car door on your finger, or you bash your thumbnail with a hammer. As blood rushes to the surface of your nail, it forms a bruise. This type of injury can open the door to other infections and needs to be watched carefully.

It'd be nice if drinking a glass of milk made your nails grow more quickly, but the reality is there's nothing you can eat or drink that will make your nails grow longer or stronger. Neither eating gelatin nor taking vitamin and mineral supplements will make your nails any stronger or grow any faster. But there are some kitchen staples that will help you keep your nails at their healthiest and alleviate nail problems.

FROM THE CUPBOARD

BAKING SODA. Clean your nails and soften cuticles by scrubbing them with a nailbrush dipped in baking soda.

SALT. Soaking painful ingrown nails in a warm saltwater solution will help ease the pain and relieve swelling. Add 1 tablespoon salt per quart of water and soak for 30 minutes. A saltwater soak can also make tough nails easier to trim. Try soaking nails in the same solution for five to ten minutes before trimming.

FROM THE DRAWER

VINYL GLOVES. Exposing your hands to moisture too often, or getting your hands in harsh detergents or chemicals, can cause brittle nails. Wearing vinyl gloves keeps your hands dry and safe from abrasive materials. To repel moisture even more, try sprinkling baby powder in your gloves.

FROM THE SINK

WATER. Hard, brittle nails need some moisture. Soak your nails in tepid water and then slather on a moisturizer with phospholipids, urea, or lactic acid.

MORE DO'S AND DON'TS

To avoid fungal infections
• Keep your nails clean and dry.

• Change your socks often.

• Use an antifungal spray or powder on your feet and in your shoes.

• Don't go barefoot in a public shower.

To avoid or treat ingrown toenails
• Trim toenails straight across.

• Don't wear shoes and socks that are too snug.

• Put small pieces of cotton under the edge of the ingrown nail. That will help the nail grow above the skin.

• Apply an antibiotic ointment to the infected area.

Nausea/Vomiting
HALTING THE HEAVES

It happens to everybody, sometime. No one gets a free pass. But that doesn't make the misery of nausea and vomiting any easier on your system.

Nausea is a warning signal; it means stop eating, let your stomach rest. Vomiting is a warning signal, too; it means something does not belong in your stomach and it's time to get rid of it. In other words, nausea and vomiting are two ways that your tummy protects itself.

Who Dunnit?

Usually nausea and vomiting are self-limiting: Once the cause is removed, the symptoms go away. So what causes these unsettling symptoms? There are many possibilities, including

- something you ate or drank
- a medication you took
- food poisoning
- early pregnancy
- a stomach disorder
- a viral or bacterial infection
- migraine headache
- head injury
- inner ear infection
- stress
- recreational drug use
- binge-purge eating disorders
- visual disturbances
- fear

The bottom line is that nausea and vomiting are not caused by any single factor. And they're not illnesses in themselves. They're symptoms of something else going on with your body.

When to Halt the Heaves

While your first inclination after vomiting is to find some way to stop it from happening again, this emetic rush is really your friend because it often literally does get rid of whatever is ailing you. On occasion, however, nausea and vomiting drag on. While you may be able to cope with ongoing nausea, there are risks to repeated vomiting. If you vomit a lot or for many days, you can become dehydrated quickly. And if vomiting accompanies morning sickness, the nutritional flow to the developing fetus may be impaired.

Because nausea and vomiting are usually just sideshows and not the main event, under most circumstances they can be remedied right in your kitchen without too much fuss or muss. Here are several ways to put them in their place.

FROM THE CUPBOARD

PEPPERMINT CANDY. Peppermint candy can remedy nausea. Peppermint anesthetizes the stomach, which reduces the gag reflex and stops vomiting. Suck on a piece or two to rid yourself of the symptoms.

POPCORN. Air pop a cup or two and place in a bowl. Skip the butter and salt. Instead, pour enough boiling water over the popcorn to cover it, then let it stand for 15 minutes. Take 1 teaspoon every ten minutes for nausea. Popcorn is a carbohydrate, which is especially necessary if you've been vomiting or skipping meals, and the added water is good for dehydration.

SALT. To stop that vomiting, mix together 1 heaping teaspoon salt, 1 heaping teaspoon red pepper, and 1 cup vinegar. Take 1 tablespoon every half hour, as needed.

SODA CRACKERS. Chewing on a few of these can help quell nausea.

VINEGAR. To stop the nausea of morning sickness, stir 1 teaspoon apple cider vinegar into 1 glass water and drink.

WHEN TO CALL THE DOCTOR

Call 9-1-1 immediately:

- If you have abdominal pain, blurred vision, muscle weakness, difficulty speaking or swallowing, or muscle paralysis. This could be botulism.

- If along with nausea and vomiting you are sweating or dizzy, have especially teary eyes or excessive saliva, are confused or have abdominal pain 30 minutes after eating. This can be pesticide poisoning or other deadly contamination.

- If you vomit blood or your vomit contains material that resembles coffee grounds

Call your doctor for:

- Bloody or tarry stools
- Symptoms of dehydration
- Swelling or pain in the abdomen or rectum
- Symptoms that recur or that last more than two to three days
- Symptoms and a fever of 101.5°F or higher

NAUSEA-FRIENDLY FOODS

Even though you're queasy, you've got to eat something. Isn't that what your mother always told you? Well, she was right. Nausea and vomiting can lead to dehydration and a depletion in vital nutrients, so unless you're fully engaged in a bout of vomiting, here are some foods that might go down easily: rice, cooked cereal, crackers, puddings, low fat milkshakes, fruit salad, cottage cheese. Also, try mixing a little white rice with cottage cheese. It digests easily.

FASCINATING FACT

Smell can exacerbate nausea and bring on vomiting. If you're feeling a little queasy, stay away from cooking smells, especially fried and spicy foods. Also skip the foods about which you have negative thoughts. Just the thought of those foods really can make you sick.

FROM THE REFRIGERATOR

CRANBERRY JUICE. When you're nauseated and vomiting, don't give up the fluids. Drink cranberry juice; it's generally easy on your digestive tract.

LEMON JUICE. Mix together 1 teaspoon honey and 1 teaspoon lemon juice. And this cure comes with a folkish instruction: Dip your finger into the mix and lick it off so that you take it in slowly.

LIME JUICE. For an immediate nausea and vomiting stopper, mix 1 cup water, 10 drops lime juice, and ½ teaspoon sugar. Then add ¼ teaspoon baking soda and drink.

MILK. Don't drink it straight. Instead, try this vintage milk toast recipe for a bland food that's easy to eat when combating nausea and vomiting. Heat 1 cup milk until hot but not boiling. Put it in a bowl. Then take 1 piece of toast, slightly buttered, and crumble it into the milk. Eat slowly.

ONION. Juice an onion, and mix 1 teaspoon juice with 1 teaspoon grated ginger. Take for nausea.

FROM THE SPICE RACK

ANISEED. This helps cure nausea and vomiting. Brew aniseed into a tea by putting ¼ teaspoon in ½ cup boiling water. Steep for five minutes. Strain and drink once a day. Or sprinkle some aniseed on mild vegetables such as carrots or pumpkin. If your stomach will tolerate fruits, try aniseed on baked apples or pears.

CARDAMOM SEEDS. To relieve nausea, chew 1 to 2 cardamom seeds. Another cardamom cure is to mix 2 pinches ground cardamom and ½ teaspoon honey into ½ cup plain yogurt. It's a nutritious food to eat when you can't keep anything else down.

CINNAMON. Steep ½ teaspoon cinnamon powder in 1 cup boiling water, strain, and sip for nausea. Do not try this remedy if you're pregnant.

CLOVE. For a nausea-fighting tea, brew a cup using 1 teaspoon clove powder in a teacup full of boiling water. Strain and drink as needed.

CUMIN. Steep a tea with 1 teaspoon cumin seeds and a pinch of nutmeg to soothe tummy troubles.

FENNEL. Crush 1 tablespoon seeds and steep for ten minutes in 1 cup boiling water. Sweeten to taste with honey. Sip as necessary for nausea.
GINGER. Ginger is the best stomach woe cure of all. Taken in any form, it will relieve nausea. Try ginger tea, gingerbread, or gingersnaps. If you're traveling, take along ginger sticks or crystallized ginger instead of travel sickness pills or patches. Studies show ginger to be more effective than anything you purchase at the pharmacy. Skip the ginger ale, though, unless it contains real ginger; most ginger ale today does not.
MINT. Mint tea relieves nausea. Simply steep about 1 tablespoon dry leaves in 1 pint hot water for 30 minutes; strain and drink. Don't toss out those mint leaves when you drink the tea. Instead, eat them. Eating boiled mint leaves can help cure nausea, too.

MORE DO'S & DON'TS

- Go to bed. Rest is the best cure for whatever's causing your nausea or vomiting.

- Skip the booze. It can be hard on a stomach even under the best of circumstances. While you're at it, avoid these gut-wreckers, too: fatty or highly seasoned foods, caffeine, cigarettes.

- If you must take an over-the-counter remedy, try one with bismuth, such as Pepto-Bismol. It will coat the stomach and relieve discomfort. Skip the fizzy seltzer stuff. It contains aspirin, which may be an irritant.

- After you vomit, rinse the remaining particles out of your mouth with ¼ cup water and ¼ cup vinegar in a 4-ounce glass. The stomach acids in vomit can be harsh on tooth enamel. Just rinse, don't gargle. This freshens your breath, too.

BACK IN THE SWING OF EATING

When the vomiting starts, eating stops. You do have to start again, though, and unless you're a glutton for more gut-wrenching punishment, starting out easy is the best way. Here's how to resume eating after a bout of vomiting.

- Try clear liquids first. You can take them during your bout of vomiting, although they may come back up. When you can keep them down, take nothing but clear liquids for 12 hours. Water, broth, flavored gelatin water, and noncitrus fruit juices work well.

- After 12 hours, switch to bland foods: rice, cooked cereal, clear soups with rice or noodles, cottage cheese, baked potatoes, flavored gelatin. Eat these for 24 hours.

- After a day of bland foods, add mild foods, such as baked or broiled lean meats and steamed vegetables, back into your diet. Skip greasy and spicy foods for a few more days just to make sure your stomach is ready to handle them.

Nosebleeds
STOPPING THE FLOW

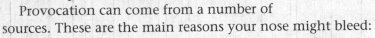

Nosebleeds can run the gamut from a tiny
trickle to a big gush. But while it may be disturb-
ing to see blood drip from your otherwise placid
nose, there is usually no need to worry. Nosebleeds are typically harmless annoyances. And
while it may look like you're losing lots of blood,
the amount is usually insignificant.

The inner nose is one of the more sensitive
parts of the body. Lined with hundreds of blood
vessels that reside close to the surface, the nostrils
don't take kindly to being harassed and will bleed
with little provocation.

Provocation can come from a number of
sources. These are the main reasons your nose might bleed:

- Trauma, such as a fall or a sports-related injury
- Dry air
- High altitudes
- Nose picking
- Sneezing
- Nose blowing
- Rubbing the nose
- Allergies
- Upper respiratory infection
- Age (Older people have more nosebleeds because the body's tissues
  have shrunk and are more dry.)
- Tumors, but this is a rare occurrence.

The main way to stop a nosebleed is to firmly but gently pinch your
nostrils closed, holding them tightly together for at least ten minutes.
Lean forward to prevent blood from running down the throat. In addition to this first line of treatment, there are other means to help stop a
nosebleed as well as prevent one.

FROM THE CUPBOARD
BAKING SODA. Used for nasal irrigation. See "Salt" on the next page.
COTTON. One folk cure that seems to work involves a simple piece of

cotton. Place it inside your upper lip against the gum during a nosebleed. What's the secret behind this cure? Location, location, location. A major blood vessel that supplies the interior of the nose runs right through the upper lip. The slight pressure of the cotton wad can help stop bleeding.

VINEGAR. Take a cloth or cotton ball and wet it with white vinegar. Plug it in the nostril that's bleeding. Vinegar helps seal up the blood vessel wall.

WHOLE-WHEAT BREAD. Zinc is a nutrient known to help maintain the body's blood vessels. Eat whole-wheat bread and brown rice, two foods high in zinc. Or, for a snack, try some popcorn, which also contains zinc.

FROM THE FREEZER

ICE. Ice is nice for stopping bleeding, constricting the blood vessels, and reducing inflammation (if the nose is injured). Place crushed ice into a plastic zipper-type bag and cover with a towel. (A bag of frozen vegetables works fine, too.) Place the compress on the bridge of the nose and hold until well after the bleeding stops.

FROM THE REFRIGERATOR

DARK GREEN, LEAFY VEGETABLES. High in vitamin K, these are essential for proper blood clotting.

ORANGES AND ORANGE JUICE. Keeping those blood vessels in top form is one way to prevent them from breaking so easily. Vitamin C is necessary to the formation of collagen, which helps create a moist lining in your nose. So drink and eat vitamin C-rich foods to help stave off nosebleeds.

FROM THE SINK

WATER. Dry winter air and mountain air can dry out the nose in no time. Being well hydrated helps. Always drink 8 glasses of water a day, but have a few more during the driest times and in the driest places.

FROM THE SPICE RACK

SALT. Nasal irrigation, commonly used by allergy sufferers to rid the nasal passages of mucus, dust, and other gunk, also helps soothe and moisturize irritated nasal membranes. You'll need 1 to 1½ cups lukewarm

WHEN TO CALL THE DOCTOR

- If the nose gushes blood and can't be stopped after five minutes
- If the victim has high blood pressure, diabetes, or blood-clotting problems
- If nosebleeds become frequent, since this may indicate a blood clotting disorder or hypertension
- If blood runs down the throat instead of out the nose
- If the nosebleed is the result of a nose, face, or head injury

TAKING A NOSE DIVE

New scuba divers often are alarmed when they experience a nosebleed. While many blame the salt water, the real problem usually stems from inadequate equalization of pressure in the sinuses and middle ear. Without proper equalization during descent, the delicate blood vessels in the lining of the nose can burst. Divers with sinus troubles, allergies, past nose injuries, or a deviated septum may find equalization a problem and experience nosebleeds more frequently. A slow, gentle descent into the deep blue with frequent equalization can stop the nose from turning red.

water (do not use softened water), a bulb (ear) syringe (typically found with baby products in the pharmacy), ¼ to ½ teaspoon salt, and ¼ to ½ teaspoon baking soda. Mix the salt and baking soda into the water, and test the temperature. To administer, first suck the water into the bulb, then squirt the saline solution into one nostril while holding the other closed. Lower your head over the sink and gently blow out the water. Repeat this, alternating nostrils until the water is gone.

FROM THE STOVE

STEAM. Take every opportunity to breathe steam . . . be it from your morning tea or from a mini steam bath. To do the latter, boil ½ pot water and place on a sturdy surface. Place a towel over your head, lean forward, and breathe gently. Don't lean in too far or you'll burn your sniffer!

FROM THE SUPPLEMENT SHELF

VITAMIN E. Keep your nasal membranes moisturized by applying vitamin E several times a day. Break open a capsule and coat your pinky finger or a cotton swab and gently wipe it just inside your nostrils. This is especially good to do at night before going to sleep.

MORE DO'S AND DON'TS

• Resist the urge to blow your nose or touch it after a nosebleed.

• Pick flowers, not your nose. Fingers only irritate the nose. Use a soft tissue or nasal irrigation if you need to remove debris.

• Blow gently, one nostril at a time, and only when necessary.

• Don't smoke. Smoking irritates and dries out nasal passages. Avoid secondhand smoke, too.

Osteoporosis
BOLSTERING YOUR BONES

More than 28 million Americans are at risk for osteo-porosis, and more than 10 million already have been diagnosed with this bone-degenerating disease. Women make up an astounding 80 percent of those who are affected by osteoporosis. Though most people associate osteoporosis with older people, the disease strikes young and old alike. But osteoporosis does become much more common as you age—affecting one in two women over age 50.

Bone Up on Osteoporosis

As you grow your bones get stronger and longer. By the time you reach the age of 20, you've got 98 percent of your bone mass; by the time you reach your thirtieth birthday, your bones are their strongest. If you were able to take a look inside your bones during those peak years, you'd see a hard outer shell and something that looks like a honeycomb on the inside. About 80 percent of your bone mass is that tough, hard outer bone called cortical bone. The rest of your bone makeup is the honeycomblike material called trabecular bone. After you hit 30, your bone mass begins to decline. Trabecular bone is typically the first to lose critical density, and as you get older, cortical bone mass also declines, but at a slower pace.

Osteoporosis literally means porous bones. That means someone diagnosed with the disease has lost so much density that there's not much there to hold their bones together, putting them at greater risk for bone breaks and fractures. The National Osteoporosis Foundation calls osteoporosis the "silent disease" because there are virtu-ally no symptoms of bone loss. Unless you're aware of the risk factors and take action, you may not know you have the disease until some benign bump against a door turns into a fracture.

WHEN TO CALL THE DOCTOR

- If you are at risk for osteoporosis. There are tests that can determine your bone density, and your doctor can advise you about prevention and treatment of the disease.
- If you have sudden pain in your back, which may indicate a fracture in a bone in the spine

THE CALCIUM CONNECTION

You've heard it over and over: "Drink milk for strong bones." But what's the catch? Why is calcium so vital for your bones? For one, your body contains more calcium than any other mineral, and 99 percent of that calcium is in your bones. When you eat or drink calcium, it goes into your bones and then gets taken out for other bodily functions.

Making sure you get enough calcium means you have enough to feed your bones and some reserve for times when your nervous system needs a little of the mineral to help pass messages from your brain to your big toe. You also need a reserve for times when you simply don't get enough in your diet.

THE ETHNIC EDGE

Five percent of African American women older than age 50 have osteoporosis. Ten percent of Hispanic women in that age-group have the disease. Compare those numbers to the 20 percent of nonHispanic Caucasian or Asian women over 50 who have osteoporosis.

Who Gets Osteoporosis?

When you think of osteoporosis, you probably picture a petite, silver-haired Caucasian woman. And, in reality, that woman could be the poster child for the disease—being Caucasian or Asian, female, small-framed, and underweight are major risk factors for thinning bones. And so is being postmenopausal. That's because estrogen is vital to bone strength, keeping bones strong by stimulating bone-building substances called osteoblasts and suppressing the bone-destroying substances called osteoclasts. Estrogen also helps the body absorb and use calcium more efficiently. As women approach menopause, estrogen production steadily declines and the protection it provides against osteoporosis is lost. But one of the greatest risk factors for osteoporosis is something you can't see and you can't control—heredity. Other risk factors include: not getting enough calcium, not exercising, having an eating disorder, using certain medications such as corticosteriods, and smoking.

Thankfully, there are many ways you can combat and even reverse the damaging effects of this bone-thinning disease, and the earlier you start the better. Why not try some of these bone boosters in your kitchen?

FROM THE CUPBOARD

BEANS. Take a can of beans—or any one-pound can—and do a few biceps curls. These cans are a perfect weight for beginners and will help you begin to build a little muscle. And strengthening your muscles helps strengthen your bones.

PEANUT BUTTER. A recent review of studies on nutrition and osteoporosis found that magnesium was a vital component to strengthening, preserving, and rebuilding bones. You can get 50 mg of magnesium by eating 2 tablespoons of peanut butter.

FROM THE FRUIT BASKET

APPLES. Boron is a trace mineral that helps your body hold on to calcium—the building block of bones. It even acts as a mild estrogen replacement, and losing estrogen is instrumental in speeding bone loss. Boron is found in apples and other fruits such as pears, grapes, dates, raisins, and peaches. It's also in nuts such as almonds, peanuts, and hazelnuts.

BANANAS. Eat a banana a day to build your bones. Studies have found that women who have diets high in potassium also have stronger bones in their spines and hips. Researchers think this is related to potassium's ability to keep blood healthy and balanced so the body doesn't have to suck calcium from the skeleton to keep blood up to par.

MOOOVE OVER, MILK

Milk isn't the only way you can load up on calcium. There are plenty of nondairy, calcium-rich foods out there. If you're lactose intolerant or simply don't like the taste of milk but you want to be sure you're getting enough calcium, check out these calcium-rich choices.

FOOD	CALCIUM CONTENT (MILLIGRAMS)
Salmon, with bones (3 ounces)	205
Blackstrap molasses (1 tablespoon)	185
Tofu (½ cup)	130
Turnip greens (½ cup)	100
Dried figs (3)	80
Okra (½ cup)	50
Orange (1)	45

FROM THE REFRIGERATOR

BROCCOLI. Eat ½ cup broccoli to get your daily dose of vitamin K. Studies are finding that postmenopausal women with low levels of this vital vitamin are more likely to have osteoporosis.

MARGARINE. Slather a teaspoon of low trans fatty margarine on your toast for a dose of vitamin D. Vitamin D helps the body absorb calcium, a necessary ingredient to bone health.

MILK. When it comes to strong bones, getting enough calcium is a must. One cup of milk can provide 300 mg of the 1,000 to 1,200 mg of calcium the government recommends you get every day. But milk is not the only calcium-rich food on the market. See "Mooove Over, Milk," above, for more ideas on how to add this bone-strengthening mineral to your diet.

ORANGE JUICE. Grab a glass of OJ to get your vitamin C. Necessary for the body processes that rebuild bones, getting enough vitamin C is vital to preventing osteoporosis. Grab some calcium-fortified orange juice and get a healthy dose of bone-building nutrients.

PINEAPPLE JUICE. Drink a cup of pineapple juice and give your body some manganese. Studies are finding that manganese deficiency is a

CALCIUM BOOSTERS

There are plenty of calcium supplements on the market. Look for supplements containing calcium citrate or calcium carbonate.

- Calcium citrate. This type of calcium is better absorbed by the body and doesn't require you to eat when you take it. Look for a brand that contains vitamin D.
- Calcium carbonate. This is probably the type of supplement you'll come across most often. You can get it in capsules, tablets, and even chocolate chews. You do need to eat something when you take these supplements to allow your body maximum absorption. This form is common in many over-the-counter antacids, such as TUMS.

  To maximize the benefit of calcium supplements

- Spread them out. Your body can't absorb more than 500 mg of calcium at a time, so don't take a supplement that contains more than that. And if you need to supplement with more than 500 mg, take them at different times of the day.
- Calcium at night. If you only take one supplement a day and it's made of calcium carbonate, take it with dinner or before bed. Your digestion is slower when you're asleep, so taking it then will ensure your body absorbs the calcium and vitamin D. If you have heartburn, though, you might want to take your supplement at another time of day.
- Try this test. If your supplement doesn't have a code saying it meets United States Pharmacoepia (USP) standards, try this test: Place one tablet in a cup of vinegar. Stir every five minutes. If it doesn't disintegrate within 30 minutes, don't take it. It probably won't dissolve in your tummy either.

predictor of osteoporosis. Other manganese sources are oatmeal, nuts, beans, cereals, spinach, and tea.

TOFU. Soy is showing promise as a potential bone strengthener. Soy contains proteins that act like a weak estrogen in the body. These "phytoestrogens," or plant-based estrogens, may help women regain bone strength.

FROM THE SUPPLEMENT SHELF

CALCIUM. If you don't get enough calcium in your diet, be sure to use a supplement to help prevent osteoporosis. See "Calcium Boosters," above, for information about selecting a supplement.

MORE DO'S AND DON'TS

- Restrict your salt. Salt may actually steal calcium away from your bones.

- Abstain from alcohol. Alcohol interferes with the way your body absorbs calcium.

- Don't smoke. Nicotine works like alcohol in railroading your body's need to absorb calcium.

- Cut the caffeine. Caffeine is a diuretic, and some experts believe drinking too much can cause your body to excrete too much calcium. Don't drink more than 2 cups of coffee or 4 cups of tea a day.

DON'T FORGET THE GUYS

Men have 25 percent more bone mass than women. But they begin to lose bone mass as they age, just like women do. Only in guys, the process is much slower. Any man over age 65 could be at risk for osteoporosis.

- Keep your weight on track. Here's one time when having a few extra pounds works to your advantage. Women who are underweight for their height are at a higher risk of getting osteoporosis.

- Get some sun. To up your supply of vitamin D, be sure to catch a few rays. Spending 15 minutes a day in the sun will give you an adequate supply without causing your skin to suffer.

- Forget the phosphorus myth. A prevailing myth about osteoporosis is that the phosphorus in carbonated drinks can deteriorate your bones. Not true! Too much phosphorus can hinder your body's absorption of calcium, but soda doesn't have enough phosphorus to cause any problems.

Poisonous Plant Rashes
LIMITING THE SPREAD

Contact with poison ivy, poison oak, or poison sumac often goes hand-in-hand with camping and other outdoor activities. Outdoor enthusiasts by the tentful have had to cut trips short after an unfortunate encounter with one of this threesome. The problem stems from the plant's colorless oil called urushiol. Whenever one of these plants is cut, crushed, stepped on, sat on, grabbed, rolled on, kicked, or disturbed, the oil is released. Once on the victim, the toxic oil penetrates the skin and a rash appears within 12 to 48 hours after exposure. This is a true allergic reaction to compounds in the urushiol. The rash starts as small bumps and progresses into enlarged, itchy blisters. No body part is immune to the oil, although areas most often irritated are the face, arms, hands, legs, and genitals.

Don't Touch!

Touching the oil after initial contact is what spreads the rash—something easily done. For example, pretend you unknowingly walk over poison ivy and the oily residue sticks like glue to your hiking boot. Later, you remove the boot, unwittingly touching the residue in the process. Since few people wash their hands after removing boots, the oil easily spreads from the hands, to the face, and even to the genital area should you make the unfortunate decision to use the bathroom. The damage is done by the time the rash breaks out. Touching the rash once it appears does not spread the oil—or the rash.

Warning! Since poison plant oils don't just disappear, it's crucial to wash anything that has had contact with the victim or the oil, including clothing, boots, pets, other people, sleeping bags, fishing poles, walking sticks, etc. Use gloves when cleaning pets, people, and objects that may have had contact with the oil.

> ### WHEN TO CALL THE DOCTOR
>
> - If the skin rash hasn't improved in a week
> - If you develop swelling, feel weak, or have trouble breathing after exposure to the plant

Outdoor expeditions need not be ruined if people learn to recognize the terrible three-some. Here are some pointers:

Poison ivy. Poison ivy plants have serrated, pointed leaves that appear in groups of three leaflets. The leaves are green in summer but are reddish in spring and fall. While their appearance can vary, poison ivy plants are found everywhere in the United States. In the East, Midwest, and South, it grows as a climbing vine. In the West and northern states, poison ivy resembles a shrub. Poison ivy rarely appears above 5,000 feet.

Poison oak. Like poison ivy, poison oak has leaves of three and the shrub's size differs depending on location. In the Southeast it appears as a small shrub, while in the West, poison oak appears as a large shrub. It has greenish-white berries and oaklike leaves.

Poison sumac. The leafy one of this three-some is poison sumac, a small shrub with two rows of 7 to 13 leaflets. Sumac prefers swampy bogs of northern states and swamps in southern states. Its leaves are smooth-edged and remain red; the plant has cream-colored berries. Unlike poison ivy and oak, poison sumac does not produce leaves in groups of three.

Even experts can be fooled by the poisonous three, so here's some relief from the kitchen.

FROM THE CUPBOARD

BAKING SODA. To relieve itching, concoct a paste of 3 teaspoons baking soda and 1 teaspoon water, and spread it on the affected area. Before going to bed, pour a cup of baking soda into a lukewarm bath and take a soak.

COFFEE. If you have any leftover (cold) coffee in your cup, pouring it on a poison ivy rash may be a good way to get rid of the coffee and the rash. Appalachian folk medicine followers believe in washing the affected area with a cup of cold black coffee. Coffee beans contain chlorogenic acid, an anti-inflammatory. This coffee cure hasn't been proved, as there haven't been any studies done on it.

VINEGAR. Be it from plant, insect, or allergic reaction, itches of all sorts are tamed by a simple vinegar rinse. First wash the affected area with

ON-THE-GO KITCHEN REMEDIES

Before heading off into the wild, grab a few items from the kitchen for a poisonous plant first-aid kit. Include a small bag of baking soda, a container of vinegar or rubbing alcohol, a bar of plain soap, an old but clean towel, and a water bottle.

OVER-THE-COUNTER ITCH RELIEVER

Calamine lotion has long been used to take the itch out of poisonous plant irritation. Calamine contains zinc oxide and acts as a drying astringent to reduce the swelling of the rash. It's also a mild disinfectant, which helps prevent infection from settling in.

RUBBING ALCOHOL TO THE RESCUE

Oil from the poisonous plant doesn't sink in immediately, so try to get off as much as you can. If you move fast enough, you can use rubbing alcohol to extract some oil from the skin. Wash down the exposed area with the alcohol and rinse well. Air-dry the skin. Do not use rubbing alcohol near mucous membranes or near the eyes.

soap and lukewarm water, then rinse. Apply vinegar with a cotton ball, rub gently, and rinse.

FROM THE SINK

SOAP AND WATER. Waste no time in getting the poisonous plant victim in contact with soap and water. Quickly, but gently, wash the affected area with lukewarm water and mild, plain soap. Air-dry the skin. Any towels used for cleaning should be washed immediately in hot water and detergent since the oil can linger.

FROM THE WINDOWSILL

ALOE VERA. According to the folk medicine taught by Seventh-day Adventists, aloe vera sap helps treat poison ivy rash through its anti-inflammatory constituents. Break off a leaf and apply the sap to the affected area. Allow to dry and gently wash off. Reapply every two hours.

MORE DO'S AND DON'TS

- Cover up. Expose your flesh to the elements and suffer the consequences. When working and playing outdoors in prime poisonous plant territory, wear long pants, long-sleeved shirts, protective footwear, and if gardening, gloves.

- Remember the pet connection. Often a mysterious case of rash can be traced to that furry family member who diligently patrols the outdoors: Fido or Fluffy. The oil gets on the animal's fur and is transferred to you via petting.

- Consider using a product called IvyBlock, which is a protectant that helps diminish contact with urushiol. This can be applied before heading out into potential poison plant territory.

Poor Appetite

Arousing Hunger

What do you mean you're not hungry? You've probably heard this response when you declare no desire to eat. While the response may sound like nagging, it is an understandable one. Humans have a physical need for food and nourishment, so when an appetite is lacking, something is amiss...and that alarms people who care about you.

A poor appetite can stem from many factors. Perhaps the most common causes are emotional upset, nervousness, tension, anxiety, or depression. Stressful events, such as losing a job or a death in the family, can also make the appetite plummet. Diseases such as influenza and acute infections play a role in appetite reduction, as do anorexia nervosa and fatigue. Illegal and legal drugs, including amphetamines, antibiotics, cough and cold medications, codeine, morphine, and Demerol can take a toll on the appetite. Sometimes poor eating habits, such as continuous snacking, can lead to a poor appetite at mealtimes. A poor appetite can also be one symptom of a serious disease.

Fortunately, for minor cases of poor appetite, the kitchen is the best place to get the appetite back into gear.

From the Refrigerator

Bitter greens. Mama always told you to eat your greens. If she knew you weren't eating properly, she might add, eat your "bitter" greens. Bitter greens consist of arugula, radicchio, collards, kale, endive, escarole, mizuna, sorrel, dandelions, watercress, and red/green mustard...in other words, all those leaves you find in fancy restaurant salads. Stimulating digestion is the name of the game with bitter greens. They prompt the body into making more digestive juices and digestive enzymes.

When to Call the Doctor

- If your appetite doesn't improve in several days
- If emotional problems are causing you not to eat
- If involuntary weight loss exceeds seven percent of total body weight in the previous month. (To calculate the percent of weight lost, divide pounds lost by your previous weight and multiply by 100.)

Bitter foods also stimulate the gallbladder to contract and release bile, which helps break fatty foods into small enough particles that enzymes can easily finish breaking them apart for absorption. This is important because fats carry essential fatty acids, such as heart-healthy omega-3s, along with fat-soluble vitamins A, D, E, and K and carotenoids such as beta-carotene.

FROM THE SINK

WATER. The wonders of water never cease. Water helps control the appetite, especially when you drink your recommended daily allowance: 8 glasses! Don't skimp, even if you don't feel like drinking.

FROM THE SPICE RACK

CARAWAY. The early Greeks knew caraway could calm an upset stomach and used it to season foods that were hard to digest. Today unsuspecting cooks who simply love the flavor of caraway continue the tradition by adding caraway to rye bread, cabbage dishes, sauerkraut and coleslaw, pork, cheese sauces, cream soups, goose, and duck. The Germans make a caraway liqueur called Kümmel and serve it after heavy meals. One of the easiest ways to enjoy caraway is with a good helping of sauerkraut. Sauté ½ medium onion in 1 to 2 tablespoons butter. When onions turn deep golden brown, add 1 can sauerkraut and its liquid along with 1 or

---

Recipe Box

BITTER GREENS SALAD
WITH
FENNEL DRESSING

1 cup quinoa, a high-protein grain
  often compared to couscous
3 cups water
1 carrot, chopped
2 cups peas, fresh or frozen
½ cup chopped purple onion
2 cups shredded arugula,
  a bitter green
1 orange and zest

2 tablespoons maple syrup
2 tablespoons sesame oil
1 tablespoon balsamic vinegar
½ teaspoon cumin
2 heaping tablespoons fresh
  fennel greens or 1 tablespoon
  ground fennel seeds
½ cup nuts (walnuts, almonds,
  or pine nuts)

Boil quinoa in water until soft. Drain and place in a salad bowl with carrot, peas, onion, and arugula. Chill. Place 1 to 2 tablespoons orange zest into a blender. Add the rest of the orange, taking care to remove any pith and seeds. Add maple syrup, sesame oil, balsamic vinegar, cumin, and fennel. Puree. Toss in salad with nuts and serve.

2 tablespoons brown sugar and 1 teaspoon caraway seeds. Let the mixture simmer (covered) for 1 hour. Serve as a side dish with meat, poultry, or sausage.

CAYENNE PEPPER. Cayenne pepper has the power to make any dish fiery hot, but it also has a subtle flavor-enhancing quality. There is some evidence that eating hot pepper increases metabolism and the appetite. Add a few shakes of cayenne pepper to potato salad, deviled eggs, chili, and other hot dishes such as stews and soups.

FENNEL. Fennel, like its cousin caraway, relieves stomach upset and boosts the appetite. For a delicious, nutritious salad topped with a fennel dressing, see the Recipe Box on the previous page.

GINGER. Ginger helps stimulate a tired appetite, both through its medicinal properties and its refreshing taste. Try nibbling on gingersnaps or sipping ginger ale made with real ginger. Ginger tea is also a way to start the day off on an appetizing note. To make, place ½ teaspoon powdered ginger into a cup and fill with boiling water. Cover and let stand ten minutes. Strain and sip. If needed, sweeten with just a little honey. Don't take more than three times daily.

Warning! Pregnant women should consult a doctor before taking ginger.

MINT. Peppermint refreshes the palate and revives the appetite. Make a cup of mint tea and enjoy anytime you don't feel like eating. Place 1 tablespoon mint leaves in a 1-pint jar of boiling water. Let stand 20 to 30 minutes, shaking occasionally. Strain and sip as needed. If you're tired of teas, make a glass of mint lemonade by adding a few sprigs to the lemonade mixture and letting it sit for ten minutes before sipping.

THE FRENCH CONNECTION

The culinary-minded French have a highly seasoned stew of meat or fish called ragout. The name is derived from the meaning, "to restore the appetite of."

THE RIGHT SPOT

If you visit an acupuncturist, they might press on a point on your head to control your appetite. This point is located in the hollow just in front of the earflap.

MORE DO'S AND DON'TS

- Try comfort foods. Sometimes a poor appetite can be remedied by those foods you adored during childhood: macaroni and cheese, mashed potatoes, green bean casserole, roast chicken, or a big slice of chocolate cake. A favorite dish or dessert can be just what you need to get out of a digestive slump.

- Reduce stress. Keeping anxieties, worries, and other stresses bundled up inside causes your appetite to plunge. Look at ways to relieve your stress.

- Exercise. Take a vigorous walk each day, and your appetite will kick in.

Postnasal Drip
TURNING OFF THE FAUCET

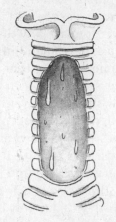

You may wake up with a sore throat, a hacking cough, or a need to clear your throat every morning—or you may just feel as if something has settled in the back of your throat. Any of those experiences could mean that you've got postnasal drip.

On any given day, you've got one to two quarts of mucus running down the back of your throat. That's an awful lot of slime running through your head, but it serves a significant purpose. Mucus cleans out the nasal passages. It kicks out bacteria, viruses, and other infection-causing invaders and clears out other foreign particles. Mucus also helps humidify the air that travels in your body, keeping you and your insides comfortable. Unless you think about it, you probably don't even notice all that mucus making its way down your throat. But if you become acutely aware of mucus in the back of your throat, or feel as if someone has turned on a faucet in your head, you're probably dealing with postnasal drip.

What Fuels the Faucet?

Postnasal drip happens when mucus production goes awry. There may be an overproduction of mucus, which gives you that typical drip, drip, drip feeling in the back of your throat. The mucus is clear, thin, and very runny. At the other extreme is thick, sticky mucus that is yellow or green. This kind of mucus occurs when mucus production slows down and thickens, hanging around in the throat.

Many factors can trigger a change in mucus production, including the following:

Air pollution. Some major pollutants in smog, such as nitrogen dioxide and sulfur dioxide, can make your mucus go haywire.

Allergies. If you can tell spring is coming by the amount of tissue on your dashboard, you've probably got a hay fever allergy—one of the most common causes of postnasal drip.

Cold air. When you step outside on a cold wintry day, your nose is likely to start drip-

> ### WHEN TO CALL THE DOCTOR
> - If your mucus is thick and yellow. You may have a sinus infection, which will require an antibiotic.
> - If you have a chronic problem with postnasal drip

ping. The same increase in mucus production happens when you're in any cold, dry environment.

Colds and flu. Your nose runs during a cold or the flu to get rid of unfriendly bacterial or viral invaders. So, if you think about it, postnasal drip is actually a great defense. Try to remember that when your nose is raw from blowing it.

Deviated septum. This is a technical term that means the cartilage that divides the nose into two sides has moved. It may be an innate structural problem, or it may be caused from that thwack in the nose you got while playing patty-cake with your one-year-old. Whatever the cause, a deviated septum can alter mucus flow.

Dusty or smoky conditions. Dust and smoke can dry out your nose and make it tough to produce an adequate amount of mucus, so the mucus you do produce gets thicker. As a result, you end up clearing your throat every few seconds.

> ### SAY NO TO NASAL SPRAYS
> Sure you feel better after squirting an over-the-counter nasal spray up your honker. These sprays restrict blood flow to your nasal passages, reducing inflammation and swelling. But if you use these sprays for more than a few days, you may make your problem worse. Avoid nasal sprays that contain phenylephrine, hydrochloride, oxymetazoline, and xylometrazoline. Saline nasal sprays are the only exception; they are safe to use and won't exacerbate your problem.

Getting older. Another one of the joys of passing years is that your mucus production slows down and your mucus gets thicker. That's why you might hear older people hacking when they wake up. Thicker mucus takes some time to get moving through the throat. Swallowing muscles get weaker as you get older, too, so you may not be able to get rid of mucus as well as you once could.

Nasal or sinus polyps. Okay, so polyps is not a word you really like to hear, especially when they're growing in your nose. But polyps are typically noncancerous growths that simply obstruct or change mucus flow.

Pregnancy. A change in hormones seems to cause postnasal drip problems in some pregnant women.

Sinus infections. Your doctor calls it "sinusitis." Infection in the four cavities surrounding your nose can make you miserable. Sinuses can become swollen or blocked, and bacteria set up shop, causing a mean infection. Thick green or yellow mucus is a good indication that you have a sinus infection. Don't let this one go without seeing a doctor. Antibiotics are the only way to completely clear it up.

Some medicines. Antihistamines, diuretics, and some tranquilizers can dry up mucus production. When those commercials warn that a product gives you "dry mouth," you can bet it will give you a dry nose and throat, too.

Most problems with postnasal drip are merely irritating and will eventually go away. But you can alleviate some symptoms with remedies in your kitchen.

From the Cupboard

SALT. Gargling with salt water can help soothe your sore throat. Add ½ teaspoon salt to 1 cup water and gargle away.

From the Refrigerator

BAKING SODA. If you're willing to do anything to clear up your mucus problem, try this remedy. Mix 1 cup warm water, 1 teaspoon salt, and a pinch of baking soda. Using a nasal syringe, squirt the mixture into your nostril, closing off the back of your palate and your throat. Tilt your head back, forward, and to each side for eight to ten seconds in each position to get the solution through all four of your sinus cavities. After you swish everything around, blow your nose. Try squirting in three or four bulbs full of the solution on each side of your nose. If you don't have a bulb syringe, you can snort the mixture out of your cupped hand. Try this process up to six times a day when you're dealing with postnasal drip. If you want to avoid future problems, do it twice a day.

WATER. Drinking enough water keeps your mucus thin and your body, including your nasal passages, well hydrated. Drink at least eight 8-ounce glasses of water a day.

From the Stovetop

KETTLE OF BOILING WATER. To keep the humidity high and stable in your house, keep a kettle of water on low boil.

More Do's and Don'ts

- Away with allergens. If cat dander tends to make your mucus start multiplying, it's logical that you can avoid postnasal drip by avoiding that allergen. If you're not sure what allergies aggravate your nasal passages, do a little detective work and find out.

- Skip the smog. Smog contains known nasal irritants. Try to stay indoors as much as possible on days when the air quality is poor.

- Skip the smoke, too. Secondhand smoke can have just as bad an effect on your throat, sinuses, and nasal passages as firsthand stuff does.

- Do a decongestant. This magic medicine can help drain your sinuses and make you feel loads better. Just be sure to use the pill kind and avoid nasal sprays.

- Consider a cough syrup. Some cough medicines thin mucus.

Premenstrual Syndrome (PMS)

SUBDUING SYMPTOMS

That soon-to-be-time of the month, and all of a sudden you do the Jekyll and Hyde switch. Your mild, calm demeanor is replaced by rages or crying jags, and your emotions become unstable. Sometimes you just feel out of control. At this time of the month, friends and loved ones may do their best to avoid you.

These mood swings, along with a host of other symptoms such as water retention, breast swelling and tenderness, depression, irritability, fatigue, food cravings, and headaches, are known as premenstrual syndrome (PMS). They typically begin a few days to a week before menstruation and end when the menstrual period begins.

Researchers believe that about 40 percent of women of child-bearing age experience PMS in some form. Symptoms and severity vary from mild and manageable to severe and disruptive. Some women only have one symptom, while others have a whole constellation of symptoms. But PMS can be downright brutal for about 15 percent of women. They're the ones who experience many symptoms to a debilitating degree, causing serious problems on the job and in interpersonal relationships.

What Causes PMS?

Well, doctors don't really know what causes PMS, but they believe it is a result of hormonal changes, particularly in estrogen, that occur around the menstrual cycle. Some believe that PMS mood swings may be related to deficiencies in vitamin B_6 and magnesium. One theory of PMS suggests that its symptoms are due to an ovarian hormone imbalance of either estrogen or progesterone.

Even though it's not fully understood, PMS is now recognized as a legitimate condition,

---

WHEN TO CALL THE DOCTOR

- If symptoms are severe enough to interfere with your normal daily activities
- If you're suddenly plagued by symptoms different from your regular PMS symptoms, especially abdominal, ovarian, or breast pain

WANT TO KNOW A SECRET?

There's a hush-hush cure that can relieve the cramping and abdominal pain associated with PMS. It's sex, particularly orgasmic sex. But don't ask your doctor for a prescription for this one.

FASCINATING FACT

Ninety percent of all aggressive actions by women happen right around the time of their periods.

not something that's all in a woman's head. There are medications available that can mitigate or stop many of the harshest symptoms. Like so many other conditions, though, there are simple kitchen treatments that will work in relieving symptoms. So try them and see what happens.

FROM THE CUPBOARD

OATMEAL. It breaks down slowly and gradually releases sugar into the bloodstream. This slow, steady release combats the cravings that come with PMS. Rye bread, pasta, basmati rice, and fruit produce the same effect.

PASTA. Pasta is enriched with magnesium, which is important for normal hormonal function. A lack of magnesium may be the cause of muscle cramps. Other magnesium-rich foods include green vegetables, breakfast cereals, and potatoes.

SUNFLOWER SEEDS. They're rich in omega-6 fatty acid, which may be missing in women who suffer with PMS. Pumpkin and sesame seeds are also rich in it.

FROM THE DRAWER

KITCHEN TOWEL. Soak it in water, wring it out, then warm it up in the microwave. Applying moist heat to your belly is soothing when you have abdominal or ovarian cramps. Be careful not to burn yourself.

FROM THE FREEZER

ICE. If you're suffering tension or extreme anxiety, a nice cooling drink may be relaxing. Or, wrap some ice in a kitchen towel to use as a cold compress on aching muscles and PMS headaches.

FROM THE REFRIGERATOR

AVOCADOS. These contain natural serotonin, which may supplement the mood-lifting brain chemical naturally produced by the body. Dates, plums, eggplants, papayas, and pineapple are also sources of serotonin.

BANANAS. Rich in potassium, they can relieve the bloating and swelling of water retention from PMS. Potassium also helps relieve heart palpitations, a PMS side effect, by evening out heart rhythm.

CHERRIES. An Ayurvedic remedy to relieve PMS symptoms, including bloating and mood swings, is to eat 10 fresh cherries on an empty stomach each day for one week before the start of the menstrual period.

CHICKEN. It's rich in Vitamin B6, which may be depleted in women who suffer from PMS. Vitamin B6 may help relieve depression by raising levels of serotonin, a mood-enhancer, in the brain. Other B6-rich foods include fish, milk, brown rice, whole grains, soybeans, beans, walnuts, and green leafy vegetables.

TURKEY. It supplies tryptophan, an amino acid that converts into serotonin, a mood-enhancer. Cottage cheese is another source of tryptophan.

> ### FASCINATING FACT
> The earliest known PMS symptoms were recorded by Hippocrates in ancient Greece 2,500 years ago.

FROM THE SPICE RACK

BLACK PEPPER. Add a pinch to 1 tablespoon aloe vera gel, and take three times a day with meals to relieve symptoms such as backache and abdominal pain. A pinch of cumin in aloe vera gel works well, too.

CINNAMON. A brew of cinnamon tea is relaxing just before bed. Sweeten with honey. Chamomile tea is also a relaxing bedtime choice.

MORE DO'S & DON'TS

- Exercise. Endorphins, which are brain chemicals responsible for improving mood, are released during aerobic exercises such as walking, swimming, and bicycle riding. Exercise once a day starting the week before your period to help relieve or prevent PMS symptoms.

- Sleep tight. Interruption in regular sleep rhythms can interfere with your regular cycle and cause irritability and fatigue.

- Forgo fats. They may make PMS symptoms worse. Limit fat to less than 20 percent of your daily calories.

- Crunch on carbs. Fresh fruits, vegetables, and whole-grain cereals and breads can reduce cravings and help elevate mood.

- Cut the caffeine. Caffeine, whether it's in coffee, cola, or chocolate, contributes to breast pain and anxiety, two of the leading PMS complaints.

SUPPLEMENTS WITH A PMS PUNCH

Studies show that symptoms of PMS may be relieved by certain vitamin and mineral supplements.
Check with your doctor before you take any of these.
They all can have serious side effects.

VITAMIN/MINERAL	DAILY DOSAGE
Vitamin E	400 IU
Vitamin B6	50–100 milligrams
Calcium citrate	1,000 milligrams
Magnesium	300–500 milligrams

Prostate Problems
PAMPER YOUR PROSTATE

It's a sad fact of growing older for men. Most men over the age of 60 (and some in their 50s) develop some symptoms of prostate problems. The three most common disorders are benign prostatic hyperplasia (BPH), a noncancerous enlargement of the prostate; prostatitis, an inflammatory infection; and prostate cancer. BPH is so common that some physicians consider it a normal consequence of aging in males.

The prostate's main role is to produce an essential portion of the seminal fluid that carries sperm. This walnut-shape gland located just below a man's bladder starts to kick in near puberty and continues to grow and grow. This enlargement doesn't usually cause symptoms until after age 40, and it usually doesn't cause problems until age 60 or later.

An enlarged prostate is problematic because it presses on the urethra, creating difficulties with urination and weakening the bladder. Some of the symptoms of prostate problems include

• difficulty urinating

• frequent urination, especially at night

• difficulty starting urination

• an inability to empty the bladder

• a dribble of urine despite the urgent need to urinate

• a burning sensation when urinating

• uncontrolled dribbling after urination

• pain behind the scrotum

• painful ejaculation

Ignoring prostate problems, as some men are wont to do, isn't a smart idea. Left untreated, prostate problems can get progressively worse, become more painful, and can lead to dangerous complications, including bladder and kidney infections.

Changes in diet can help relieve some prostate discomforts and, in some cases, may reduce the chances of developing prostate cancer. Check out how the kitchen can help.

FROM THE CUPBOARD

PUMPKIN SEEDS. Pumpkin seeds are used by German doctors to treat difficult urination that accompanies an enlarged prostate that is not cancerous. The seeds contain diuretic properties and plenty of zinc, which helps repair and build the immune system. The tastiest way to enjoy pumpkin seeds is to eat them plain. Remove the shells and don't add salt. You can also try a tea. Crush a handful of fresh seeds and place in the bottom of a 1-pint jar. Fill with boiling water. Let cool to room temperature. Strain and drink a pint of pumpkin seed tea a day.

> ## WHEN TO CALL THE DOCTOR
> - If you experience one or more of the symptoms listed on the previous page
> - For an annual prostate cancer test

FROM THE REFRIGERATOR

CORN SILK. The silk from corn has been used by Amish men for generations as a remedy for the symptoms of prostate enlargement. When fresh corn is in season, cut the silk from 6 ears of corn. (Corn silk can be dried for later use, too.) Add to 1 quart water, boil, and simmer for ten minutes. Strain and drink 3 cups a week.

FISH. From the deep comes a way to fight prostate cancer and tumor growth. Try to get 2 servings a week of fish high in omega-3 oils (the good oil) such as tuna, mackerel, or salmon.

SOY. Learning to like and use soy foods is an easy and good way to help nip prostate problems in the bud. Soy-based foods contain phyto-estrogens, which are thought to help reduce testosterone production (believed to aggravate prostate cancer growth) and to limit the growth of blood capillaries that form around tumors of the prostate.

TOMATOES. Seize that salsa! Pour on the spaghetti sauce! Down that tomato juice! Learn to add more tomatoes to your diet. Studies have shown that as little as 2 servings of tomatoes (including cooked tomatoes) a week can help men reduce their risk of prostate cancer by half. These red orbs are full of lycopene, an antioxidant compound that helps fight cancer.

WATERMELON SEEDS. The Amish use watermelon tea to flush the system out and help with bladder problems and prostate problems. Enjoy a slice of watermelon, and spit the seeds in a cup. When you have ⅛ cup fresh watermelon seeds, put them in a 1-pint jar and fill with boiling water. Let the tea cool, strain, and drink. Drink 1 pint of the tea every day for ten days.

FASCINATING FACT

Approximately 1 out of every 10 men in the United States develops cancer of the prostate. Despite this alarming statistic, more men die with prostate cancer than from the cancer. Most pass away due to other ailments such as heart disease and stroke.

FROM THE SUPPLEMENT SHELF

SAW PALMETTO. The extract of the berries of this plant has been shown to work as well or better than prescription drugs in improving urinary flow rates and reducing the symptoms of BPH, such as urinary hesitancy and weak flow. The extract works by altering certain hormone levels, thus reducing prostate enlargement. Palmetto extracts can be purchased at the health food store. Consult your physician for recommended dosages.

STINGING NETTLE. Stinging nettle has been used in Europe for more than a decade, and studies have shown it to reduce symptoms of prostate problems. Nettle helps by inhibiting binding of testosterone-related proteins to their receptor sites on prostate cell membranes. Take stinging nettle in extract form (as capsules). Check with your physician for the correct dosage.

MORE DO'S AND DON'TS

- Drink 8 glasses of water a day.
- Limit your intake of fatty foods and red meats.
- Schedule an annual prostate exam. Catching problems early is vital.
- Watch your alcohol intake. Studies have shown that beer can raise prolactin levels in the body, which in turn can eventually lead to prostate enlargement.

Psoriasis

Softening the Scales

Imagine having an unwanted guest show
up on your doorstep. No one knows who
invited him, and no one really wants
him there. He's one of the most annoying people you've ever met. And his
personality is so abrasive, you're embar-
rassed to take him anywhere.

If you have psoriasis, or know anyone
with this frustrating skin condition, you
know that it's much like that uninvited guest. It shows up in the form of
dry, inflamed, red, scaly patches of skin. Not only are psoriasis flare-ups
aggravating, they make people with the condition so self-conscious
about their appearance that they're reluctant to go to the grocery store
without ample covering. Probably most frustrating of all is that there's
no magic formula to kick this guest out of town indefinitely. You have to
learn how to deal with flare-ups as they come and take good care of
yourself and your skin.

The Psoriasis Puzzle

Normally, your skin cells go through a month-long life cycle. New
cells are formed deep within the skin, and over a period of about 28 to
30 days they make their way to the top of the skin. By that time your old
skin cells die and are sloughed off by everyday routines such as shower-
ing and toweling yourself dry.

The skin of a person with psoriasis, however, goes into fast-forward.
The entire skin cell process happens in three or four days, causing a
buildup of dead skin cells on the surface of the skin. Thankfully, this
quickening of skin cells usually happens in patches, mostly on the scalp,
lower back, elbows, knees, and knuckles. The technical term for these
dry, irritating, scaly patches is plaques.

No one really knows what psoriasis is: an allergy? an infection? And,
even with all the advanced medical knowledge in the world today, the
causes of the condition remain a mystery. In about 32 percent of psoriasis cases there's a family history of the condition, which means there is a
significant genetic link. Doctors do know that there are specific lifestyle
factors that can trigger psoriasis or make symptoms worse. Drinking
alcohol, being overweight, stress, a lingering case of strep throat, anxiety,

WHEN TO CALL THE DOCTOR

- At the first sign of a psoriasis-like patch. Psoriasis can mimic more serious skin conditions and even certain types of skin cancer.

some medicines, and sunburn all tend to make psoriasis even more unbearable.

Psoriasis isn't contagious, though it looks like it might be. Some people end up with mild cases of the condition that produce small patches of red scales. Others are plagued by psoriasis—it covers large areas of their body with thick scales. Some people even get psoriasis in their nails, which causes the nails to become pitted and malformed, and even to break away from the skin. And in some rare cases, a type of arthritis called psoriatic arthritis develops.

Though there is no way to get rid of psoriasis, you can help your body recover more quickly and ease your symptoms with some kitchen staples.

FROM THE CUPBOARD

APPLE CIDER VINEGAR. Add 1 cup apple cider vinegar to 1 gallon water. Soak a washcloth in the mixture and apply it to the skin to ease itching.

BAKING SODA. To take the itch out of scaly patches, mix 1½ cups baking soda into 3 gallons water. Apply to itchy patches with a washcloth soaked in the solution.

EPSOM SALTS. Add a handful of these healing salts to your bath. They'll keep swelling down.

MINERAL OIL. This is another time-proven skin soother. Add a bit to your bath and soak your aching skin.

OLIVE OIL. An old favorite for easing psoriasis outbreaks is mixing 2 teaspoons olive oil with a large glass of milk and adding the concoction to your bathwater. Or, if you are dealing with psoriasis on your scalp, massage some warm olive oil on your scaly patches. It will help soften the dead skin and make it easier to remove.

PLASTIC WRAP. After you douse your patches in moisturizer, wrap them in plastic wrap to help hold the moisture in. Change the wrapping often.

VEGETABLE OIL. Get in the tub and add a cupful of vegetable oil to your bath to ease your psoriasis.

WHITE VINEGAR. Vinegar has soothing properties that can help ease the itch. Add 1 cup to your bathwater.

FROM THE SPICE RACK

CAYENNE. Capsaicin, the substance that gives cayenne pepper its heat, helps relieve pain and itching by blocking the communication system of sensory nerves. Studies have found that a cream containing capsaicin helped relieve itching and got rid of psoriasis plaques. Look for a cream containing .025 to .075 percent capsaicin—any more than that and you risk burning your skin. It takes about a week for the cream to work.

FROM THE SUPPLEMENT SHELF

FISH OIL. There have been numerous studies linking the omega-3 fatty acids in fish oil to improvement in psoriasis patches. The people in these studies had to take large oral doses of the supplement to show any results, but one study did find simply slathering fish oil on a psoriasis patch helped with healing. There are also commercial creams available that contain fish oils or derivatives of the oils.

MORE DO'S AND DON'TS

- Keep skin supple. Moisturizing your skin helps keep swelling to a minimum, makes your skin more flexible, keeps your psoriasis from getting worse, and makes scales less apparent. Look for moisturizers that are thick and lock moisture into the skin— ingredients such as lactic acid seem to work best. Or you can use cooking oils, lard, or petrolatum. Apply a moisturizer right after you step out of a bath or shower to hold on to natural oils and water.

- Sunbathe. The sun can work magic in clearing up psoriasis patches. But be careful; getting sunburned can cause more psoriasis problems.

- Try tar. Coal tar creams, shampoos, and bath items seem to work by helping to loosen scales, which makes them easier to slough off. Try an over-the-counter brand.

- Use shampoos and creams that contain salicylic acid. They're known to get rid of scales.

- Use "superfatted" soaps that contain moisturizers, or go for soap-free cleansers. They'll both be kinder to your skin.

- Medicate that itch. Over-the-counter cortisone creams or antihistamines may help ease some of the itch and inflammation.

- Keep the indoors tropical. Dry indoor air can make psoriasis more unbearable. Humidify your house to help make you more comfortable during a psoriasis flare-up.

- Slim down. Being overweight makes psoriasis more uncomfortable and harder to control.

- Watch the medicines. Antimalarials, beta blockers, lithium, and some other drugs can make psoriasis worse.

THE SKIN THEY'RE IN

Psoriasis affects more than 7 million Americans. Women tend to get the disease more often than men. About 150,000 to 260,000 new cases of psoriasis will be diagnosed this year. Though most people may link psoriasis with the elderly, the average age of a first-time psoriasis sufferer is 28 years old. But the condition can happen in every stage of life from birth to old age. In fact, 10 to 15 percent of people who get psoriasis are younger than 10 years old.

Seasonal Affective Disorder
LOOKING FOR LIGHT

Ho hum. Another day, so much to do. But you can't seem to drag yourself out of bed. In fact, the only thing you'd really like to do is burrow in between the covers for a long winter's nap.

If that's how you feel every winter, you could be suffering from seasonal affective disorder, or SAD. It's a poorly understood condition that affects some people during the winter months, when there is less sunlight. In addition to a depressed mood, symptoms of SAD include cravings for carbohydrates, inability to concentrate, irritability, lethargy, weight gain, and a lack of interest in sex.

Although the link between the gray, short days of winter and SAD is well-established, no one knows why only some people are affected. Current thinking associates SAD with having too much melatonin, the hormone that causes you to be sleepy. Normally, sunlight stops melatonin production in the body, and darkness starts it. When there's not enough sunlight, as often is the case in the winter months, melatonin kicks into overtime production. Some medical researchers compare SAD to hibernation. During the winter, many animals store up on carbohydrates, crawl into a cave, resist the mating urge, and snooze until spring. That's exactly the way people who suffer SAD react, only in a modified version.

Another theory is that SAD is a result of a delay in the timing of the body clock. In SAD patients, the body's lowest temperature occurs at 6 A.M. rather than at 3 A.M. as it normally should. As a result, they are awakening when physiologically it is the middle of the night. When treated with light from 6 A.M. to 8 A.M., these patients experience a shift in minimum temperature to an earlier time and an associated shift in mood.

WHEN TO CALL THE DOCTOR

- At the first SAD symptom. Other ailments, including underactive thyroid gland, low blood sugar, chronic fatigue syndrome, chronic viral illness, and some strains of flu, mimic SAD and must be ruled out.

- When symptoms, such as depression, prevent you from performing your daily activities

Doctors often treat SAD with antidepressants. For some, they work. For others, the side effects are overwhelming, often worse than the SAD itself. So if you've got SAD, look in the kitchen for some relief.

FROM THE CUPBOARD

BASMATI RICE. The sugar in this rice is slow to release into the bloodstream, which helps blood sugar levels stay constant. Drastic changes in blood sugar can lead to weight gain, which is a side effect of SAD. Other foods with a similar effect on blood sugar are rye bread and pasta.

> **FASCINATING FACT**
> While seasonal affective disorder is typically a condition of winter, symptoms may start as early as September and continue all the way through April.

BOUILLON. When the carbohydrate craving is just about to defeat you, drink some hot bouillon or broth. Hot liquids in the belly are filling, and consuming them before a meal is an old diet trick that reduces food consumption. Better the bouillon than the banana cream pie.

CEREALS. Cooked cereal, unsweetened muesli, and bran flakes are slow to release sugar into the bloodstream, which helps raise serotonin levels.

HERBAL TEAS. Any herbal tea is a better choice than teas with caffeine. Your reduced energy level may cause you to turn to caffeine for a boost, but it can also cause anxiety, muscle tension, and stomach problems. Those side effects will only compound your problems. You can also drink a cup of herbal tea instead of giving in to your carbohydrate cravings.

FROM THE FREEZER

ICE. When you can't get going no matter what you do, try sucking on some ice. Its chill can give you a wake-up call. Or, splash your face and wrists with ice water.

FROM THE REFRIGERATOR

APRICOTS. This fruit gradually raises serotonin levels and helps keep them there, as do apples, pears, grapes, plums, grapefruit, and oranges.

AVOCADOS. They are high in natural serotonin, which seems to suppress appetite. Also high in natural serotonin are dates, bananas, plums, eggplant, papayas, passion fruit, plantains, pineapples, and tomatoes.

COTTAGE CHEESE. It's high in tryptophan, which is lacking in people with SAD. Other foods just as high in tryptophan are turkey, fish, and eggs.

LEGUMES. These help maintain an even serotonin level throughout the day and night.

SHELLFISH. These are high in tyrosine, which forms chemicals that act on the brain cells to improve concentration and alertness, both of which become sluggish with SAD. Other foods high in tyrosine are fish, chicken, skinless turkey, cottage cheese, plain yogurt, skim milk, eggs, tofu, and very lean ham, pork, and lamb.

TURKEY. Protein-rich foods such as turkey, low fat cottage cheese, chicken, and low fat dairy products can reduce the carbohydrate cravings of SAD as well as control the weight gain that occurs during SAD months.

FROM THE SPICE RACK

PEPPERMINT OIL. Or lemon oil. Steep in water and inhale. These are stimulating and may give you a little extra zip.

FROM THE WINDOW

CURTAINS. Open them, or remove them, especially if your kitchen window has a southern exposure.

DIRTY DISHES. If your sink is near or under the window, save all your dishes from the night before and wash them the next day, during the brightest sunlight.

MEAL PREP. Prepare your meals in the brightest light of the day, in front of the kitchen window.

MORE DO'S & DON'TS

- Take a walk in the sun. Morning or early afternoon sun is the best.

- Cut trees and bushes away from your windows. Remove heavy drapes that block the light.

- Lighten your home with light-colored fabrics, walls, and rugs.

- Add more light to your home or office.

- Exercise. Aerobic exercise has a positive effect on moods. Try walking or biking. Even better, exercise in the sun or near a nice, sunny window.

- Vacation in a warm, sunny spot during the winter months if you can.

BAD SAD FOODS

Because overeating and weight gain often go hand-in-hand with SAD, you need to take extra care to avoid the foods that trigger carbohydrate cravings. Here's a list of some of the worst offenders and what they do:

- **Sweets:** Sugar, honey, soft drinks, cookies, candy, cake. These quickly raise blood sugar levels and provide a quick serotonin boost that falls off rapidly. When this happens, the brain wants another quick fix and you crave more. This can turn into a never-ending cycle, since the body wants a serotonin high all the time.

- **Simple carbohydrates:** Bread, bagel, potato. Starchy foods also cause a rapid rise in blood sugar, which gives the brain its fast serotonin high, then drops you like a rock.

- **Fats:** Butter, margarine, oil, and fatty foods. These can cause the weight gain that accompanies SAD. Weight gain may also contribute to the depression associated with SAD.

Sore Throat
RELIEVING RAWNESS

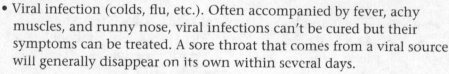

It's scratchy, tender, and swollen, and you dread the simple task of swallowing. But you must swallow, and when you do, you brace yourself for the unavoidable pain. If you've got a sore throat, you're in good company; everybody gets them, and 40 million people trek to the doctor's office for treatment of one every year.

The mechanics of a sore throat are pretty simple. It's an inflammation of the pharynx, which is the tube that extends from the back of the mouth to the esophagus. The following are the leading causes of sore throat:

- Viral infection (colds, flu, etc.). Often accompanied by fever, achy muscles, and runny nose, viral infections can't be cured but their symptoms can be treated. A sore throat that comes from a viral source will generally disappear on its own within several days.

- Bacterial infection, especially from a streptococcal bacteria (strep throat). Symptoms are much like those of a viral infection but may be more severe and long lasting. Often a bacterial infection is accompanied by headache, stomachache, and swollen glands in the neck. A strep infection is generally treated with antibiotics because permanent heart or kidney damage can result. Culturing the bacteria is the only way a doctor can determine the cause of the sore throat.

While those are the primary reasons for a sore throat, there are others, including

- Smoking
- Acid reflux
- Allergies
- Dry air, especially at night when you may sleep with your mouth open
- Mouth breathing
- Throat abuse: singing, shouting, coughing

> ### LARYNGITIS? SHUSH!
> If you've got laryngitis, don't whisper. The whispering movement on your vocal chords is just as bad for you as shouting. To get that voice back, talk quietly or be silent. And moisturize those vocal chords to help them heal. Drink 8 to 10 glasses of water a day, and drink ginger tea and inhale the steam.

WHEN TO CALL THE DOCTOR

- If you have a swollen throat and are having difficulty breathing, call 9-1-1 or seek immediate emergency treatment
- If your sore throat lasts more than four days
- If you suspect a serious infection such as strep
- If you have a fever over 103°F or any fever lasting more than three days
- If you have a skin rash
- If swallowing is very painful
- If the sore throat is accompanied by an earache
- If you have achy joints
- If you have blisters or pus in your throat
- If you're spitting up bloody phlegm
- If the sore throat interferes with normal activities
- For any sore throat in infants, young children, people with weakened immune systems, or older people

- Polyps or cancer
- Infected tonsils
- Food allergy

Whatever the cause, you want a cure when your throat's on fire. In some cases, medical attention is definitely required to cure the underlying infection. But there are soothing remedies to be found in the kitchen that can stand alone or work side-by-side with traditional medicine to stifle that soreness.

FROM THE CUPBOARD

CIDER VINEGAR. This sore throat cure is found in several different remedies. Here are a few of the more popular ones:

For sipping: Mix 1 tablespoon each of honey and cider vinegar in 1 cup warm water.

For gargling: Dissolve 1 teaspoon salt in ½ cup cider vinegar, then mix in 1 cup water. Gargle with the solution every 15 minutes as necessary.

For soaking: Soak cheesecloth or gauze in ⅔ cup warm water with 2 tablespoons cider vinegar. Wring out and apply to the throat, covering it with dry gauze or an elastic bandage. Wear it all night.

HORSERADISH. Try this Russian sore throat cure. Combine 1 tablespoon pure horseradish or horseradish root with 1 teaspoon honey and 1 teaspoon ground cloves. Mix in a glass of warm water and drink slowly.

LEMON JUICE. Mix 1 tablespoon each of honey and lemon juice in 1 cup warm water. Sip this mixture.

LIME JUICE. Combine 1 spoonful with a spoonful of honey and take as often as needed for a sore throat.

SALT. Yes, when your mother told you to gargle with salt water, she knew what she was talking about. It cuts phlegm and reduces inflammation. Dissolve ½ teaspoon salt in ½ cup warm water and gargle every three to four hours.

FROM THE FREEZER

JUICE BAR. This is cold and soothing to a hot throat. Don't suck, though. Sucking may irritate the throat even more. Simply let small pieces melt in your mouth.

FROM THE REFRIGERATOR

BEETS. Make a poultice by grating 2 to 3 tablespoons red beets and covering them with 2 cups boiling water. Soak a clean towel in the warm solution, wring it out, and apply to the throat. Remove when cold and reapply as often as necessary. Beets will stain the cloth (and your skin) so use a towel that you don't mind turning reddish purple.

ONIONS. This tear-promoting veggie contains allicin, which can kill the bacteria that causes strep. Eat them raw or sautéed.

RASPBERRIES. These can make a great gargle. Combine 2 cups raspberries with 2½ cups vinegar, and leave in a cool place for three days. Place the mixture in a saucepan, add 1 cup sugar, and bring to a gentle boil. Simmer 15 minutes, remove from heat, and cool. Strain through a sieve, pressing the berries down. Store the juice in a bottle, refrigerate, and use as needed. Do not drink any liquid you have used as a gargle.

GIVE IT SOME ZINC

Zinc lozenges may relieve a sore throat. Suck on 1 lozenge every two hours. And because high doses of vitamin C are often recommended in treating a sore throat (it doesn't cure the throat problem but it does boost the immune system), ask your pharmacist about vitamin C lozenges.

FASCINATING FACT

The Roman emperor Nero wasn't just fiddling while Rome burned. He was singing, too. But his operatic attempts were met with failure, resulting not in applause but in a chronic sore throat and hoarse voice. To treat his often-ailing throat, he ate nothing but leeks soaked in oil for several days each month.

FROM THE SINK

WATER. Gargle with 4 parts water to 1 part three-percent hydrogen peroxide two to three times a day. Also, sip plain water throughout the day to prevent your throat from becoming dry.

FROM THE SPICE RACK

CINNAMON. Mix 2 parts cinnamon, 2 parts ginger, and 3 parts licorice powder. Steep 1 teaspoon of this mixture in 1 cup boiling water for ten minutes, then drink as a sore throat cure three times a day.

GARLIC. This Amish remedy can treat or prevent a sore throat. Peel a fresh clove, slice it in half, and place 1 piece in each cheek. Suck on the garlic like a cough drop. Occasionally, crush the garlic against your teeth, not to bite it in half, but to release its allicin, a chemical that can kill the bacteria that causes strep.

HERBAL CURES

Chamomile.
Make a tea
by adding
1 teaspoon
chamomile to
1 cup boiling water. Steep
for ten minutes, strain,
then gargle three to four
times a day. Make a poul-
tice by mixing 1 table-
spoon chamomile flowers
in 2 cups boiling water.
Steep five minutes, then
strain. Soak a clean towel
in the warm solution,
wring it out, and apply to
the throat. Remove when
cold and reapply as often
as necessary.

Horehound. This is a
great remedy for sore
throat, but it's not a
common herb found on
store shelves. If you do
happen to find it, make a
tea with 1 tablespoon
horehound leaves and
1 cup boiling water. Steep,
strain, and gargle. Or, suck
on some horehound hard
candy.

FASCINATING FACT

Don't add boiling water to
vinegar. The boiling water
drives off volatile acetic
acid, which, along with
the added water, dilutes
the vinegar too much.

MARJORAM. Make a soothing tea with a
spoonful of marjoram steeped in a cup of
boiling water for ten minutes. Strain, then
sweeten to taste with honey. Drink as
needed.

PEPPERMINT OIL. Add 2 drops each of peppermint and eucalyptus oils to 2 teaspoons
olive oil and massage on the throat and
upper chest for a nice, relaxing throat-
soother.

SAGE. This curative herb is a great sore throat
gargle. Mix 1 teaspoon in 1 cup boiling
water. Steep for ten minutes, then strain.
Add 1 teaspoon each cider vinegar and
honey, then gargle four times a day.

TURMERIC. Try this gargle to calm a cranky
throat. Mix together 1 cup hot water, ½ teaspoon turmeric, and ½ teaspoon salt. Gargle
with the mixture twice a day. If you're not
good with the gargle, mix ½ teaspoon
turmeric in 1 cup hot milk and drink.
Turmeric stains clothing, so be careful when
mixing and gargling.

FROM THE STOVE

STEAM. With or without herbs, inhaling
steam can relieve the discomfort of a sore
throat. Heat a pot full of water, remove from
heat, make a tent with a towel, and place
your face over the steam. Then breathe.
Adding 1 to 2 drops eucalyptus oil can be
soothing.

MORE DO'S & DON'TS

• Drink plenty of fluids, especially fruit
juices.

• Nix the colas and scratchy foods, such as
chips and pretzels. They'll irritate an
already irritated throat.

• Rest. This will allow your body to build up the defenses to fight off
whatever's causing your sore throat.

Stomach Upset
TACKLING TUMMY TROUBLES

You celebrated your promotion with dinner at your favorite barbecue joint. You've been working hard for months, you think, so you deserve to cut loose a little. On the way home you groan and mutter that you wish you had stopped after that first barbecue platter. Your partner shrugs. You both know the price for your revelry will be a painful night of bloating, gas, and heartburn.

But sometimes your tummy can turn on you even when you haven't made too many trips to the buffet table. Here's how to distinguish between simple indigestion and something more serious.

The Digestive Dance

The digestive process begins in your mouth. Your salivary glands produce digestive juices that lubricate your food and prepare fat for digestion. The food travels through your esophagus into your stomach, where digestive juices continue to break food down even further so it can travel on to the small intestine. The pancreas and liver secrete other digestive juices that flow into the small intestines. In the small intestine, vital nutrients including vitamins, minerals, water, salt, carbohydrates, and proteins are sucked out of the food and absorbed into your body. By the time your dinner makes its way to the large intestines, it's mostly bulk and water. The large intestines absorb the water and help you get rid of the, umm, excess.

But sometimes things in the digestive system go awry and cause indigestion, a catchall term that means you have trouble digesting your food. When you eat too much, or you eat the wrong foods, you may get one or more symptoms of indigestion, including nausea, vomiting, heartburn, bloating, or gas.

Those unpleasant feelings may send you running to the drugstore for relief, and if they do, you've got plenty of company. The American Gastroenterological Association says that digestive problems are one of the most common reasons Americans take over-the-counter medications. Indigestion can be a symptom of something more serious, such as gastritis, an ulcer, severe heartburn, irritable bowel syndrome, or diverticulitis. But if it's just the result of overdoing it at dinner, try some of these kitchen cures for relief.

WHEN TO CALL THE DOCTOR

- If you have excessive abdominal cramping that doesn't go away after 30 minutes or gets worse with time. You may have an intestinal obstruction.
- If you have vomiting, fever, extreme nausea, or abdominal cramping. You could have food poisoning or an ulcer.
- If your stomachache lasts for longer than a day
- If your indigestion is accompanied by pressure in the chest, nausea or vomiting, sweating, or breathing trouble. You could be having a heart attack.

FROM THE CUPBOARD

BAKING SODA. Make your own antacid with baking soda. Mix ½ teaspoon baking soda in ½ glass water and drink away. But read the antacid instructions on the baking soda label before you take this home remedy.

CRACKERS. If you haven't eaten anything all day, and your stomach is churning and burning, you probably have overactive stomach acids. Your best bet is to eat something bland, such as crackers.

RICE. If an overflow of stomach acid bothers you, try eating ½ cup cooked rice with your dinner. It's a complex carbohydrate that keeps the stomach busy churning, diverting excess acid. Plus it's a bland food that tends to be easy on the stomach.

FROM THE DRAWER

ANTACID. Antacids can help neutralize stomach acids, which can cut that burning sensation you feel when you have an empty stomach. But be careful what kind of antacid you choose. Antacids can cause other trouble if you're not careful. If you tend to be constipated, try an antacid with magnesium listed first on the list of ingredients. If diarrhea tends to be more bothersome for you, pick an antacid that has calcium listed first.

FROM THE FRUIT BASKET

BANANA. If you have a sensitive tummy, bland foods such as bananas seem to ease the pain. One study found that half the people who took banana powder capsules every day for two months eased their tummy pain. You can get similar results by eating a banana or plantain every day.

FROM THE REFRIGERATOR

APPLE. Adding fiber to your diet will help alleviate stomachaches and keep your digestive system healthy. One study of fiber's effect on the tummy discovered that people who ate fiber-rich foods at the first sign of a tummy ache cut their chances of getting a full-blown upset stomach in half. If you haven't been eating much fiber, be sure to start slowly, adding fiber gradually over a few months and drinking plenty of water to avoid overloading your system. To get started, grab an apple and nosh away, peel and all—that's where you get most of your roughage.

SODA POP. Sipping on a can of decaffeinated soda can help settle your stomach. This trick is especially useful if you've eaten too much. The carbonation in the soda causes you to burp, which is the quickest way to get relief from an overfull belly.

WATER. Drinking water is your best bet for avoiding tummy trouble. It helps move things through the digestive system smoothly. Try drinking at least six to eight 8-ounce glasses of water a day.

FROM THE SPICE RACK

CARAWAY SEEDS. These help with digestion and gas. You can either make a tea from the seed or simply chew on the seeds after dinner. Caraway seed tea: Place 1 teaspoon caraway seeds in a cup and add boiling water. Cover the cup and let stand for ten minutes. Strain well and drink up to 3 cups a day—be sure to drink on an empty stomach.

CINNAMON. This aromatic spice stimulates the digestive system, helping things move along the digestive tract smoothly. You can make a cinnamon tea by stirring ¼ to ½ teaspoon cinnamon powder into 1 cup hot water. Let the tea stand for up to five minutes and drink.

FENNEL SEEDS. This remedy is one of the most commonly prescribed by medical herbalists for gas and stomach cramps. Try a fennel tea for your stomach: Place 1 teaspoon fennel seeds in a cup and add boiling water. Cover the cup and let stand for ten minutes. Strain well and drink up to 3 cups a day—be sure to drink on an empty stomach.

GINGER. Ginger helps stomach ailments of all types, particularly nausea and gas. Ginger helps food flow smoothly through the digestive tract, so it can better absorb nutrients. Drink a cup of ginger tea to get your stomach back on track. To make ginger tea: Add ½ teaspoon ground ginger to a cup of hot water, let stand for up to three minutes, strain, and drink.

MINT. A folk remedy for indigestion, mint (in the form of peppermint or spearmint) can soothe a troubled tummy. Mint helps food move through the intestines properly and eases stomach cramps. Sip a cup of mint tea to let the herb work its magic: Put 1 teaspoon dried mint in a cup and add boiling water. Cover the cup and let it stand for ten minutes. Strain and drink up to 3 cups of the warm tea a day. Be sure to drink it on an empty stomach.

LIFE AND TIMES OF YOUR LUNCH

You ate tuna fish on rye at noon, and that tuna will be with you for a while before it's digested. Take a look at how long food takes to get from entrance to exit.

Esophagus: One bite slides down the esophagus in eight seconds.

Stomach: Carbohydrates take two hours to digest. Proteins take four hours. Fatty foods stick around for six hours.

Small Intestines: Foods stay in this winding road for three to five hours.

Large Intestines: That sandwich will stay in the staging room of the large intestines for 4 to 72 hours before it departs.

FOODS MOST LIKELY TO CAUSE TUMMY TROUBLE

German researchers wanted to know which foods caused the most trouble for people. So they asked people what foods tended to create an aching tummy. The top three offenders for normal, healthy eaters were mayonnaise, cabbage, and fried and salted foods.

THYME. Thyme stimulates the digestive tract, helps with stomach cramping, and relieves gas pressure. Place 1 teaspoon dried thyme leaves in a cup. Fill the cup with boiling water and let stand, covered, for ten minutes. Strain and drink on an empty stomach up to three times a day.

FROM THE STOVE

HOT WATER. Heat some water and pour it into a hot water bottle. Place the bottle on your stomach after you eat to help increase circulation to the abdominal area. The improved circulation should help improve digestion.

MORE DO'S AND DON'TS

- Think twice about milk. People who are lactose intolerant have trouble digesting milk and end up with bloating, gas, and cramping.

- Cut the coffee. Coffee causes stomach irritation in some people.

- Ax the alcohol. Alcohol is also a stomach irritant. If you have a sensitive tummy, skip the after-dinner drink.

- Pass on pepper. Red or black pepper may add a kick to food, but it can also kick you in the tummy. Avoid it if it bothers your stomach.

- Choose produce carefully. Some vegetables and fruits are notorious for their ability to produce tummy trouble. Watch out for broccoli, cabbage, brussels sprouts, and melons.

- Wash your beans. You can take the "music" out of beans. Let them soak overnight in water, then drain the water and replace it with fresh water before cooking. Rinse canned beans, too. This simple technique will help avert gassy problems.

- Get busy. Exercise helps get your digestive system moving as it should.

- Banish the aspirin. Aspirin and nonsteroidal anti-inflammatory drugs such as ibuprofen have been known to cause ulcers. If you're prone to tummy trouble, avoid both of these drugs.

- Relax. Many people get stomach troubles because they react poorly to stress. Learn some techniques for relaxing your mind and body.

- Eat up. Don't skip meals. It allows acid to build up in your stomach and can leave you with an aching tummy.

- Quit smoking. Smoking makes you more at risk for painful heartburn.

- Slow down. Take time to enjoy your meal and allow your food to digest properly.

Stress

Putting Pressure in its Place

Some people thrive on a stressful lifestyle, but others don't, and the stresses in their lives begin to take a toll, physically and mentally. Stress alters body chemistry and affects immunity. You know that heart attack someone suffered because he was "all stressed out"? Stress changed his body chemistry. It contributed to a hormonal imbalance that increased the rate at which plaque was hardening his arteries, and it altered the production and distribution of his body fat.

And that psoriasis she suffers? Stress caused her nerve cells to produce a chemical that stopped immune cells from fighting the itchy skin disease.

Find out your stress level by answering the following questions. Your answers will reveal whether you might benefit from some kitchen cures.

Stress on the job:

1. Are you overworked, underappreciated, or both?
2. Does it take everything you've got, physically, mentally, or both, just to make it every day from 9 to 5?

Stress at home:

1. Do you feel you don't have enough time for the fun things?
2. Do people expect more from you than you want to give?
3. Are there some important relationships that should be better?
4. Are there some changes you'd really like to make in yourself?

If you find yourself muttering "yes" to half of these, you're stressed. To what degree depends on your ability to cope with stress. But if you need a little stress relief, here it is.

From the Cupboard

Baking soda. A soothing bath in baking soda and ginger can relieve stress. Add ⅓ cup ginger and ⅓ cup baking soda to a tub of hot water and enjoy the soak.

Oats. Besides fighting off high cholesterol, oats produce a calming effect that fights off stress. Use them in bread recipes and desserts or for thickening in soups. Or just eat a bowl of oatmeal!

WHEN TO CALL THE DOCTOR

- When you're experiencing symptoms. Stress symptoms mimic the symptoms of other serious illness, including thyroid disease, so it's vital that your doctor determine the cause of your problem.

- When stress interferes with normal daily activity and home treatments do not work. Medications can help remedy symptoms.

- When stress causes any kind of chest pain, even mild pain

PASTA. When you're faced with eating a late-night meal, choose pasta. It causes a rise in the brain chemical called serotonin, which has a calming effect on the body. Rice produces the same effect.

SALT. Try this muscle-soothing bath to wash that stress away. Mix ½ cup salt, 1 cup Epsom salts, and 2 cups baking soda. Add ½ cup of the mix to your bathwater. Store the dry mix in a covered container, away from moisture.

SESAME OIL. For a nice relaxation technique, warm a few ounces and rub it all over your body, from head to toe. Sunflower and corn oil work well, too. After your massage, take a long, hot soak in the tub.

WHOLE-WHEAT BREAD. It's high in the B vitamins, which sustain the nervous system. Other B-rich foods include whole-wheat pita bread, whole-grain cereal, pasta, and brown rice. For a good stress-fighting diet, about 60 percent of your daily calories should come from these starchy foods.

FROM THE DRAWER

BALLOON. To make a stress ball, fill a small balloon with baking soda, tie off the opening, and simply squeeze your stress away.

FROM THE REFRIGERATOR

CELERY. The phytonutrients called phthalides found in celery have a widely recognized sedative effect.

CHERRIES. They soothe the nervous system and relieve stress. Eat them fresh or any way you like them.

LETTUCE. This stress-reducing veggie has a sedative effect. A small amount of lacturcarium, a natural sedative, is found in the white, milky juice that oozes from the lettuce when the stalk is snapped.

FROM THE SPICE RACK

CARDAMOM SEEDS. These are said to freshen the breath, speed the digestion, and cheer the heart. But they also bust the stress. To make a tea, cover 2 to 3 pods with boiling water and steep for ten minutes. Or, add the pods to a regular pot of tea. You can crush the pods and add to rice or lentils before cooking, or use in a vegetable stir-fry. Cardamom is a good addition to cakes and biscuits. Instead of pods, use 1 teaspoon powdered cardamom; it's available in the spice section of the grocery store.

PEPPERMINT. Drink a cup of peppermint tea before bed to relieve tension and help you sleep. Chamomile, catnip, or vervain works well, too. Place 1 teaspoon of the dried leaf in a cup of boiling water. Sweeten with honey. To reap the fullest benefits, sipping this soothing tea should be the last thing you do before you tuck yourself in for the night. And during the day, if you don't have time for a cup of tea, try a peppermint candy. Read the label first, though, and go for one with peppermint, sugar, and little else. The more extra ingredients, the less the relaxing benefit.

TARRAGON. A tarragon tea calms the nervous system. Add ½ teaspoon dried tarragon to 1 cup boiling water. Or use it fresh, snipped into salads or vegetables. It's a good seasoning for creamy soups, too, or added to a salad dressing of balsamic vinegar with a dash of honey.

> ### WHERE'S THE BEEF?
> If you're stressed, it shouldn't be in your meal. Foods with high protein content, such as beef, release an amino acid called tyrosine that activates the production of norepinephrine and dopamine, two hormones that can cause anxiety, hyperactivity, and high blood pressure. So skip the beef and choose pasta or a veggie.

MORE DO'S & DON'TS

- Seek support. It's easier to cope when someone is there to hold your hand.

- Choose control. You can't control everything in your life, but that doesn't mean you should relinquish all control. Take control where you can. You'll find that a little control can go a long way in fighting stress. Make a list with two headings: Things I Can Control and Things I Can't Control. When you see it in print, you'll be surprised how much of your life is already under your control. That, in itself, should relieve some stress.

- Find your purpose. Knowing your purpose can relieve stress, and if nothing special comes to mind, create a purpose. Volunteer at a homeless shelter, make new friends at a nursing home. When you involve yourself in something other than your stress, your stress will actually decrease.

- Exercise. The endorphins released in 20 minutes of aerobic exercise have a feel-good effect that reduces stress.

- Nix the artificial stimulants. Caffeine, nicotine, alcohol—it may seem like they relieve stress, but the effect is only temporary. In the long run, they can make you anxious and cause you more health problems.

- Relax. Take some deep breaths. Give your stressed-out muscles a break, and soak in a nice warm tub or listen to relaxing music. Indulge in a flight of fantasy, read a book, meditate or pray, or take up a hobby.

Sunburn

SHIELDING YOUR SKIN

A sunburn is one of the most common hazards of the great outdoors. The unappealing and painful lobster look results when the amount of exposure to the sun exceeds the ability of the body's protective pigment, melanin, to protect the skin. What makes sunburn different from, say, a household iron burn? The time factor. A sunburn is not immediately apparent. By the time the skin starts to become red, the damage has been done. Pain isn't always instantly notice-able, either. You may feel glowing after two hours sitting poolside without sun protection. But you'll change your tune (not to mention color) when the pain sets in, typically 6 to 48 hours after sun exposure.

Like household burns, sunburns are summed up by degree. Mild sunburns are deep pink, punctuated by a hot, burning sensation. Moderate sunburns are red, clothing lines are prominent, and the skin itches and stings. Severe sunburns result in bright red skin, blisters, fever, chills, and nausea.

Being burned to a crisp can lead to serious consequences later in life. In fact, one severe, blistering sunburn during childhood doubles your chances of developing malignant melanoma, a deadly form of skin cancer, or other types of skin cancer such as basal cell and squamous cell carcinomas. If cancer doesn't frighten you, then the specter of developing premature wrinkling and age spots just might.

Obviously, covering up and applying a waterproof sunscreen with a high SPF (sun protection factor) is the best way to prevent sunburn. But if you slip up and expose your tender flesh to the fierce sun, these kitchen cures should help you chill out.

FROM THE CUPBOARD

BAKING SODA. Adding a few heaping tablespoons of baking soda to cool bathwater makes a sunburn-soothing remedy. Just keep your soaking time down to 15 to 20 minutes. If you soak any longer, you risk drying out your already lizardlike skin. When you've emerged from the bath, resist the urge to towel off. Air-dry your skin instead, and don't wipe the baking soda off.

CHAMOMILE TEA. Brew dried chamomile in a tea and sponge onto affected areas. Make the tea by combining 1 teaspoon dried chamomile with 1 cup boiling water, or use a prepackaged chamomile tea bag. Cool and apply. Do not use chamomile if you have pollen allergies, or you may suffer a skin reaction atop the burn.

CORNSTARCH. Sunburns often strike where skin meets bathing suit. Sensitive and hard-to-reach spots you've neglected to smear with suntan lotion (along bikini lines, underneath buttock cheeks, or around the breasts and armpits) often fall victim. These burn spots then have to face daily irritation from tight elastic in bras and underwear. To ease chafing, cover the burned area with a dusting of cornstarch. Don't apply petroleum jelly or oils, which can exacerbate the burn by blocking pores. If the burn is blistering, however, don't apply anything.

> ### WHEN TO CALL THE DOCTOR
>
> - If there is extensive blistering with the sunburn
> - If you feel nauseated or weak, run a fever, or have chills
> - If a moderate or severe sunburn covers the face, hands, feet, or genital area

OATMEAL. Oatmeal added to cool bathwater offers wonderful relief for sunburned skin. Fill up the bathtub with cool water, not cold water since that can send the body into shock. Don't use bath salts, oils, or bubble bath. Instead, scoop ½ to 1 cup oatmeal—an ideal skin soother—and mix it in. Another option is to buy Aveeno, an oatmeal powder found in the pharmacy. Follow the packet's directions. As with the baking soda, air-dry your body and don't wipe the oatmeal off your skin.

POTATOES. The plain old potato makes for a wonderful pain reliever. It's a time-tested technique known throughout the world. Take two washed potatoes, cut them into small chunks, and place them in a blender or food processor. Blend or process until the potatoes are in liquid form. Add water if they look dry. Pat the burned areas with the pulverized potatoes. Wait until the potatoes dry, then take a cool shower. Another less messy method is to apply the mash to a clean gauze and place on the burn. Change the dressing every hour. Continue applying several times a day for a few days until the pain is relieved.

VINEGAR. Adding ½ cup vinegar to your cool bathwater should also take the sting out of the sunburn.

FROM THE REFRIGERATOR

MILK. Cool off with cold milk. Soak a facecloth in equal parts cold milk and cool water, wring it out, and gently press it on the burned areas.

FROM THE SINK

WATER. As the sun fried your skin, it also dehydrated it. Be sure to replenish liquids by drinking plenty of water while recovering from a sunburn. Being well hydrated will help burns heal better.

FROM THE WINDOWSILL

ALOE VERA. The thick, gellike juice of this plant can take the sting and redness out of a sunburn. Aloe vera causes blood vessels to constrict. Simply slit open one of the broad leaves and apply the gel directly to the burn. Apply five to six times per day for several days.

MORE DO'S AND DON'TS

- Avoid being out in the sun between the hours of 10 A.M. and 3 P.M. because that's when the sun's rays are the strongest.

- Don't think you're protected if the skies are cloudy. Damaging rays aren't inhibited by clouds, and you can still get burned.

- Use a waterproof sunscreen if you'll be swimming or if you'll be sweating a lot. Reapply frequently (follow the directions on the label).

- If you're taking any medications, be sure to check about side effects from sun exposure. Some medications, such as tetracycline, cause a rash on areas exposed to the sun.

WAYS OF THE RAYS

Here on earth we're exposed to two types of ultraviolet (UV) rays: UVA and UVB rays. Unlike visible light, these rays are shorter in wavelength, are higher in energy, and fall outside the visible spectrum (so you can't see what's hitting you). When these high-energy rays strike your skin, they generate free radicals, which can damage DNA. UV ray damage can be short-term (a painful burn) or long-term (premature aging of the skin and skin cancer). What's the difference between UVA and UVB rays?

UVA: Ultraviolet A
- has a longer wavelength
- penetrates the deep layers of the skin and produces free radicals
- is linked to premature aging of the skin
- can pass through window glass in cars, houses, and office buildings
- is the most common ray used in tanning beds

UVB: Ultraviolet B
- has a shorter wavelength
- doesn't penetrate deeply into the skin
- can cause significant damage to DNA
- is the primary cause of sunburn and skin cancer
- cannot pass through windows

Ulcers
HEALING THE HOLE

It's only in the last decade that scientific evidence conclusively proved that ulcers are most often caused by a bacterial infection, not by the Type-A, pressure-cooker personality that was the subject of countless jokes. Misconceptions and myths die hard, though, so there are some people who haven't gotten the word yet and still believe that the demanding boss or the overachiever are more likely to work themselves into an ulcer. While these personality characteristics may aggravate an existing ulcer (not to mention the people they associate with), they don't cause one.

There's a Hole in the Bucket

An ulcer is a sore or hole in the protective mucosal lining of the gastrointestinal tract. Ulcers appear in the area of the stomach or the duodenum, the upper part of the small intestine, where caustic digestive juices, pepsin, and hydrochloric acid are present. Today we know that the majority of ulcers are the result of an infection with a bacteria called *Helicobacter pylori (H. pylori)*. This bacteria makes the stomach and small intestine more susceptible to the erosive effects of the digestive juices. The bacteria may also cause the stomach to produce more acid.

There are some lifestyle factors that can contribute to the development of an ulcer. These include alcohol consumption, eating and drinking foods that contain caffeine, significant physical (not emotional) stress such as severe burns and major surgery, and excessive use of certain over-the-counter pain medications such as aspirin or ibuprofen. Studies have shown that smoking also tends

WHEN TO CALL THE DOCTOR

- If you experience severe and sudden abdominal pain
- If your bowel movements are black or bloody
- If you vomit blood
- If you feel cold or clammy with no other explanation
- If you develop persistent nausea or vomiting
- If you lose weight for no reason
- If you have pain that radiates to your back

DOWN WITH DECAF

Just when you thought you were being good by ordering decaf, along comes this discouraging news: Decaffeinated coffee may do as much harm to ulcers as the full-strength brew. The effects of decaffeinated coffee were compared to those of peptone, a strong stimulant of acid secretion in the stomach.

Researchers found that drinking unleaded brew produced more gastric acids than were produced by peptone.

to increase the chances of developing an ulcer, slows the healing of existing ulcers, and makes a recurrence more likely. Family history of ulcers also appears to play a role in susceptibility.

Who Gets Ulcers?

If Type-A folks don't automatically get ulcers, then who does? The cause lies less in personality and more in stomach makeup. Researchers believe some people just produce more stomach acid than others. If stomach acid production isn't the problem, then a weak stomach may be. The stomach lining in certain individuals may be less able to withstand the onslaught of gastric acids. Lifestyle factors mentioned above can also weaken the stomach's lining.

Signs and Symptoms

The most typical symptom of a brewing ulcer: a burning or gnawing pain between the breastbone and navel. This pain is more common between meals (it improves with eating but returns a few hours later) and in the middle of the night or toward dawn.

Less typical symptoms include nausea or vomiting, weight loss and loss of appetite, and frequent burping or bloating.

If you have an ulcer or suspect you may have one, you should be under the care of a physician. But between visits to the doctor, there are ways to care for your digestive tract.

FROM THE COUNTER

BANANA. This fruit contains an antibacterial substance that may inhibit the growth of ulcer-causing *H. pylori*. And studies show that animals fed bananas have a thicker stomach wall and greater mucus production in the stomach, which helps build a better barrier between digestive acids and the lining of the stomach. Plantains are also helpful.

GARLIC. Garlic's antibacterial properties include fighting *H. pylori*. Take two small crushed cloves a day.

FROM THE REFRIGERATOR

CABBAGE. Researchers have found that ulcer patients who drink 1 quart raw cabbage juice a day can often heal their ulcers in five days. Researchers also found that those who eat plain cabbage have quicker healing times, too.

PLUMS. Red- and purple-colored foods inhibit the growth of *H. pylori*. Like plums, berries can also help you fight the good fight.

FROM THE SPICE RACK

CAYENNE PEPPER. Used moderately, a little cayenne pepper can go a long way in helping ulcers. The pepper stimulates blood flow to bring nutrients to the stomach. To make a cup of peppered tea, mix ¼ teaspoon cayenne pepper in 1 cup hot water. Drink a cup a day. A dash of cayenne pepper can also be added to soups, meats, and other savory dishes.

LICORICE. Several modern studies have demonstrated the ulcer-healing abilities of

> ## FASCINATING FACT
> About 20 million Americans develop at least one ulcer during their lifetime, according to the National Institute of Diabetes and Digestive and Kidney Diseases. Each year more than 40,000 people have surgery because of persistent symptoms or problems from ulcers, and about 6,000 die of ulcer-related complications.

licorice. Licorice doesn't reduce stomach acid; rather, it reduces the ability of stomach acid to damage the stomach lining. Properties in licorice encourage digestive mucosal tissues to protect themselves from acid. Licorice can be used in encapsulated form, but for a quick cup of licorice tea, cut 1 ounce licorice root into slices and cover with 1 quart boiling water. Steep, cool, and strain. (If licorice root is unavailable, cut 1 ounce licorice sticks into slices.) You can also try licorice candy if it's made with real licorice (the label will say "licorice mass") and not just flavored with anise. Don't eat more than 1 ounce per day.

MORE DO'S AND DON'TS

- Be like a bunny and nibble throughout the day. The key to keeping gastric juices from attacking the digestive tract lining is to keep them busy with food. Snacking on healthy treats, such as carrot sticks and whole-wheat crackers, should do the trick. Also, consider becoming a six-small-meals-a-day type person rather than a three-meals-a-day type.

- Don't smoke. Smokers have double the risk of developing ulcers. If that's not bad enough, ulcers heal more slowly in smokers, and their relapse rate is higher than normal.

- Limit alcohol intake. The question of alcohol's impact on ulcer formation remains unanswered, but many medical experts believe individuals who drink heavily are at higher risk for ulcer development compared to light drinkers or abstainers.

- Control your stress. All that frustration and anxiety you carry around can aggravate ulcers or make the conditions ripe for one to appear. Work on ways to effectively control (and eliminate) stress. Take a stress management course, learn to meditate, do yoga, or exercise regularly!

Urinary Tract Infection
BLASTING BACTERIA

You stand in front of the bathroom door for the twentieth time in the last hour. You've got to go, but every time you do, you end up with only a painful trickle. You recognize the burning sensation that makes every trip to the toilet an ordeal. You've got a urinary tract infection.

Urinary tract infections (UTIs) are the second most common reason people visit their doctors each year. Men get UTIs, but they are much more common in women—more than eight million women head to their doctor for UTI treatment annually. And 20 percent of these women will get a second UTI.

If you've ever had a UTI, you'll probably never forget the symptoms. It usually starts with a sudden and frequent need to visit the toilet. When you get there, you can squeeze out only a little bit of urine, and that's usually accompanied by a burning sensation in your bladder and/or urethra. In more extreme cases you may end up with fever, chills, back pain, and even blood in your urine.

Bladder Control

UTIs are a result of bacteria, particularly *Escherichia coli (E. coli)* bacteria, taking temporary control of your bladder and your urethra (the tube that allows urine to flow from your bladder to the toilet). Women tend to get more UTIs for two reasons: They have a shorter urethra than men, and their urethral opening is precariously close to the vagina and the bacteria-loving anus, where *E. coli* and other bacteria normally hang out without causing harm. That means everyday body functions and sex are more likely to push bacteria into your urethra. Being pregnant also ups your risk of a UTI because your bladder is under a lot of pressure from your uterus and is more susceptible to an infection. And if you use a diaphragm to protect against pregnancy, you put more pressure on your urethra and are more likely to end up with a UTI.

> **SIZE DOES MATTER**
> The urethra in the average woman is about one inch long. The urethra in the average man: nine inches.

Men get UTIs but not for the same reasons. If a man suspects he has a UTI, he should call his doctor; the UTI may be due to a bladder stone, an enlarged prostate, or a sexually transmitted disease such as gonorrhea. A prostate infection may also make its way to the bladder, causing a bladder infection.

When you have an infection in your lower urinary tract, the medically correct term for the condition is cystitis. If the infection is in your urethra, you've got urethritis. UTIs typically combine both cystitis and urethritis. But sometimes the infection is at the top of your urinary tract, closer to your kidneys. If you end up with this type of infection, it can easily spread to your kidneys, causing a condition called pyelonephritis. Pyelonephritis can cause more severe symptoms, including back pain, fever, nausea, and vomiting.

UTIs that last longer than two days require medical intervention. Untreated UTIs can infect the kidneys and turn into a much more serious problem. To help prevent a UTI from developing or nip one in the bud, try some of the remedies available in your own kitchen.

FROM THE CUPBOARD

BAKING SODA. Add 1 teaspoon baking soda to a glass of water to help ease your infection. The soda neutralizes the acidity in your urine, speeding your recovery.

WHEN TO CALL THE DOCTOR

- If you have symptoms and also have shaking spells or have vomited in the last 12 hours
- If you have symptoms and a fever that get worse after a couple of days of home treatment
- If you have blood in your urine
- If you have symptoms of a urinary tract infection and you have a history of kidney disease
- If you have symptoms of a urinary tract infection and have diabetes or are pregnant
- If you experienced a stomach or back injury within two weeks before your symptoms started. This may indicate a kidney injury.
- If you have symptoms and high blood pressure
- If you have symptoms and are a man over age 50
- If you suspect you may have a sexually transmitted disease

FROM THE REFRIGERATOR

BLUEBERRIES. Blueberries and cranberries are from the same plant family and seem to have the same bacteria-inhibiting properties. In one study, blueberry juice was found to prevent UTIs. If you can't find a gallon of blueberry juice at your local store, try sprinkling a handful of these flavorful, good-for-you berries over your morning cereal.

CRANBERRY JUICE. Many studies have found that drinking cranberry juice may help you avoid urinary tract infections. It appears that cranberry juice prevents infection-causing bacteria from bedding down in your bladder, and it also has a very mild antibiotic affect. Drinking as little as 4 ounces of cranberry juice a day can help keep your bladder infection-free. But if you tend to get UTIs or are dealing with one right now, try to drink at least 2 to 4 glasses of cranberry juice a day. If pure cranberry juice is just too bitter for your taste buds, you can substitute cranberry juice cocktail. It seems to have the same effect as the pure stuff. Take note: If you have a urinary tract infection, cranberry juice is not a replacement for doctor-prescribed antibiotics in treating your infection.

PINEAPPLE. Bromelain is an enzyme found in pineapples. In one study, people with a UTI who were given bromelain along with their usual round of antibiotics got rid of their infection. Only half the people who were given a placebo plus an antibiotic showed no signs of lingering infection. Eating a cup of pineapple tastes good, and it may just help rid you of your infection.

FROM THE SINK

WATER. If you tend to get urinary tract infections, be sure to drink plenty of water—about eight 8-ounce glasses a day. You should be urinating at least every four to five hours. If you are currently dealing with an infection, drink buckets of water to fight it off. Drink a full 8 ounces of water every hour. The river of water in your system will help flush out bacteria by making you urinate more frequently.

FROM THE STOVETOP

HOT WATER. Heat up some water on the stove, and pour it into a hot water bottle. Place the water bottle on your lower abdomen to help ease any pain caused by the infection.

FROM THE SUPPLEMENT SHELF

VITAMIN C. Some doctors are prescribing at least 5,000 mg or more of vitamin C a day for patients who develop recurrent urinary tract infections. Vitamin C keeps the bladder healthy by acidifying the urine, essentially putting up a no-trespassing sign for potentially harmful bacteria.

MORE DO'S AND DON'TS

- Don't wait. When you've got to go, go. It sounds simple, but how many times have you held it—when you're in a business meeting, when you're stuck in traffic, when you're at a concert and the lines are too long. If you hold your urine, you're more likely to get a backup of bacteria and end up with an infection.

- Consider cotton. Anything that comes into close contact with any of those ultra-personal areas should be cotton. Wearing cotton underwear or cotton-lined panty hose will help you stay fresher and dryer. Guys should go for boxer shorts.

- Don't drink alcohol. Alcohol is an irritant to your bladder, just what you don't need when you're dealing with an infection.

- Cut the caffeine. Also avoid caffeine-loaded drinks such as caffeinated soda pop, coffee, and tea. Caffeine can irritate the bladder, which is the last thing you need when a UTI has taken hold.

- Pull out a nonprescription pain reliever. Taking acetaminophen, ibuprofen, or aspirin can help ease the pain during your infection.

- Follow the rules for making love. If you have trouble with UTIs, be sure you and your partner clean up before making love. After you make love, head to the bathroom to urinate and get rid of any potentially harmful bacteria. And try using a condom instead of a diaphragm. Diaphragms may promote UTIs.

- Go with the flow. After urinating, be sure to wipe from front to back to keep bacteria from getting close to the urethra.

WHY'S THAT LINE SO LONG?

You've been slurping sodas through the entire circus performance. But like everyone else under the big top, you don't want to miss the human cannonball, so you hold it until intermission. As soon as the lights come up, you run to the restroom, only to discover there's already a line around the corner. As your eyeballs begin to float, you glance over at the guy's restroom, where there's nary a man standing around waiting for a chance at the porcelain throne. You wonder what in the world the magic is that makes guys get in and out so quickly.

Well, a group of researchers at Cornell University wanted to know if girls indeed spent more time in the restroom than guys. They set up shop at highway rest stops and counted the seconds each sex spent doing their duty. Men spent an average of 45 seconds using the toilet. Women spent almost twice as much time, an average of 79 seconds. Why the difference? It could be panty hose, primping, or some other reasons. No one knows.

Warts

BANISHING BUMPS

Witches are usually depicted with a wart at the end
of their nose, and you've certainly heard the old
wives' tale that claims you can catch a wart
by touching a frog or toad. But witches
didn't get their warts from toads, and toads'
bumps aren't actually warts. How, then, do
people get warts?

Warts are caused by the human papillo-
mavirus (HPV), and there are more than 60
varieties of it. You get a wart from coming into
contact with the virus through skin-to-skin contact. You can get the virus from another person,
via a handshake for example, or you can actually give one to yourself if
you already have a wart. You can spread the wart virus to other parts of
your body by scratching, touching, shaving, or even biting your nails. All
it takes is a little break in the skin for the virus to enter the system.

Culprit Categories

Before you can attempt to get rid of your wart, you have to be sure
that little bump actually is one. There are three common varieties—
common, plantar, and flat—according to the American Academy of
Dermatology.

Common warts are found in areas where the skin has been broken:
where fingernails are bitten down to the quick or hangnails are picked
until they bleed. Often, they look like they have little dots or seeds in
them, which is why they're frequently called "seed warts." But what you
see aren't seeds; they're merely dots produced by the blood vessel supply-
ing the infected area.

Common warts are

• Small

• Flesh-colored

• Hard

• "Seedy" and rough to the touch

• Raised

• Usually found on kids, because they always have some kind of sore on
  their fingers, and people with immune system deficiencies, since they

are more susceptible to all types of viral infections.

Plantar warts do not stick above the surface the way common warts do. That's because the pressure from walking keeps pushing them back into the skin.

Plantar warts are

- Usually found on the weight-bearing areas of the foot (plantar means bottom of the foot)

- Usually gray or brown

- "Seedy" and rough to the touch

- Hard

- Flat

- Painful. At the very least, a plantar wart can feel like a stone in the shoe. It can also cause a sharp, burning pain. At worst, the repetitive pounding of simple footsteps can irritate these nuisances, sometimes so badly they bleed.

- Able to grow to an inch in circumference or more and spread out into clusters called mosaic warts.

Flat warts are the smallest of the warts. They are

- Found in clumps of 20 to 100, usually on the face and neck, but also on the chest, knees, hands, wrists, and forearms. In men they're common in the bearded area, most likely picked up from shaving irritations and nicks. In women, they're common on shaved legs.

- Tiny

- Flat

- Smooth

- Flesh-colored, gray, or brown

There are dozens of other kinds of warts, as well as other problems that may look like warts. If you have any concerns, consult your physician. What looks warty to you could be something much more serious, such as a skin cancer.

Waiting Them Out?

Warts can take a long time to go away, but most will if you wait long enough. Unfortunately, they also have a tendency to recur. Doctors

WHEN TO SEE THE DOCTOR

- If the wart is causing problems: If it's unsightly or sore or it's in a place where it's constantly irritated, which increases the likelihood of spreading it

- If the wart changes colors or bleeds

- If you're more than 45 years old and a new wart pops up. The doctor may want a peek to make sure it's not skin cancer.

- If you have a plantar wart and also have diabetes or poor circulation in your feet

WART STATS

- 10 percent of us get warts
- 50 percent of all warts disappear without treatment within 6 to 12 months

THOSE EMBARRASSING STRINGY THINGIES

You know those fat little strings of flesh that pop up on your face, neck, or eyelids? They're called filiforms, and yes, they're warts, too. You may be tempted to clip them right off, but don't! Clipping off any wart can cause the virus to spread and reinfect the area.

aren't sure why, but some speculate that the "mother" wart sheds "babies" into the surrounding skin. And some people seem to have a susceptibility to warts. Adults get warts less frequently than children do, but warts in adults take longer to go away.

Wart Be Gone

There are many ways to rid yourself of a wart. Doctors can zap them with a laser, burn or freeze them, or give you topical medications that might do the trick. You can pay a pretty penny for these medical treatments, but if your warts are painful or multiplying rapidly, you may want to go the medical route. If not, and you have some time, there might just be a remedy from the kitchen that will send your unsightly little nuisance into wart oblivion.

FROM THE CUPBOARD

BAKING POWDER. Mix baking powder and castor oil into a paste, then apply it to the wart at night, covering it with a bandage. Remove the bandage the next morning. Repeat as necessary.

BAKING SODA. Dissolve baking soda in water, then wash your wart-plagued hand or foot in it. Let your hand dry naturally, with the baking soda still on it. Repeat often, until the wart is gone.

FOODS. Eat foods that strengthen the immune system, such as garlic, sweet potatoes, whole-grain breads, sunflower seeds, and rice. (See also foods in "From the Refrigerator" on the next page.)

GARLIC. Rub crushed garlic or onion on your wart. Or, eat fresh garlic. If you don't want to smell like an Italian cookery, munch on some breath-freshening parsley afterward—or try swallowing 3 garlic capsules three times a day.

FROM THE DRAWER

ADHESIVE TAPE. Wrap a finger wart with four layers of adhesive tape. Wrap the first strip over the top of the finger and the second strip around the finger. Repeat both wrappings. Leave the adhesive in place 6½ days, then remove and let the wart breathe for half a day. Repeat the process until the wart is gone.

FROM THE REFRIGERATOR

CARROT. Finely grate a carrot and add enough olive oil to it to make a paste. Dab the paste on your wart twice daily for 30 minutes for two to three weeks.

FIGS. Mash up a fresh fig and place some on your wart for 30 minutes. Do this daily for two to three weeks.

FOODS. Eat foods that strengthen the immune system: broccoli, red meats, oranges, onions, scallions.

LEMON JUICE. Squeeze a little lemon juice on your wart, then cover it with fresh, chopped onions for 30 minutes once a day for two to three weeks.

PINEAPPLE JUICE. Soak your wart in pineapple juice. It has a dissolving enzyme.

THE DANDELION CURE

If you've scorned the lowly dandelion growing in your lawn, you may change your mind if you've got recalcitrant warts. Pick a dandelion, break the stem, and rub the white milky juice on your wart two or three times a day until the wart is cured.

FROM THE SUPPLEMENT SHELF

VITAMIN C. Crush 1 vitamin C tablet, and add water to make a thick paste. Apply it to the wart, then cover. The acid in the vitamin C may irritate the wart away.

VITAMIN E. Break a vitamin E or A capsule, rub a little of the oil on the wart, and cover it with an adhesive bandage. Repeat three times a day. Remove the bandage at night to let it breathe, then start over with the oil in the morning.

FROM THE WINDOWSILL

ALOE. Break open an aloe leaf, and soak up the clear juice from the inner leaf on a cotton ball. Apply the cotton ball to the wart, and cover with a bandage. Repeat daily until the wart is gone.

MORE DO'S & DON'TS

- Don't scratch existing warts.
- Don't shake hands with someone who has an obvious wart.
- Wash your hands with soap and hot water if you've touched a wart.
- Don't go barefoot in public places, including showers. Wear sandals.
- Use an electric razor if the area you shave has a wart. This helps to avoid the tiny nicks that will allow the virus to gain entry.
- Keep your wart dry. Warts love to multiply in moist areas.

Water Retention

BEATING THE BLOAT

If you feel like the Goodyear blimp around "that time" of the month, join the millions of other women who feel likewise. Water retention is part of the premenstrual syndrome (PMS) package. During this time, hormonal fluctuations can cause havoc in a woman's body. In some women the monthly rise in estrogen turns on the faucet for the hormone aldosterone. Aldosterone, in turn, causes the kidneys to retain fluids and the woman to suddenly gain a few water-filled pounds.

While PMS is the major cause of water retention in women, water retention for both men and women can also be related to kidney problems, both serious (kidney disease) and commonplace (not drinking enough water). Heart, liver, or thyroid malfunctions can also play a role in water retention. And, of course, eating too many salty foods can turn your body into a water-storage tank.

Thanks to the effects of gravity, retained water tends to flow southward and pool in the feet, ankles, and legs, although no area of the body is immune. Try to elevate your legs frequently. If you suffer from the occasional bloated-cow feeling due to PMS, eating too much, or not drinking enough water, the kitchen is the place to deflate yourself.

FROM THE CABINET

SALT. Around the time you expect your period, drastically reduce your salt intake. Sodium increases fluid retention, so don't use the saltshaker. And if recipes call for salt, try adding more pepper or another spice instead. But, most importantly, cut down on processed foods and fast foods, all of which are overflowing with salt. For a salt-free cooking substitute, see the recipe on page 178.

FROM THE COUNTER

BANANAS. Go ape and grab a few bananas. Slice 'em on your cereal, make a smoothie, or just peel and eat them plain. Bananas contain high amounts of potassium, which helps eliminate fluid retention. Not a banana fan? Gobble down a handful of raisins instead.

FROM THE FREEZER

ICE. When ankles puff up, applying an ice pack can help bring them back to normal size. Place ice cubes in a plastic bag with a zipper seal, wrap a light towel around the bag, and apply for five to ten minutes. A bag of frozen veggies also works well. In summertime, dip legs (ankle-deep) into a bath of ice water. People who have diabetes or poor circulation in their feet should skip the ice bath, however, unless directed to use it by their physician.

FROM THE REFRIGERATOR

CABBAGE. A natural diuretic, cabbage can be added to salads or sandwiches. Enjoy a side of coleslaw for lunch.

CRANBERRY JUICE. Another natural diuretic. Drink it straight from the bottle.

YOGURT. Too many rich treats will cause stomachs to bloat. If you've overindulged and are feeling the effects, treat your stomach to a cup of plain, low fat yogurt that contains active cultures. The active cultures aid in digestion and increase the good bacteria in the gut.

FROM THE SINK

WATER. When you feel waterlogged, guzzling a glass of H_2O might be the last thing on your mind. But it may be the best thing for you. Water flushes out the system better than anything else and can reduce premenstrual bloating. Drink 8 to 10 glasses a day; more when you exercise.

FROM THE SUPPLEMENT SHELF

VITAMINS A AND C. When you feel like a balloon, try to increase your intake of vitamins A and C, both of which help diminish the fragility of capillaries and decrease water retention.

MORE DO'S AND DON'TS

- Lift your legs! Ankles can swell like sourdough bread thanks to water retention. Luckily, avoiding la baguette look just takes a little movement. Exercises that work the calf muscles help move blood and excess fluid out of the ankle area. Regularly walking, running, bicycling, and aerobic dancing can work wonders. If ankles swell while seated at work, try lifting your legs up parallel to the floor every few minutes.

WHEN TO CALL THE DOCTOR

- If you are older than 45 and suddenly experience bloating and swelling, especially of the ankles
- If you are pregnant and experience water retention
- If water retention is disrupting your daily life
- If you're taking blood pressure medications or birth control pills and are retaining water. These can cause fluid retention.

FASCINATING FACT
In an odd tribute to dandelion's diuretic effect, the French call it pissenlit, meaning to urinate in bed.

During breaks, walk around the office or up the stairs. Spend a portion of the lunch hour on your feet, exercising.

• Keep your feet up. While resting, reading, or watching television, prop a pillow under those tootsies. A little help from gravity can go a long way in draining fluid from swollen limbs.

• Forget sitting ladylike! Cross off the notion that crossing your legs is the dainty way to sit. Doing so limits the blood flow through the thigh veins, in turn aggravating the swelling in the lower legs.

• Toss out tight clothing. If you have to squeeze into your pants, you can be guaranteed that pressure is being placed on your upper thighs and waist, in turn restricting the removal of fluids from the lower legs.

• Limit alcohol intake.

• Don't smoke.

• Stay away from junk food. Not only is it bad for you, but the excess salt tips the scales.

• Try to eat 6 small meals a day rather than 3 big ones.

BE KIND TO YOUR KIDNEYS

Kidneys, the two small bean-shaped organs located at the back of the abdominal cavity on either side of the spine, are the filters of the human body. Whatever enters the body, the kidneys sort like two efficient secretaries into a "Keep and Use" pile and a "Throw Out" pile. The "in" items are sent into the bloodstream, while the "out" items leave with body waste.

Unlike administrative assistants today, the kidneys are on duty 24/7 and hold down the extra job of making sure every office in the body is getting its share of water. When the water supply is cut down (for various reasons, including not drinking enough), the kidneys become sluggish and the entire body is put into panic mode. Every single cell and tissue holds dearly to the water it already has.

Managing the kidneys is relatively easy. Keep them happy and functioning efficiently by drinking eight 8-ounce glasses of water a day, more if you exercise or are in hot or humid weather.

Yeast Infection
ACHIEVING A BALANCE

No one wants to talk about a yeast infection, and no one wants to admit they have one. That's probably because it's known as one of those "personal" things that only affects women.

Well, in most cases that's true, but yeast infections are not restricted to women only. You know that diaper rash covering the cutest little bottom you've ever seen? Guess what? Yeast. And that condition called thrush that babies often develop in the mouth? Yeast again. So you see, yeast is a fungus that can proliferate anywhere the breeding ground is right. And the breeding ground is right in the genital and oral areas because that's where *Candida albicans,* the fungus that causes a yeast infection, lives.

Yeast happens when the acidity of normal fluids is altered. Usually they're acidic enough to keep the yeast from flourishing. But when the balance is tipped, the yeast have a party, multiplying over and over. What causes the imbalance? Here are the common factors:

- Weakened immune system
- Diabetes
- Overuse of antibiotics
- Steroids

In vaginal yeast infections, there may be additional factors:

- Hormonal changes, such as those that occur at puberty, pregnancy, or menopause
- Inadequate vaginal lubrication during intercourse
- Soap sensitivity
- Feminine hygiene deodorants and douches
- Spermicides

THE THUMBS-UP FOOD LIST FOR YEAST INFECTIONS

It's important to keep the immune system strong when fighting off a yeast infection. Here are some immune-boosting foods to add to your grocery list:

- Raw vegetables and juice
- Green leafy vegetables
- Winter squash
- Whole grains

Yeast infections can also be transmitted between sexual partners. Use condoms or abstain from sex during the infection to prevent spreading it.

WHEN TO CALL THE DOCTOR

- If you have abdominal pain
- If you have bloody discharge between menstrual periods
- If discharge gets worse or lasts longer than two weeks
- If you think you've been exposed to a sexually transmitted disease
- If you have recurrent yeast infections. This could be a sign of diabetes.
- If you have chills or fever
- If you have back pain
- If your symptoms resemble those for trichomonas or gardnerella

Typical symptoms of a vaginal yeast infection include intense itching and soreness accompanied by a thick white discharge. Symptoms of a genital yeast infection in men include irritation and itching in the genital area, sometimes accompanied by white discharge under the foreskin and/or swelling at the end of the penis. In the throat, yeast looks like creamy white patches.

Most yeast infections can be cured with creams or suppositories found on the pharmacy shelf. And some prescription medications will stop the problem in as little as three days. But there are also simple kitchen panaceas that can bring relief or cure and even stop the disease from recurring.

FROM THE CUPBOARD

BAKING SODA. For thrush, brush your teeth after every meal with a toothpaste of baking soda and water. Commercial toothpaste may be too harsh if sores develop. Pour a little baking soda in your hand and add just enough water to make a paste. Rinse with ½ cup warm water and 1 tablespoon 3 percent hydrogen peroxide. Do not swallow. Replace your toothbrush when the infection is cured.

GARLIC. Eating 2 fresh garlic cloves a day, either plain or minced and tossed in a salad or sauce, may prevent yeast infections or help clear up a case of thrush. Garlic has antifungal properties.

LICORICE POWDER. Boil 1 pint water and add 1 teaspoon licorice powder. Steep it, strain, but don't drink. Use the liquid as a vaginal douche.

VINEGAR. Make a mild vinegar douche and use at the first sign of problems. Mix 1 to 3 tablespoons white vinegar with 1 quart of water.

FROM THE REFRIGERATOR

CRANBERRY JUICE. Drink this one. Unsweetened, it may acidify vaginal secretions and equip them to fight off the yeast.

YOGURT. The live culture in plain yogurt is a great remedy for a yeast infection, helping to restore the acid/bacteria balance in more ways than one. Of course, you can eat yogurt. But you can also insert 1 to 2 tablespoons into your vagina, apply it externally to the affected area (anal or vaginal), or use it as a douche by diluting it with warm water.

FROM THE SINK

WATER. For a baby with thrush, give ½ ounce boiled, cooled water after a feeding to wash away milk remnants that contain milk sugars, which yeast love to feed on.

FROM THE SPICE RACK

BASIL. For thrush, make a basil tea and use it as a gargle. Boil 3½ cups water, remove from heat, and add 1¼ teaspoons ground basil. Cover and steep for 30 minutes. Cool and gargle. Or sweeten to taste with maple syrup and drink 1 cup twice a day.

ROSEMARY. To relieve itching and burning, make a tea of rosemary, and use it as a douche or dab it onto the external area.

SALT. If mouth sores develop with thrush, gargle with a mixture of ½ cup lukewarm water and ½ teaspoon salt to foster healing.

THYME. Make thyme tea using 1 teaspoon dried thyme per 1 cup boiling water. Steep and drink 1 to 4 cups per day if you have a yeast infection.

MORE DO'S & DON'TS

- Avoid stressful situations. They can bring on infection.
- Dry yourself thoroughly after a shower.
- Skip the nylon undies; they hold in moisture and heat. Instead use breathable cotton.
- Trade in the tight jeans for baggies. Tight clothes can create the perfect breeding ground for yeast: moist and hot.
- Remove a wet bathing suit as soon as possible.
- Skip the feminine hygiene products, including sprays, soaps, and perfumes. The chemicals in them cause irritation.
- Check with your doctor about your contraceptive choices. Some people who take birth control pills or use the contraceptive sponge are more prone to getting yeast infections.
- Yeast is contagious. Don't share towels, and don't bathe with anyone.
- Try an over-the-counter antifungal cure.

ALL ABOUT DIAPER RASH

Diaper rash is caused by either a yeast or bacterial infection, and it happens to almost all babies because those warm soggy diapers are a great yeast-friendly environment. Some babies seem more prone to them, but no one knows why. It could be their immune system isn't quite strong enough to fight it off yet. One thing is known, however: Breast-fed babies are less likely to get the infection.

Symptoms of a yeast-induced diaper rash are:

- Small, pimplelike bumps
- Sores that ooze and may smell bad
- Crusting or scaling eventually covering the sores

Be sure to call the doctor if the affected area is unusually red or sore to the touch, if pus-filled sores develop, or if the baby has fever or diarrhea or is lethargic.

Index